A SIGNET BOOK

Pal Hal

Dick Beddoes was born in Sheep Tracks, Alberta, did a brief stint in the army, and attended the University of Alberta until he was kicked out in 1952. He immediately joined the staff of the Edmonton *Bulletin*, which folded six months later. He went to Vancouver, where he worked in the newsroom of the *Sun*, later transferring to the sports department, where he worked for ten years. In 1964 he moved to Toronto to work for the *Globe and Mail*. In recent years he has worked extensively in radio and TV, as a sports director, interviewer and sports talk-show host.

He has written four books, won a National Newspaper Award for sports writing, and received two Can-Pro Awards for excellence in sports programming. His most recent book is entitled *Dick Beddoes' Greatest Hockey Stories*.

PAL HAL

An Uninhibited, No-Holds-Barred Account of the Life and Times of Harold Ballard

WRITTEN BY HIS GREAT AND IRREVERENT FRIEND
Dick Beddoes

A SIGNET BOOK

NEW AMERICAN LIBRARY

Published in Canada by
Penguin Books Canada Limited, Markham, Ontario

First published in Canada by Macmillan of Canada, 1989
Updated for this edition

The publisher and the author gratefully acknowledge
permission to reproduce material from the following
publications: *Ballard* by William Houston (1984),
published by Summerhill Press; *Conn Smythe: If You
Can't Beat 'Em in the Alley* by Conn Smythe and Scott
Young (1981), used by permission of the Canadian
Publisher, McClelland and Stewart Limited, Toronto;
and *It Was Warm and Sunny When We Set Out*,
copyright by the author, Joan Finnigan.

   Additional books consulted include: *The Trail of the
Stanley Cup*, volume two, by Charles Coleman
(National Hockey League, 1969); *A Picture History of
Ontario* by Roger Hall and Gordon Dodds (Hurtig,
1978); *Songs from the Front and Rear* by Anthony
Hopkins (Hurtig, 1979); *Toronto Remembered* by
William Kilbourn (Stoddart, 1984); *Maple Leaf
Gardens, Fifty Years of History* by Stan Obodiac (Van
Nostrand Reinhold, 1981); *Bassett* by Maggie Siggins
(Doubleday Canada, 1967); *Tiger, A Hockey Story* by
Tiger Williams with James Lawton (Douglas and
McIntyre, 1984); *Canada's Sporting Heroes* by S.F. Wise
and Douglas Fisher (General Publishing, 1974); *Hello
Canada: The Life and Times of Foster Hewitt* by Scott
Young (Seal Books, 1985).

Signet, Signet Classic, Mentor, Onyx, Plume, Meridian
and NAL Books are published in Canada by Penguin
Books Canada Limited, 2801 John Street, Markham,
Ontario L3R 1B4

First printing October, 1990   Printed in Canada

10 9 8 7 6 5 4 3 2 1

Canadian Cataloguing in Publication Data
Beddoes, Dick, 1926-
   Pal Hal

ISBN 0-451-16884-4

1. Ballard, Harold, 1903-1990. 2. Toronto Maple Leafs
(Hockey team). 3. Maple Leaf Gardens Ltd. - History.
4. Sports team owners - Ontario - Biography. I. Title.

GV848.5.B3B4 1990   796.96'2'092   C90-094160-X

Contents

◆

Acknowledgements

♦

I have known Harold Ballard for twenty-five years, and much of the information in this book is culled from provocative conversations I've had with him through the years in hotels and planes, on radio and television, and especially in Maple Leaf Gardens.

The genesis of the book was in a telephone conversation I had with Carel Arcus, an associate in the Helen Heller Agency, who heard me talking about the Battling Ballards on the CBC and believed there was a tale to be told. Helen sold the idea in the fall of 1988 to then publisher Linda McKnight and president Arnold Gosewich at Macmillan of Canada.

I am indebted to them and to my hands-on editor, J.R. Colombo, the all-time All-Canadian at publishing fascinating Canadiana. Sheldon Fischer and his colleagues at Macmillan were uncommonly cooperative in giving me time to portray Pal Hal my way.

I am grateful to Ann Mason-Apps, an old friend and prodigal researcher, who found the court documents pertinent to the Battling Ballards in litigation.

William Houston of the Toronto *Globe and Mail* was a particular source of information from his 1984 book, *Ballard*, and in many conversations about his own prickly association with Pal Hal.

Clay Powell, a prominent Toronto lawyer, generously shared his recollections on Ballard, whom he prosecuted in a trial for fraud and theft as a crown attorney in Toronto in 1971–72.

Many others, through the years, fleshed out the fascination I have for Ballard's role in the myth of Maple Leaf Gardens. They are:

Officials of the Gardens: directors Don Giffin and Paul McNamara, treasurer Don Crump, building superintendant Don MacKenzie, the late Leaf publicist Stan Obodiac.

Owners and hockey officials: Harry Ornest, Jim Gregory, Frank Bonello, Gordon Stellick, Bob Stellick, Rudy Pilous, John Brophy, the late Punch Imlach, and especially the deceased Conn Smythe.

Maple Leafs: Bob Davidson, Bert Olmstead, Bob Baun, Bill Harris, Dick Duff, the late Babe Pratt, George Armstrong, Gary Leeman, Wendel Clark, Sweeney Schriner, the late Gord Drillon, and the ever obliging and always laughing King Clancy.

Friends and rivals in the press box: Rex McLeod, Scott Young, Frank Orr, Milt Dunnell, Jim Proudfoot, Tom Murray, Jim Coleman, Jim Christie, Jean Sonmor, Al Strachan, Maggie Siggins, Scott Morrison, Wayne Parrish, Barbara Moon, Foster Hewitt, Dave Hodge, Ralph Mellanby, Brian McFarlane, Jim Kernaghan, John Kernaghan, Earl McRae, Jeffrey Goodman, Stan Fischler, Bob McKenzie, Trent Frayne.

Colleagues in the field otherwise unacknowledged: Ralph Allen, Pierre Berton, Ted Blackman, Tim Burke, Jack Cahill, Adrienne Clarkson, Clark Davey, Jack Dennett, Richard Doyle, Joan Finnigan, Barbara Frum, John Gault, George Gross, Anthony Hopkins, Jim Hunt, John Iaboni, Paul Kaihla, Joe Morgan, Al Purdy, Don Ramsay, Ted Reeve, John Robertson, John Temple, Jim Vipond, Bruce West.

Others: Murray Dryden, lawyers Bill MacDonald and John Chapman, Judge John Kerr, ticket host Mike Wassily, Hall of Fame president Scotty Morrison, Hall of Fame curator Lefty Reid, comic Mike Banks, television producer Phil LaChappelle, television host Kathy Renwald, camera lady Cecelia Carter-Smith.

The word, everybody, is thanks.

Preface

Hockey is a Canadian specific.

AL PURDY, "Hockey Players"

Harold Ballard was famous for being famous in Canadian jocktocracy, the custodian of a hockey team from the yearless region of Canadian dreams until the hounds of oblivion caught him. He died on April 11, 1990, his kidneys shot, his heart sluggish, diabetes gnawing at him. He was rising 87 and, filled with black-assed melancholy, pulled the plug on himself in Toronto's Wellesley Hospital.

Ballard's team was the Toronto Maple Leafs, winners of eleven Stanley Cups, second only to the Canadiens of Montreal. Generations of Canadians have childhood memories of Leaf players who were Toronto demigods moving through a golden haze in which their sweaty jerseys seemed pure white. We were kids hooked on hockey as the most wonderful game on earth and on the Leafs as the most wonderful team and on Maple Leaf Gardens as the mother temple of the game.

The Leafs have played 64 storied seasons in the National Hockey League and Ballard spanned all those years. Sometimes, lying in a hospital bed, puzzled and fretful and frail, he wondered why the franchise he had owned since 1972 and had begun to operate in 1961 had grown frowzy and degraded. The night after his death, the 1990 Leafs were eliminated in the first round of the Stanley Cup playoffs by the St. Louis Blues.

Toronto has not won the Cup since 1967 when, against the odds, the Leafs beat the Montreal Canadiens in six absorbing games. Ballard's critics contended the team would not win another Cup as long as he was alive and meddling.

He pondered the critics during lucid moments in the four months he lingered on before his death. Once, visiting him, trying to recall old laughs, I heard one last Ballard bomb-mot.

"You know, Rich," he said, "I've just been thinking how many assholes there are in the world."

He may have been thinking about those who would quarrel over his estate. Or of the obituary writer who found it difficult to speak well of the dead.

"There is no reason to waste tears on Pal Hal," Jim Proudfoot wrote in *The Toronto Star*. "He's now dead after almost nine decades of running roughshod over anybody — absolutely anybody — who got in his way. You will read and hear that his callous exterior was a mask, concealing a warm and giving heart. This is mawkish nonsense, the kind of sentimental claptrap the Maple Leafs' owner detested. . . ."

Ballard could be, by turns, mean and warm, tough and demanding, proud and comic, rude and unpredictable, outrageous and generous. There were warts on him, but when he showed his philanthropic face, as he did in his will, you couldn't catch a better person with a bear trap in a cathedral. Through the twenty-six rewarding years that I knew him, I called him Pal Hal. He called me Rich, as in his opening gambit in person or on the phone, "Hey, Rich, how the hell are ya?" or "Rich, what the fuck's new?"

Ballard rarely pondered the Leafs of yesteryear, but he cannot be considered in isolation from them. He must be seen in the context of the institution he commanded.

The Leafs *are* their prickly founder declaring, in the brazen tone of a trumpet, "If you can't lick 'em in the alley, you can't beat 'em on the ice!" Those fighting words were uttered by Constantine Falkland Cary Smythe, a belligerent little bull who always carried his own china shop with him.

The Leafs *are* the dressing-room slogans, Smythe's defiant "Defeat Does Not Rest Lightly on Their Shoulders" and Ballard's own papal bull, "Success Comes in Cans, Not Can'ts."

They are "Hockey Night in Canada," Foster Hewitt introducing a game with the sure readiness of a poised hockey stick, "Hello, Canada, and hockey fans in the United States and Newfoundland!" And, with a dramatic flourish when a Leaf unloaded, "He shoots! He scores!"

The Leafs, across 'ie century, are Big Chas and Wild Bill,

Ace and King, Buzz and Busher, Bingo, Bucko and Baldy, Turk and Teeder and Tiger, Pep, Punch and Pully, Boomer and B.J., Hinky and Howie, Red, Flash, Hap, The Chief, Bigfoot and Mahov, Babe and Bud, Sweeney, Shakey and Squid, Windy and Waldo, Motor City Smitty and Clear-the-Track Shack. They are The Hound Line, The Kid Line, The Rocks and The Gold Dust Twins.

They are the fans of four Stanley Cups in the 1960s, yelling for dapper number 14: "When in doubt, send Keon out!"

Maple Leaf Gardens isn't a hockey rink. It's a temple, a Tajmahockey, the Old Cashbox on Carlton Street. Canadians beyond Quebec are wrapped in a Maple Leaf flag. Who wants to be prime minister if he can be Maple Leaf captain? Even a real prime minister, Mike Pearson, would rather have been Punch Imlach, a Stanley Cup coach. Punch Imlach didn't want to be prime minister. He wanted to be Punch Imlach, too.

The Leafs are kids on winter-pink Saturdays in neighbourhood driveways choosing up heroes. "Okay, you be Borje Salming and I'll be Gary Leeman!" "No, I don't want to be Salming again! If I got to be somebody, I want to be Wendel Clark!"

The Leafs are controversy in the off-season. "How come that sumbitch general manager traded Russ Courtnall for John Kordic? That's giving up a flashy gem for a klutzy zircon. How come Harold Ballard let his general managers make stupid trades, like giving up Lanny McDonald in 1980 and not drafting Mike Bossy when the Leafs had the chance in 1977? I'm gonna ask my cousin, who knew that old bastard Ballard personally before he cashed in."

The Leafs aren't a religion, but you've got to have faith — especially in the way they keep raising the ticket prices. They haven't won a Stanley Cup in twenty-three seasons. They aren't a one-night stand, they're a lifelong commitment. We Leafs fans are married to a shared delusion.

Somewhere, sometime maybe, the Leafs will revisit 1967. Hope leaps eternal, loud and resounding. "We want Wendel! If his bum back is better! We'd have given Ballard's right eyeball for a winner! Now Pal Hal's gone, we'd give the right eyeball of the new boss, Don Giffin!"

The last thing Ballard coveted was a Stanley Cup with his own imprimatur on it. But he was caught in the eye of Hurricane Harold, buffeted by his lover on one side and by his three children on the other, the Ballards battling with a sitcom zaniness — money and power, sex and greed at the Gardens.

With Harold Ballard gone, two Canadian breweries now covet the Gardens, Molson and Labatt, always at lagerheads. Molson has an option to buy, conferred on it in 1980 when Ballard needed money to pay off earlier loans. Molson also supplied the $15-million Ballard needed in 1989 to buy out his daughter, Mary Elizabeth, from the family company, H.E. Ballard Ltd.

Molson plays down a thirst for the Gardens and the Maple Leafs franchise because of possible conflict-of-interest charges. Molson owns the Montreal Canadiens, and multiple ownership in the NHL is no longer fashionable.

Labatt battles Molson on all fronts in a brewery war, and in the stock exchanges. Labatt controls the Toronto Blue Jays baseball team for the purpose of selling the Labatt Blue brand. If the brewery owned the Maple Leafs, it would peddle a Labatt Blue and White brand.

Toronto politicians have declared the Gardens a historic site — and for hockey fans, it is — but the politicians were slightly off the mark. They should have designated Harold Ballard himself the historic site.

A small tarnished trophy among his souvenirs is inscribed: "OLD ORCHARD Speed Skating Club/ 880 Yards City Championship 1920/ Won by HAROLD E. BALLARD." That made Pal Hal at least slightly historical, in Toronto.

Near the end, flat on his back and kept alive by machinery, he no longer boasted a ripe jauntiness. His steakhouse belly was gone. He was as pale as the old print of a Maple Leafs hockey team nailed to an out-of-the-way wall in the Gardens.

The Ballard hockey fans care to remember was captured the day after his death by Rex MacLeod in the *Toronto Star*. There has not been a more literate hockey writer in Canada than the MacLeod who wrote:

By now, Harold Ballard is telling God that the Pearly Gates badly need a paint job, or he's showing Him how He can double the number of seats in Heavenly Gardens without even using up one of His miracle timeouts.

Or Ballard is advising the Devil the Red-Hot Stove Lounge, on the outskirts of Hades, could use more microwaves, more scalding soup on the menu — that "the goddam place" in general could be fixed up. "This joint looks like hell," Ballard growls.

The Devil tells him where to go, Ballard counters with a few profane ripostes and they fall down laughing. . . .

Rex MacLeod's Ballard is the one I knew, too, a Pal Hal who could be blistering, blighting, and blasphemous. When he died it was as if a painting had fallen out of the Maple Leafs frame. Suddenly you were left staring at an incredible amount of vacant space. This unauthorized biography written in the last year of his life attempts to recreate Harold Ballard in that space.

CHAPTER 1

Mammon of the Mint

♦

I left the flamboyant *Vancouver Sun* before the 1963–64 hockey season and landed on the first bounce at the Toronto *Globe and Mail* to produce a sports column, considerably underpaid but grossly overprivileged.

The sports editor was Jim Vipond, a tall, decent man who pointed me in the direction of Maple Leaf Gardens. "You'll want to meet Punch Imlach," Vipond said. "Good coach, very full of himself."

Full of himself, indeed. When Rex MacLeod was writing the liveliest stories on the hockey beat for the *Globe*, he referred to Imlach as "The Big I." "Punch's square name is George F.," Rex wrote of the team's profane and perverse dean of men. "The F stands for his favorite word."

Jim Vipond said, "You'll also want to aquaint yourself with the club president, Stafford Smythe. Good hockey man, but a strange sort, trying to outdo his father."

Smythe's father was the clamorous Conn, who invented the Maple Leaf franchise in 1927 and built the Gardens in 1931. Stafford grew up similarly short and cocky, but never outdid his dad. He reached maturity but forgot to touch second base, unable to escape the long shadow of a legend. There developed in his character a soft little spot that, in the turmoil of the late sixties, would collapse under pressure.

Vipond told me, "But the guy you'll really want to see is Harold Ballard. He's the executive vice-president, the money man. He makes the Gardens go. Inclined to exaggerate. He'll tell you some pretty good stories."

The Gardens is in midtown Toronto, a prime location at the intersection of Church and Carlton Streets, serviced in all directions by public transit. A stranger riding a northbound subway train from downtown to the Gardens gets off at College Street station and notes a Toronto aberration. College, running east and west, stops abruptly at Yonge Street, a north-south thoroughfare best described as Canada's original hardened artery. East of Yonge, College becomes Carlton Street.

The stranger strolls a long, curving block along Carlton and, of a sudden, near the end of the curve at Church, comes upon a domed rococo pile, mouldering in the baked brownish-orange color of terra cotta, the most famous cold-storage locker in Canada. Maple Leaf Gardens.

Not every witness is impressed. Barbara Moon expressed a disdainful view in the now departed *Globe Magazine*, in 1966. "The building that means Toronto, and even Canada to a good part of the outside world is — to the probable despair of architects, culturati, and definers of the native ethos — the Gardens.

"It's a sports palace with a gross, unlovely silhouette; no historical associations unless you count visits by the Beatles in 1964 and 1965 or the time Stafford Smythe had Howie Young of Chicago Black Hawks suspended for unsavory language and spitting at Mrs. Smythe; and no unassailable distinction, even among sports palaces, except that of being the cleanest rink in North America."

The Gardens, built at the depth of the Depression for $1.6 million, has a dome rising 13 storeys above centre ice. The structure contains 750,000 bricks, enough to make a strip four inches wide and 23 miles long. Builders used 77,500 bags of cement, 70 tons of sand, 11,000 tons of gravel, 950,000 board feet of lumber and 540 kegs of nails. There are 14 miles of conduits in the floor for making artificial ice. The huge scoreboard clock beneath the dome weighs 7.5 tons. Harold Ballard, pursuing a buck with a hustler's enthusiasm, increased the crowd capacity from 12,586 to 16,182. Good luck getting a ticket on a big night, or even an average night.

Those are all the facts about Maple Leaf Gardens, but none of its essential flavor. It is not merely an arena of mortar, muscle and masonry, with Big Bucks Ballard playing a merry tune on his cash register; it is more than Barbara Moon's sardonic sketch of greed piled upon gluttony. Profits make the proprietor's heart go pit-a-pat, but you can't put a price on the playpen of our daydreams. Not on a place where a Canadian child cherishes the remote hope of becoming famous in a harmlessly spectacular way. For us, it is Make Believe Gardens.

William Kilbourn, a Toronto historian, came close to the essential flavor in a 1966 essay. He wrote:

> There is a religious cult that celebrates the Gardens' reason for being – Hockey Night in Canada.
>
> It is unlike all other cults in that it unites Canadians of all ages and classes, from coast to coast: the tribal howl in the hollow of the eardrums in the darkened rooms of Depression and Wartime, as Foster Hewitt's nasal radio voice winged above the roar of the crowd.
>
> Then there was the Saturday night TV ritual of the fifties and after, in millions of homes across seven different time zones, as two or three gather together before the household altar's moving screen to watch their gods and heroes locked in mortal combat, about the only gods and heroes left whose actions can actually be seen, rather than taken on faith or by second-hand report.

On the winter day 25 years ago, when I first met the Mammon of the Maple Leaf Mint, I had more than a reporter's instinct going for me. I had the demigods of boyhood, staring down from the Gardens' gallery of the great, going for me as well. Charlie Conacher, Big Chas, the big shooter, a master blaster. Francis Michael Clancy, King of the capers. Babe Pratt, a Hall of Famer who could take a drink, or several. Stylish Busher Jackson, who became a drunk and died a derelict. Ted Kennedy, a fierce Leaf Captain, hard as a hockey puck.

The executive offices in the Gardens are on the second floor, back of the red seats, reached by escalator. In 1964, I noticed ads for Schick razor blades festooned the risers on the escalator, proof that Ballard had fashioned one of the sharpest deals ever honed on a rising staircase.

"How are ya?" he said, bluff, hearty, shirt sleeves rolled up to the elbow, beefy as a burly bartender. "You're a new guy on the beat, eh? Maybe you'll last, if you're lucky."

Ballard shook hands like a Rotarian, hail-fellow, gimme-five-and-glad-to-meetcha. Brian Mulroney, the general manager of Canada, has perfected such a greeting into a gesture of fine old fakery to make you think he cares.

"You'd like a story, eh?" Ballard said. "Why not do one on Staff Smythe and me? We run this joint. You could call it Mike and Ike, the Gold Dust Twins."

"But isn't there a third chap involved in controlling the Gardens?" I asked. "What about John Bassett?"

"Oh, yeah," Ballard said, off-hand, as though he'd just remembered an old-pal postscript. "Our old buddy Bassett. We cut him in for a third when we bought the 60 per cent of the Gardens which Old Man Smythe owned. Bassett's chairman of the board, but he doesn't have any say running the place. He's too busy cosying up to the Eatons for money to run the *Tely* and his TV station."

Bassett's coziness with the Eatons had paid off in the purchase of the *Telegram* in November, 1952. Eaton guaranteed a bank note of $4,250,000 to buy the newspaper, the 23,999 shares to be held in trust for Eaton's four sons and Bassett's three.

In 1960, when a Tory federal government awarded Tory Bassett a television license in Toronto, the station – lucrative CFTO – was operated by a company called Baton Broadcasting. The "Ba" stood for Bassett, the "ton" for Eaton.

John White Hughes Bassett was publisher of the Toronto *Telegram*. A lofty, capricious, ebullient man, unable to catch *The Toronto Star* in afternoon circulation, he finally sold out to the *Star* in 1971. *The Toronto Sun* rose as a tabloid Phoenix from the *Tely* ashes, brash and insolent, thriving on a readership eager for bosom-and-bullets journalism, mammary majesty protruding daily on page three. The surefire formula, suitable for lip readers, is called T and A; tits and ass.

"You can say," Ballard said at our first meeting, "that our old buddy Bassett got lucky in his Eaton connection."

"I hear you've been lucky, too," I said. "Somebody said you have the balls of a burglar."

Ballard turned on a high-beamed grin, big smile wrapped around teeth. "I treasure the compliment," he said. "Let me tell you about the time I stole the Olympic flag."

Ballard was 25 in 1928, the year Toronto's Varsity Grads, all-conquering among Canada's senior amateur hockey teams, were chosen to represent this country in the Winter Olympic Games. The quadrennial snowball fight was held in the

Swiss mountain spa of St. Moritz. About then, Ballard's
prolonged rivalry with Conn Smythe began. Smythe, strut-
ting about with a very consequential air, managed the Grads
to the Canadian title in 1927, but was too busy manipulating
the Maple Leafs in 1928 to share the Olympic adventure.
W.A. Hewitt, father of broadcaster Foster, replaced Smythe
as manager of the Grads and Ballard tagged along as assistant manager.

There was Pal Hal, out in front, carrying the Canadian flag
in the splashy opening parade of the Swiss Games. It was
unusual for Ballard, a non-competitor, to carry the Canadian
banner, but the Grads insisted upon it.

The late Joe Sullivan, who tended goal for the Grads and
became a Tory appointee to a snug sinecure in the Canadian
Senate, said, "We were wearing skates made by Ballard's dad
and Harold was part of the team. He was amiable, likeable.
We just told the Canadian Olympic Association to go to hell
and that Harold would carry the flag, and that was that."

The Olympic tournament was a romp. The Grads were
granted a free pass into the championship round while nine
other hockey nations, mediocre bushers, played off in
groups of three. The group winners qualified to join Canada
in the medal round. Dr. Joe Sullivan, in goal, would later
have more difficulty removing a burst appendix in Toronto
than he did stopping Olympic pucks. The Grads won gold
prizes by slathering Sweden 11–0, Switzerland 13–0 and
Great Britain 14–0.

Ballard, bored between games, decided to steal the Olympic flag, the large bunting bearing five linked circles which
flew over the athletes' village.

"I wanted a souvenir," he said, "so one night, near the end
of the Games, I hid in a snowbank close to the flagpole. Two
Swiss guards marched around the Olympic Village. I timed
them and rushed out of the snowbank when they marched
off. I cut down the rope on the goddam flagpole with a
jackknife, then hauled in the flag and stuck it in my windbreaker."

It is Ballard's story that, years later, when he and Staff
Smythe grabbed the Gardens, the Olympic flag decorated
one wall of his office. Still later, when Harold moved into the

studio apartment in the Gardens with his lover, Yolanda Babik MacMillan, he used the Olympic flag as a massive bedspread.

"Can I see it?" a guest once asked.

"You can't," Ballard said. "Some son of a bitch stole the Olympic flag I swiped."

CHAPTER 2

The Young Hal

Reach down the wellshaft of the years and draw up images by the bucketfull; recapture time from Harold Ballard young.

He was young when the century was, born on July 30, 1903, one more bouncy citizen in a Toronto bustling with 209,000 slightly immortal souls. In Ottawa, a latter-day buddy, Francis Michael Clancy, was five months old.

Ballard was born in a city based on a White Anglo-Saxon Protestant ethic, although a Pennsylvania sociologist named E. Digby Baltzell didn't coin the term WASP until 1964. Toronto the Good had a reputation for stuffy rectitude that clung like a clergyman's cloak, Godfearing but unfrightened.

"By 1900," Roger Hall and Gordon Dodds wrote in *A Picture History of Ontario*, "to spend a week in Toronto on Sunday had become a standard Montreal joke."

Drums of commerce beat along Yonge Street, where T.P. Loblaw had his first self-service grocery store at 511. Timothy Eaton had a men's furnishings department that was tip-top tacky, and still is. Pollution spewing from smokestacks in the warehouse district made the atmosphere on the Toronto waterfront as clear as the driven smog.

Cricket and rugby were popular with muscular sportsmen, while more genteel jocks convened in long pants the color of vanilla ice cream to toss, underhand, bowls on the lawn.

Members of the Toronto Hunt Club, vaguely British, rode to the hounds along Front Street in comic pursuit of foxes that never did them any harm. Maybe they were kidding, or unaware of Oscar Wilde's dictum that hunting a fox represents the unspeakable in search of the inedible.

The Toronto Hunt has quaintly persisted since 1843 and once had the aforementioned John W.H. Bassett among its riders. One afternoon, a skittish horse bucked off the esteemed Mr. Bassett and broke his leg. One Toronto sports writer, no special fan of Bassett's, voted for that Toronto Hunt dromedary as horse of the year in Canada.

The Salvation Army — the good old Sally Ann, up the Red Shields, bang those tambourines, round up cheerful out-of-tuners to sing Christmas carols on street corners — originated in Toronto in 1882 and marched into the 1900s with a purposeful left swing.

"My parents gave to the Sally Ann," Ballard said, long years after, when he was a practising atheist. "Me, too. I like the Army's slogan, 'From Soup to Salvation.' "

His parents were Sidney Eustace Ballard and Mary (Manie) Garner, a high-spirited woman, saving and energetic, who decided one child was sufficient. She baptized him Edwin Harold, but he rebelled at the "Edwin" when he realized the name had a sissy sound. A good thing, too; you can call him Pal Hal but Pal Edwin, he told me, "would sound sort of faggy."

Sidney Ballard and his three brothers — George, Owen and Herbert — had been raised by an undertaker father in the hamlet of Paris, 61 miles southwest of Toronto as the slapshot flies. Paris was noted for knitting mills in the 1890s and, later, as the birthplace of Sylvanus Apps, the beau ideal of the Maple Leafs from 1936 to 1950.

The Ballard boys worked in the mills. Sidney, learning on the job, became a superb machinist. George moved a few miles down the road to Hamilton, where he played for and presided over the Hamilton Tigers in ORFU, the Ontario Rugby Football Union.

Harold's Uncle George was an operator in his own obstreperous right and, in 1907, engineered the formation of an Eastern football league know colloquially as the Big Four. The new federation included the Tigers, the Toronto Argonauts, the Ottawa Rough Riders and the Montreal Winged Wheelers. Historians manage to contain their enthusiasm for Uncle George's roughshod role in giving the ORFU a cavalier kick-after-lack-of-gate receipts.

"George Ballard was the driving force behind the Big Four," wrote S.F. Wise and Douglas Fisher in *Canadian Sporting Heroes*, first printed in 1974. "In that sense, Ballard was a builder. Since Ballard was president of the ORFU when he assumed the same office with the new league, he was also a wrecker."

J.B. Hay, next president of the ORFU, said of his pushy predecessor, "Ballard displayed a narrow club spirit. He held the presidencies of both the team and the league at the same time."

Harold was four when his uncle organized the Big Four that survived in the same cities until 1987, when the Montreal Alouettes abruptly abandoned Canadian football. When he was 74, Harold said, "No question George was my favorite uncle. He was like me. He fucking got things done."

In 1978, honoring Uncle George's memory, Ballard bought the Hamilton Tiger-Cats for $1.5 million so he and his constant companion, F.M. (King) Clancy, could have fun in the summertime. The Ticats were purchased in the name of Maple Leaf Gardens, without serious opposition from any shareholder. Ballard exercises 80 per cent control over the Old Cashbox on Carlton Street.

Some memory, Uncle George's, some latter-day losses. The Ticats are the biggest basket-case in the history of Canadian football, losers of roughly $18 million since Ballard assumed command. Hamilton investors, offered a chance to buy the Ticats for $1.5 million in 1988, scorned the team as a disgusting side dish of turnips they hadn't ordered. A Hamilton industrialist, David Braley, bought the Cats in 1989 for one dollar.

Young Ballard lived with his parents on Sherbourne Street, toddling distance from the grubby shops located on the future site of the Gardens. His father was a foreman, at a munificent $15 a week, for the Eastman Machinery Co. His mother catered to nine boarders, each of whom paid $3 a week to live in the spacious Sherbourne Street home. Harold and his parents slept in the living room to accommodate the paying guests upstairs.

Money, in a perspective of the time, went far. Bread was five cents a loaf, milk five cents a quart, meat six to twelve cents a pound, coal $4.50 a ton. A meal ticket guaranteed the user 21 restaurant meals for $2.75, although, as Bruce West noted in his caressing centennial look at Toronto in 1967, "At least one Toronto dining place rather snootily informed its

customers in a sign over the counter that napkins would not
be provided to anyone ordering a meal under 15 cents."

The headline athlete when Harold was still bumping his
head under his mother's table was Tom Longboat, a resolute
marathon runner from the Six Nations Indian Reserve near
Brantford. On April 19, 1907, Longboat won the famous
Boston bunion derby in two hours, twenty-five minutes and
one-fifth of a second, record time for the rigorous 26-mile
route.

Longboat, draped in a Union Jack flag, returned to a tri-
umphal reception in Toronto on April 23, was greeted loudly
at Union Station, and paraded up Bay Street to City Hall,
where Mayor Emerson Coatsworth pinned a medal on his
manly chest. Riches promised by blowhard civic politicians
were not paid and Longboat, a few years later, sought solace
in alcohol. In middle age, Longboat was a garbage collector in
north Toronto, a weary genius with a well-bent elbow.

Harold Ballard, middle-aged, rode the same triumphant
road to City Hall, executive vice-president of the Maple
Leafs, champions of hockey's mercenary world in 1962-63-
64-67. The only garbage he collected was his Leafs after 1967.

Harold was eight when his family moved to Norristown,
Pa., where Sid Ballard worked for the Wildman Manufacturing Co., a firm producing sewing machines for the textile
industry. They returned to Toronto before the First Great
War, upwardly mobile, settling at 44 Parkway Avenue in the
city's swanky west end.

Sid established the Ballard Machinery Company downtown on Lombard Street, east of Yonge between King and
Queen. The four-floor factory employed more than 50 people making machinery for the garment district on Spadina
Avenue and, as a sideline, ice skates.

Sid possessed an inventive bent and developed a straight-
knife cloth-cutting machine for garment makers. He sold
textile supplies and, generally hustling, prospered as a
small-time industrialist.

His penchant for invention was later reflected in Harold,
who made a meat-cutting machine for Jenny and Harry
Shopsowitz. He was a corned-beef junky whom Mrs. Shopsowitz favored with choice cuts in the kitchen of Shopsy's

Delicatessen on teeming Spadina. Harold noticed that Jenny Shopsowitz had a laborious time slicing the meat.

"That machine you got," he said, "is too goddamn slow. I'll invent you a faster one." Sam Shopsowitz, a son, marvelled at the speed of the machine Harold brought back from Sid Ballard's shop. "Fast?" Sam said. "When Harold's machine whacked off sausage meat, the sausages came shooting out like machine-gun bullets. My mother ran the slicer while my father stood back catching sausages."

Harold was a bumptious 11 in the summer of 1914 when a Serbian nationalist let the air out of Austrian Duke Franz Ferdinand with a bullet. It was a popular murder, in Serbia, but the impetuous assassin coincidentally pulled the trigger on the guns of August which blasted the world's innocents into a four-year holocaust.

Harold patrolled a paper route, door to door carrying the war-mongering *Globe* which, on January 22, 1915, demanded that Ontario farmers and laborers join the European crusade.

"Is rural Ontario losing its Imperial spirit?" the *Globe* cried. "Must the stalwarts of the breezy uplands, the vigorous manhood mountain and plain be branded as laggards in the Empire's shoulder-to-shoulder march to the trenches?" Always, always there is some valiant editorialist prepared to have you bleed for his country.

Thousands of Torontonians, thus encouraged, went down the red gullet of the First Great War in the spring of their years. More than 10,000, their dreams lost in military madness, were consigned forever to the boneyards of Western Europe.

Ballard was too young for combat, but a subsequent ally and future foe marched off to save civilization. The nineteen-year-old Conn Smythe's self-esteem in 1914 was hippopotamic, but he was bold enough to buckle a swash with any man alive.

Lieutenant Smythe was a little pistol, seven abrasive inches over five feet, when Canadian troops stormed imposing Vimy Ridge in northern France on April 9, 1917. The Canadians won the whaleback ridge but lost 3,598 lives. Smythe, unscathed, won the Military Cross for bravery, transferred to the Royal Air Force, got shot down behind

German lines and finished the global dispute as a prisoner of war.

In Toronto, stay-at-home patriots sang melancholy melodies, the bittersweet "It's a Long, Long Way to Tipperary" and "Carry Me back to Dear Old Blighty" and "Oh, Oh, It's a Lovely War." Ballard attended Howard Public School, where the graduating class of 1916 raised money to buy the colors for Toronto's 204th Battalion. The students marched briskly to class, brave backs straight, eyes firmly fixed on the Union Jack. *The Toronto Star*, greasing up the Howard parents in a circulation drive, reported that "the children at this school come from an excellent class of people who take a warm and intelligent interest in the pupils."

Harold and his well-scrubbed chums swam at nearby Sunnyside Beach and romped in spacious fields not far from High Park. On winter nights, the air peppermint cold in their nostrils, they tested their Ballard Skates on Grenadier Pond or the Old Orchard Rink between Ossington and Dovercourt Avenues.

Adventuresome kids, often led by Ballard, travelled to Toronto Islands in the old-time summertime to angle for perch and bass in the tranquil lagoons. They speared catfish with table forks tied to poles or caught bullfrogs with hooks baited with red flannel. The fish and frog-legs were cooked over driftwood fires on the beach. A scow moored to Centre Island sold ice cream, yellow, flavored with vanilla, food for boisterous young gods born to the *Star's* "excellent class of people."

In 1917, a large 14, Harold enrolled at Upper Canada College, up Avenue Road, beyond St. Clair Avenue. UCC was established in 1829 as a private boys' school, run by people out of English academies whose academic requirements ranked money and pedigree above brains and ambition.

William (Choppy) Grant came limping back from the war in 1917 to rehabilitate himself as principal of UCC, where he had taught history. Grant was a splendid educator, "A man of character," novelist Robertson Davies wrote, "old warrior, ripe scholar." Grant made Christianity seem exciting, muscular. His charges were startled to hear the headmaster shout one night in Prayer Hall, "Live in the large! Dare greatly, and if you must sin, sin nobly!"

Harold heard his master loud and clear, cheerfully admitting to noble sinning through the century in a grand wide swath. He was less inclined to listen to the edict of UCC's minister, Reverend Ernest Voorhis, who preached that swearing is a disease, "mighty contagious." Reverend Voorhis claimed "a true gentleman never swears, and I mean a gentleman like Sir Douglas Haig." His reference was to the commander of the British forces on the Western Front, a homicidal dullard who may have hated dirty words but didn't mind dirty war. Haig was the Allied hero who, in 1917, sent 2,700 Canadians to die in the bloody mud of Passchendaele.

One of Haig's subordinates, seeing the Belgian swamp that sucked in soldiers, blurted, "Good God, did we really send men to fight in that shit?"

Harold properly jeered when he discovered that the clean-mouthed Imperial commander dispatched troops into filthy fights. "When I heard what a prick Haig was," he said, "I began to swear like a son of a bitch."

Ballard boarded at UCC and, in his freshman year, was a spare on the junior rugby team that won four games and lost three. He was an outsized junior, big and ebullient, called Old Smiley because of his perpetual grin. He was also called Ball-ox, as when a kid beneath him in the scrum bawled, "Hey, Ball-ox, get off me, you big lummox."

Allan Lamport, contemporaneous with Ballard at UCC and later the mayor of Toronto, remembers Harold as "abrasive. Mess with him and he'd get very severe."

Mess with Mayor Lamport, years distant at City Hall, and he'd get verbally wild and wonderful in swooping language. "If you're gonna stab me in the back," Lampy'd say, "I want to be there." Or, "Getting decisions through this damned Council is like pushing a car uphill with a rope."

The war was over by 1919 and Ballard, at 16, abandoned UCC halfway through his third year, never to crack the cover of a book again. "He had itchy feet," Lamport said, "and wanted to get cracking."

Harold got cracking in his father's machine shop and, bright and booming, sold Ballard Rockered Tube Skates and textile equipment. He was hearty in the fashion of Mary, his mother, absolutely devoid of asceticism, ready to shoot craps wherever the action was. He came roaring into the Roaring Twenties, a mythic decade of change and invention that shattered old puritanical bonds.

"Look up the word 'whoopee,'" Harold once said. "That was the twenties. Plenty of drinking and dancing and fucking. I had a hell of a time."

Everything came up for him smelling like a banana split, his favorite meal, topped with rich, creamy marshmallow. He owned a Pierce-Arrow roadster before he was 20 and, when he tired of road touring, cruised Lake Ontario on Sid Ballard's expensive motor yacht, the *Torcan*, short for Toronto, Canada.

Sexual conquests, given freedom in cars and boats, were easier than if he'd been some poor romantic slob riding his girl home on a Toronto streetcar. "Oh, I got a few bumps, all right, Richard," he told me.

"Pardon me?" I said. "Bumps?"

"I forgot," he said. "You're from a later generation. In the twenties if you got bumped, it meant you'd got laid."

The pattern of Ballard's adult existence began to form. Conn Smythe came swaggering home from the war, mustered out of the military as a major. He married a patient woman named Irene Sands and, in 1921, their first son, Conn Stafford, was born, who would grow up to play like Ike to Ballard's Mike.

In Ottawa, in the season of 1921–22, King Clancy began to play a rousing game of defence for the prehistoric Senators in the National Hockey League. Clancy, too, in a later guise, would play Ike to Ballard's Mike.

In 1922, in the real world beyond fun and frolic, Dr. Frederick Grant Banting and colleagues at the University of Toronto perfected one of the medical marvels of the century. Their discovery of insulin prolonged the lives of millions of diabetics, Ballard among them. Diabetes was the ultimate price he paid for a lifelong addiction to chocolates and ice-cream sundaes, his system so clogged with sugar that, at 80, he couldn't feel the bottoms of his feet.

He could feel them fine at 20, though, smoothly moving through the winters on Ballard speed skates. He does not dispel the myth that he was a Canadian champion over a quarter- and half-mile, but the feats are myth.

Sam Shefsky knew Ballard in the twenties and the Toronto sportsman, who used to own a Goodyear Tire franchise, told William Houston in 1984, "I used to fool around with skating like Ballard. He'd come to skating carnivals in his big coon coat and try to put on a show, but he was a lousy skater. That stuff about the Canadian championship is a lot of bullshit."

Shefsky was giving Ballard's skating competence all the worst of a bitter appraisal after their friendship ceased. At Maple Leaf team parties during Christmas week at the Gardens, after Ballard gained control, he skated with the ease of any player for two or three laps. No champion, but smoother than any falling-down klutz of a sports writer, at that.

Ross Robinson and his sister Gladys were prominent Canadian speedskaters in the twenties, and Ballard trained with them at the Old Orchard rink. Robinson could not recall for William Houston that he ever saw Ballard compete anywhere.

"We'd get together after practice for a drink or two," Robinson said. "Harold seemed to have all the breaks. His father was wealthy. Everything was laid in his lap."

About then, Harold revealed a penchant for rowdy friends and gross misconduct. He was there one night in Lake Placid, 1,881 feet up in the Adirondack Mountains of upper New York state, when several Toronto drunks decided to skate on the carpets of the hotel where they were bivouacked. Management humored that caper but called for a riot squad after the inebriates began hurling empty champagne bottles through plate-glass windows.

Another time at another resort in upper New York, the town's convivial police chief took the Toronto visitors on a tour of the local jail. Harold, joking around, locked the chief in one of the cells and disappeared with the key. It was not his last experience with prison. Fifty years later he would be incarcerated in the Crowbar Motel at Millhaven, Ontario, and no jailer was joking.

Harold was somewhat tamed, but not entirely domesticated, in 1924, after meeting Dorothy Higgs at a dance in Toronto. She was 17, the impoverished daughter of a Methodist minister, in training at Wellesley Hospital to be a nurse. Her escort this night was another young man comfortably on the make. Ballard barged in, mobile as a nimble moose, and Dorothy spent the rest of the night dancing with him.

"Your name's Higgs, eh?" he said. "They call me Old Smiley. I'll call you Jiggs. Jiggs Higgs."

They were a handsome couple — Jiggs lively and lovely, Harold a laughing six-footer smitten by the woman he would call "the love of my life." He took his time sanctifying their relationship, to the consternation of her stern father, Reverend William Higgs of Belleville, Ontario. Their courtship lasted 17 seasons, one of the longest warm-ups for a wedding in Canadian history, not certified by marriage until 1941.

"How come," I asked, "you kept a nice woman like that waiting so long?"

"Christ, Richard," Harold said, "I was having too much fun to get married."

His peers had fun in their fashion in the golden high time of their lives. Smythe coached the University of Toronto Blues and sought a Toronto franchise in the National Hockey League. King Clancy, a clown prince, led the Ottawa Senators to the Stanley Cup in 1923 and 1927. Ernest Hemingway left *The Toronto Star* to settle in Paris and, carving words in a hard spare prose, wrote *The Sun Also Rises*. Foster Hewitt stayed at the *Star* and, in a vivid staccato voice, began broadcasting hockey games for the paper's radio station, CFCA.

In 1927, Smythe gave birth to the blues he called the Toronto Maple Leafs. Early in January, with the Toronto St. Pats incurably addicted to losing, one of the Toronto owners asked Smythe to supplant Mike Rodden, a sports writer, as coach.

"No," Smythe told Jack Bickell. "Coaches are too easy fired. I'll run the team only if I can buy part of it."

Jack Paris Bickell was a substantial Toronto broker who invested in a northern Ontario gold property that became the mother lode of McIntyre-Porcupine Mines Ltd. He shared ownership of the St. Pats with N.L. Nathanson, Paul Ciceri and a broadcasting blatherskite, Charles Querrie.

Philadelphia promoters offered $200,000 for the St. Pats, on the condition that the team be transferred to the Pennsylvania city. Smythe rushed around, buying time, telling any Torontonian who would listen that if the city lost its NHL franchise, another might never be available.

Jack Bickell listened. "Okay," he said. "You can't afford the St. Pats yourself, but I've got $40,000 in the club. You find $160,000 to pay off the others and I'll leave my money in, if you'll run the team."

Smythe put down $10,000 he had won in racing bets the previous November. He grubbed for other investors who, on February 14, 1927, paid another $75,000. The deal was consummated on the understanding that the remaining $75,000 would be paid in 30 days.

On February 15, the Toronto *Globe* carried news of the sale under a banner headline. A subhead in the story read:

> Goodbye, St. Pats!
> Howdy, Maple Leafs

Smythe spoke of the name change as though he were designating a new army battalion.

"St. Patrick's doesn't mean a thing," he declared. "The name was hatched as a sop to the Toronto Irish. Our Olympic team in 1924 wore maple leaf crests and won. I wore it on military insignia during the war, and Canada won. The maple leaf means something proud across Canada."

The St. Pats played their first game as Maple Leafs on February 17, 1927, home in the cramped Arena Gardens on Mutual Street to the New York Americans. It was overcast and bleak, down to 17 above. Sleds driven by horses skidded on Yonge Street. Most of the 8,500 fans swayed to the game in streetcars for two cents a ride.

Fans who remained downtown dined at malnutrition manors, such as Child's on Yonge or the Stoodleigh at Mutual and Shuter Streets. Coffee sold for 27 cents a pound, and people wondered if inflation would ever stop.

There was civil war in China but the only battling in Toronto was for choice hockey seats: $2 grandstand, $1 rush. Hot dogs were five cents, soda pop five cents, a program twenty-five cents. There were few women and children in attendance. Harold Ballard was there, but not Jiggs Higgs.

In the Toronto dressing room, under the stands, the first

player signed as a Leaf felt a rookie's trepidation. Carl Voss
was 20, a junior who had played the previous season in
Kingston. Smythe signed Voss the day before, $1,200 for the
balance of the 1926–27 season. His mother had to endorse
the contract because her son wasn't the legal age of 21.

"I'm against professional sport," Mrs. Voss told Smythe.

"But the money's not bad," he countered. "Besides, your
boy's big enough to be out earning a living."

Now Voss looked around the dressing room, at the new
coach, Alex (Porky) Romeril, at the team's only established
pros — goaltender John Ross Roach, forwards Clarence
(Hap) Day and Irvine (Ace) Bailey.

Before the game, Smythe instructed Romeril, "Move Day
back to defence. That's where he starred at Varsity." Day
would captain the Leafs, perfect the clutch and grab, and
never again play forward.

Referee William O'Hara, the game's sole official, picked up
his cowbell and clumped to the ice. Whistles would not
replace cowbells for 10 more years. Fans jeered the referee
cheerfully, then cheered as the residue of the St. Pats skated
out as Maple Leafs.

The Leafs and Americans warmed up, then lined up for
the anthem, "God Save the King." Referee O'Hara rang his
bell and the legend of the Leafs began. The Americans
poured pucks at goalie Roach, who was beaten in the first
period by Lionel (Big Train) Conacher, a formidable name in
Canadian sport, remarkable in lacrosse, baseball, boxing and
hockey.

The Americans led 1–0 after the first period, but the reborn
Toronto Irish rebounded to win 4–1. George Patterson, who
lived on to 1977, scored the first Maple Leaf goal midway in
the second period in alliance with Bill Brydge.

Then Bert Corbeau, rushing up from the Leaf defence,
escaped one-eyed Leo Reise at the New York blueline. Corbeau broke clear and passed the puck to Ace Bailey. His shot
beat Jake Forbes in the New York net: 2–1, Leafs up for the
first time in their history.

"Up the Irish!" yelled fans who still recognized the players
as St. Pats.

Goalies Roach and Forbes were unbeatable in the last

period until, after 16 minutes, Bailey scored again. A few seconds later, Corbeau combined with Bailey for the last goal in the first Leaf game. Carl Voss, the rookie, played mostly left end on the bench. "Toronto fans couldn't believe," he said, "that different jerseys and a name change could make such a turnabout in the team's luck."

The change was brief. The Leafs limped home last, 29 points behind King Clancy and the first-place Ottawa Senators.

Conn Smythe won, however, on another hockey front in 1927. He guided the Varsity Grads to the Allan Cup, emblematic of the Dominion senior hockey championship. The Grads subdued Fort William in a series played in Vancouver and returned to rejoicing in Toronto.

The Toronto Star ran a picture of Coach Smythe on the first sports page. The cut line under the picture read, "He's uncanny at handling players."

Uncanny Conn and his conquering Grads were paraded from Union Station up University Avenue to the University of Toronto campus.

"The next time I do this," Smythe vowed, "it'll be a Maple Leaf parade."

There would be longer parades later that spring for an American pilot who flew an airplane from New York to Paris alone, without stopping. He possessed, romanticists wrote, "the look of eagles in his eyes."

John Lardner, the essayist, wrote in *The Aspirin Age*: "The pilot's performance was instantly recognized as the climactic stunt of a time of marvellous stunts, of an epoch of noise, hero worship, and the sort of individualism which seems to have meant that people were not disposed to look at themselves and their lives, in general, and therefore ran gaping and thirsty to look at anything done by one man or woman that was special and apart from the life they knew."

The flimsy Spirit of St. Louis flew 3,610 miles to Paris in 33 hours and 29 minutes, and wobbled out of the sky at Le Bourget field at dusk. "Well, we are happy to be here," the American pilot said. "I am Charles A. Lindbergh."

Hockey players relaxed strongly in the summer of 1927 with wine and women, "climb in, Mabel, and let's get stinking." They sang "Roll 'Em, Girlie, Roll 'Em" as their flapper friends peeled their stockings down to their brazen knees. They danced to the absurd Mississippi Mud ("It's a treat/To beat your feet/On the Mississippi Mud").

Women were enticed by movie ads to dream of "brilliant men, beautiful jazz babies, petting parties in the purple dawn" or "white kisses, red kisses, the truth." Impassioned preachers denounced the motor car as "a house of prostitution on wheels." On wheels, Ford offered a fancy touring model for $515. The Studebaker company, celebrating 75 years of homage to the internal combustion engine, slashed prices on all models.

The Prince of Wales, wilful playboy of the Western world, surrounded by flatterers and flunkeys, visited Toronto in midsummer to open the Princes Gates at the Canadian National Exhibition. The gates were ugly then, and now. It would be nine years before the Prince became King Edward VIII and, quitting the throne because he couldn't place his twice-divorced American bride on it, became a candidate for Upper Class Twit of the Century.

Lindbergh's epochal flight across the Atlantic inspired others, including Harold Ballard, to ride the skies. One flight north of Toronto prompted one of the tales he tells.

"We're in this farmer's field, me and the pilot, and he's having a hell of a time getting this rickety two-seater off the ground. We finally get up, maybe 70 feet off the ground. Then we hit the top of a tree, which ends the flight. As we're falling out, I see a haystack and dive for it. I make it and live. The pilot? He damn near got his ear ripped off."

On September 30, 1927, a lumbering libertine named Babe Ruth hit his 60th home run of the year for the New York Yankees. His single-season standard for belting baseballs beyond the fences stood until another Yankee in a distant generation, Roger Maris, hit 61 in 1961.

On November 15, 1927, Toronto hockey players, wearing blue-and-white sweaters with a maple leaf on the chest, began a 44-game NHL schedule. They lost 4–2 to the New York Rangers, and Conn Smythe knew the Leafs needed all his spare time. He could not afford to accompany the Varsity Grads to the 1928 Winter Olympics in Switzerland. Ballard joined the Grads in Smythe's absence and, as he has said, the Grads won and he stole the Olympic flag. Jiggs Higgs, he said, was impressed.

A fresh passion consumed him in 1928. He joined his friends at the National Yacht Club (NYC) in racing dinky runabouts off the Toronto waterfront, a sport guaranteeing risk and excitement. Lou Marsh, writing a sports column at the *Star*, called the boats "sea fleas."

"Sea flea, hell," Ballard said. "It was like riding a fucking plank with a motor attached."

One of his sea-flea partners was Harry (Red) Foster, who played for nothing for the Toronto Argonauts, and subsequently scored in the advertising game.

"Hydroplaning suited Harold," Foster said. "He knew boating, he was a strong swimmer, he knew about motors. And he liked to take a chance."

Marsh beat gums and drums for the sport in a *Star* column, "Sea Flea Bites." "This is the most sensational water sport developed in 20 years. To see these little craft tear through the water is a revelation to landlubbers. ...Watch Ballard, a West End boy." The West End boy was admitted to the Hell Driver's Club at the NYC in 1929. In the spring, he drove *Cracker Jack* in a B class race on Frenchman's Bay, 18 miles west of Toronto on the north side of Lake Ontario.

William Houston, who has no trouble restraining his applause for Ballard, was moderately impressed by his sea-flea research. "Ballard made a strong showing on Frenchman's Bay, then competed a few days later at the Brule Lake Regatta. He pushed the favorite before finishing second. He was rated a favorite for B class in a NYC meet in June for the R.B. Maybee trophies. But Jimmy Rogers, a Toronto teenager, beat Ballard handily. That evening, the entire NYC fleet ran a series of mile heats outside the sea wall off the Exhibition grounds and a crowd of close to 10,000 attended."

"It was," Ballard said, "a hell of a fast way to get your ass wet."

In August, 1929, Ballard got his rear end wet and his ego burnished when he won a sea-flea free-for-all, Toronto to Oakville, 22 miles of flailing through six-foot seas.

"We were dumb to race in that danger," Ballard said. "But

no Hell Driver could be called a coward, so 21 of us took off."

Twelve boats finished the course, one sank and several drivers were rescued by lifesaving crews. Ballard drove *Torcan's Pup* and, near the finish, duelled for the lead with Wes Kelly of Peterborough, Ontario.

Ballard had a 15-second edge at the finish, but both drivers crossed the line on the wrong side of the flag. *Torcan's Pup* swirled around to cross properly, but Kelly watched from the pier because his battered boat had sunk.

"Son of a bitch," Ballard exulted, "it felt good not to crash."

The real world beyond Lake Ontario, in early October, 1929, did crash. Money markets collapsed. Money losers began to jump out of windows. In England, 12.5 million men were thrown out of work. In Toronto, people sang the words to pianist Ernest Siet's popular song, "The World Is Waiting for the Sunrise."

But for 10 Depression years, the world would know only sunsets.

CHAPTER 3

Riding out the Depression

◆

The depressed decade between the stockmarket shatter in October, 1929, and the advent of the Second Great War in September, 1939, was called by Barry Broadfoot, in his oral history of the dirty thirties, "Ten Lost Years." Everybody fell into the Valley of Debts. The poet Al Purdy wrote of "riding a boxcar through the depression," of the unemployed riding the rods, scarred and scared, growing older, hopeless.

Seldom Seen Gene, a racetrack tout, said, "Pay was $2 a week and nobody had $2. Streetcar tickets were five cents each and everybody was walking." Gene was called Seldom Seen because he was occasionally in jail for theft, which he called "finding something before it is lost."

Ten lost years, but not for Harold Ballard and buddies. His prayer was "Give us this day our daily circus." In 1930, on a raw April day, he entered a long-distance outboard race in New York state, 129 miles down the Hudson River, Albany to New York City.

"This," he said, "was another wet-ass special." He was driving a new boat, the *Buttercup*, belting along on power supplied by a Johnson Seahorse motor. "I'm in the lead for 35 miles or so, when, son of a bitch, a fucking log ripped off my propeller. I yanked the motor into the boat and jammed on another propeller. Cost me goddamn near a half-hour."

Ballard gunned *Buttercup* back to contention when a large, motorboat cut across his course, churning waves. *Buttercup* hit a wave, flipped up, tossing Ballard onto the bow.

"Son of a bitch, I had to hustle my ass back and grab the steering before the boat turned over! Finished 19th, which ain't bad, the trouble I had."

His 19th overall placed him second in the B class for amateurs. Two other Toronto drivers also had respectable finishes. New York newspapers called them "the Canadian

Polar Bears." Mayor Bert Wemp held a civic reception for
them when they returned to Toronto.

Racing boats represented Ballard's drives and dreams, foi-
bles and follies, his sad, mad escapades. He fought to survive
in frigid Lake Ontario a few weeks after the City Hall hooray.
On a Friday night, with the worn old teeth of winter still in
the wind, he joined Red Foster and Jimmy Rogers in a death-
bound ride off the Toronto waterfront. They overreached for
danger.

William Houston sketched the vivid details.

> Foster was steering from the front of the six-metre,
> flat-bottomed craft, Ballard sat beside him, and Rogers
> was at the back beside the motor. About a mile out, the
> boat lurched and turned into one of its waves. The three
> were thrown in the water. It was a chilly evening and all
> three wore sweaters and overcoats. Ballard, a strong
> swimmer, set out for a buoy 100 metres away, appar-
> ently under the impression that he was the only one in
> the water.
>
> Foster, seeing that Rogers was in trouble, turned back
> to help him and called to Ballard to do the same. Ballard
> returned and they managed to keep Rogers afloat. They
> couldn't go near the boat because the motor was still
> running and the boat was cutting crazily in circles
> through the water. Minutes later, Red Orde, operating a
> sailboat called the *Tigris*, saw Foster's boat running loose
> and the men struggling in the water. It took Orde 15
> minutes to manoeuvre close enough to pick them up.

Foster was half-conscious when rescued. Rogers slipped
away and sank, finished. Ballard had gone down twice and,
gasping, was hauled aboard. They were returned to the
NYC, shivering from exposure, waiting for word of Rogers'
fate. Searchers never found his body.

When they heard the bad word, death, they wept. "I never
bawled again like that for 35 years," Ballard said, "after my
wife died." Dorothy (Jiggs) Higgs Ballard succumbed to cancer in 1969.

The Depression did not daunt Harold at a time when most
Canadians were flatter than a bankrupt's bastard. He danced

the summer nights away with Jiggs at the Palais Royale or the Silver Skipper on the Humber River. He won prizes at dances at the Prince George Hotel, downtown at King and York Streets. He won a ton of coal in a raffle, proof indeed that them as has, gets.

King Clancy said, "Everybody else is singing 'I Can't Give You Anything but Love, Baby,' and Harold wins a ton of fucking coal he didn't need."

Harold earned a good living at his father's machine shop and, through the NYC boaters, got his first job running a hockey team.

The boaters backed a senior team, the Toronto National Sea Fleas, in the Ontario Hockey Association in 1930–31. Red Foster, involved and eager, recruited the players for manager George McFarlane, a notable lacrosse player. Ballard was business manager, his first experience at strumming a lively tune on a hockey cash register.

"You can bet I made the register ring, all right," he said. "We sure put asses in the seats."

In 1931–32, the Nationals, as they become known, were loaded with some of the best players outside the NHL. Norbert (Stuffy) Meuller tended goal. Doug (Weiner) Lough was a nimble centre. Wiry Ken Kane played a slambang left wing. Bruce and Ross Paul, fired up, were a robust pair. The playing coach, Harry Watson, considered superior to many in the NHL, had been an Olympic star in 1924. The Nationals rolled to the Allan Cup, the all-conquering senior amateur champions of Canada.

The season, 1931–32, was a vintage year, hockey style, in Toronto. After the Sea Flea conquest, the Maple Leafs stormed the mercenary heights and won the first of the team's 11 championships. Conn Smythe, exulting, had pulled off his longest chance. The Leafs beat the New York Rangers three successive times in a best-of-five series, all by tennis scores, 6–2, 6–4, 6–2. There was a champagne celebration in the Toronto dressing room, jubilation unconfined. Smythe felt someone tug his arm.

"Put 'er there, Dad!" Stafford Smythe, the stickboy, then 11, thrust out a small hand. Father and son embraced, Stafford enjoying his father's sweaty glory, never as close again.

Before 1931–32, Smythe, rather than his players, was the dominant performer on the Toronto team. He was from the slash-and-burn school, atomic tempered and rash. There was the time on Christmas Day, 1928, when the Leafs beat the Montreal Maroons in the Mutual Street Arena. Rough antics belied the goodwill — 23 penalties were called.

Smythe was in feisty form. He berated the referee for failing to call fouls committed by the Montreal bully, Nelson Stewart. Smythe did not subside until the referee, an unfortunate named O'Leary, socked him with a $100 fine. Stewart hollered at the tyrannical Toronto manager, "Whyn't you take your fucking spats and go home for Christmas with your kids?" Smythe wore pearl-gray spats around his ankles, regarded as fashionable, if comic.

The NHL did not consider Christmas official unless games were played on December 25, and Smythe was not about to take his spats anywhere. His wife Irene, patient and serene, gift-wrapped the day for their three children, Stafford, Miriam and Hugh.

Smythe built towards his 1932 champions with hockey planks supplied by his loyal subaltern, Frank Selke, an electrician at the University of Toronto. Selke was short and cunning, masking his shrewdness with the unctuous demeanor of a business agent for an embalmers' union.

"Smart little bastard," Ballard said of Selke Sr. "You had to watch him."

"Selke could goose you with the old soft soap," Smythe said, "but he could be disloyal."

Disloyal or not, Selke started the junior Toronto Marlboroughs in 1924 and directed the best of them to Smythe. Selke was an admirer of the first Duke of Marlborough, a British general who drove his troops to bleed and beat the French at Blenheim in 1704. The noun "Marlborough" was too long for short newspaper headlines. Toronto sports editors breezily pruned the word to "Marlboros," or, in a tight squeeze, "Marlies."

Graduating Marlboros were prominent in Smythe's first championship year. Reginald (Red) Horner played defence with a muscular malice that turned the Gardens into a Basilica of Brawn. Charlie Conacher and Harvey Jackson formed two-thirds of the celebrated Kid Line. Joe Primeau, a gentleman centre, was the other third.

Four days before Christmas, 1928, Horner played a junior game on a Saturday afternoon. He was a sturdy six feet, 190 pounds and 19 years old. Smythe scouted the junior game and, afterwards, approached Horner.

"You think," Smythe said, "you'd be in shape to play another game tonight? For the Maple Leafs?"

Horner was hooked on the budding Maple Leaf vision and, startled in the presence of the Great Man, mumbled, "It'd be a pleasure, sir."

Smythe drove Horner to the Mutual Street Arena, where the redhead started on defence against the Pittsburgh Pirates, a decrepit team which knew the word "win" only by hearsay.

First shift for Pittsburgh came Frank Fredrickson, a crafty Manitoba Icelander carrying the puck into Toronto territory. Fredrickson dropped his head one way, faked the other way and left Horner immobile in his jockstrap, rooted to the ice. Fredickson shot wide of the Toronto net and the puck rebounded off the boards into the Pittsburgh zone. Fredrickson retrieved it and, his ears flapping intelligently, tested Horner again.

Horner, moving with the play this time, hammered Fredickson like a roof caving in. Horner's check was sufficiently brutal to earn him his first penalty in the NHL. He thought Smythe would cuss him out between periods, but he was disabused of the notion.

"Don't stop, kid!" Smythe said. "What do penalties matter? We write 'em off as mistakes. No man ever made a million if he didn't make the odd mistake."

About then, Smythe, bristling, minted his maxim, "If you can't lick 'em in the alley, you can't beat 'em in the rink!"

Ballard, watching the Leafs whip the Pirates, said, "Smythe always said Red Horner was the greatest goddamn body-checker he ever saw. Me, too."

Horner eventually served 1,254 minutes in NHL penalty boxes, slightly less than one day. Ballard told me, "You should look up the poem Ted Reeve wrote about Horner's first game. A hell of an epic."

A mock epic, anyway. Reeve, the poet laureate on the sports pages of the Toronto *Telegram*, was delighted to salute Horner's arrival in suitably hilarious verse.

> Our Reginald Horner
> Leaped from his corner
> Full of ambition and fight,
> He broke up the clash with a furious dash
> While the stockholders shrieked with delight.

Smythe retained Clarence (Hap) Day, who never seemed especially happy and who became a minority partner in C. Smythe for sandpits. Day played defence in the style of a lovelorn octopus, clutching and grabbing, and stayed on until 1938, then became the most successful manager-coach in Leaf history. Day's early-day friends included Smythe and Ballard, although both abandoned him when they considered him no longer useful.

Off the ice, Smythe insisted in 1928 that Billy Barker be listed as the Leafs' first vice-president because of "his gallantry in wartime." He was listed in Leaf programs as "Lt. Col. W.G. Barker, V.C., destroyer of 53 German planes with his Sopwith Snipe."

Smythe believed an occasional pep-talk from the famous warrior would inspire the Leafs to win. Barker's first exhortation was his last. The air ace was an alcoholic who frequently, Smythe said, "got plastered." "Like a parched fish," Ballard said, "Barker drank. The night he was supposed to goose the Leafs, his car skidded on Jarvis Street and turned upside fucking down."

Barker arrived dishevelled at the Mutual Street rink, clothes torn, face bloody, much the worse for wear. He gave what Smythe called "a hell of a speech on the importance of morale."

Smythe added, "I don't know how it helped morale, but it probably made a few of the players think about the dangers of drinking and driving."

"Pep-talks aren't worth a shit," Ballard said. "What Smythe needed was pep. He got it when Clance came to Toronto."

King Clancy was 28 when Smythe obtained him in 1930, small, wiry, five-feet-seven, 155 pounds, with, in the argot of the game, "guts to burn." A story, as Mark Twain said, goes with Clancy's acquisition from the Ottawa Senators.

The Senators would collapse in the death throes of the Depression, but they rebuffed rigor mortis by offering Clancy to any buyer for two players and $35,000. Smythe's partners, pinched for cash, wouldn't go beyond $25,000. Smythe got lucky with a race horse he owned, a claiming stiff named Rare Jewel.

Rare Jewel, in the fall of 1930, was nominated for Canada's premier juvenile race, the Coronation Futurity. She was the longest shot in the field. Smythe owned the filly in partnership with a gambler, Dave Garrity. Smythe's trainer, Bill Campbell, did not trust Garrity, who had scant use for Campbell.

Before the race, at Old Woodbine, Garrity slipped into Rare Jewel's stall and forced half a bottle of brandy down her throat. She liked it. Campbell returned to the stall after Garrity left and administered another half flask of brandy to Rare Jewel. She pranced to the post with more inspirational chemicals inside her than sprinter Ben Johnson had in the 1988 Summer Olympics. He got caught; Rare Jewel did not, since she wasn't required to give a sample of her urine.

Smythe won about $11,000 in bets, plus the Coronation Futurity purse of $3,570. "Now," he said, "I can buy King Clancy and win the Stanley Cup."

"Typical Smythe luck," Ballard said. "Rare Jewel, the horse, bought him a rare jewel of a hockey player. My buddy, Clance."

Smythe sent $35,000 to Ottawa, accompanied by two dispensable pros of modest distinction, defenceman Art Smith and forward Eric Pettinger, in sum roughly $50,000. Clancy was worth it, cheap at double the price. When he walked through the dressing room door, Maple Leaf apathy jumped out the window.

The Leafs jumped to second in the Canadian Division in 1930–31, then subsided to the Chicago Black Hawks in a preliminary playoff. For Smythe, the 9,000 fans attracted to a post-season game in the cramped Mutual Street Arena indicated he needed a larger cold-storage locker.

Equally significant was his decision to hire Foster Hewitt to broadcast every Maple Leaf game, first on CFCA in Toronto, later on a national network. Every time, for the next 49 seasons, Hewitt talked into a microphone, he was selling stock in the Maple Leafs. His agreement with Smythe was a handshake.

The building of the Gardens was a monumental piece of financing in depressed 1931. Smythe was an irritable scold, fuming and cajoling, rounding up financiers, refusing to retreat from his dream. The tale is told in the late Stan Obodiac's scholarly *Maple Leaf Gardens*, published in 1981.

> Smythe had help, initially advised by Toronto businessmen Larkin Maloney, Alfred Rogers, J.P. Bickell, Ed Bickle and his assistant, Frank Selke. . . .
>
> Smythe decided he wanted a block of land at Church and Carlton Streets, owned by the Eaton department store. He got it, underpriced, for $350,000. Eatons also bought $25,000 worth of Gardens' stock.
>
> Now the land was there waiting. All Smythe needed was money to pay for it and build the rink. He began knocking on doors. Bankers were offered the security of a good investment and profits. The city was approached with the idea that Toronto would have a major arena to be proud of, one that might also attract conventions. Unions were swayed by the idea for employment. At various times 1,300 men were employed on the project. The large number of unemployed workers at the time and the fact that costs were 20 to 30 per cent lower than they had been a few years earlier made it possible to erect the building in five months . . . for $1.5 million.

Ballard said, "I came to dislike the Smythes, but I admired Conn then. He got a hell of a rink built on time."

Smythe said, "The workers believed in what they were doing because part of their wages was Gardens' shares. There was only one dissident. He got into an argument one day with Cecil Shaw, the business agent for the electrical union who wanted the guy to work faster. They went at it with their fists, right under where we installed the time clock. At the end Shaw was on his feet and the other guy on his back looking up. It was maybe the best fight ever staged in Maple Leaf Gardens."

By November 12, 1931, when the Chicago Black Hawks visited for the first game, the Gardens was a clean, well-lighted place, rosier than Smythe's fondest hope. He had much pride in the warp and woof of Empire and had a portrait of the British king, George V, hung at one end of the Gardens.

George V's successors also had their portraits festooning the Gardens until Ballard gained absolute control in 1972. Then he removed Queen Elizabeth's picture in order to construct more seats. "I just booted her ass out of the Gardens," Harold said. "She never gave me anything. Never paid any taxes for me."

His antipathy for British royalty did not surface on opening night. He was 28 then, and impressed. "Smythe had bands from the Royal Grenadiers and the 48th Highlanders march on making a hell of a bagpipe racket. Everybody got a kick out of it when one of the Highlanders slipped on the ice and fell on his ass. We all sang 'Happy Days Are Here Again.'"

The Leafs fell, too, losers 2–1 to the Black Hawks. Harold (Mush) March, a Chicago forward no bigger than a handful of liver, had the distinction of scoring the first goal in Smythe's pleasure palace. Five months later, on April 7, 1932, the Hawks were nowhere and the Leafs were Stanley Cup champions.

"The Leafs won, we Sea Fleas won and we had a joint party," Ballard said. "In the Royal York. Everybody tied one on. Each player was given a jug of whisky before he entered the party room. Christ, we wound up with guys swinging from the chandeliers."

In 1932–33, a chiropodist could have got rich treating all the toes Ballard stepped on. Harry Watson retired as coach of the Sea Fleas and Ballard, coaxed by his players, replaced him.

Pal Hal was a reluctant candidate. He was 29 and had no back-of-the-bench experience. He didn't know, either, that a woman who would influence him later was about to arrive in

Fort William, at the top of the Great Lakes. Yolanda Babik was born on January 3, 1933, to Yugoslav immigrants who owned a hotel. She would, in 1987, have her name changed to Yolanda Ballard.

Ballard said of his hockey background, "I never played much. I don't know any more about coaching a hockey team than St. Peter knows about African golf." William Houston observed, "Ballard's coaching was a fiasco. Dress up the Keystone Kops in hockey uniforms, throw in several scenes from the movie 'Slapshot' and you get the idea of what Ballard's attempt at coaching a hockey team was like. It was something of an omen, because there would be many more tragi-comic seasons after Ballard controlled the Maple Leafs."

The Canadian amateur champions were chumps. Defections and injuries caused the Sea Fleas to flunk. One reporter, watching them lose 5–1 to the Hamilton Tigers in January, 1933, was somewhat acerbic: "It was a sorry display by a team that was the Allan Cup and Ontario winner. They floundered around like a bunch of schoolboys and were out-classed, outplayed and generally outed right out of the rink."

Missing the playoffs, the Sea Fleas permitted their tempers to come untied. "You should have seen Kenny Kane one night," Ballard said. "He had lots of pepper in the old pot. He jumped a referee and beat the shit out of him."

The referee, Frank McCurry, assessed Kane a penalty for slashing in a game against the Toronto Marlboros. Kane argued that the limping Marlboro had clumsily moved his ankle into Kane's stick.

"You're gone!" the referee said, pointing to the penalty box.

"Fuck you!" Kane said, loudly aroused.

Kane shot the puck at the astonished referee, then dropped his stick and attacked McCurry. Slapshot, indeed. Kane throttled the official and beat upon him as a drum. The Ontario Hockey Association, aghast at the boyish ogre, suspended Kane for life.

Ballard, ever nimble between his head bones, told Kane not to worry. "So we miss the OHA playoffs? So what? I'm going to take the Sea Fleas overseas for the world tournament. You're coming along. The OHA ban won't apply overseas."

There was one word for the Sea Fleas' behavior in Europe in 1933, and William Houston found it. "Notorious," he wrote. "Ballard's gang was notorious." They scourged Europe like Asian flu, the first Canadian rowdies to sack arenas in London, Zurich, Berlin, Paris and Prague.

The Sea Fleas played two exhibition games in England and two in Paris prior to fetching up in Prague for the world tournament. Rambunctious, provocative, they beat the intimidated Czechoslovaks 8–0. The United States, represented by the Massachusetts Rangers, shut out Austria 4–0. In the final, in overtime, Ballard's bruisers lost 2–1. They did not like it much. From Prague, they invaded Berlin, where a goose-stepping Austrian corporal had pranced to power two months earlier as chancellor of Nazi Germany. Adolf Hitler was preparing to lead another Teutonic migration across Europe.

"We should have clubbed that Nazi son of a bitch," Ballard said, "but we were too busy stoning German hockey players."

A brawl, one of those messy bench-clearing battles, inspired German fans to strafe the Canadians with bottles, beer steins and slightly used bratwurst buns. In Zurich, Swiss fans became agitated when Kenny Kane raised, as it were, Cain. He tripped the referee; he bodychecked the U.S. goaltender; he flailed passers-by with his stick. Swiss fans retaliated by pelting the Canadians with snowballs and pickled frost.

Ballard did not blame the petulant Swiss. He reasoned that Switzerland's age-long neutrality must be a very frustrating condition. Since the first referee fell out of a tree, and began chasing the nearest blonde, Canadian hockey players have been big, overgrown boys with clubs in their hands, forever stimulating hostility among the spectators.

Ballard was more benign in his international relations than several latter-day Canadian tourists. Team Canada, en route for the first series at the summit, in downtown Russia in 1972, paused for two spirited games in Sweden. Wayne Cashman, among other Canadians, addressed the Swedes in uncouth terms. "Where," Cashman demanded upon landing in Stockholm, "were you Swedes in World War II?"

The Swedes did not care for such Canadian charm. The next night, in the game, Cashman inhaled six inches of a Swedish stick thrust down his throat. He was unable to eat solid food or talk much for several weeks thereafter.

Ballard's marauders, in 1933, retreated from Europe through France, delighted to confront the Paris police. There was a chaotic scene in a Paris hotel.

"We're having a party with the Americans," Ballard said, "on the mezzanine floor. A fan, one of those pushy frogs, wanted to join in. We said, 'Screw you,' so he called the cops." Gendarmes rushed up the stairs, nightclubs brandished in the belligerent manner of a highsticking hockey player. Ballard met the top cop at the top of the stairs, not at all pacific.

"I knocked that cop ass over teakettle down the stairs," he said. "Then there were guts to clean.

"My players came to help out," Ballard said. "We shove down to the lobby where three cops grab me. One hits me on the head with his goddamn stick. I'm woozy when they lug me to the can. It was war."

French authorities asked the Sea Fleas never to infest Paris again. Ballard was released after officials from the Canadian embassy intervened.

"I had to give them something to do," Harold said, "to earn their money."

The Fleas cheefully dismissed their antics after arriving home, blithely claiming the European press exaggerated their vulgarity. Ballard was not contrite, glad to be home in time for the longest game played in Maple Leaf Gardens.

The Leafs had finished first in the Canadian Division in 1932–33 and played the Boston Bruins, winners of the American Division. They were tied two games each in a best-of-five semifinal. The deciding game was played in the Gardens on April 3, 1933.

Charles Coleman picks up the story in Volume 2 of his seminal trilogy, *The Trail of the Stanley Cup*:

> ... The fifth and final match was a thriller. It left 14,500 fans, as well as the players, limp with exhaustion ... The Bruins thought they had won late in the third

period and netted the puck, but it was ruled offside. Then followed five overtime periods.

The closest thing to a goal came in the fourth overtime period when King Clancy rifled the puck past Tiny Thompson in the Boston net, but a whistle had sounded just before he shot. At this stage, past midnight, NHL president Frank Calder suggested that the team toss a coin to decide the winner. Boston was agreeable, but Toronto elected to play to a finish. . . .

Conn Symthe, worried and weary down to his spats, went into the Leaf dressing room. "We can toss for it, boys," he said, "or we play 'er out."

Many of the Leafs lay on the floor, their legs up on the cow stools they sat on to dress, resting, tired. One of them, Baldy Cotton, leaped to his feet when Smythe mentioned the coin-toss.

"No goddamn way!" Cotton said. "Let us out there, Conn, and we'll beat their ass."

Smythe instructed his coach, Dick Irvin, to use the fresh legs of Ken Doraty in the sixth overtime period. Doraty was a utility forward from the Ontario town of Stittsville, so small he resembled an emaciated fifth-grader.

Up in the gondola, Foster Hewitt made a memorable call at 1:51 a.m. "Andy Blair intercepts! Blair has the puck! Ken Doraty takes it! He shoots! He scores!"

The Leafs had won 1–0 after 104 minutes and 46 seconds of overtime. In mid-Toronto, a radio fan, Harry Fyfe, took out the family garbage at 1:45 a.m. and forever regretted missing Hewitt's hoarse dramatics. The last four words — "He shoots! He scores!" — became Foster's signature call. He was the first of the best hockey broadcasters, and modern moose-callers are still cribbing from his locutions.

Ballard knew the reason for the prolonged Boston-Toronto marathon. "Awful ice. The Gardens couldn't remake ice between periods in the thirties. So Clance and those guys were skating in slush up to their ankles."

One longer game occurred two years later, in the Montreal Forum on March 24, 1936. The Detroit Red Wings beat the Montreal Maroons 1–0 on a goal by Mud Bruneteau after 116 minutes and 30 seconds of overtime. Fans who remained for the finish did not escape the Forum until 2:25 a.m.

In 1933, after barely escaping Boston, the Leafs subsided in the Stanley Cup final, beaten three games to one by the New York Rangers. "Hockey Night in Canada" was born on November 10, 1932, and, across Canada, Foster Hewitt's broadcasts caught us by the scruff of our imaginations.

CHAPTER 4

Skating through a Golden Haze

♦

I was a small boy on an Alberta farm, still bumping my head under the table, when the Leafs relinquished the Stanley Cup to the Rangers. I bawled, distraught as only a childish partisan could be when the Leafs lost the last game of the 1933 Stanley Cup final, 1–0, the Ranger goal scored by hard-boiled Bill Cook.

Harold Ballard wouldn't range into my orbit for 30 years, but the blue-and-white robes of the Leafs were the garments I wanted to touch. Coast to coast, on radio, Foster Hewitt made the Leaf team Canada's team. They still are, for a certain generation, on nights when they are athletically respectable.

In Alberta, two time zones behind Toronto, Hockey Night in Canada came on the air at 7:00 p.m. We'd burrow into the old megaphone attached to a battery radio to hear, "Hello, Canada, and hockey fans in the United States and Newfoundland!" God, it was grand to be transported on Foster Hewitt's staccato tones to the peak of Maple Leaf excitement.

My parents, immigrants from Wales and the Cheshire hills, were scrambling, as all farmers were, on the ragged edge of survival. Their 480 acres were part of the prairie west, that vast patch extending north from the U.S. border to central Alberta, Saskatchewan and Manitoba. It is Big Sky country, nothing but miles and miles of miles and miles to every horizon.

Poor, my parents were, and I didn't know it. Sometimes they could not afford to have radio batteries charged. On those winter Saturday nights, I'd race a half-mile across a field to the neighbors' place, there to join a childless couple who humored a small boy in front of a large Marconi radio. "Hello, Canada. . . ." How delighted, how rich I felt.

They were demigods, those Leafs of Hewitt's description, beyond ordinary mortals, heroic. Only afterwards, when I

too would be bruised by humiliation and reality, did I realize
that athletes could be human and frail and funny and, therefore, more interesting than the inflated immortals of a child's
imagination.

Joan Finnigan's father, Frank, played for those Maple Leafs
and, in one of the best hockey poems ever written, she
evokes how it was to be the child of a Leaf luminary. "Grey Is
the Forelock Now of the Irishman" was published in *It Was
Warm and Sunny When We Set Out*, in 1970.

> Grey is the forelock now of the Irishman,
> stickhandler of my roaring Twenties birthright,
> F. Scott Fitzgerald of the sporting world,
> (and, between games, father to me).
> My beautiful brain-washed Canadian sons
> are bringing in the whole neighborhood
> to see the old pro alive,
> the all-round right-wing Maple Leaf god,
> Adonis of an arena now crumbled
> and fallen into the cannibal maw of mobs.
>
> The boys, crowding in at the door,
> surround him with a fiery ring of worship,
> envying his eyebrows,
> thick with scars inflicted by the high sticking
> of old idols, Clancy, Morenz, Horner —
> (and, my god, one of them is standing at attention!)
>
> When I was their age, unholily dreamful,
> full of the same power of innocence,
> I saw crowds pick him up and carry him away,
> policemen trampled down,
> hysterical women following their infatuation
> to the barricaded hotel-room doors,
> crying in the corridors
> their need for illusion.
>
> And I remember the millionaires who courted him
> whose money had not bought them youth
> and the golden skates of fame;

one of them used to invite him
into his suite at the Royal York for an oyster feed,
then ordered up by phone,
crustaceans, wine, stove, pans, chef and all;
another used to send him every Christmas
suitably engraved silver dishes
which my mother never used.

I remember my father, too, in the headlines,
on the gum cards, in the rotogravure,
and how, in the pasture, there was nothing
to charge but shadows and, in the dark beyond the night,
bright enormous butterflies crossing the moon
of his disenchanted vision; I heard him
cry out to them in another room but they stayed in his eyes
until we were well-marked by the days
of his going down into ruin.

Wrinkled now is the brow of my all-star father
standing in the doorway
of his grandchildren's generation
who must yet learn,
in smaller forums with less limelight,
how heroes are really made.

Joan Finnigan's mood is melancholy, something I wouldn't have understood at six. At six, all dreams seem possible. Only after, bearing scars, do we understand Joan Finnigan saying, as W.B. Yeats did, "I have been to the funeral of all my hopes, and buried them one by one. . . ."

Harold Ballard, not being of a retrospective nature, is rarely trapped in melancholia. He remembers the Leafs of my childhood for the joyous ribaldry of King Clancy, always the chairman in charge of good humor.

To see Clancy, in his eighties, was to start laughing. There was a perpetual grin on his map-of-Ireland mug, akin to the expression on everybody's favorite uncle who shows up at family reunions a little bombed.

"Oh I'm 40 years a sailor," King would burble in silly moments, "and never lost a raft!"

"King was involved in all the capers," Ballard said. "Son of a bitch, he almost fixed a game in the Gardens."

The caper was vintage Clancy, perpetrator of The Glorious Fix that Failed. And out in the hinterlands, we believed the players were superserious superstars ready to die for the blue-and-white, Toronto banners flying. Who would have thought our beau ideals would try to help a player from a rival team?

Eddie Convey had been briefly a Maple Leaf, a journeyman forward not competent enough for the champions, sent away to the abysmal New York Americans. His nicknames were Slider and Cowboy. The Americans would demote Convey to the minors, but not before Clancy tried to keep him in the NHL. The Americans visited Toronto on November 28, 1933 and, Clancy heard, Convey needed a big game to keep browsing on big-league sirloins.

Clancy's concern inspired him to conspire with Charlie Conacher, the burly, humorless right wing, and Lorne Chabot, the tall, dour goaltender.

"Look," Clancy told Conacher and Chabot before the game, "Eddie's in trouble. Also, his mother and girlfriend are sitting up in the blues. If we get a few goals up, like we should against these bums, let's make it easy for Convey. Let's help him score a couple."

The Leafs jumped ahead in the first period, 4–0 or something, far enough for Convey to get his chance in the second period, with Clancy's skilled collusion. Convey got off the New York bench and, for several droll minutes, hockey's stage was manipulated. He came on against Conacher on the Toronto forward line, Clancy on the Toronto defence, Chabot in the Toronto goal.

"Now!" Clancy called to Conacher as Convey skated down left wing. Conacher fell down to oblige Convey, who shifted towards Clancy. Convey hit the Toronto blueline with the puck and Clancy conveniently neglected to check him. Convey walked in on Chabot, who didn't move. Convey had a clear shot at the vacant side of the net. He wound up and drove the puck 20 feet wide.

"One more chance!" Clancy yelled and, on a return rush, Cowboy Convey came riding down the wing. Conacher faked a bodycheck, and missed. Clancy stumbled, and fell down. Convey swept in on the stationary Chabot, who left one side of the net invitingly open. Convey unloaded a wicked shot, high into the end blue seats.

"One more time!" Clancy told his conspirators and Convey got it, the next time he appeared on the ice.

"Let him through!" Clancy shouted at Conacher, who permitted Convey to skate past him. Convey escaped Clancy's bogus check. Telling it, in Ballard's hotel suites long past midnight, Clancy would be on his feet, aping the Cowboy Convey of 56 years ago.

"He flew by me, really dangling. He went cruising in on Chabot, who stepped aside and gave him the whole goal to shoot at. Chabot moved aside and whap! Convey hit him right in the Adam's apple with the fucking puck! Down Chabot went, choking and gagging. His tongue went down his throat!"

Tim Daly, the Leaf trainer, skidded on the ice to aid the stricken Chabot. Daly reached his fingers down Chabot's throat to retrieve Chabot's tongue.

"Any more of this," Chabot muttered, when he was up and could speak, "and that goddamn Convey'll kill me."

Clancy agreed. "I guess we better knock off trying to make the Cowboy look good."

"Yeah," Conacher said, disgust plain. "Fuck Convey."

Two weeks later, in Boston, Clancy and the Leafs played a boisterous game against the Bruins that had a nation-wide repercussion. On December 13, 1933, morning news-drinkers gulped down strong black headlines in the Toronto *Globe*. The blackest read:

FISTS FLY, HEADS SPLIT, AS LEAFS TRIM BRUINS 4–1.

Below it were the grim details in a dispatch with a Boston dateline: how the night before, surly Eddie Shore of the Bruins dumped Ace Bailey of the Maple Leafs on his head, how Bailey landed with crushing impact on the ice and was knocked unconscious, how a Boston neurosurgeon feared excessive brain damage. Bailey required three operations to relieve pressure on his brain. Conn Smythe kept a feverish vigil outside Bailey's hospital room in Boston.

Six nights after the incident, Smythe phoned hockey writer Bert Perry at the *Globe* in Toronto. "Have Toronto radio stations broadcast a prayer across the nation," Smythe said. "It is the only thing that will save the boy now."

Melodramatic, in hindsight, such gravity. The power of prayer was more fashionable in 1933, especially when it involved English Canada's hockey team. The request for prayers for Bailey was heard, in northern Alberta, over the Edmonton station, CJCA. My mother, a devout Methodist, responded to Smythe's request. That night, when my brothers and I knelt for prayers, she had us add, "Please, God, save Ace Bailey."

Bailey was saved. The next morning in Boston, at 2:30 a.m., a nurse stepped into the corridor where Smythe and a few reporters waited. "I think you can all go home now," she said. "He's gone to sleep. We think the crisis is over."

So was Bailey's hockey career. He never played again. He served in the Gardens for 47 years as an assistant to the penalty timekeeper. Abruptly, in 1984, Ballard dismissed him.

"Ballard fired four of us," Bailey told Paul Hunter of *The Toronto Star*. "He didn't say why. He just sent me a letter saying that my services were no longer required."

Bailey added, "Ballard's getting too mean. He used to be such a gentleman. I'm not surprised his Leafs do poorly."

Bailey was reacting to one side of a many-sided person, the chintzy side. Another of Ballard's sides, the generous side, was reflected in the senior hockey team he ran after the Sea Fleas became an endangered species. They merged with the West Toronto club as the West Toronto Nationals in 1934, coached by Dr. Horace McIntyre. Ballard managed the tickets, the schedule, the recruiting, the travel plans and the financing, all with the gusto of a weight-guesser at the Canadian National Exhibition.

Ballard signed Phil Stein to play for the Nationals. "I told Harold I'd play for him," Stein said, "but I was 20 and needed a job. He said, 'Stick with me and I'll get you $20 a week.' So he got me a job with a paper company owned by Reg N. Boxer, who was president of the Argonaut football team. The paper company paid me only $16 a week. Every Friday I'd go down to the Gardens to see Harold. He'd reach in his pocket and give me $4 to make up the $20."

Compared to NHL players, Stein was rank poor. "Least I ever made in the Depression was $7,000 a year," King Clancy said. "Felt I was rich as Rockefeller. Hell, I lived in the Royal York Hotel for $25 a month."

Ballard, in his 1934 hockey guise, was more fan than suave hockey executive. He'd barge into the Nationals' dressing room to exhort, "Jesus, c'mon you guys. We gotta beat these bastards." The players, clumping past him to the ice, heard his admonition, "Skate fast, shoot hard, knock the sons a bitches down, score often and don't get hurt!"

Off the ice, Ballard ran the machine shop for his ailing father. Sid Ballard died of lead poisoning in late March, 1936, victim of a lifetime of factory pollution. He was the first of the Ballards buried in Park Lawn Cemetery, on a shaded knoll west of the Humber River.

Harold inherited the machine business. His mother was left $80,000 in cash and the title to the family home on Parkway Avenue. She spent her summers in Canada House, a tourist hotel in Penetanguishene, on Georgian Bay. The proprietor of Canada House, Mrs. Mary Cloutier, remembered Mary Ballard as "close with her money, but kind."

Ballard shared a hockey prize in 1936, the Memorial Cup, awarded to the champion junior team in Canada. He managed the West Toronto Redmen, allied with Hap Day, who coached the Redmen when he wasn't playing for the Leafs.

"Harold had energy," Day said. "Wasn't afraid to work. When we needed stories in the papers, he'd stir things up. 'I can get ink,' he said."

Day and the Leafs had a memorable night in the playoffs on March 26, 1936. The Leafs were matched against Boston in a two-game quarter-final, total goals to count. The Bruins won the first game 3–0 and in the second game, in the Gardens, they scored another goal in the first period.

The Leafs came off for the intermission, sullen, behind 4–0 on the round. There was a one-seat toilet off the main dressing room and Charlie Conacher wandered in for a cigarette. He was the team's booming shooter.

King Clancy was on the toilet ahead of Conacher, camped

on the only available seat. "Get off there," Conacher muttered.

"Get off?" Clancy said, bristling. "Waddaya mean, get off?
Why should I get off for a bum who's playin' like you are
tonight?" He blew a puff of smoke. "I'll not be gettin' off."

Conacher had been restricted by a Boston shadow in the
series, followed around like a yappy terrier by Red Beattie.
He mentioned how he was being checked. Clancy turned
solicitous and stood up. "Well, now," King said, "sit down
and I'll tell you how to handle Beattie."

Conacher sat down and Clancy perched on his knee.
"Why don't you go out and belt Beattie? Go out and slug the
son of a bitch."

"The hell with that," Conacher said. "I'd get a penalty."

"So what's a penalty?" Clancy said. "I'll get the puck and
pass it to you just when Beattie's beside you. When he gets
close, whack him."

Conacher followed the instructions of his Irish collabora-
tor. He jammed an elbow into Beattie's astonished expression. Odie Cleghorn, a tolerant referee, overlooked the
infraction. A few minutes later, Clancy tripped Eddie Shore,
the meat and sinew of the Bruins. Cleghorn missed that foul,
to Shore's monstrous chagrin.

Clancy, skating in malicious circles, stimulated Shore's
wrath. "The man's blind, Eddie! He's robbin' you, sure as
hell. Look how he fucked up the call on Beattie!"

Shore, agitated, shot the puck at Cleghorn and hit the
official square in his ample ass. "You're gone!" the referee
shouted. "That'll cost you a two-minute penalty!"

Injustice nagged at Shore's short temper. He picked up the
puck and hurled it into a delighted Toronto crowd. "And
that'll be 10 minutes more!" the referee added "Misconduct
penalty for you!"

While Shore was gone, Charlie Conacher laid hold of the
Bruins with his meaty paws and, in two periods, simply
ripped them apart. The Leafs tied the score 4-4 in Shore's
absence. They kept scoring after he returned, finally winning
the game 8-3, and the series 8-6.

Conacher scored three goals and assisted on two others,
the sort of performance instantly caught in memory, like an

insect perfectly preserved for all time in a piece of clear amber.

The next week, in a pickup game on a prairie school-ground, one kid bumped another into a snowbank and romped on to drive a frozen chunk of horse manure between two pieces of coal used to mark the goal.

The other kid hollered, "Aw, who d'you think you are? Charlie Conacher?"

"Yes!" I said. "Oh, yes!"

No matter how big hockey seemed to Ballard and Smythe, and the rest of us absorbed in the Leafs via radio, the fate of the civilization in the late thirties turned on extraneous events. Several million Chinese couldn't have cared less how the Leafs made out. They were too busy repelling a Japanese invasion.

In Britain, in the political wilderness, Winston Churchill warned that Adolf Hitler's menacing gibberish written in *Mein Kampf* represented "the most malignant hatred ever to corrode the human breast."

In Spain, 1,293 Canadian volunteers in the Mackenzie-Papineau Battalion fought for the Loyalist Government against General Franco and his overpowering Fascists. Only 649 returned from the battlefields of Jarama, Brunete, Quinto, Belchite, Teruel and Fuentes de Ebro.

W.B. Yeats echoed in poetry what Churchill was writing in majestic prose. "Irrational streams of blood are starving earth." England slept, when it wasn't listening to a senseless Walt Disney song, "Three Little Pigs."

> Who's afraid of the big bad wolf, big bad wolf,
>   big bad wolf,
> Who's afraid of the big bad wolf? Tra la la la!

In Alberta, my parents and their rural contemporaries sought political salvation in a bombastic Calgary preacher, William Aberhart. His moral majority, the Masonic Marines, formed the world's first Social Credit government.

My father's passion for the Maple Leafs was matched by my mother's infatuation for the wilful Prince of Wales, who decided that he couldn't rule as Edward VIII without the woman "I love." The woman he loved was a twice-divorced American, Wallis Simpson. She had slept upward to reach the bedroom of a king.

Once more, on the Alberta farm, the power of prayer was invoked. My mother had my brothers and me add to our nightly prayers, "And please don't let the King marry that American woman."

But he did, and abdicated to become a useless royal derelict. British women of his generation, smitten by him, never forgave his failure to do what they considered his duty.

You cannot win them all with prayer, of course. We couldn't save the king on our knees but perhaps divine intervention helped save Ace Bailey, which for hockey fans was more important.

CHAPTER 5

The Tug of War

◆

A few observers 50 years ago regarded Ballard, in contemporary argot, as a suck for Conn Smythe.

George Parsons played left wing for the Maple Leafs from 1937 to 1939, before the loss of one eye ended his pro career. Parsons remembers Ballard's cordial attempts to ingratiate himself with Smythe. "Harold seemed to be with Conn all the time. At parties and dos and funerals and marriages and everything else."

Smythe like to be romanced, but he rebuffed Ballard's effort to become part of the Gardens' command. "Harold's an old-fashioned buccaneer," Smythe said. "If there's gold on that ship, it doesn't matter what flag you fly, Harold is going aboard and get that gold."

Smythe considered Ballard's business ethics the color and texture of a black rubber boot. "Harold might do a lot of good things with that gold, but that doesn't make his piracy right."

Perhaps it took a rogue to know one; Smythe, too, cut the odd ethical corner. He tossed away old colleagues such as Frank Selke and Hap Day as though they were wads of used Kleenex. He refused recognition of his son Stafford's wife, Dorthea, because she was a Catholic. When he talked about Catholics, Smythe used words you had to put out with a fire extinguisher.

He had similar pungent words for Ballard. "I've known Harold most of his life as a good giver, a good friend, but I would not give him a job at 10 cents a week." Smythe's compliments often had a fishhook in them. "Harold's way of doing things," he said, "is not mine."

One spring, when the Leafs and the Detroit Red Wings were eliminated from Stanley Cup contention, the teams toured western Canada by train. The train would pause at way-stations so the hicks could gawk at the big-leaguers. "Say, Hank," one farmer would say to another on the railroad

platform at Cornflake, Manitoba, "who's the little dude in
the fucking spats?"

"That's Smythe, Fred, the Little fucking Pistol. They say
he runs the Leafs like he would a world war."

The storied Leafs were on that trip, the Kid Line and
Clancy and Horner and the rest and they were royalty to the
rubes. Radio was the major link between Toronto and the
boondocks of Moose Jaw and Otter Haunch, Medicine Hat
and Sheep Tracks, Alberta. "We'd stop somewheres," Charlie
Conacher said, "and we thought the prairie fans would
climb all over us big stars. No goddamn way. The guy they
wanted to see was the little squirt, Foster Hewitt."

Conn Smythe understood our adulation of Hewitt. "Of
course, Foster was the biggest guy in our lineup," Smythe
said. "His broadcasts made us the toast from coast to coast."

These players were from the timeless region of daydreams, and I yearned to see the Leafs confront the hated
Red Wings on the vast surface of the Edmonton Gardens.
The rink was 215 feet long and 90 wide, the largest body of
frozen water south of Great Bear Lake. Attending the game,
from a farm 100 miles southeast of Edmonton, was beyond a
family budget that was rock-bottom depressed. We read
about it in the sports section of the Edmonton *Bulletin*.

The *Bulletin* was the poorer and more desperate of two
Edmonton papers. The other was the *Journal*, still in existence, an Alberta link in the Southam chain. In the mid-
thirties, an itinerant peddler came to the farm, in a Model A
Ford, selling newspaper and magazine subscriptions.

"We don't have money to buy shoes, let alone papers," my
dad said.

"Hell," the salesman said, "I'll take anything."

"Yeah? What, from a broke shit-heel of a farmer?"

The salesman gazed across the farmyard, where a flock of
turkeys was noisy with gobbledegook. "How about," he
said, "three turkeys for three years' subscription to the *Bulletin*?"

Dad considered the offer for, oh, five full seconds. "Okay,"
he said. "We'll take the *Bulletin*."

Twelve years later, for me, the *Bulletin* experience came full turn. I joined the paper as a cub reporter after being kicked out of the University of Alberta two steps ahead of the dean's shoe. The Dean of the Faculty of Education, noting my lack of attendance, said, "We need the space you aren't using. It'll help if you leave."

Radio, in 1938, was where it was beyond Hockey Night in Canada. Jack Benny played a comic tightwad for Jell-O on Sunday nights. Bob Hope gleamed brightly for Pepsodent, as risqué as the censors allowed with smart-ass lines like, "Oh, girls go out with guys like me/'Cause only God can make a tree."

Amos 'n' Andy were two white radio actors playing in black face as Amos, a cab driver, and Andy, a bum. We laughed at another of their characters, the Kingfish, represented as a big, shiftless deal afraid of his own black shadow. "Cold feet?" the Kingfish told Andy one night. "Man, Ah got pneumonia clear up to my gall bladder." We didn't realize, on those western farms, or didn't care, that blacks bleed the same color as whites, and show it in wartime. In peacetime, too, although Joe Louis did not bleed much in the early years of his heavyweight championship. Few foes beat him.

On radio, on June 22, 1938, the black man destroyed a white man from Germany. North Americans of all colors cheered when Louis knocked out Max Schmelling inside one round. Hitler's Hessian was clubbed by a two-fisted attack of unexampled ferocity.

I can hear Clem McCarthy now, taut and disciplined, describing the knockout from Yankee Stadium in New York: "Schmelling is down! ... The count is three! ...The German is hurt! ... Seven ... Eight ... Nine ... Ten! ... It's all over! ... Joe Louis, still world champion!"

Louis young was like that, fighting fast, punching with the hardest right hand in heavyweight history, eight disabling inches to the jaw. He was, in T.S. Eliot's word, "succinct." Eliot won the Nobel Prize for distinguished literature, but always regretted never meeting Joe Louis.

WASP Toronto, at the time, didn't want blacks or persons of any other pigmentation or nationality or creed to become too uppity. Ballard was good-natured about referring to Jews as Hebes, Italians as Wops, Frenchmen as Frogs, Englishmen as Limeys, Orientals as Slants. The first time Harold saw a Sikh wearing a turban, he said, "There goes a rag-top."

Ballard did not expect his Jewish friends to be offended. Sam and Israel Shopsowitz, heirs to Shopsy's deli on Spadina Avenue, were delighted with his attention. He advised them to buy property at Highways 400 and 401, on the beltway north of Toronto, for an expanded plant to smoke meat. He obtained a choice site for a fast-food booth on the CNE grounds and went into partnership with the Shopsy brothers.

"More than anyone else," Israel Shopsowitz has said, "Harold made Shopsy's the success it is today. He guided us when we needed it."

Ballard brought his thrust to bear on the CNE general manager to secure the CNE Shopsy site. The general manager was Bert Powell, and a broad stroke of irony goes with his assistance to Ballard. Powell's son Clay was the crown prosecutor who, in a subsequent generation, sent Ballard to jail in 1972.

In 1938, Ballard and Smythe and Maple Leaf zealots everywhere were fascinated by new boys on the hockey block. Syl Apps came off the campus of McMaster University in Hamilton to pivot tough-checking Bob Davidson on left wing and lazy, opportunistic Gordon Drillon on the right.

Foster Hewitt had Drillon shooting and scoring 26 times in 1937–38. Drillon added 26 assists in the 48-game schedule, for a total of 52 points and the NHL scoring title. No Leaf, through the ensuing 51 seasons, has finished first in points.

"Drillon couldn't get his ass off a dime," Ballard said. "But he'd pop the puck in the net, if Apps got it to him. He was one of Smythe's playboys."

Drillon was from Moncton, New Brunswick, and, glad to be away from there, made for the big league's bright lights. "What a hell of a thing," he said once, "a kid from Moncton playing in New York. It was something to meet Jack Dempsey, the old champ."

A player could, then and now, meet a new woman in New

York. "I felt pretty good once," Drillon said, "dating an actress in Manhattan. We had some laughs after closing up the bars."

"We had 15 guys on a club in my time," Drillon told me one night in Montreal in 1964, in Ballard's Stanley Cup suite. "Most of 'em better not smoke or drink, or Smythe'd kill you. But there's exceptions to every rule, eh?"

Smythe would order Drillon into his Gardens' office for regular reprimands. The boss would say, through his customarily clenched teeth, "I know we've got to have a few on any team who lush it up, Gordon."

Drillon would stroll out beaming, glad Smythe understood his boyish proclivities. At the door, he'd hear Smythe caution, "But Gordon, don't do it too many times, eh?"

Drillon was fat and middle-aged when we met. His hair had gone away and he was a biceps bureaucrat back home with the New Brunswick Department of Recreation. But his second wife, treasuring his dream, insisted that he always attend one or two Stanley Cup games a year. He said, "It keeps me part of what makes Canada, eh?"

I was unaware of any of this as a schoolboy in 1938. All I knew was that Drillon was the NHL scoring champion, a Maple Leaf eminence you could get a glossy picture of in exchange for one label from a pail of Bee Hive Golden Corn Syrup. Drillon was the first of countless pictures I collected, each requiring one label from a Bee Hive can. My mother had sufficient syrup in the cupboard to last until 1958, 13 years after I'd left home.

Drillon remembered, "Bee Hive really treated me good. They gave me $25 for using my picture and threw in a case of syrup. It cost me $16.50 to ship the syrup home to my mother, so I cleared $7.50 on the endorsement."

Deals were simpler then, when there were fewer wheeler-dealers, like R. Alan Eagleson, fewer pragmatists, idealists everywhere you turned. Or was the farm boy only young and glamor only a word?

About then, in 1938, Ballard was advised on a good deal to make. George Braden was the president of Canadian Cycle and Machine (CCM), a company that competed against Ballard's in the skate business. "Buy as many used sewing

machines as you can for that machine shop," Braden said.
"There's a war coming and there'll be a shortage of sewing
machines."

"Braden was right," Ballard said. "I bought every used
fucking Singer machine I could, and did all right in the war."

The dream world, on human balance, has always weighed
heavier than the real world. Mackenzie King, the quaint
Canadian prime minister in 1938, governed the country by
ouija board. He was a devious dreamer. He had met Hitler in
1937 and declared the German dictator was "a simple sort of
peasant . . . who isn't contemplating a world war."

So much for ouija boards. "The bleak fact," historian Polly
Toynbee more accurately wrote, "is that civilization is but a
stone's throw from barbarism."

Canada had a benign early summer of pageantry in 1939,
before stones hurled by Nazi barbarians smashed out the
lights all over civilization. King George VI and his impressive
Queen, Elizabeth, toured the Dominion in a corny demonstration of royal public relations. Not as big as Gordon Drillon winning a scoring crown, but big.

It was a command performance in the outback. Pupils
from rural school districts in central Alberta were piled into
trains and buses to get a glimpse of the meandering mon-
archs during their pause in Edmonton. School trustees had
us showing the flag, the Union Jack, even though many had
roots under other flags, in Scandinavia, Galicia, the Ukraine,
Quebec.

The regal circus appealed to my mother for the incontest-
able fact that she had been born on the same day, month and
year as the Queen — August 4, 1900. Mom was, I guess,
radiant when the imperious pair stepped out on the second-
floor porch of the Macdonald Hotel to wave to thousands of
prairie paupers.

We clapped and cheered politely in the long, cool Alberta
twilight, some of us anxious to get to the basketball game.
The Edmonton Grads, undisputed champions of women's
basketball from 1915 until they disbanded in 1940, made a
royal exhibition of themselves in the Edmonton Gardens.

There was nothing polite in our partisan cheering as the
Grads subdued the Tulso Stenos, best of their sex in the

United States. Stately Noel Macdonald, nimble Babe Belanger and their Grad playmates were Edmonton ornaments. Not as shining as Eddie Shore, who roared out of Alberta to Boston as Edmonton Express, but shining. Shore was a Grad fan, too. His first wife, Kate McRae, was one.

Queen Elizabeth, up close, seemed to appreciate the collective curtsy she got from the Grads. King George looked preoccupied, as though he wished his defected brother, Edward Windsor, was here and he could be off shooting a helpless grouse on a Scottish moor.

George was a reluctant king, his tongue tied in a stammering half-hitch. His good fortune was his wife. She covered his oversights and embarrassments. Gus Siverts covered the royal tourists for the Vancouver *Sun*, three feet away from them when they left a function in Hotel Vancouver.

George wandered down the front steps, heedless of the sycophants around him. Elizabeth was a half-step behind. Reporter Siverts heard her murmur, "Don't forget to thank our host, George."

"Ah, yes," George VI said to the beaming manager of the hotel. "Well . . . thanks."

The King was more eloquent in Toronto at the King's Plate, Canada's premier horse race, promoted in 1939 at Old Woodbine. Horse degenerates now call it old Greenback Downs. The Plate was named for the British monarch, whoever he or she might be, by the stuffed sports shirts who direct the Ontario Jockey Club. The race was the Canadian highlight for the Windsors. Most royals since the womanizing King Edward VII have been horsey people. I hold that a monarch who can read the Racing Form can't be all bad.

George VI, perusing the Form in 1939, noted that Archworth had the best form in a mediocre field of 12 rivals. Archworth romped through the chilly afternoon, 10 lengths ahead for owner George McCullagh. He was the dapper publisher of *The Globe and Mail*, aggressive enough for Conn Smythe to name him a director of Maple Leaf Gardens.

"I was there with Smythe," Ballard said. "We made a bundle on McCullagh's nag. Got back more than $5.00 for every two bucks we bet."

George VI gave McCullagh a purple sack containing 50 gold coins, a traditional Plate prize from the housekeeping satchel at Buckingham Palace. "I congratulate you, sir," the King said. "You have a great thoroughbred, there."

Elizabeth added, "Your horse is a real champion. He was never extended." Ralph Allen covered the race for the *Globe* and composed, for so literate a sports writer, a fulsome first paragraph: "Royalty saluted royalty with the timeless love of a good man for a good horse."

George McCullagh was jubilant. He was never a man to do things by half: his king, his horse, his gold coins, his sports writer.

Reality intruded in the late sunburned summer of 1939. Hitler's barbarism dawned on Canadians, perhaps even on Mackenzie King, when Nazi armies crushed Poland.

On September 10, a Sunday, CBC radio scheduled a mellow midday program, "Smoke Gets in Your Eyes," exported by the National Broadcasting Company. The program was interrupted for announcer Austin Willis to read, from a Toronto studio, a Canadian Press report.

"Canada," Willis read, cool, imperturbable, "has declared war on Germany." Then, Knowlton Nash wrote in *Times to Remember*, " . . . the CBC went back to the NBC music show, picking up the strains of 'Inka Dinka Doo.'" It was a mindless return to comfortable idiocy.

Smythe was 44 in 1939, considered too old for service a second time overseas. The first time, 1914–18, he got shot at often enough to win the Military Cross. This time he couldn't get to the war zone until he formed his own unit, the 30th Battery of the Royal Canadian Artillery. It was called, because of Smythe's prickly presence, "The Sportsmen's Battery."

English Canada's patriotism was sustained by an early outrage. The ship *Athenia*, outbound from Britain with 1,412 passengers, was torpedoed by a German submarine on September 3, 1939. There were 1,300 survivors, among them 12-year-old Billy Gadsby and his mother from Calgary. Gadsby grew up to play 20 scarred years on defence for the Chicago Black Hawks, the New York Rangers and the Detroit Red Wings.

Ballard was 36 when the world went down the menacing

road of a new decade, too old for any wartime draft. He worked hard in the machine shop, by Red Foster's account, or briskly hustled his hardware to the garment-makers on Spadina Avenue.

He built a large home on a medium-sized lot on Montgomery Road, a fashionable street in Etobicoke. The property is now worth $1.5 million. Over the front door, carved in the frame, is Harold's handiwork — "Woodycrest 1941." One windy fall day, when fallen maple leaves were turning cartwheels on the lawn, he phoned Dorothy Higgs. "Jiggs," he said, "let's get married."

She was 34 and she'd known him 17 years and she must have wondered if he'd ever invite her to nest. They were married in Avondale United Church in Tillsonburg, a tobacco town in southwestern Ontario. Dorothy's sister was the wife of the local doctor, C.A. Richards. The marriage vows were toasted in Mary Richards' home.

"Then," Harold said, "we went to Niagara Falls for the honeymoon." He couldn't resist re-working an old honeymoon gag. "We had a good look at the Falls, after we came up for air."

War beckoned Stafford Smythe, who was 20 in 1941, and aware of how perverse his male parent could be, Staff told a friend, "I'll see which way the old man is going in the war. Then I'll enlist in the other direction."

When Conn opted for the army, Stafford joined the navy as an ordinary seaman, on duty four years. In 1942, on leave from the Halifax naval base, Staff married a constant girl friend, Dorthea Gaudette. He was a nominal Protestant, she a Roman Catholic.

"You wouldn't believe it," Peg Christie, a Smythe family friend, said. "Staff couldn't have got a nicer wife. But Conn tried to break it up, right up to the morning of the marriage."

Family wheels turn inexorably into fresh generations. More than 20 years later, Conn's granddaughter, Candace Hoult, married Mike Walton, a Maple Leaf player and a Catholic. Conn proposed a toast to the bride, gallant and conciliatory.

"Religion is important," the old man said, "but other things are more important. Getting along with each other, that's what's important. We, as Smythes, welcome Mike, a Catholic, into this Protestant family."

The bride's aunt, listening at the back of the hall, wept. "I wish," Dorthea Smythe said, "Mr. Smythe could have said that to me, 25 years ago."

Major Smythe, bustling around in 1941, didn't ask what religion a recruit was. He only asked a man if he was brave enough to bleed. His combat credo was cut from his hockey motto: "If you cant' lick 'em on the ice, you can't kill 'em in the slit trenches."

Smythe might have thought many of his Maple Leafs would volunteer for his battery. Few did. He was joined by lacrosse players and softball players, by football players and sports writers, but ignored by big-league hockey players. The Leafs would wear his straitjacket in the NHL but not his uniform in WWII.

His uniform was worn by Ted Reeve, the lanky lyricist of the *Toronto Telegram*, and Ralph Allen of *The Globe and Mail*. They humored Smythe's truculence. The battery was shipped to Vancouver Island for guard duty in 1942, after an insolent Japanese submarine hurled a couple of firecrackers at the Canadian weather station on Estevan Point.

The assignment included building some shelters, lest Hirohito's henchmen return. Corporal Allen was one of Canada's best writers and the world's worst carpenter, as Smythe discovered, not quietly.

The Major inspected the wobbly jerry-built installation thrown up by the corporal's killing-knife carpenters. Smythe paused before it, in wonder. "Corporal Allen," he said, "it's not exactly like the Taj Mahal. . . . "

Before enlisting, Smythe dismissed Dick Irvin as coach and replaced him with reliable Hap Day. He believed Day would also watch Selke's machinations in the business office. Ballard was an amused bystander.

"Smythe always felt Selke was about to screw him," Ballard said. "But little Frankie, he gave me my first big break around the Gardens."

Selke appointed Ballard president and manager of the Toronto Marlboros, thriving through the war in junior competition. Staff Smythe played briefly for Ballard before enrolling in the navy. Afterwards they would carouse and conspire as, Ballard said, "Mike and Ike, the Gold Dust Twins."

The Selke connection remained tight even after Ballard served a jail term for himself and the dead Stafford. Selke, as chairman of the Hockey Hall of Fame selectors, supervised Ballard's admission to the hall in 1977. Conn Smythe, far removed from hockey power then, stifled a powerful urge to throw up.

Abroad, in 1941, Winston Churchill kept offering embattled Britons nothing except "blood, toil, tears and sweat." He was prime minister at last, a lion raging around London, rumbling through rousing speeches, defiant. "He marshalled the English language," John F. Kennedy would say, "and marched it into battle."

Churchill could not win with words alone. He needed the Americans. He needed the colossal break the Allies got when Hitler, 21 miles away across the English Channel, opted to attack the Soviet Union, Nazi armies grapevining all over the Eastern Front like cancer. The dictator was indeed demented. How Soviet citizens fought off the military malignancy, at the expense of 24 million dead, is remarkable in the annals of bloodshed.

Pacific isolationists kept American blood from shedding through the first 11 months of 1941. There were athletic diversions. Joe DiMaggio, swinging a bat as unerringly as a seagull flies, hit safely through 56 successive games, a monumental baseball record.

Cocky Billy Conn won the heavyweight title from Joe Louis across 12 rounds. In the 13th, the impetuous Pittsburgh prizefighter elected to slug with the champion. Conn's mandible disintegrated the first time Louis got a clear, short, succinct shot at it.

An early teenager on a western farm heard the dramatics on radio, the vivid impressions life-lasting. The tug of war began to pull older teenagers into armed service. It was an exciting time, briefly blighted after the coach deemed I was too weak a skater to play regularly for the high-school hockey team.

Goodbye, hockey illusions. Sometimes, in games easily

won against teams from rival towns, the coach permitted the scrubs to play. He installed me in bulky pads and sent me to the net, where I played a static but well-meaning game of goal.

The coach had empathy with the chagrin of a high-school hockey failure. He redirected my hockey hope. "We've got that high-school paper," he said. "You get the best grades in English, so I appoint you to write up our games." It was my first tentative, cliché-ridden step toward the Maple Leaf press box and Harold Ballard.

Ballard ingratiated himself with Hap Day after Smythe marched off to war. Harold, hearty and jovial, was an emotional opposite to stern, serious Hap. Ballard drove Day to games at the Gardens, and drove him home. Their wives were friends. Occasionally, Ballard travelled with Day when the Leafs were on the road.

Day told Bill Houston that Ballard always sought adventure. Only Harold and random milk-wagon horses would be up at 4:00 a.m. By 6:00 a.m., he'd be knocking on Day's door. "He'd be standing there with a big smile, ready to go. He loved to see the town."

War did not shake the NHL's enormous preoccupation with its mercenary tournament. The league contrived to skate around the Japanese hell of Hong Kong, the fall of France in a futile fight, the Jap bashing of the American fleet at Pearl Harbor, gas rationing, and restricted train travel without missing one league game, safe on the frozen backwater of reality. It was business as usual in never-never land.

The playland in April, 1942, pivoted on Make Believe Gardens, site of a Stanley Cup climax in stirring circumstances. The Leafs lost the first three games in a seven-game series against the Detroit Red Wings, then rebounded to sweep the next four, a feat unique in NHL chronicles.

The Sportsmen's Battery, training towards Europe, was stationed at Petawawa, a sandy barrens 99 miles northwest of Ottawa. Major Smythe, his uniform brass gleaming, took Stanley Cup leave. Hap Day was the coach, but every Toronto coach heard incessant advice from Smythe. His prod had the thrust of a bayonet.

"Bench Drillon and McDonald," Smythe snappishly advised after Detroit beat the Leafs three in a row. "They're swinging the goddamn lead."

Gordon Drillon had led the Leafs in scoring through the 48-game schedule, but in the final he fired blanks. Bucko McDonald was an immobile defenceman with the largest set of jug ears in NHL history.

Coach Day figuratively saluted the Major. He replaced Drillon and McDonald with fresher speed supplied by Henry Goldup and Don Metz, a remarkable replacement. Metz scored four goals in the last four games.

The teams came to April 18, a Saturday, tied three games each. Everybody in Toronto walked nine feet high, civic hope hooked to the resilient Leafs. There were 16,218 aroused spectators in Smythe's Tajmahockey, a rink record to that time.

Fans far-flung across the country shared the surging sense of comeback. "Hello, Canada, and hockey fans in the United States and Newfoundland . . . and to Canadian troops overseas!"

Ballard drove Day to the Gardens before the climactic seventh game. A bulldog ebullience was upon him. "Hap," Harold said, "you're going to knock those Detroit fuckers on their ass."

Smythe expressed similar sentiment in his pre-game peptalk. "Men," he said, the word bitten off hard as a cannonball, "I expect no redshirt to knock down one — not one — blueshirt."

The Detroit redshirts, stuffed with belligerents, knocked the Toronto blueshirts on their collective keister early. Syd Howe, no kin to Gordie, drove the puck beyond the struggling reach of Walter (Turk) Broda in the Toronto net. "The Wings one," Foster Hewitt, feverish in the gondola, was saying, "the Leafs no score."

Howe had beaten the best money goaltender in hockey. "If I had one game to play for the world championship," Smythe would say, "there's only one goalie I'd want. I'd only want Broda, the Turkey Man."

Broda played up to that praise through the final two peri-

ods of the most important game in 1942. Smythe walked
around the Leaf quarters druing the first intermission, agitated, swearing a brisk series of damnits.

He paused in front of Sweeney Schriner, an eight-year
NHL veteran, quicksilver smooth on left wing, unruffled,
confident. "What about it, Sweeney?" Smythe said, "Can
we win it for my guys in the Battery?"

Schriner gazed at Smythe with a smoke-ring calmness.
"Hey, boss," he said, "keep your chin up. Polish those but-
tons. You're going to have a Stanley Cup parade."

Few Maple Leaf pros have endorsed their confidence with
Schriner's niftiness. How he did it kept me hopping out of
my seat at the moving-picture show in my hometown. I was
double-dating with the best hockey player on our high-
school team, innocently sedate stuff at a time when we were
hooked more on shinny than sex.

Our best player's name was Bob Hanrahan, clever-skating
and red-haired, good enough later to have a brief cup of
coffee in the Montreal junior system. Bob kept the girls company while I ran across the street to the town garage to hear
Foster Hewitt holler out of a mantle radio.

"What's happening?" I asked the town's grease monkey.

"Leafs tied it, 1–1," he said. "On a power play. Schriner
scored."

I ducked back and forth across the street with the news,
oblivious to the black-and-white scenes flickering on the
movie screen. In Toronto, pesky Pete Langelle scored from a
scramble to produce a Leaf lead, 2–1. The noise coming out
of the radio suggested the Gardens had gone slightly nuts.

Then it was the third period and I stayed in the garage with
the grease jockey and a few of his farmer clients, all rustic ears
tuned to Toronto. I forget the name of that old movie. Next
week, the girl, miffed at my inattention, forgot me. I'll never
forget Foster Hewitt's hurray, late in the game, "He shoots
. . . He scores! . . . Sweeney Schriner scores the insurance
goal! . . . Leafs lead 3–1!"

They won 3–1, their fourth consecutive conquest after
three consecutive defeats, an unmatched Stanley Cup deed.
On the prairie, the picture show blinked to "The End."

"How'd the game end?" Bob Hanrahan said.

"Wonderful!" I said. "Leafs won 3–1. Schriner scored two."

"Swell," Bob said. "That's a better ending than the movie had."

"I hope," one of the girls said, "you guys have enough money for a piece of banana cream pie." We barely did have enough, 40 cents for a victory banquet in Ben Chow's cafe. The girls are faceless now, grandmothers I guess, but I still cut up memories with Bob Hanrahan of a star-bright Alberta night when Sweeney Schriner promised Conn Smythe a Stanley Cup for the Sportsmen's Battery.

In Toronto, there was champagne by the case, and the Leafs guzzled it in the elbowing presence of exuberant hangers-on, some of them late arrivals who hadn't been on the bandwagon when the band began to play.

Harold Ballard hugged Hap Day. "I told you you'd knock those bastards on their ass!" Day guided Leaf teams to four more Cups before the forties ended, the most successful decade in club history.

Smythe called Schriner into the Gardens the Monday after the Saturday celebration. Sweeney was two days hung over. "Geez," Smythe said, "the smell of you would paralyze a platoon of goats."

Then Smythe said, "I'm going back to the Battery and pretty soon we'll be going overseas. You're 34, the oldest and best I got here. Keep up the good work."

Schriner's work had sufficient guile for admission to the Hall of Fame, in 1962. He had been born in 1908 in the tiny town of Saratov in the Soviet Union, the first Russian admitted to hockey's version of Valhalla. Trivia experts are wrong when they insist Anatoli Tarasov was the first. Schriner's family, escaping the thuggish czars, emigrated to Calgary when he was eight months old.

The Stanley Cup spring of 1942 was a loaded pause before Canadians faced the sickening realization, for the second time in this century, that soldiers get killed uselessly because their generals are stupid. Lord Louis Mountbatten of the Allied high command was just clever enough to be stupid on a fairly large scale.

Mountbatten sent .. Canadian force, in mid-August 1942,

to raid the fortified French port of Dieppe. Intimidating lime-stone cliffs rise from stony benches where the Canadians landed for a suicidal frontal attack. Enemy artillery, mortar and machine guns turned the beaches into a killing ground. It was a pornography of blood.

Mackenzie King, the prime minister wearing sly boots, called a national plebiscite to release his Liberal lackeys from their anti-conscription promises. Quebec residents voted *no* by 72.9 per cent; the *yes* vote won by 80 per cent in the other provinces. Divided, King's Canada stood. "Conscription if necessary, but not necessarily conscription."

Maple Leafs began to enlist, the 1942 champions drifting away to manning depots — Nick and Don Metz, Johnny McCready, Bingo Kampman, Ernie Dickens and Frank Eddolls. Wally Stanowski, a rushing defenceman from Win-nipeg, joined the airforce. Bob Goldham, the first and per-haps best of defencemen who sprawled to block the puck, went in to the navy.

Irving Berlin composed "White Christmas," the big smarmy song of the Second Great War. Every time Bing Crosby warbled "White Christmas," homesick guys in the Sportsmen's Battery "dreamed of white Christmases we used to shovel."

Spencer Gaylord Evans, known as Spiff, uttered those words. He survived the war and returned with Smythe to the Gardens as director of public relations.

"Men," Smythe said, when he got them overseas, "we're here to beat Germans. After we beat 'em, any of you who don't get killed and want a job, come and see me at the Gardens."

Spiff Evans was one of those. So was Shanty MacKenzie, who apprenticed for war by fighting hand-to-hand battles in the line for the Toronto Argonauts. Len Heath joined the Battery after a Grade 12 bookkeeping course in Mimico, on the west Toronto lakefront. Post war, Heath was the Gardens' accountant, prominent in revealing the fraud and larceny executed in the 1960s by Staff Smythe and Pal Hal.

Pal Hal, in the 1940s, maintained his cosy connection with Hap Day and Frank Selke. Hockey is best described as warfare under wraps, and the Leafs began to lose when the wraps came off their players who volunteered for a real war.

Jack Fox, a hay-pitcher on a Leaf farm, was the first pro-hockey player to die. Fox was killed serving with the Princess Pats regiment in Italy, one of those avenging Canadian cherubs who knew all about death before he knew very much about life.

A future Ballard partner served in Italy with a certain swaggering distinction. John Bassett was a brash, flamboyant major commanding a company of Canadians. He had the audacity to force a pause in the war.

Sergeant-Major S.A. McKim told Maggie Siggins for her Bassett biography, "Bassett wanted to have a look at the German fortifications so he arranged with the enemy, who were yelling distance away, to have a truce for 10 or 15 minutes. We flew a white flag while John and the German commander met at the top of a dike and surveyed each other's installations to see what effect our mutual harassment was having."

There is a four-letter word for that sort of boldness and Ballard, who can now barely utter Bassett's name without spitting, would utter it. The four-letter word is guts.

Bassett returned from battle inflated with his considerable self, convinced he could become a media mogul if he could find an angel. He found heaven in the richbuck Eaton family.

Bassett came up bingo, too, in his association with Ballard and Staff Smythe. He made millions in 1971 from a 1961 investment of $700,000 in the Gardens, most of it because of Ballard's aggressive promoting.

Material success was beyond their gaudiest dreams in 1943. Bing Crosby burbled "White Christmas" to the top of the wartime charts while a skinny rival began knocking the sox off the bobby soxers. Frank Sinatra was dubbed "Swoonatra."

Sinatra survived, as Pal Hal has, a pair of Golden Oldies. A woman I knew, intimate and passionate, once murmured within two inches of my ear, "When Sinatra sings, I feel like I'm naked and being massaged all over with cold cream." We made love, naked, to the soothing sound of his long-play records.

Frank Selke attempted to keep the Leafs competitive in 1943 and 1944. He obtained Babe Pratt, a lusty, imposing defenceman from the New York Rangers. He recruited Ted (Teeder) Kennedy, a rugged teenager from the Lake Erie town of Port Colborne.

Kennedy had a Hap Day determinism, implacable and flinty, always wanting the piece of ice you were standing on. He led Day's teams to five Stanley Cups, but not in 1943 and 1944.

Those NHL years belonged to the Montreal Canadiens. Few Canadiens went to the real war, reflective of the Québécois who declined to participate in what they insisted was a foreign fight. Those Canadiens included Maurice Richard, a Habitant hothead who believed putting on a Montreal jersey was a declaration of hostilities on English Canada.

Richard was a flaming rocket from the blueline to the goal, his nickname earned in bursts of crackling hate. He fixed goaltenders with the Rocket's red glare, rarely more baleful than on March 23, 1944. He scored five times in a 5–1 slathering of the Leafs in a playoff game.

Foster Hewitt was among the mightily impressed. The Toronto broadcaster, asked to choose the three stars, intoned, "First star, Maurice Richard. Second star, Maurice Richard. Third star, Maurice Richard." That night every cretin in the country knew the word "unanimous" meant Maurice Richard.

The embarrassed Toronto goaltender was Paul Bibeault, a wartime substitute who chartered new dimensions for ineptitude. Walter Broda, Toronto's money goaltender, had been hustled reluctantly to war.

Broda, facing induction into the army, was a money goaltender indeed. He bargained himself between military districts in Toronto and Montreal, aware that many officers commanding service centres were jockstrap sniffers anxious to assemble strong hockey teams.

Broda decided to play for the Montreal Army. He left Toronto near midnight on October 15, 1943, on a train, accompanied by a sergeant-major attached to the Montreal Army. His draft notice was about to expire. Finks from the

Toronto Army, Military District No. 2, contacted the Royal Canadian Mounted Police.

Mounted cops apprehended Broda and his Montreal escort at Don Station, east of Toronto. Caught, a draft evader, Broda was quickly inducted into the army in Toronto. There was a period of brisk training, long enough for the Turkey Man to learn the difference between a Lee Enfield rifle and a CCM goalstick.

Then, still shouldering a goalstick, Broda was shipped to Europe. War stormed, but army authorities nonchalantly allocated hockey players to assorted service teams. Broda was safely assigned to the Fourth Division team in Holland, proof that sportsmen were indulged, even at the front.

Not all sportsmen sought or got the authorized favors allotted to privileged players. Albert (Red) Tilson, a fleet, compact forward with the Ottawa Generals, was the premier junior in Canada in 1943, a potential Maple Leaf.

Tilson graduated from the Generals to the Army base in Cornwall, Ontario. One of his instructors was the loudest second lieutenant in the history of the Canadian military, George F. (Punch) Imlach. Punch was apprenticing for peace, which he subsequently shattered by yelling at hockey players instead of footsore fusiliers. Recruits saluted the Imlach-style martinets in a jeering song, "Fuck 'Em All."

> Fuck 'em all, fuck 'em all,
> The long and the short and the tall;
> Fuck all second looies with their bloody bren guns,
> Fuck all the captains and their bastard sons,
> For we're saying goodbye to them all,
> As back to our barracks we crawl,
> There'll be no promotion, this side of the ocean,
> So cheer up my lads, fuck 'em all . . .

Red Tilson, on the other side of the ocean, fired guns rather than goals. He was killed during the hard-won Canadian sweep to liberate Holland. Top scorers today in the Ontario Hockey League, pursuing his snuffed-out dream, compete for the Red Tilson Trophy.

The Gardens was in the front line of the home front. There

were rallies to sell war bonds and victory stamps. Ballard remembers playing bingo to buy bullets. He would, in the rattle and roll of 1980 politics, refuse Russians the right to play hockey in the Gardens. That seemed ironic: in 1943, the Gardens was the scene of "A Salute to Our Russian Ally." War veterans offered prayers of thanksgiving for Soviet victories over Nazi invaders.

Those of us in the hither and yons of Canada kept in touch with Toronto by ubiquitous radio. Every night at 10 o'clock Toronto time, we heard the National News read by Lorne Greene, the Voice of Doom. His deep, bottom-of-the-barrel tones had the rumble of distant thunder, especially when the war news was grim.

In 1944, by June, our long losing crusade took a U-turn. By then it looked as though, in the song's words, "Yes, There'll Always Be an England." D-Day was June 6.

We can sit on the spring ground, on any D-Day anniversary, and think about the 1944 death of men we knew. If they weren't kings, they were princes at the very least. They hit France in waves rolling up the Normandy beaches, Canadian troops in the massive assault on a tyrant's Europe.— the 1st Hussars and Canadian Scottish, the Reginas and North Novas and Glengarrians, the Fort Garrys and Sherbrooke Fusiliers and Chaudières, the North Shores and the Queen's Own Rifles.

They struck French towns with names that have acquired an archaic sound, thin and far away as a trumpet on the Douai Plains beyond Vimy Ridge — Courselles and Bernières and St. Aubin and Beny-sur-Mer.

The forecasts were for 1,800 Canadian casualties the first day, but a thousand soldiers got momentarily lucky. Only 800 were killed or maimed on D-Day. "Only." The word has an insensitive ring, the corpses nothing more than numbers in the logistics of generals.

D-Day, 45 years away from guts spilled, is for elderly survivors who might pause to reflect that it was the beginning of the end for many comrades. For the dead, it was the shortest day. No more hockey nights in Canada.

The Sportsmen's Battery, bivouacked at Eastbourne on the southeast English coast, was held in reserve. Major Smythe chafed for action. He got it in a softball game, playing third base for the headquarters' team.

Smythe was the victim of a Sportsman's assault and battery, as recorded by his biographer, Scott Young.

> . . . The other team had a big happy guy from Peterborough, Joe Dwyer, to whom I'd assessed a few hours pack drill from time to time. He reached second base with none out. The next pitch was a high hopper hit to me.
>
> I faked a throw to first to get Joe running for third, and then blocked him off for the out. There's no way I expected him to take it easy because I was an officer, and there's no way that he, as buck private, was going to think I expected him to take it easy. Our unit wasn't built that way. So he sailed into me.

Smythe was knocked ass over spats, as it were. "When I woke up I had four broken ribs. One knee had hit my chest and knocked me back across third base and right across the coaching box. I passed out and swallowed my tongue."

Ted Reeve, keeping score, reached the fallen Smythe first. Reeve used his pencil to pry out Smythe's tongue and hold it. Smythe came out of his daze to hear someone say, "The Old Man's hurt bad. We got to get him to hospital."

Smythe spat out Reeve's pencil. "The hell you say, and that's an order. Get a civilian doctor."

Smythe told Scott Young, "The pain was tremendous and I was thinking, if I'm hurt that much they'll take the Battery away from me and send it to Normandy under somebody else. . . ."

In hospital, Smythe was visited by a colonel. "I hear your ribs are broken," the colonel said. "I can't let you go to France hurt."

Smythe reached for his holster beside his bed. He put his hand on the revolver and said, "Now listen. I've been through a tough two and a half years to get here. If I'm not going to France, you're not going."

The colonel, cowed as the referees whom Smythe used to taunt, retreated. Smythe was aching and taped up and riding a padded chair rigged up by Shanty MacKenzie when his Battery embarked for Normandy on July 7, 1944.

"The Toronto papers made a hell of a deal of it when Smythe got to France," Ballard said. "He was some kind of hero in *The Globe and Mail.*"

The story belongs to Ralph Allen, who had been discharged from the Battery to serve as the *Globe*'s war correspondent. There is a mouldering headline in the paper's morgue for June 28, 1944:

CONN SMYTHE WOUNDED TRYING
TO SAVE BURNING AMMUNITION

Ralph Allen's report was datelined "With the Canadians in France," and began:

> War has never been far away since that terrible miraculous morning called D-Day. Today it seemed closer than it had ever been before. This was a personal feeling, bound up with that most impersonal of all war's byproducts, the official casualty lists.
>
> Up near the top of a coming casualty list, under the heading "Wounded in Action," will appear the name of Major C. Smythe, M.C., of Toronto. A little further down will be the names of a Toronto corporal and a Peterborough gunner, Red O'Connor and Les Clark, dispatch riders for Smythe . . .

Modern readers of Toronto sports pages will note how coincidence piles up on facsimile. Les Clark, no kin to the dead dispatch rider, is the father of an implacable Maple Leaf, Wendel Clark. This Les Clark, on vacation from a 5,400-acre farm near Kelvington, Saskatchewan, watches games from Harold Ballard's bunker in the Gardens.

Ralph Allen explained the random chance in a butcher's game without rules. " . . . My story is about three men, all of them athletes, who were knocked out of this war before they killed a single German. Most men who are knocked out of the war . . . get it pretty much the same way, scrambling in the dark hardly knowing what's coming at them. . . ."

Then Allen caught the Major Smythe he cared about. "Those who know him as manager of the Maple Leaf hockey team know him as a dynamic little ball of fire, who drives his team hard, screaming well-rounded insults at the referees

... generally giving the impression he expects his team to win every game it plays. It is not a misleading impression."

Smythe, in the Battery, "wasn't an easy to man to work for. If somebody goofed, everybody heard about it. 'Second place in war,' he said, 'isn't good enough.'"

Then, after a measured windup, Allen followed through with a dispassionate pitch. He had the good writer's taste to know that hyperbole is for hacks.

> The trouble started about midnight on July 25 while the Battery's Bofors guns straddled the jumping-off line for the Canadian thrust south of Caen. Enemy air activity was intense. It was a hot night for all the ack-ack guns on the beachhead ...
>
> At Battery headquarters a German plane dropped a flare on an ammunition truck. Through its light two other German planes flew back and forth, strafing. The burning tarpaulin of an ammunition truck threatened to blow up the piled boxes of ammunition and Battery headquarters ...
>
> Major Smythe did exactly what anyone who knows him would have predicted he would do. He was out of his quarters in his greatcoat and into the middle of it at once, tugging at the flaming tarpaulin of the truck, directing the dispersal of transport over his shoulder.
>
> The other headquarters people were in it, too, doing what they could in the red confusion. A few yards away the crew of one of the major's guns was blown right off the gun by a bomb and scrambled right back and resumed firing.
>
> When the ammunition truck went up the major caught a piece of shrapnel in the back. When they found him his body was partially paralyzed, but the major's spirit will never be paralyzed by a truckload of ammunition and a few bombs and machine-gun bullets.

Smythe was helpless on the ground, Allen wrote, but loud. "I'm all right!" he shouted. "Get those fires out!" Then they carried him to shelter, and out of the war.

Smythe was evacuated to England, dead from the waist down, perhaps saved by constant injections of penicillin.

"Conn might have been paralyzed in the legs for a while," Ballard said, "but you'd never paralyze his tongue. He kept yelling, in hospital, about the fucking zombies."

The word was peculiar to Canada in the Second Great War, the result of Mackenzie King's split-lip military. The Prime Minister had volunteers, and he had zombies.

Anthony Hopkins explained in his rollicking *Songs from the Front & Rear*, published in 1979: "In Canada, when conscription was instituted, conscripts could not be sent overseas unless they volunteered for overseas service. Zombies were the 70,000 men who chose to wait out the war at home. They were not much loved, either at home or among the troops, particularly not among infantry regiments which in 1944 and 1945 were sometimes desperately short of reinforcements to replace men killed or wounded in battle."

Smythe, recuperating, compiled complaints from other invalids about the shortage of replacements for casualties suffered on the Western Front. He raised his voice. Before he set it down, he had called Mackenzie King every sort of grubby little fat toad.

George McCullagh, who fought a brave fight behind the headlines, published Smythe's pungent comments in the *Globe*. George Drew, the Conservative premier of Ontario and a wounded alumnus of the First War, was delighted to chime in.

All were anti-Zombie, anti-Liberal, anti-King. The Prime Minister, a spiritualist and solid gold cornflake, confided to his diary that "Smythe-Drew-McCullagh are an unholy alliance." King added, "Maybe we should have cashiered Conn Smythe."

The craven King did not possess the boldness to dismiss Smythe from the army. In the field of political hipper-dipper, Willie Mac always ran around the ends. His style was to dissemble rather than confront. Smythe's insistence that well-trained Zombies be sent overseas forced King to cave in. A few were sent before the war ended, dragging their feet, whipped aboard troop ships in Halifax.

Smythe's corrosive antipathy for Liberals extended to the next generation. Staff Smythe had a withering scorn for Liberals, coarse and impious. When the Liberals had a chance to nail Stafford on an income-tax rap in the 1960s, they hammered him.

He was the Ike in Ballard's Mike-Ike blend, and Pal Hal said, "Ike drank himself to death before they could throw him in jail." Mike did the time for both of them.

That was a long time after the high time of 1945, when Lieutenant S.C. Smythe was discharged from the navy's Fleet Air Arm. In Europe, Canadians wheeling through Holland and Belgium were astonished to hear Foster Hewitt's hockey broadcasts transmitted by German radio. A female Nazi broadcaster, playing to the homesick, breathed into a microphone, "Why not call off the war, Canadian boys, and go home to see the hockey games?"

Hewitt had a response on December 23, 1944, before the Detroit Red Wings beat the Leafs 5–4. His call to Europe began, "Christmas greetings to our men overseas, and an extra big hello to Calamity Jane of Arnhem."

CHAPTER 6

The Silver Seven

A deep muffler of silence fell on Calamity Jane and other Nazi propagandists in the climactic spring of 1945, but not before Foster Hewitt broadcast another hockey exploit to fans on the Western Front. The Maple Leafs, wartime misfits, finished 28 points behind Montreal in the final NHL standing.

"Son of a bitch," Ballard said, "those Leafs were brutal. But they beat Canadiens in six games and Detroit in seven for the Stanley Cup. It was a hell of a homecoming gift for Smythe."

That was the poetic-justice thing to say; reality is harder-eyed. The 1945 Leafs won for themselves first, ego-ridden as all winners are. Smythe was a gimpy postscript to their party. His paralysis had subsided, but old wounds tormented him until he died in 1980, a limping 85.

Anyone who could see lightning and hear thunder and avoid an army draft was an acceptable big-leaguer in 1945. Jackie McLean, Jackie Hamilton and Thomas B. (Windy) O'Neill formed a line of little leaguers described in 1945's brand new word as "atomic." Vern DeGeer, in *The Globe and Mail*, tagged them "The Mighty Atoms," as though they crackled like something left overnight in a plutonium pile.

Ballard was inclined to less bloated rhetoric. "Windy O'Neill was a hell of a guy," he said. "A music man. Banged away on the piano. Windy, in fact, was the best fucking piano player who ever played right wing in the NHL."

O'Neill's professional aspirations abandoned him when the pros came home. He became a jolly Toronto lawyer who attended to George F. Imlach's hockey contracts. In the Stanley Cup years of the 60s, when Ballard's hospitality flowed 24 hours a day, Windy O'Neill was among those of us who committed dawn attacks on "Mother Machree" and other

72

songs suitable for boozing by. Deadheads, camp followers, a stray priest or two and the occasional small-time whore joined in. The Leaf celebrations in 1945 were more muted. Still to come were the Satiated Sixties when the Leaf leaders invited their intimates to the twin dens of debauch, Sodom and Gomorrah West.

Goaltending represents at least 65 per cent of a hockey team's strength, and a goaltender was the reason the 1945 Cup was won. Frank McCool was a lean Calgary player excused from military service because his warm batch of ulcers would have burned a hole through an army uniform.

In Toronto, soothing his ulcers with a milk poultice, McCool held a hot hockey hand. He shut out the Red Wings three consecutive times, 1–0, 2–0, 1–0, a Stanley Cup record. Then the war ended and McCool went home to Calgary, a man who passed by, now merely a line of agate type in the NHL guides, dead since 1974.

The Leafs won the 1945 cup on April 22. Fifteen days later, Churchill's Hinge of Fate slammed shut the war in Europe.

V-E Day uncorked the tensions of war in Europe, but a few Canadians were scheduled to help the Americans finish what the Japanese had started in the Pacific. We were saved from that perilous adventure when Harry Truman certified the dropping of atomic superbops on the doomed cities of Hiroshima and Nagasaki.

Retrospection and second-guessing of our inhumanity to a wicked enemy came later. Now it was time to get on with the rest of our lives. We sang "Pack up Your Troubles in Your Old Kitbag," teenagers very drunk. We had yet to learn it is easier to smash an atom than patch a quarrel. For one shining, selfish moment it was forever summer.

Staff and Dorthea Smythe purchased a house in mid-Etobicoke, five minutes away from the Ballards. Vicky Smythe and Mary Elizabeth Ballard were born near the end of the war. The Smythes produced a son, Tom, in 1946, then two daughters, Mary and Elizabeth. Bill Ballard was born in 1946 and Harold Junior in 1947. Harold Junior was called Bobby to distinguish him from Harold Senior.

The reader is struck, reeling off the names, by similarities.

Dorthea Smythe and Dorothy Ballard; Mary Elizabeth Ballard and Mary and Elizabeth Smythe; Mike Ballard and Ike Smythe, as Harold referred to himself and Stafford.

It is conventional, since the Battling Ballards have become Canada's longest running soap opera, to regard Harold as a callously negligent parent, too busy with business for family affairs. His children, groping towards him, believe he has an underdeveloped heart.

Too often he has said, "Children are like dogs. They come up, sniff your crotch and you pat 'em on the head and say 'Nice Fido, now screw off.'"

He admitted to Earl McRae in *Today* magazine 10 years ago, "My kids don't bother me, I don't bother them. I don't understand them or their friends, they don't understand me. I don't want to be a burden on them."

Harold Junior (Bobby) claims that when he was a small boy, his father stuck one of Bobby's fingers into an electric socket as shock treatment for a misdemeanor. Harold Senior dismisses his kid's claim as "pure bullshit."

Ballard signs more autographs for more children than any of his hockey players, but seems to have scorned gentleness with his own progeny. Stafford Smythe, too. They were not willing to be vulnerable enough to reach down to a child and say, "I love you." Their macho world had no room for softness towards their own.

Ballard's brood did not suffer from lack of maternal attention. Dorothy Ballard was an embracing woman, full of grace, glad to hold the many she cared about. Harold supplied the material things, unaware perhaps that you cannot buy filial devotion.

Tom Smythe, growing up with the Ballards, remembers Harold as an amiable uncle. He recalls what Ballard called "a day for the men" in New York.

The boisterous Ballard was at his affable best squiring his sons and the son of his closest friend around Manhattan, to the Empire State Building, the Statue of Liberty, the sights seen at whirlwind speed. There were frequent stops to inhale the junk food Ballard prefers. Tom Smythe told Bill Houston that the excitement ended in exhaustion. "And," Tom said, "I had a stomach ache for two days."

The peace won in the Second Great War was not peaceful for Ballard and Staff Smythe. "We began to travel at a million miles an hour," Harold said. "That was with the Marlboros and the Leafs." There was wine, women and so long, after what furniture stores call an occasional piece. Harold drove his cars the same way, recklessly.

Harold and Stafford were driving towards control of Maple Leaf Gardens, but not yet. Conn Smythe returned to his hockey shrine in 1946, impatient to stamp his fresh imprint on the altar. His first heedless act was to stamp out Frank Selke, whom Smythe regarded as competent but devilishly sly. Smythe demanded partisanship from an associate, or, at most, absolute acquiescence. He suspected Selke of a tunnel job while Smythe was at war, undermining him as managing director.

"Sure, Conn thought Selke was screwing him," Ballard said. "Frankie'd done a good job running the Leafs with Hap Day while Smythe was away. They won Stanley Cups in 1942 and 1945, for Christ's sake."

Conn Smythe did not own enough stock to exert total control of the Gardens. It was his story that Selke refused to back him in the stock fight he believed he'd have with other directors who didn't want Smythe as president.

It was Selke's story, before he died in 1985, that he caught Smythe in an indiscretion which led to his departure. Selke confided that he went to a spare room on the executive floor of the Gardens to get paper for printing a hockey program. The door was unlocked. Selke is supposed to have walked in, surprised to find Smythe on a sofa in the comradely embrace of a secretary.

Each man interpreted their dispute in his own wilful way. Smythe considered Selke disloyal; Selke knew about too many skeletons in Smythe's closet. Smythe found it convenient to pick a fight. "If you didn't work for me," Smythe said, "you'd starve to death."

Selke cracked back, in rare candor, "I'd rather starve to death than work for you."

Rather than starve to death, just then, Selke went to lunch. He returned to find a mean note on his desk from Smythe chastising him for leaving the Gardens without Smythe's permission.

Selke resigned in a scholarly snit. "Lincoln freed the slaves in 1865," he wrote Smythe. "I'm gone. Goodbye."

Selke, hired to rebuild the Canadiens, went as far as Montreal in the summer of 1946, finally given his own way. His way meant spending for a productive farm system, "the grey-flannel business way," Trent Frayne called it in *Maclean's* magazine. He fooled everybody with his soft velvet hand in a velvet glove. The Canadiens were artfully mobilized to win five successive Stanley Cups, 1955 to 1960, an unmatched span of conquests. Frank Selke's legacy is the sustained class of Canadiens since 1946.

Conn Smythe got his way as well, supported by Percy Gardiner, a Toronto stockbroker canny enough to turn blue chips purple. Gardiner sold Smythe 30,000 Gardens' shares for $10 a share, a bargain that gave Smythe the Ultimate Clout. He became unchallenged boss of the Gardens in November, 1947.

Smythe increasingly became both the conscience and straitjacket of the NHL. He encouraged Mervyn (Red) Dutton, the league president in 1946, to suspend Smythe's best defenceman for gambling. Babe Pratt played defence with a big roving insouciance, in the same carefree way he lived off the ice. He was among the Leafs who bet on hockey games.

"It was simple," Pratt said. "We'd lay our bets with the old guy who sold papers at the corner of Yonge and Carlton. He'd lay off his action with bookmakers in Montreal, who made the betting line for hockey."

Pratt convinced Red Dutton that he had never wagered against the Maple Leafs. He was expelled for 16 games for "conduct prejudicial to the welfare of hockey."

The league's explanation was pious claptrap, not lost on anyone who paid attention in the Gardens. Charles Coleman explained in *The Trail of the Stanley Cup*: "The Pratt matter precipitated an uproar from all sides, particularly when it was generally known that a so-called 'bull ring' operated in Maple Leaf Gardens."

Coleman added, "This betting centre was said to be frequented by some of the most prominent men in Toronto despite the efforts of police to suppress it."

Ballard filled in the blanks. "The bull ring was no bullshit. Gamblers had full run of the area behind the red seats. You could go up there and bet on anything that moved."

There is scant evidence that Conn Smythe discouraged the money lenders and bettors from infesting his temple. You can carry hypocrisy only so far. Smythe and his partners in the NHL cartel might not have wagered on hockey games, but they plunged into horse-racing. He had thoroughbreds, Selke had thoroughbreds, Jim Norris in Chicago had thoroughbreds. The horses were four-legged playthings to bet on. The owners were guided by a feudal law — "we'll tell our players what to do, and we'll do what we want to do."

Babe Pratt, to pay for his Toronto sins, was sent to Boston and later exiled to the American League. He had never been paid more than $6,500 a year. One year, 1944, he had been chosen as the most valuable mercenary in the NHL. His was a classic case of the NHL owners looting a player's clock of all his useful hours, then ripping off the hands.

To approve their arbitrary deeds, the owners needed a compliant commissioner. They got one in Clarence Sutherland Campbell, who replaced Red Dutton as NHL president in 1947. "Campbell is the right man," Conn Smythe said, "because he'll take orders."

Stafford Smythe, seldom inclined to echo his father lest he be considered weak, agreed about Campbell. "Where else," Staff said, "could we find a Rhodes scholar, graduate lawyer, decorated war hero, and former prosecutor at the Nuremberg trials, who'll do what he's told?" NHL owners, their eyes red-rimmed with power and greed, prefer their commissioners to make the sound of one hand clapping.

Campbell did so the next time the NHL had a gambling scandal. The league discovered in 1948, through illegal wiretaps on a Detroit bookmaker's phone, that members of the Boston Bruins were betting on games. The ringleader was slick and shopworn Bill Taylor, considered a glossy prodigy when he graduated to the Maple Leafs from the junior Oshawa Generals in 1940. Taylor grew up knowing where the action was.

Sweeney Schriner told me in Calgary last year, "We'd be

sitting at a beer table when Billy was a Leaf. Most of us would bring out $2 to buy. Billy'd bring out a roll with fifties and hundred-dollar bills."

Schriner once asked Taylor, "Geez, Bill, where'd you get that wad?"

Taylor was casual, as though big money was no big deal. "Oh," he said. "I know a few bookmakers."

Taylor's accomplice in betting in Boston was Don Gallinger, large, gifted and imprudent, a centre from Port Colborne, Ontario. Gallinger would bet, if the odds were high enough, on Tuesday not following Monday.

Clarence Campbell had evidence from Detroit police that Taylor and Gallinger gambled against their team, the Bruins. Gallinger, caught, admitted he had bet against the Bruins "five or six times." Campbell, taking his cue from Conn Smythe, barred Taylor and Gallinger from the NHL for life. They were given no chance to atone for admitted misdeeds. Scott Young, practically alone among fair-minded journalists, argued in *The Globe and Mail* that life was too long a sentence.

Conn Smythe would say, when he was asked about the harshness of the penalty, "The NHL must be kept clean of gamblers. Keep Taylor and Gallinger where they are, right under here." Then he would make the bully's gesture of pressing down with one thumb.

Far along, in 1970, 22 years after the lifelong bans imposed on Taylor and Gallinger, Smythe understood mercy. His older son, Stafford, was facing a jail term. Smythe was at his horse farm in the billowing Caledon Hills north of Toronto when he telephoned Campbell at NHL headquarters in Montreal.

"It's time," Smythe told Campbell, "to pardon Taylor and Gallinger. I saw little Billy at a sports dinner not long ago. I can't die before the NHL rehabilitates him."

Campbell was still obedient to a man who had not been an NHL governor for 10 years. He ordered the reinstatement of Taylor and Gallinger. Taylor was glad to return to the NHL as a scout for the Pittsburgh Penguins. Gallinger sought a few NHL jobs and was rebuffed. He remains beyond the NHL pale, loquacious and obsessed about his expulsion, forever spiritually scarred.

Herb Carnegie was a polished amateur hockey player in Toronto during the Maple Leaf boom after the war. He could have been a Leaf if the team had not had an unspoken policy on qualification-by-pigmentation.

Conn Smythe spoke it. "Too bad about Carnegie," Smythe told observers. "Too bad he's black."

Jackie Robinson, a flaming competitor, had broken the color barrier in baseball, but the NHL remained lily-white. Carnegie, still bitter, said, "They didn't want a black fly in white milk."

A color bar no longer exists in the NHL. Tony McKegney had been a useful left wing for 11 seasons in Buffalo, Quebec, Minnesota, New York and St. Louis. Grant Fuhr, a Stanley Cup champion in Edmonton, has been the best goaltender on earth.

Harold Ballard, on the racial scale, is color-blind. "I don't care if a guy is black with yellow spots all over him and hairy arms down to his knees," Harold says. "If he could help me win the Stanley Cup, I'd sign the son of a bitch."

The Leafs won with whites in the high time after 1945, four Stanley Cups in the heady seasons between 1947 and 1951. In 1950, when the Leafs didn't win, Ballard managed the senior Toronto Marlboros to the Allan Cup.

His coach was Joe Primeau, the hub 15 years earlier of the Leafs' Kid Line. His star was George Armstrong, the rangy son of a Scots father and Ojibwa mother, from Skead, Ontario.

Ballard managed the Marlboros with a familiar flair when they arrived in Calgary to play the local Stampeders for the Allan Cup. He knew there were Indian reserves near Calgary, Stoneys at Sarcee, Blackfeet at Morley.

"I told reporters that the Marlies might be from the East," Ballard said, "but we had a genuine Indian in our camp. We bussed out to Morley to meet Chief Bearspaw or Duckfoot or Moosegroin . . . I forget who the hell he was."

Whoever the Morley chief was, he was delighted to meet the Marlie brave. He decorated Armstrong with a chief's ceremonial headdress and solemnly proclaimed George "Chief Shoot-the-Puck." Armstrong was 19 and impressed; he went on to shoot 296 pucks for goals in 20 NHL seasons.

The 1950 Marlboros stymied the Stampeders four games to one for the Allen Cup. Ballard coached them in their solitary loss. Harold was back of the bench in the second game while Coach Primeau flew home to Toronto for his father's funeral.

"There were a lot of chuckles in Harold," Armstrong said. "Primeau came back and restored discipline. We won the last three games straight."

Primeau was rewarded with elevation to the Leafs as coach in 1950–51 while Hap Day remained as general manager. Those Leafs were Conn Smythe's last champions, the climactic club in the string of four Stanley Cups in five seasons. Smythe would preside over the Leafs for 10 more years but never again be close.

The 1947–51 teams possessed two of the notable defencemen in Toronto history, Gus Mortson and Jim Thomson. Turk Broda made his last grand stands in goal. Toronto centremen through that halcyon period were stylish Syl Apps, robust Cal Gardner, fancy Max Bentley and resourceful Ted Kennedy, the team's soul and guts.

Kennedy had a fierce concentration, especially when he had a bet riding on the Leafs. "If we were a goal behind after two periods," Babe Pratt once said, "Hap Day or Conn Smythe didn't need to come in our dressing room to give the pep talk. Kennedy'd take care of that. He'd rage around bawling out the guys who missed his passes. 'Goddamn it!' Ted would say, 'you guys are costing me money!'"

Kennedy's nickname was Teeder, hung on him by Smythe. During lulls in the Gardens, when the Leafs were in peril, a fan would call, "C'mon-n, Tee-der-r-r!" It was the signal for the Leafs to rally behind the most combative captain in their history, hard, cold and competent.

I asked Smythe when he was an old stone eroded by obstinancy, who was the quintessential Leaf of his time. I suggested that he might select Syl Apps, whom he cherished, or King Clancy, a loyal retainer.

Smythe fixed me with a glittering blue gaze. "As usual, Richard," he said, "you've got it all wrong."

"So who," I persisted, "was your all-time Leaf?"

Smythe replied in a wartime metaphor. "If World War III

broke out tomorrow, and I was going over the top again, there's only one Leaf I'd want at my right side."

"C'mon, Major. Who?"

"Teeder," he said. "Only Teeder. When it came to laying guts on the line to win, Teeder Kennedy laid on the most."

Smythe's appraisal of Kennedy was shared by fans across Canada who knew the Leaf captain only through Foster Hewitt's voice. I was leaving the Gardens after a game on February 23, 1988, when, out of the milling crowd in the lobby, a fan from Nova Scotia got my attention.

He was in his early 20s, in town from Halifax, his first visit to, for him, the most important building in the country. "Who," he said, "was the best player the Leafs ever had?"

I pointed to the team picture of the 1951 Leafs hung high on the wall behind us. "See the guy in the middle of the front row, cradling the Stanley Cup? They guy with the big C on his jersey? That's Teeder Kennedy. Conn Smythe, who invented the franchise, says Kennedy was the best all-time Leaf."

The fan from Nova Scotia looked up at Kennedy for a reflective moment, then reached into his jacket for his wallet. He thumbed it to find his driver's license.

"My dad's name," he said, "is Enos Wellwood. He only heard about Kennedy on the broadcasts, but he was impressed. When I was born, look what my dad named me."

The name on the driver's license was Teeder Wellwood, named after Teeder Kennedy. "C'mon-n, Tee-der-r-r!" That is true fame, hockey-fashion.

Smythe's last good team won the Stanley Cup with a gaudy flourish. The Leafs beat the Canadiens four games to one, but the Canadiens could have won four games to one. Every game went into sudden-death overtime.

The Leafs won the last game, the fifth game, with a heart-attack finish. They tied the score, 2–2, in the last 32 seconds of regulation time. Bill Barilko untied it, 3–2, after 2 minutes and 53 seconds of overtime. He was a robust, rough-cut defenceman from Timmins, another of the many Leafs from northern Ontario.

That summer, Barilko knew real sudden-death. He and a companion were killed on a fishing trip when their small plane crashed in the northern Ontario bush. He was 24, in his hockey prime.

The last of Smythe's good teams died with Barilko. The Leafs would not win the Cup again until 1962, and Smythe no longer commanded the Gardens. His son Stafford, Harold Ballard and John Bassett were in command then.

Smythe's monument is the Gardens, but he has others. He stumped around, barking orders and seeking money for crippled children. His energy was the inspiration for Variety Village on Kingston Road in Scarborough, home for handicapped young persons learning life skills.

"We owe it to them to give them the one thing we all need," Smythe said. "A chance."

Ballard was among the many Smythe touched for donations. "Not many better givers than Harold," Smythe said. Harold turned 50 in 1953 and there was more of him than formerly. He was growing a steakhouse belly, although he rarely ate steak. He was a gluttonous junkfood junky.

"Laura Secord chocolates are the best," he'd say. "If you've got any Laura Secord goodies on you, I'll steal them." He regarded himself as an expert on peanut butter.

"There's only one kind of peanut butter that's any goddamned good," he told John Gault in *Toronto Life* in 1972. "And that's Jack and Jill."

Ballard's generosity towards people he liked became legend in Toronto's garment district. Milton Kahn of Reliable Sewing Machines said, "If Harold likes you, the sky's the limit. He never really wants anything back from anyone. He's a mensch, a Yiddish word meaning a decent person."

Kahn started his own machinery business in downtown Toronto in 1955 and became a competitor of Ballard's. "What are you going to sell?" Ballard asked. "You got any inventory?"

"None," Kahn said. "We're buying it as we can pay for it."

"The next thing I knew," Kahn told Bill Houston, "there was a truckload of machinery at my store. It was from Ballard. I phoned him and said, 'Harold, I can't afford to pay for this stuff.'"

Ballard said, "Don't give me any goddamn arguments,

Milt. I'm going to help you get started. Pay me when you can. Just get started."

The good deed came full circle. In the early 1970s, when total control of the Gardens required all of Ballard's time, he sold his machinery business to Milton Kahn.

Staff Smythe was a foreman in his father's gravel pits in the Caledon Hills but covetous of his father's hockey club. He aped his father, the same raspy voice, the same go-to-hell swagger, a similar arrogance. He exhibited a rudeness which is the weak man's imitation of strength.

Milt Dunnell, well hooked to the NHL Establishment as sports editor of *The Toronto Star*, had a perceptive appraisal. "Staff decided to be like his old man," Dunnell said. "He was going to be a dictatorial little son of a bitch. But he wasn't really like Conn. He couldn't pull it off."

Buck Houle worked for Smythe in the gravel pits, served with him in the war and later managed minor teams in the Maple Leaf system. Houle believed Stafford was misunderstood. "He had a lot of his old man's ability. If he had some of Ballard's personality, he'd have been better off. People forget how good a hockey man he was."

Jim Norris owned the Chicago Black Hawks when Stafford came to power as Leaf president. "He was a good hockey man," Norris confided to Frank Orr of *The Toronto Star*. "But he was always looking to get laid. Staff was governed by his groin."

Staff Smythe's wretched public relations masked how his scouting in the fifties produced the Leafs who won Stanley Cups in the sixties. He had the rare ability to visualize how a junior of 17 might develop into a professional at 23. Not many hockey scouts have that foresight, which is why lush contracts are inflicted upon ultimate mediocrities. Often, in arenas and press boxes, you'll hear scouts mention a flash who has flamed out, "God," the scouts will say of a miss out, "that guy was a hell of a junior."

Staff Smythe found players who endorsed their junior precocity when they jumped to the pros. He ran with Ballard in gearing junior Marlboros to win the Memorial Cup in 1955 and 1956 — Bob Nevin and Billy Harris, Carl Brewer, Bob Baun and Bob Pulford.

St. Michael's College in Toronto was another proving ground for Leaf prospects. St. Mike's priests, with a bent for play rather than piety, sent Tim Horton, Dave Keon, Dick Duff and Frank Mahovlich to join Marlboro grads in winning four Stanley Cups in the sixties.

Entertainers, including the crowd-pleasing Princess Elizabeth, played the Gardens in the fifties. Elvis Presley, however, was an entertainer more to Ballard's florid tastes. The twitching Caruso, in front of a microphone, behaved like an outboard motor suitable for attaching to Ballard's sea-flea speedboats.

Presley's pelvic gyrations were suggestive of a man coming to a sexual climax. He wore his sideburns long. When he sang, he bisected the notes, as in:

> Lo-uving yo-ou e-uternally
> Wi-yith a-ull my-igh har-ut!

Presley wore blue suede shoes, and sang about them. Charles Templeton wore two-toned brown-and-white brogues and, on a loftier level, sang and preached about salvation with Reverend Billy Graham, the bullthroat of the Baptists. Templeton later recanted and became a distinguished broadcaster, editor, novelist and agnostic.

By 1957, the excitement was drained from the Leafs managed by Hap Day. Conn Smythe undercut Day in a cheapshot critique in *The Toronto Star*. Day resigned after 30 years of playing, coaching and managing for Smythe. Out of the Gardens, he discovered that Ballard abandoned him, too.

"Staff Smythe was replacing me," Day said. "I understood about blood being thicker than water. I understood Harold hitching himself to the Smythes."

Day may have understood, and nursed his hurt as proprietor of a tool-handle company in the southwestern Ontario town of St. Thomas. He could, in 1988, forgive Ballard. He came to Toronto on opening night, at Ballard's invitation, to drop the ceremonial first puck. Day was 87 and spry and elegant in a black tie and tuxedo. We stood, those of us with long memories and, for a long warm minute, applauded a Maple Leaf original.

Conn Smythe yielded to his son's bid in 1957 for a youth-movement in management. Staff Smythe was appointed to a Leaf hockey committee. John Bassett and lawyer Ian Johnston, approved by Conn because of their wartime service, were on the committee.

There were four others, all Gardens' shareholders, all well-heeled. George Gardiner was a stockbroker and horse owner, son of Percy Gardiner, the financier who backed Conn Smythe a decade earlier.

Bill Hatch knew about thoroughbreds from his family and was vice-president of McLaren's Food Products. George Mara, a gold-medal hockey player for Canada in the 1948 Olympics, was president of his family's wine distributorship. Jack Amell was vice-president of a large firm manufacturing jewelry.

Ballard was excluded from the hockey committee when it was formed, still not high on Conn Smythe's list. He bided his time, chuckling along, until Smythe needed Ian Johnston's legal skill to thwart the threatening NHL players' union. The threat was to the NHL shareholders' profits. Ballard replaced Johnston on the hockey committee in November, 1957.

The hockey committee, seven chaps prepared to party, were supposed to give championship direction to the Leafs. Toronto newspapers called them The Silver Seven, after the renowned Ottawa Silver Seven, winners of the Stanley Cup in 1903–4–5. A few of the Toronto Silver Seven knew what makes a hockey team. Most of them never opened their mouths about the game without subtracting from the sum of hockey knowledge.

Ballard set the tone. "The Silver Seven were a glorified glee club," he said. "It was girls, booze, fun and frolic." He was exaggerating, as usual. Only 4.5 members of the Silver Seven were known to carouse.

Rex MacLeod, covering the Leafs for *The Globe and Mail*, agreed about the frolic. "It was a never-ending party," MacLeod said. "Their mission was to boost the team morale.

Mostly it was morale-boosting for the Silver Seven. They were anonymous in their business successes but, suddenly, they were hockey celebrities."

Jim Thomson was Leaf captain in 1957, a solid defence-man held over from the championship years, 1947–51. He was among the players who dared to form a union. Conn Smythe, a many-sided character, could be graceful and graceless. Smythe interpreted Thomson's union activities as disloyalty. He defrocked Thomson as captain and shipped him to Chicago with a scurrilous endorsement.

"Thomson," Smythe said, "is a Quisling and a traitor." The reference was contemptible, graceless, unworthy of Smythe. Vidkun Quisling had been a pro-Nazi Norwegian who sold out his country to the Germans in 1940. Jim Thomson did not deserve the Quisling slur. All he sought was a better deal for NHL players who were underpaid by NHL owners whose emblem was a locked purse on a field of pinched pennies.

Yolanda Babik, 23 in 1953, weaved her way from Fort William to Toronto. She was employed as an operator by Bell Telephone. One right number seemed to be William MacMillan, the young lawyer she married on January 12, 1957.

CHAPTER 7

Buying the Gardens

◆

Harold Ballard bloomed during the social insurrection of the sixties. The decade confirmed Conn Smythe's estimation of him as a fast operator who would have thrived in the high noon of buccaneering, when pillage and patriotism went fist in glove.

He shared Shopsy's CNE Deli with the Shopsowitz brothers, often getting behind the counter to hustle corned beef and hotdogs. He invented, as an appetizer, a pickle-on-a-stick. He plowed his profits from the annual Exhibition into Gardens' stock.

Ballard came to 1958 with 3,606 shares of Gardens' stock in his portfolio, peanuts compared to the 147,000 outstanding. Staff Smythe, a working stiff in the Smythe gravel pits, owned 500. Their partner-to-be, John Bassett, owned 1,000 as proprietor of The Telegram Publishing Co., the journalistic tentacle of the Eaton octopus.

Ballard, Bassett and Stafford sought to buy out Conn Smythe in 1958. They offered $4 millon if he would relinquish his principal ownership and the presidency. Conn rebuffed their bid.

Undeterred, Bassett and Ballard kept buying stock. They were almost double-crossed by Stafford, who was prepared to side with his father. A block of 14,000 shares in the estate of a man named Webster were about to be sold. Ballard was mooching around the boardroom of the Gardens when he overheard Conn and Stafford talking about buying the 14,000 shares for $24.50 each. Ballard's ears perked up like an astonished donkey's.

"Right away," he said, "I rushed out of the boardroom to a pay phone and called Bassett at the Tely. John phoned the trust company handling the Webster estate and offered $25 a share for the whole kaboodle and we bought it all."

Old glee is on him when he recalls the squeezing of Conn

Smythe. "Conn was so bloody mad he told Stafford to stay to hell out of dealing with Bassett and me. I got a third of the 14,000 and Bassett two-thirds."

On the ice, it was ebb-tide for the Leafs in the late fifties as it is in the late eighties. They chopped and changed coaches and players; each fresh change was only a fresh mistake.

Then, in 1958, George F. Imlach arrived to restore the Leafs to Stanley Cup eminence. He was surpassingly bald, pot-bellied and bright, so full of himself that Rex MacLeod referred to him in *The Globe and Mail* as The Big I. The apt nom-de-goon was spun off The Big M, which Stan Houston of the *Telegram* called Frank Mahovlich, a prodigal left wing. Mahovlich on a big night was a great stallion leaping across bluelines, the most vivid player of his time, 1956 to 1974.

Imlach, cussing and cajoling, making trades, playing hunches, drove the Leafs back to Stanley Cup prominence by the spring of 1962. He ran the team as though he owned it, a pushy approach not guaranteed to ingratiate himself with Staff Smythe, who had his own ego to strut.

Stafford needed Ballard's balls in a continuing slanging match with his father in 1961. Ostensibly, the family feuded over how Harold and Staff manipulated the junior Marlboros, but that masked the real reason. Staff, at 40, wanted what he considered his hockey legacy. Conn, at 66 refused to accept that he no longer occupied the bully's pul-pit at the Gardens.

"Okay, Stafford," he said, after a directors' meeting, "if you're so smart, why don't you buy me out?"

Stafford was working for wages and had no financial swat of any kind. He asked Ballard, "Any way we can buy out my father?"

"You bet your ass there is," Ballard said.

They adjourned to the Silver Seven penthouse in the City Park Apartments behind the Gardens to think and drink. The penthouse was the playroom for the Silver Seven, but there were no playgirls this night. They needed more than $2 million to buy out Conn Smythe.

"Staff didn't have a dime to spare," Harold said. "He had no collateral. We decided I'd try to get the $2 million from my bank."

Ballard arrived home in Etobicoke at 3:30 a.m., but could not sleep. That is not unusual. He is accustomed to sleeping in four-hour snatches, then getting up "to make sure the sky isn't caving in."

He got up at 5:30, shaved and showered and put on a glaring white tie festooned with bright blue maple leafs.

He drove to the office of Harold E. Ballard Textile Machinery Company on Adelaide. He pored over the Gardens' books. He convinced himself that he could turn the Tajma-hockey into a Mint. Conn Smythe kept the building open for hockey and wrestling, and the odd bible-punching binge. Ballard had other notions on the fall morning in 1961 when he made the decision which made him rich and nationally notorious.

"By 8 o'clock that wet fucking morning," he said, "I was on the step of the bank where I dealt, the Bank of Nova Scotia branch at Spadina and Adelaide. I'm sweating. I can't wait for the manager to arrive."

The manager, G.J. (Robbie) Robinson, appeared at 9:00 a.m. Ballard gave him the big hello and wondered why he'd got up so early. "Did'ja wet the bed or what?"

Inside the bank, Robbie Robinson said, "So what do you want this early in the day?"

Ballard said, "I want two and a half million bucks."

The bank manager sat down. He gazed at Ballard in some amazement. Ballard's bank balance was a modest $19,000 and casual change.

"Harold," Robinson said, "you don't have enough money to buy lunch. What have you got for collateral?"

Ballard played his ace. "For collateral," he said, "I've got Maple Leaf Gardens."

Robbie Robinson was further amazed. "You've got what? Maple Leaf Gardens, you say?"

"I will have," Ballard said, "when this fucking bank where I've done business for years comes up with the cash."

"This," Robinson said, "is a deal for head office."

Ballard never tires of relating his coup. "So we phoned the head office of the Bank of Nova Scotia and they said come right over. We made an appointment for 10:30."

Ballard was so certain he would get the loan that he

telephoned Staff Smythe, who was up to his hips in gravel in a Caledon pit.

"Staff?" Harold said, unable to conceal his excitement. "Are you standing or sitting down?"

"Standing," Staff said at his end of the blower. "You know my old man never lets anybody sit down on the job."

"Well, grab a chair," Harold said. "I got good news!"

"Like what?" Staff wanted to know. He sounded hung over from their plotting the night before.

"Like," Ballard said, "we got the fucking money. Two and a half big ones. You better get down here to the head office of the Nova Scotia Bank. You'll need to sign some documents."

Staff Smythe was in Toronto within the hour. He came with Ballard to the headquarters of the Bank of Nova Scotia in rubber boots and a mackinaw, de rigueur for the foremen of gravel pits of a teeming November day.

"It was pissing down," Ballard said, "and we were laughing. We talked to the assistant manager and the accountant and said we needed two and a half mil. They said when do you want it? I said, 'Goddamn it, we want it now!' They jumped smartly and 20 minutes later we had the money to buy out Staff's old man."

Ballard and Stafford left the bank to inform John Bassett of the loan. The *Telegram* was situated at Bay and Melinda streets, not far from the canyons of Bay Street. They stopped in Rutherford's Drugstore, across the street from the *Telegram*.

"It was a cold day," Ballard said, "but I was hot. We had a couple of soft drinks to cool off. Then Stafford threw a swifty. He said, 'We really don't need Bassett in this deal.'"

Harold said, "We don't do business that way. You take the whole thing if you want, it's okay with me. But I made a deal with John that he's in if we get the money."

Ballard phoned Bassett and the publisher said come right over. Bassett met them in the boardroom of the newspaper, a high-volt smile on his I'm-in-charge expression.

Bassett's first words, after hearing Ballard's story, were, "Do I get cut in for a third?"

"You do," Ballard said. "We borrowed $2.5 million from

the bank. Your third's about $900,000. The loan gives us enough to buy out Staff's old man."

They would pay Conn Smythe $2.5 million, or $40 a share for stock selling at $33. They acquired, in return, 59 per cent of the best-known arena and most-prized athletic team in Canada.

Bassett wanted lawyers to arrange a complex contract, but Ballard refused to sign a complicated pact. They settled on a simple bargain, buddy-buddies pledging to vote their shares as one. A pertinent clause stated that if one of the three partners wanted to sell his shares, or if he died, his shares would first be offered to his two partners. Each of the three owned roughly 20 per cent of the stock.

From the *Telegram*, Harold and Stafford confronted Conn Smythe at the Gardens. "We told him we had the money to buy him out," Ballard said. "You never saw such a surprised look on a guy's face. Conn liked to shit a brick. He never thought we'd get the money to get rid of him."

Conn Smythe insisted that he thought he was dealing with his son and his son's close friend. He professed not to know that John Bassett was part of the triumvirate.

"After we told Conn," Ballard said, "Staff and I went out and tied one on. I was going to make the Gardens take off at a million miles an hour."

After midnight, much the worse for wear, Ballard staggered into his Montgomery Road home. He made a commotion groping up the stairs. Dorothy Ballard woke up, aroused, fearful that a herd of unruly elephants was clumping through her bedroom.

"You're drunk," she accused Harold.

"Jiggs," he said, "I had reason to celebrate. I just bought the Maple Leaf Gardens."

Dorothy Ballard sat up in bed. "You're not only drunk," she told her errant spouse. "You're also crazy."

He was as crazy, it developed, as a 20th Century fox. John Bassett's *Telegram* printed many extraordinary stories in 1961. The Berlin Wall was erected as an obscene barrier in a divided city. John F. Kennedy was inaugurated president of the American Camelot. Ernest Hemingway, unable to summon grace under pressure, put a shotgun in his mouth and blew out his brains in Ketchum, Idaho. Roger Maris, slugging on behalf of the New York Yankees, hit 61 home runs to break Babe Ruth's single-season record of 60.

But the story which gave Bassett the biggest kick in 1961 was published in the *Telegram* on November 23. It announced the Bassett-Ballard-S. Smythe takeover of the Gardens. A press conference had been called that morning to announce the changing of the Gardens' guard. Rex MacLeod, covering for the *Globe*, recalls someone running in to blurt, "This goddamn deal is already on page one of the *Tely*."

MacLeod overheard Conn Smythe say, "If I'd known Bassett was part of this, there wouldn't have been any god-damned deal."

Staff Smythe replaced Conn as president, receiving $45,000 a year to supervise the hockey operations. Ballard received $35,000 a year as executive vice-president in charge of making money. Bassett was paid $15,000 as chairman of the board. Conn Smythe was pensioned off with an office, a secretary, a car and driver, which seemed reasonable sever-ance.

He had his thoroughbreds, which included his wife. He still controlled selections for the Hockey Hall of Fame. He received high praise for his philanthropy towards the handi-capped. But he mourned the severing of his roots in the Gardens.

"What's it like," I asked him, "to no longer run the Gar-dens?"

"It's like," Conn Smythe said, "being widowed after the death of a wife you loved a lot."

Ballard hustled the Gardens as Smythe had not, starry-eyed as a loan shark. He sold advertising space on the walls to CCM and the Ford Motor Company. He peddled Schick razor blades on the escalator risers and on the bottom of the tip-up seats. Dominion Stores advertised "Mainly Because of the Meat" on the Zamboni ice-conditioning machine. More advertisements were sold in the Gardens' program.

Ticket prices constantly escalated. Red seats, best in the house, were $5 each in 1961. Ballard ultimately added gold to the red-blue-green-gray color scheme, and gold became the

most expensive. The comic Johnny Wayne, a season sub-
scriber, twitted Ballard with a sharp line, "Oh, when your
hair has turned to silver and your seats have turned to gold."

A Gardens' gold, for the 1988–89 season, was $29. If the
Leafs had qualified for the playoffs, a gold pew would have
cost $40. If the Leafs had qualified for the minimum number
of playoff games, two, the gate would have approached
$800,000, more than enough to pay the annual salaries of two
principal players, Borje Salming and Wendel Clark.

In 1961, Ballard negotiated a radio-televison contract for
$700,000 a year. In 1965, he signed a six-year radio-TV con-
tract with McLaren Advertising Company for $9 million. The
Leafs have not been an attractive TV draw for 10 years, but
televised games earned the Gardens shareholders millions
in 1987–88.

Conn Smythe rarely consumed alcohol, perhaps submit-
ting to an occasional sip of champagne when the Leafs won a
Stanley Cup. Ballard repealed Smythe's Dry Law by demol-
ishing stores on the east side of the Gardens to provide space
for a gamey watering hole, the Hot Stove Lounge. Member-
ship in the Hot Stove Lounge is so exclusive that anyone
listed in the Metro Toronto telephone directory can get in.

On the ice, Punch Imlach drove a team of Geritol Follies to
the 1961–62 championship. Goaltender Johnny Bower,
whose real name was Johnny Kishkan, was 37 by his own
admission and several years older by common consensus.
Defenceman Allan Stanley was 35, his partner, Tim Horton,
31. Red Kelly was 34, Bert Olmstead 35, captain George Armstrong 31.

Coupled with age, though, Imlach had the marvellous
Mahovlich, hard-playing Bob Nevin, sprightly Dick Duff, a
solid defence pairing of Carl Brewer and Boomer Bob Baun,
industrious Bob Pulford, entertaining Eddie Shack, utility
centre Billy Harris, and Dave Keon, the concentrated quintes-
sence of forechecking and endless skating. They were
young, and defeat did not rest easily upon them.

The 1961–62 Leafs finished second to the Montreal Canadiens and eliminated the New York Rangers four games to
two in one semi-final. The Chicago Black Hawks, defending
the Stanley Cup, beat the Montreal Canadiens in the other

semi-final. The Toronto-Chicago final gave Ballard the chance to party with the Chicago owner, James Dougan Norris.

Norris was a wilful heir to millions made by his father, James Norris, a grain baron born in St. Catharines, Ontario. The junior Jim inherited $55 million and admitted, in response to a question, that his ambition was to run it down to $53 million.

At one time in the six-team NHL, the Norrises owned franchises in Chicago and Detroit, and pieces of the New York Rangers and Boston Bruins. The family's influence was all-strangling, so pervasive that Jim Coleman, in *The Globe and Mail*, referred to the NHL as the "Norris House League." Besides the Black Hawks, James D. Norris owned, in 1962, the International Boxing Club (IBC), the most powerful monopoly in pugilism. Mobsters, killers and hoodlums were among his boxing associates, reasons for Norris to be investigated by the U.S. Federal Department of Justice.

Government agents were fascinated by the appearance in their Norris files of names like Golfbag Sam Hunt, an alumnus of the Al Capone gangs; Sh'h, the sobriquet of a racetrack goofbucket; and, above all, Frankie Carbo, a dapper figure of mystery who was twice tried for murder.

Norris's wayward ties to the underworld impressed Ballard and Staff Smythe. Stafford, who wore no man's collar, sometimes not even his own, said, "Beside Big Jim, I'm a boy scout."

Ballard was enchanted by the bodyguard who accompanied Big Jim to hockey games in the cavernous Chicago Stadium. "You wouldn't believe it," Harold said, "but the bodyguard brought a goddamn violin case with him. Inside, I guess, was a gun."

I wondered if the gunsel with Norris might have been Golfbag Sam Hunt, who was known to carry a sawed-off shotgun in a golfbag. "Naw," Harold said. "I think Jim said this guy's name was Greasy Thumb Guzik."

One night, in the Chicago section of the series, the Hawks seemed to score a goal but the goal judge did not flash his red light. Yahoos in the Stadium erupted. "To kill! To kill!"

Ballard was sitting between Jim Norris and Greasy Thumb

Guzik. Guzik picked up the violin case containing his gun and, above the din, said to Norris. "Shall I go ventilate that goal judge now, Jim?"

Norris said, "For God's sake, Greasy, put that thing away. We don't want any trouble here tonight."

The Hawks, behind the Leafs 3–2 in games, had trouble on the ice in the sixth game of the 1962 final, played in Chicago. This was a Chicago club of distinction — acrobatic Glenn Hall in goal, crafty Pierre Pilote and lumbering Moose Vasko on defence, artful Stan Mikita at centre, Robert Marvin Hull unloading slapshots at 118 miles an hour.

Hull unloaded one midway in the third period to break a scoreless tie. Lofty Bob Nevin, an underrated right winger, tied it 1–1 two minutes later.

Then, as Scott Young described it in *The Globe and Mail*, Dick Duff won the game and the Stanley Cup. "Tim Horton handled the puck three times on that rush, then finally got the puck to Duff, which is earning an assist the hard way."

They had won, those Leafs, for Smythe and Ballard and Bassett and the baldhead behind the bench, but mostly they had won for themselves.

Scott Young listened to a bruised Leaf winner, Bert Olmstead, an iconoclast who showed contempt for any Leaf less combative than he. Olmstead had helped the Montreal Canadiens win four previous Cups.

"It's been a long haul to win this one," Olmstead said. "But when you win the last game you play, you'll never go wrong."

It was the last NHL game for Murray Bert Olmstead. He went home to raise wheat in the dry belt of southwestern Saskatchewan, but the slab-sided farmer left much of himself imprinted on the minds of young Leafs. Olmstead's attitude was that if you lose tonight, the experience should increase your appetite for winning tomorrow.

Other stories occupied interest in 1962. The prolonged Wilt Chamberlain scored 100 points in a basketball game for the Philadelphia Warriors. A corrupting drug, thalidomide, caused thousands of birth defects. John Glenn was the first American astronaut to orbit the earth. The Winnipeg Blue Bombers beat the Hamilton Tiger-Cats in the Fog Bowl, the only Canadian football final that required parts of two days to play because fog socked in thick as porridge on the first day on the Toronto lakefront. John Kennedy and Nikita Khruschev went eyeball to eyeball over Soviet missiles installed on Cuban soil. Khruschev blinked first.

Bob Dylan tipped the impending revolt of North American young. He sang of a melancholy time with many questions, and of answers, perhaps, "blowin' in the wind."

For Harold Ballard, the crass answer was in the bottom line of money made and a Stanley Cup won. He hired a short, dark, subtle man name Joey Faraco to administer the prospering Hot Stove Lounge. Faraco had been in charge of the Polo Lounge in the Westbury Hotel, a pleasant inn on Yonge Street, two blocks west of the Gardens.

One of Faraco's chores was to maintain the penthouse in the City Park Apartments where the Silver Seven convened to play. Faraco kept the keys, paid the rent and provided stag films for raunchy parties.

Faraco told Bill Houston of a day when one of the seven wise men came to the Hot Stove Lounge for the keys to the penthouse. Faraco said the chap was squiring a woman. The City Park Apartments are located in three buildings behind the Gardens and the man walked into the wrong building. He and his amour rode an elevator up to the penthouse, to discover that the keys did not fit the door. The resident inside opened the door, to face a surprised "couple."

The chap asked the resident what he was doing in the Silver Seven penthouse. The resident said the Silver Seven must have another penthouse. The celebrant discovered his mistake and was dead game in correcting it. He gave the other man an "honorarium" for his trouble.

"The fellow," Faraco said, "thought it was a hell of a good joke."

The Silver Seven penthouse, rented for a trivial $350 a month, was colloquially called the Marlboro Athletic Club. The lease was held under the title S.H. Marlie, a transparent mask; the S. stood for Stafford, the H. for Harold, the Marlie for Marlboro. S.H. Marlie's unofficial theme song was "Ain't We Got Fun?"

Ballard rented the Gardens to assorted promotions, some

of them bizarre. One involved miniature racing cars hurtling around a track erected through the stands and on boards covering the ice surface. A member of the "Hockey Night in Canada" television crew had a key to the Gardens and, with Ballard's permission, came in to skate after midnight.

"I skated to stay in shape," the TV operative said. "One night I entered the Gardens and heard these miniature cars running. The track hadn't been removed from the show the night before. Men were laughing and women squealing. I stole a peek and you wouldn't believe it. Here was Stafford Smythe, a member of the Gardens' executive, driving a little car naked. A naked woman perched on his shoulders, screaming. Driving right behind, naked, with a naked woman on his shoulders, was Harold Ballard. I got the hell out of there."

Maple Leaf fans, devoted to Conn Smythe's Puritan ethic, would not believe the freeway value system that existed in the Gardens in the sixties. One tattered phrase fit the extra-curricular activities at top level. The phrase is "anything went."

The players, Punch Imlach's Stanley Cup champions, did not share in the lechery of their leaders. Joe Morgan, casting sports for Foster Hewitt's radio station, CKFH, called those Leafs "the Milkshake Kids." The idolatry they earned was deserved.

No Leaf deserved it more than Frank Mahovlich in 1962. He scored 48 goals, the highest number in any season by any Leaf to that time. He skated in graceful swoops, reckless in his plunging stride, geared to vivid attack. There was, curiously, some intangible in Mahovlich's personality that made Toronto fans boo. On display, he seemed to live in a kind of desperation, vilified by Leaf partisans when he faltered from the perfection they demanded of him. He was such a prodigy that the customers settled for nothing less than prodigious scoring feats.

Mahovlich wore number 27 and, at 27, he wondered what became of the glamor he thought hockey had when he was 13. The answer was that the glamor had been rubbed away by years of living on the inside of a world that seemed magic when seen from the distance of his birthplace in Shumacher,

in northern Ontario. He was not the first pro athlete to wonder "where have all the flowers gone?" Mahovlich discovered that hockey belongs to players only when they are on
the ice. His exciting talent was an ornament to the sport, but
he resented that the schedule of his life was arranged by
calculating men.

It is the law of pro sport. Intruders decide what a player is.
Strangers arrange all their tomorrows. The Toronto owners
talked about Mahovlich on his big nights, but they did it in a
chilly way, like John Bassett bragging about a Rolls Royce he
has just had polished.

Twice, in the fall of 1962, Bassett, Ballard and Staff Smythe
tried to sell Mahovlich to Jim Norris in Chicago. Norris
flashed a tempting million dollars, which would have
relieved the loan owed to the Bank of Nova Scotia.

Negotiations began between Norris and Ballard on the eve
of the NHL All-Star Game, in Toronto on October 6, 1962.
The format for the game then matched the Stanley Cup
champions against a select squad from the other five NHL
teams.

The all-star dinner in the Royal York Hotel was followed by
a drinking marathon in Norris's suite. The place was full of
the usual NHL suspects, league governors, team executives,
sports writers.

"Goddamn it," Ballard told Norris, "we're having trouble
signing Mahvolich. Son of a bitch scores 48 goals and all of a
sudden we've got him and his old man in the Gardens holding us up. We offer a figure and old man Mahovlich says to
Frank, 'Dun't sign, Mahov.'"

No amount of cash fazed Norris. Big Jim could, as his
admirers noted, write cheques big enough to make the banks
bounce. "I'd be glad," Norris said to Ballard, "to take
Mahovlich off your hands. I'd sign him."

Liquor loosened tongues, but Norris and Ballard could
navigate carrying a full load. Fred Cederberg, a lanky press
attaché from the Toronto *Telegram*, observed their bargaining.
There was loud conversation about what Mahovlich was
worth on the hoof.

Norris beckoned Tommy Ivan, the Chicago general manager, to follow him into an adjoining room. Norris asked, "Is

Mahovlich worth $500,000?" Ivan said, "He's worth more."

"Is he worth $750,000?" Norris asked. Ivan said, "That may be high. But you get Mahovlich and, with Bobby Hull, we'd have the best left side in hockey history."

"Okay," Norris said. "I think I can get him. I think Ballard will sell."

Big Jim and Little Tom returned to the main room. Norris began to dicker with Ballard. "Will you take $250,000 for Mahovlich?" Ballard said no. "Will you take $500,000?" Ballard refused.

It was midnight. Norris's suite reeked of cigarette smoke. Boozy talk was heard out of freeloaders dipping their beaks in Big Jim's liquid hospitality. Punch Imlach and King Clancy joined the festivities.

"All right," Norris announced. "I'll give Toronto one million for Mahovlich." Ballard looked at Imlach, who held the dual portfolio of Leaf coach and general manager.

"Norris will give us a million for Mahovlich," Ballard said. "What do you think, Punch?"

Imlach surveyed a scene of alcoholics, not one of them anonymous. "Under these conditions," Punch said, "I wouldn't make any kind of deal."

Norris began to write out conditions of the sale on a red package of DuMaurier cigarettes. Someone gave him a sheet of Royal York stationery. Norris wrote, "I promise to pay $1 million for Frank Mahovlich." He signed the note, "Jim Norris." He asked Ballard and another member of the Silver Seven, Jack Amell, to sign it. Each wrote "Accepted."

Norris reached into his pockets for a roll of spare cash that would have choked one of his race horses. Ballard didn't want to accept a down payment but Norris insisted that he take $1,000, in 10 one-hundred dollar bills.

Ballard asked Imlach to seal the deal by shaking hands with Norris. "There's no way," Punch said, "I'll shake on any deal the shape you guys are in tonight."

Jim Norris asked Ballard how he wanted to announce the news. "Any way you like," Ballard answered. Norris said, "I want my publicity man to say that 'The Chicago hockey club has purchased Frank Mahovlich for $1 million.'"

CHAPTER 8

Maple Leaf Mint

◆

The Chicago publicist, Johnny Gottselig, was a former Black Hawk forward. He broke the news to Canadian Press and Associated Press. Jim Vipond, hovering around the hotel for *The Globe and Mail*, phoned the astounding story to Canada's self-proclaimed paper of record.

Ballard chortled, and he has a very snorting chortle. "This'll knock the goddamn World Series off page one! Is selling Mahovlich for a million big news or what!"

Across the continent, in San Francisco, the New York Yankees were about to beat Willie Mays and the Giants in the seventh and deciding game for the rounders championship of the planet. The World Series was an absorbing story, covered by many Canadian sports writers, but a small yarn beside Frank Mahovlich and the Leafs in 1962, in Toronto.

Stafford Smythe, occupied elsewhere all evening, walked into Jim Norris's suite after one o'clock in the morning. He was not too stiff to realize that there would be a certain hell to pay over peddling the one Toronto player who might reach superstar status.

"Before this deal is final," Staff said, "our whole Gardens' board will have to ratify it. Let's put this thing on hold until the morning."

In the morning, the $1,000 which Ballard had accepted from Norris as a binder was returned, by messenger, to Norris's suite. Norris, certain the deal was still on, arranged to get a certified cheque for $1 million from the First National Bank of Chicago. He gave it to Tommy Ivan and sent his general manager to the Gardens.

There had been loud fall-out. Conn Smythe, on the phone to the Gardens to his son, said, "Stafford, be careful. Don't roll a drunk. Don't take the million from Big Jim."

Tommy Ivan entered Staff Smythe's office to present the

cheque and take possession of Mahovlich. Ballard and Staff sat together, both reasonably sober.

"We can't accept the cheque, Tommy," Staff said. "We'd have to have a directors' meeting on a deal this big. It's off."

"They were making excuses," Ivan said. "But there was nothing I could do. I took the million back to Big Jim."

In the Royal York, Fred Cederberg visited Norris's suite to report on any postcripts for the *Telegram*. Norris asked Cederberg to order him breakfast from room service. "Make it coffee and a Danish."

Cederberg noticed the $1,000 on a side table. "Where'd this loot come from?" he wondered.

"Ballard and Smythe sent it back this morning," Jim Norris said. "But a keeper's a keeper. We work that way in the West. A deal's a deal when I put my money where my mouth is."

Ballard still wanted to cut up jackpots with Norris, but Staff Smythe prevailed. He ordered Punch Imlach to sign Mahovlich before the All-Star Game that Saturday night. Frank played for the Leafs in a contest the champions won 4–1.

Ballard seemed sheepish when he saw Fred Cederberg in the press room. He asked the Tely man, "What did Big Jim say when we sent the cheque back?"

Cederberg relished his reply. "Big Jim said you people don't keep your word and don't know the value of a handshake. He thinks you welshed."

Cederberg's answer bothered Ballard. "Damn it," he said. "God damn it. I was afraid he'd feel that way. I don't want Big Jim or anybody else to think I'd cheat on a deal." Big Jim's power, enforced by underworld muscle, made his NHL partners quaver. Ballard knew Greasy Thumb Guzik had Norris artillery in his violin case.

The 1962–63 season began and the excitement about Mahovlich subsided. Scott Young, home from the World Series, wrote in *The Globe and Mail* that the deal was "sham, flim-flam, trickery, hoax." A drunken caper, Scott thought.

Ballard had a remorseful second guess. He liked the media and confided in some of us. One of us was Joe Morgan at Foster Hewitt's station, CKFH. "The Mahovlich deal," Ballard told Morgan, "ain't dead yet."

Morgan remembered Ballard's tip when the Leafs travelled to Chicago to play the Black Hawks on a Sunday night early in November. He phoned around Toronto and could not find any of the Silver Seven at home. They were living it up in Chicago. Long after midnight the phone rang in Morgan's apartment in midtown Toronto. Ballard was on the line, just back from Chicago by plane. He sounded excited.

"What's up, Harold?" Morgan said. "Got to be something big to wake me up at this goddamn hour."

"It is big," Ballard said. "The Mahovlich deal with Jim Norris is back on. It's damn near cinched. You can go with it."

Joe Morgan was 60, an old-style rabble-rouser who had worked 20 years for newspapers in New York. He wore a snap-brim fedora inside and outside a radio studio. His breathless style was fashioned on Walter Winchell's, who went to press in brassy authoritative tones.

Joe Morgan was a Winchell in full flight on the morning of November 12, 1962. At 8:00 a.m. he attacked a CKFH microphone. "CKFH has reliably learned that the Frank Mahovlich deal is back on! Once more it's a million bucks for the Leaf left wing! My source is unimpeachable!"

Morgan's source was Ballard, on this occasion somewhat impeachable. Ballard and Staff Smythe had not quite tied up details of the sale with Jim Norris. Morgan's announcement was premature.

Staff Smythe, driving to the Gardens from his home in Etobicoke, heard Morgan's broadcast. "Son of a bitch," he thought, "somebody's leaked it. The deal's not final."

At the Gardens, Smythe began issuing denials. "No, we haven't sold Frank Mahovlich. No, we are not going to sell him. Yes, that story you heard on CKFH is all wrong. I don't know where Joe Morgan got that nonsense."

Through the day, Morgan was chagrined to have his Mahovlich flash repudiated. The Toronto newspapers, when they appeared on the street, carried Staff Smythe's denial.

Periodically, in the afternoon, Ballard phoned Morgan from a pay station outside the Gardens. He felt his friend's dismay. "You wouldn't believe what Staff's doing now, Joe. He found a bible somewhere. He's making a lot of us come into his office and swear on the bible that we didn't spill the story to you. Goddamn."

To have a story blow up, to a newsman, is to eat ashes. Humiliation gnaws at your guts. Your peers are delighted to point out, on their radio stations and in their newspapers, that your information is pure horse manure. There was no bombast in Joe Morgan when he had to announce, on his evening sportscast, that Staff Smythe denied all knowledge of any sale of Mahovlich to Chicago.

Later, consoling himself in the library of his apartment, Morgan received a phone call. "This is John Bassett," the caller said. "I know, Joe, how bad you must feel. I was in Chicago and we were close to a deal. You were 99 and 99/100ths per cent right."

No one thought, just then, to ask Frank Mahovlich how he felt. He felt like a piece of meat — high-grade meat, to be sure, but meat just the same.

The 1962–63 Leafs were Punch Imlach's best, first by a single point over the Canadiens across a 70-game schedule. They beat the Canadiens in five games in one semi-final, then the Detroit Red Wings in five to retain the Cup.

Dick Duff had a jubilee for himself in the first game against Detroit. He sprang around Doug Barkley twice in the first 68 seconds of the game and shot pucks past goaltender Terry Sawchuk. His feat stands as a Stanley Cup playoff record — Fastest Two Goals from Start of Game and Period: 1 minute, 8 seconds — Dick Duff, Toronto Maple Leafs, April 9, 1963.

Dave Keon, Toronto's good-luck cameo, won the Lady Byng Trophy as the player best combining uncommon skill with courtly conduct. He had sinned for four insignificant minutes in penalties in two seasons. Kent Douglas, a truculent freshman on the Toronto defence, won the Calder Trophy as rookie of the year.

That summer, Ballard sought permission to build 4,000 more seats by extending the Gardens over Carlton Street at one end and Wood Street at the other. Municipal politicians approved the Gardens overhanging public land, but the provincial government refused the encroachment. Ballard's old schoolmate from Upper Canada College, Allan Lamport, was a voluble controller in the City of Toronto. Lamport understood that expanding the Gardens over public property would increase tax money for the city and produce more profit for the Gardens.

"What in the world is wrong with profits?" Lamport asked. Provincial authorities decided, piously, that private profit should not be made out of an intrusion over public land. Ballard threatened to move the Gardens to the Toronto suburbs, but that was so much gaseous bafflegab spouted into the air space above the Gardens.

Toronto's Milkshake Kids prepared to defend the Stanley Cup with a late September exhibition trip to Quebec. In Quebec City, Bob Pulford and Tim Horton drank enough inflammatory liquid to inspire a boyish prank. They made sufficient noise hurling municipal garbage cans around the streets to get themselves arrested. They were fined $50 each for conduct unbecoming to Stanley Cup champions.

Municipal garbage cans, in Quebec City, are not as easily tossed as tin cans. The strength of a particularly muscular carnivore is required. Tim Horton had such strength.

It was generally supposed that Gordon Howe was the heavyweight champion of the NHL, strong as a bull moose sexually excited. I said to Howe on television, after he retired in 1980, "Everybody claims, Gordie, that you were the strongest player of your time."

"Everybody was wrong," Howe said. I persisted. "So who was stronger?"

"You should know," Howe said. "You covered him for years in Toronto. I was the second strongest in my time. Tim Horton was the strongest. I was always glad I played right wing and Horton played right defence. That means I didn't have to come down his side and get ridden off by a great bear."

The great bear and his playmates bruised the Boston Bruins in their first game of the 1963–64 schedule, 5–1. The date was October 12. In the United States, an American president widely admired in Canada had 41 days to live. Everybody remembers where he was when he heard a broadcaster say, on November 22, 1963, a Friday: "We interrupt this program for a special bulletin. John F. Kennedy has been shot today in Dallas . . .".

I was in the lush lobby of a Ramada Inn in downtown Vancouver, assigned there by *The Globe and Mail* to cover the last game of the Western football final between the B.C. Lions and Regina Roughriders. I was interviewing Bob Kramer, an aggressive farm machinist, then president of the Roughriders.

"I can't believe it," Kramer said. "Insane things like this don't happen on this continent. Assassinations happen in some Middle Eastern jerkwater."

On television, in the hotel lobby, commentator Walter Cronkite reported that it could indeed happen in North America. "It is official and without doubt," Cronkite was saying that shocking noontime. "President Kennedy is dead."

Molehills of telegraph copy, in newsrooms world wide, piled up a mountain of a story. Bob Kramer said it for all of us whose lives are given to games, whether playing or writing or watching. He said, "This puts games in their proper perspective. Sport seems so flimsy, when a big person dies."

Our banal games went on. We stood for a moment's silence the next day in Empire Stadium, before the B.C. Lions beat Regina for the Western football title. In Toronto, Harold Ballard ordered the Red Ensign over Maple Leaf Gardens lowered to half mast to signal respect for the president who lay dead in Washington. There was no pause in Saturday night TV hockey. Fans coast to coast watched the Leafs curb Boston, 4–1.

The Maple Leafs continued their Stanley Cup run through 1963–64, but the achievement was never easy. They finished third behind the Canadiens and Chicago, after Punch Imlach swapped two of his favorites to the New York Rangers. He sent away Bob Nevin, Dick Duff and three others from the Toronto system for Don McKenny, a competent forward, and Andy Bathgate, an all-star centre.

Duff and Nevin were integral parts of those championship teams, scarcely delighted at the breaking up of that old gang of theirs. They had discovered the truth about professional hockey. It is a grasshopper profession. The summers of youth are splendid, when you are winning, but the winter of middle age can be barren when you don't score.

Maple Leaf fans had special affection for Duff. They understood that the long boyhood was over for dapper number 9, a stocky athlete who left the grinding mining town of Kirkland Lake and played for the Leafs as though angels had sung at his christening. He scored 26 goals one year, 26 another, 29 in a third, all in an era when scoring 20 goals a year was the big-league norm. His production tailed down to 19 goals, 16, 17, 16 before Imlach traded him.

Bob Nevin, never a media marvel, ultimately became captain of the Rangers. Duff got a gratifying break. He left New York in a trade to Montreal, where he won four more Stanley Cup rings with the conquering Canadiens of the late sixties.

There is a Duff postscript. In Montreal, he lost money in the stockmarket and believed he could find balm in booze. He became an alcoholic. Then he bailed out of liquor and became a non-alcoholic. He is a Maple Leaf scout now, and underpaid, but the best part of his quiet existence is unpaid. He counsels people caught in a whisky whirligig.

There were dramatic moments in the 1963–64 playoffs, nights the observer can polish forever among his souvenirs. Ballard and Staff Smythe celebrated before the Stanley Cup was won, every night turned high, wide and have some, either whisky or women.

"Help yourself, boys," Ballard the bartender would offer in the Maple Leaf suite. "Name your poison. We're fucking on our way to the fucking Cup again."

Typical was the night of March 28, 1964, a Saturday, for a crackling game between the Leafs and the Canadiens in Montreal, really hockey night in Canada. The country's hottest rivals performed with rare distinction in the second game of a best-of-seven semi-final. The Leafs needed to win to tie the set 1-1.

The hockey herds were bivouacked in the Mount Royal Hotel, an old flop below the hummock which passes for a hill in downtown Montreal. Ballard was at his most hospitable in the Maple Leaf suite, the dean of men and women. The game began at eight o'clock and, at 7:00 p.m., Harold began rummaging his guests out of various bedrooms in the suite. I was there with Joe Morgan, the renowned runner from Foster Hewitt's broadcasting stable.

Ballard opened one bedroom door, charmed to see a couple in transports of sexual ecstasy. The gentleman was poised for a quick departure. He was nude except for the hat on his head and the shoes on his feet.

Ballard beckoned. "Come look at this, Beddoes," he said. The party of the second part in the energetic coupling did not care for spectators.

"Will you bastards shut that door!" the lady said.

"Hurry it up, Tommy," Ballard advised the gentleman involved. "Time to get to the game." Then he shut the door.

At the Forum, Punch Imlach was making a sage decision. He decided that, since Frank Mahovlich was stalled on left wing, he would shift Mahov to centre ice, between Red Kelly on the left side and George Armstrong on the right. The Leafs dandy little thinker never played a wiser hunch.

Mahovlich was inspired to a hard blue glow of flying purpose. He commanded Toronto's attack in a 2–1 triumph. Four minutes into the game, he put a baleful shot from 20 feet on the Montreal net. It seemed a certain score until goalkeeper Charlie Hodge, in the barest fragment of a second, flung his small torso in front of the puck.

At eight minutes, Mahovlich was back, spitefully speeding through the Montreal defence. He shot once from a sharp angle, and Hodge saved. He smacked the rebound, and Hodge kicked out the puck. Ralph Backstrom wheeled for the Canadiens on a return rush, but here came Mahovlich on an infrequent backcheck.

He retrieved the puck in the Toronto zone and swept down the left wing, untouched by three tangled Canadien defenders. Mahovlich cut over the Montreal blueline, highballing. Red Kelly went with him and got uncovered in front of Hodge.

Mahovlich passed the puck. Kelly shot it. Hodge fanned. Goal. The action was so swift that it was a blur defying accurate description. Watching, high in the press box, I perched on the edge of sweaty excitement.

Mahovlich scored Toronto's second goal, the winning goal, the culmination of a passing alliance with Kelly and Armstrong. He forced Charlie Hodge into two more big saves. He hit a goal post. He may have been a sensation on other nights, but I never saw him more sensational.

Punch Imlach, in the steamy Leaf quarters, had his gum cracking at one hundred miles an hour. He shoved his fedora back off his glossy forehead. Then he offered an instant parable to explain the frustrating valleys and impassioned peaks in Mahovlich's performance.

"Hockey is mostly a streetcar named Desire," Punch Imlach said. "Sometimes big Frank doesn't catch it."

The 1963–64 semi-final came to a seventh-game climax in Montreal, two of the towering teams on earth tied three games apiece. It was a game for historians to cherish, for John William Bower to be preserved forever in the memories of those lucky enough to have watched him.

Bower was rising 39, by his own admission, in the spring of 1964. He was several years older in hockey legend. The legend was spawned by the fact that Bower had been born Johnny Kishkan in Prince Albert, Saskatchewan. He played junior hockey in Saskatoon as Kishkan. Then his mother married a second time, to a man named Bower. John took his stepfather's surname and, in the process, his birth certificate was lost. The loss led to comic speculation about Bower's correct age.

Bower had been buried in the American League at Providence and Cleveland until he was at least 34, aware there were only six big-league goaltending jobs and he might not get one. He was content to remain in Cleveland where, in recognition of his prowess in stopping pucks, he was called The Great Wall of China. During the summers, he managed a hamburger hutch in Prince Albert National Park.

Bower felt so comfortable with the Cleveland Barons that he was reluctant to jump to Toronto. Jim Hendy, managing the Barons, had to talk him into the NHL. "Listen, John," Hendy said, "you know that hamburger stand you got in Prince Albert? Only you and a few of your neighbors know you've got it. But if you go to Toronto, and make the Leafs, Foster Hewitt will be hollering all across Canada, 'Yes, sir, Bower was Johnny-on-the-spot again for the Leafs, just as he is selling hamburgers in Prince Albert.'

"Then," Hendy said triumphantly, "every goddamn tourist in Canada will know about your hamburger stand. You can't not move." Bower moved and the rest, as the storytellers say, is history.

Historic especially on April 9, 1964, a Thursday. The Leafs won the game 3–1 and the series four games to three and they could thank a manifest classy young centremen and a mature old goaltender.

Dave Keon scored two goals for Toronto in the first period, one shorthanded, against the run of the play as the Leafs fended off a penalty to Andy Bathgate. It was all ebb and flow as the Canadiens, on the brink of elimination, came in unceasing red-shirted waves against the sagging Leafs.

You could have grated carrots on everybody's gooseflesh. There were 14,541 noisy Montreal partisans on the verge of 14,541 cardiac arrests.

The Leafs carried their 2–0 into the third period. Their defence bent for one goal, but Bower refused to break for any more. He would make a save, the Leafs would wearily clear the puck, and the Canadiens would regroup. Rex MacLeod, sitting beside me in *The Globe and Mail* seats, kept muttering, "Goddamn it, here they come again!" "They" were Jean Beliveau and Henri Richard, Ralph Backstrom, Yvan Cournoyer, Boom-Boom Geoffrion, John Ferguson and the rest in an all-star cast.

The Canadiens compelled Bower to handle the puck 18 times in the last 20 minutes. He saved it 17 times, beaten only by Backstrom. In the last minute, with the Montreal goal empty, Keon counterpunched his third score into an unguarded net. Exactly 11 seconds remained in one of the enchanting games in Toronto memory.

In the last second, Johnny Bower tore out of his goal in a ponderous rush and folded his arms around the closest Leaf, who was Bob Baun. It was like holding a boa constrictor, the way the manly defenceman thrashed about in muscular jubilation.

Then Bower and captain George Armstrong stuck their heads through a huge horseshoe of roses, 1,500 blooms from Leaf listeners to CFGM, a station in Richmond Hill, Ontario.

Up in the pigeon roost of the press box, gazing at the tumultuous scene, Joe Morgan said, "Well, that's appropriate. Bower made the Leafs come up smelling like roses."

In the dressing room, Toronto's peerless leader delivered himself of a homily. "If the NHL wasn't going to pay Bower a pension," Punch Imlach said, "I'd pay him one. He's the oldest guy in the fastest game with the quickest reflexes."

Every Leaf's reflexes would be tested in a seven-game final against the Detroit Red Wings, the Wings of Terry Sawchuk, Bill Gadsby, Alex Delvecchio, Marcel Pronovost and the great Howe, all en route to the Hall of Fame. Toronto's camp followers, in the Detroit end of the series, stayed in the tacky Book-Cadillac Hotel, in the black hub of Motown. On warm April nights, young black hookers hustled on the streets outside the Book-Cadillac. Ballard established Maple Leaf headquarters in the largest suite in the mouldering roadhouse.

Joe Morgan called the series "life and death. This is another life-and-death special, with no guarantee the Leafs will live. Remember: you heard it here first!"

The Red Wings had more life after five games. They led the series three games to two and could snatch the Cup from Toronto if they won the sixth game, at home, in the cosy Detroit Olympia on April 23, 1964. The Leafs required a win to force the seventh and final game in Maple Leaf Gardens on April 25.

I sat in the cramped press box between Foster Hewitt and Jack Dennett, part of the commentating team on radio. Upstairs, in another cramped booth, Bill Hewitt called the game on television. Pressing, under the guns, Foster was the intrinsic master of hockey broadcasting.

Once, at a smouldering juncture in the second period, the Red Wings drove the Leafs to cover around Johnny Bower. Larry Jeffrey struck the puck and, I was certain, scored. "Goal!" I thought, disciplined enough not yell over Foster's play-by-play. Upstairs, in the TV booth, Bill Hewitt announced, "Jeffrey scores!"

Foster, in the radio booth, eyes focused through the clash of sticks and bodies, said, "And Jeffrey barely shoots it wide of the open corner!" It was a classic demonstration of the older Hewitt's command of the game from blueline to goal. His reporting was so meticulous that it was noteworthy when he missed a goal, assist or penalty.

The teams were tied 3–3 beyond the middle of the third period. The Red Wings were faster, their sustained attacks leaving the Leafs limp. At 13:14 of the last period, Bob Baun was apparently knocked off the Toronto defence. He stopped a shot by Alex Delvecchio that caromed off his right ankle.

Baun recalled the scene. "When Delvecchio's shot hit me, my leg turned soft as shit. I collapsed. The next thing I knew they were carting me off on a stretcher."

An emergency team led by the illustrious Toronto trainer, Robert Haggert, carted Baun to the Leaf dressing room. Dr. Jim Murray of the Leaf medical staff consulted with Dr. Bill Stromberg, a Leaf fan in from Chicago. The patient was in anguish.

"Freeze it," Baun suggested. "Freeze the damn thing now!" Dr. Stromberg reached into his black bag and removed a hypodermic needle that to Baun looked a foot long. The doctor plunged his sick shooter into Baun's leg.

Hypoed to the hip, Baun clumped back to the Toronto bench. He hopped on the ice before Punch Imlach could restrain him. "Nothing could have stopped Baun," Imlach would say. "He had a charge in him that would have blown up the rink."

The charge did not ignite just then. The score stayed tied, 3–3. In overtime, leading off, Imlach put it up to Armstrong, Keon and Billy Harris, Carl Brewer and Baun. Keon snared the puck behind the Detroit goal. He whipped it out to Armstrong, who whacked the rubber in the air. It skittered to Baun at the Detroit blueline and he smacked it, hard and rolling towards the Detroit goal.

Terry Sawchuk, in goal, skidded to the right, with the play. The stray puck struck defenceman Bill Gadsby's stick and deflected into the net, in the spot where Sawchuk had been. Baun's goal, the 4–3 goal after 102 seconds of overtime, let the last ounce of pressure out of a boiler that belonged to Detroit.

The Leaf room, normally a sane sanctum, win or lose, was loud with relief. They weren't yet dead. They had to win this one to stay alive, and Boomer Baun won it on a broken leg. Even the good ones grow tense with fatigue and the threat of failure. Afterwards, for a long moment, he wept.

Baun has dined out on that overtime goal for 25 years. I keep telling him, "But Bob, it wasn't the big bone in your leg that was broken. It was only the fibula, the second bone."

"Go take a shit in your hat," Baun says amiably, and keeps on dining out.

Reprieved by Baun, Ballard had a party that should have got us all arrested. I returned late to the Book-Cadillac with Joe Morgan, after finishing our work in the press box at the Detroit Olympia. It was ritual. Joe would say, in the lobby, "Let's go up and see what laughs Pal Hal's having."

We marvelled, upon arriving at the Maple Leaf levee, at the black fluff running around, most of it practically naked. It was pick-your-partners time with the prosties who cruised the Detroit streets, eight of whom were there to help celebrate Baun's goal.

"Come in, come in!" Ballard boomed. He gestured at the two-legged scenery. "Help yourself, boys. Have a little fun. Two nights from now we'll have another Stanley Cup."

"Are you kidding?" Joe Morgan said. "This joint could be raided and I'm too old to be a found-in."

Ballard's guests included a Roman Catholic priest whose well-honed hockey sense sharpened big-league prospects for the Leafs. The priest should have been a hockey scout rather than a Catholic cleric because the fevers of his flesh often consumed the vows of his soul.

"Gee, Harold," the priest mentioned wistfully. "I'd sure like one of those girls."

Mine host was obliging. "You want to get laid, Father?" Ballard said. "Go to your room and I'll send one down."

The tumescent padre left and Ballard, ever obliging, doubled the order. He sent two black girls down to the priest's room. The girls returned an hour later, both dishevelled. "My God," one of them told Ballard, "that man was a tiger!"

Two nights later, on cue, as Ballard forecast, the Leafs won their third Stanley Cup, uninterrupted. Andy Bathgate scored in the first period. Keon, Armstrong and Red Kelly, limping, scored in the third, final score 4–0. Baun played, shot full of novacaine. Kelly collapsed in the shower from his leg wounds, proof it was no longer jolly to be a Geritol Folly.

There was another Stanley Cup soiree at Staff Smythe's home in the elegant Kingsway area of Etobicoke. "If we keep on winning Stanley Cups," he said, "I'm going to have to build a bigger house." He later had a mansion built in Etobicoke, with money diverted from Maple Leaf Gardens.

Another Canadian athlete raced into the headlines in the spring of 1964. Northern Dancer, a chunky bay colt owned by industrialist E.P. Taylor, won the Kentucky Derby and Preakness Stakes, the first Canadian horse awarded two of the gems in racing's Triple Crown. Taylor's initials stood for Edward Plunkett but cynics on the racing beat, with reverse English, said the E.P. stood for "Empty Pockets."

The Liberal government ordained in 1964 that Canada, 97 years after Confederation, should have a distinctive flag in place of a banner reflecting British influence.

Old soldiers grumbled, in unison with Conn Smythe, "If the Red Ensign was good enough to die under, it's good enough to live under."

Prime Minister Pearson's designers produced a Maple Leaf Flag, red and white with a red leaf from Canada's national tree. Conn Smythe was unimpressed. He met Pearson that summer and the Prime Minister said, "What are you complaining for, Connie? Our new flag has a maple leaf on it."

"But," Smythe retorted, "it's in Detroit Red Wing colors!"

Four pill-popping Liverpudlians conquered North America in 1964. George Harrison, Paul McCartney, Ringo Starr and John Lennon were the Beatles, working-class rebels who gave fresh meaning to music known as rock.

Harold Ballard was no more musical than the Beatles, but he can play a cash register. He strummed it to the tune of 18,000 admissions sold for a Beatles' concert in the Gardens on September 7, 1964.

Beatlemaniacs lined up outside the Gardens five months before the concert. Ballard, who can't distinguish a beetle from a bedbug, wore a Beatle wig and walked up and down the lineups shaking hands. Stafford Smythe joined him in silliness.

The Fab Four stimulated assorted nuttiness. Charlie Conacher, the old formidable right wing, phoned Gardens' publicist Stan Obodiac with a request. "Never mind Leaf tickets," Conacher said. "Get me Beatles' tickets." CHUM radio, through rock announcer Jungle Jay Nelson, gave roses to mothers who stood in line to buy tickets for their children.

The Beatles had three suites in the King Edward Hotel, and no quietude. A woman from London tried to crash the hotel, on the pretense of being John Lennon's babysitter. Phil Givens, the mayor of Toronto, wandered past the hotel in a forlorn quest for Beatles' autographs. Lyndon Johnson, presiding over the United States, tried to get a pass for a girl who pleaded for his intervention with Harold Ballard.

Hysteria was in the saddle the night of the concert. The Beatles avoided the Beatlemaniacs in front of the King Edward by escaping for the Gardens through a freight entrance, in a police paddy wagon. More than 900 policemen attempted to maintain order outside the Gardens. Girls swooned by the nubile hundreds.

"Goddamn, the Beatles are a hot ticket," Ballard said. "We've got to have those Limey bastards back."

He had them back in the Gardens in 1965, under acrimonious circumstances. The Beatles' manager, Brian Epstein, promised one performance only, on a hot August afternoon. Ballard sold tickets for two shows, afternoon and evening. Epstein was angry. He hollered in Ballard's office, "You cheat! One show's all you get!"

Ballard said, "Look, the tickets are sold. If you don't go on twice, this mob'll tear the Gardens down. And they'll tear you with it."

Ballard nodded to Joey Faraco, the maître d'Hot Stove Lounge, who was listening, "Joey, take this guy down to the bar and get him stiff."

Epstein continued to curse Ballard in the Hot Stove Lounge. "The fucking prick!" he said. "The absolute fucking prick!"

Faraco, defending Ballard, said, "Geezus Christ, Ballard's going to double your money. You and the Beatles are going to get $100,000 instead of $50,000. Shut up and drink."

Then Ballard, making up the rules quickly as Beatlemania raged, invoked a concessions clause. He turned off the water fountains, turned on the heat and told the concessionaires to dispense with small cups.

Mike Banks was a Beatle fanatic standing in the sweltering

August lineups. "Ballard had the concessions sell only large cups of pop," Banks said. "He sent soda butchers outside the Gardens to hawk pop and other junk. He delayed both performances so the concessions could sell more."

Money grubbing aside, the Beatles performed twice, each time to a teeming 18,000. Brian Epstein wandered off with the Liverpool Lads, drunk and incoherent.

Profits from the Maple Leaf Mint soared. Shareholders received $829,993 in 1965 and the largest dividend in the Gardens' history, $1 a share. Shares traded at $114.75 each and were split five for one. The Leafs lost in 1965, beaten by the Canadiens in the Stanley Cup semi-finals, but the shareholders won. Ballard scored financially for himself and his partners, Staff Smythe and John Bassett, collectively in for 60 per cent.

CHAPTER 9

Cash before Class

◆

Harold Ballard was 62 in 1965, in the middle of a disordered life, of buffoonery in Stanley Cup cities, of transitory loves. Then, for the first time, life began to scar and bruise him.

Dorothy Ballard, or Jiggs Higgs as he called her, was the love of his life, the balance wheel of his existence. His involvement with other women, the many other women, represented lust, horniness rampant. We fall in love, most of us; we fall in lechery, some of us.

In 1965, noticing a lump on one of her breasts, Dorothy checked with her doctor. A biopsy revealed the worst news anyone can hear. She was a victim of cancer. For her, Harold put on the old familiar ebullient face. "C'mon, Jiggs. We'll beat this. We'll knock the big C on its ass."

Privately, he was less confident. He would say, in rare reflective moments, "How the hell's it figure? Jiggs never hurt a soul in her life. I been raising hell all my life and I'm healthy as a horse. It's not fair."

Ballard, on the domestic surface, was half of what seemed a harmonious marriage. Dorothy was the other half, tolerant of his frequent disappearances, at home when he and their children needed her, the hub of Harold's chaotic existence.

Billy Harris, a good spare part among Leaf forwards, remembers the hockey wives feeling special warmth for Mrs. Ballard. He told Bill Houston, "She was just a terrific lady. She'd say, 'Call me Dorothy.' But she was always Mrs. Ballard to me."

The Ballards' social strata was upper middle class, no hardship, economic ease, summer home on Thunder Bay near Midland. Harold inherited the summer property from his mother, who died in 1956 and is buried beside his father in the family plot in Park Lawn Cemetery, in Etobicoke.

Mary Elizabeth, Bill and Bobby Ballard attended Etobicoke Collegiate, one long block up Montgomery Road from their home. Mary Elizabeth studied physiotherapy at the University of Toronto. Bill and his brother attended the University of Waterloo, where Bill earned a law degree and played football.

All reflected the strong good looks of their mother. Mary Elizabeth and Bill have the boldness of their father. Bobby (Harold Junior) is less demanding, inclined more to the artistic. He could have been a commercial artist because, as Harold Senior said, "The kid draws a hell of a chesterfield."

Ballard was never tamed by domesticity. He, like many of us in sport, was a wandering tomcat. His cronies, over time, were Red Foster, Hap Day, Sam Shopsowitz, Staff Smythe and Joey Faraco. His chums, later on, would be King Clancy and George Armstrong.

Sunday mornings, when Dorothy worshipped at Kingsway-Lambton United Church, Ballard would join Faraco for lunch and a squat on hot rocks in the Gardens' sauna. Sometimes they drove to the Ballard gravesites, where Harold once offered Faraco a plot. "You can be planted right here, Joey, right beside me." Faraco, finding the matter a bit ghoulish, declined.

Ballard remained chancellor of the exchequer and good-humor guy at the Gardens. He considered himself equal with Stafford Smythe, but Smythe always seemed the more equal. And the more complicated. Smythe needed Ballard around to make him laugh.

Ballard would say, after his partner died suddenly in 1971, "All that trouble we got into with the law, Stafford started it. I went along, but he started it."

The trouble began in 1965, when Ballard and Smythe came to randomly regard Gardens' money as their own. They were a law unto their arbitrary selves. They ransacked the Gardens, as the judge said at Ballard's trial in 1972, "by deceit, falsehood and other fraudulent means." The judge, Harry R. Deyman of Peterborough, was succinct. "... The accused [Ballard] presented Maple Leaf Gardens with invoices from suppliers which were false and from which he had the benefit, either in goods or services, and which invoices were paid by Maple Leaf Gardens. . . ."

The fraud, in the beginning, was penny-ante cheating, a tinhorn trick. On September 5, 1965 "... Maple Leaf Gardens was caused to pay an invoice of Brown Sporting Goods in the amount of $438.78 which was represented to be for 142 CCM hockey sticks for the Marlboro Junior Hockey Club, and which was, in fact, for the purchase of a motorcycle, equipment, license, insurance and repairs for a son of the accused man, Harold Edwin Ballard. . . . "

The $438.78 was chicken feed, and cheap chicken feed, at that. Harold could have paid it out of the change on his dresser. There was a similar purchase paid for in the same devious manner later in September, 1965.

Ballard bought for his son William O., known as Bill, a motorcycle for $440.83. Records from the Gardens, obtained by the court, listed the purchase of "144 CCM hockey sticks" for the Marlboro Hockey Club. The invoice was certified by Jim Gregory and George Imlach, respective managers of the Marlboro juniors and Maple Leaf pros.

The Maple Leafs failed on the Stanley Cup trail in 1965–66, detoured to defeat in four games by the Canadiens in the semi-finals. By then, Harold was negotiating for a prizefight that had international political overtones.

Cassius Clay, large and mobile and chatty, had relieved heavyweight boxing of its sleazy tedium. He annoyed American patriots by joining the Muslim faith and adopting the name Muhammad Ali. He refused induction into the U.S. Army on the reasonably sound ground that "I ain't got nothing against them there Viet Cong."

U.S. hawks still screamed that the Vietnam War was an essential conflict worth consuming U.S. troops. Ali was stripped of the heavyweight title, then denied the right to fight anywhere in the United States.

Ali took the title on tour to Canada. His promoter, New York lawyer Robert Arum of Main Bout Inc., tried to show Ali in Verdun, Quebec, Sorel, Quebec, Vancouver, Edmonton, Kingston, Ontario, and Cobourg, Ontario. Assorted rejections from two-bit athletic commissions left Ali a pugilistic orphan on Ballard's doorstep. Harold booked Ali for hostilities against the Canadian champion, George Chuvalo.

Chuvalo was 28, earnest and plodding, ranked ninth among the world's heavyweights. His manager, Irving Ungerman, a Toronto poultry processor, was not chicken.

Irving would have sent George up a mountain against a ton of sliding rock.

Ballard's business with Ali stirred a militaristic hornet. Conn Smythe, a veteran of two great wars, was appalled that a draft resister was permitted to fight in the Gardens. Smythe's role in the Gardens was minimal, but he retained 5,100 shares and a directorship. Smythe wrote John Bassett, chairman of the board: "Unless you send me assurances that Clay will not fight in the Gardens . . . please accept my resignation from the board of directors and buy out my 5,100 shares."

Bassett, backing Ballard, gave Conn Smythe a quaint hint for disposal of his resignation and his shares. Sell your shares on the open market, Bassett advised. "Perhaps it is for the best that you resign if it is difficult for you, as a director, to see us carry out policies with which you do not agree."

Smythe carried his fight to the Toronto newspapers, one of his lifelong gambits. The Ali fight confirmed for him the grubbiness of the new bosses in The House that Conn Built. He told Milt Dunnell of the *Star*, "They are putting cash before class."

There was not much cash for the Ali-Chuvalo fisticuffs, inside the Gardens or out. Toronto fans resisted buying tickets scaled from $10 to $100, ringside. Exhibitors of the fight on closed-circuit television were forced by the American Legion to limit the number of U.S. theatres showing the bout.

Gate receipts at the Gardens in 1966 were $136,000, less than half the take from one NHL game. Revenue from closed-circuit sources was a paltry $150,000. Chuvalo's total payday was $50,000, compared to $193,000 for Ali. Experts, as we often are, are never in doubt but often in error. Chuvalo was dismissed as a 6–1 underdog to be bled by the dancing, chattering champion. "Geezus, champ," Ballard said, "I hope you'll carry Chuvalo a few rounds. Make it exciting."

"Don't worry," Ali said. "I'll enjoy beating Shoovalo. He's an old washerwoman."

Chuvalo, through the fight, was more of a stubborn mule. He did not retreat one solitary inch across 15 lively rounds. He could have beaten Ali if he had unloaded the knockout drops in his right hand, which he carried curiously as though it was in a sling.

The debacle, for Ballard, was lightened by a confusing moment. Ali asked if there was a room in the Gardens where he might spread a prayer mat to address Allah.

"I didn't know what Ali meant," Ballard said. "I thought he wanted to use the can, so that's where I took him. I don't think he liked putting his prayer rug so close to the can."

Ballard frequently attended athletic socials with Staff Smythe. John Bassett invited them to a cocktail reception when Bassett presided over the Toronto Argonauts, a football team. Smythe was apparently on his worst behavior, so intoxicated his head must have felt like the inside of a motor running hot.

"Bassett had a lot of big deals at this shindig," Ballard said. "One of them was John Turner, who was in the fucking federal cabinet. Stafford began to insult Turner."

The federal Liberals had opened a hockey branch to form Hockey Canada, designed to improve this country's abysmal representation in world tournaments. Staff Smythe, an insufferable Tory, was offended by government intrusion into hockey, specifically by a Liberal Government.

Ballard said, "Staff asked Turner what the fuck business the government had in hockey. He finished up calling him a 'Goddamn fucking son of a bitch!' "

John Turner was not intimately involved in the Liberal lunge into hockey. His sport was sprinting, in the late 1940s, as Chick Turner at the University of British Columbia. Ballard always felt that Turner remembered Smythe's insults.

"You better goddamn believe Turner never forgot," Ballard said, "when we got jammed up in an income-tax beef with the feds. When he got a chance, he nailed us."

In March, 1967, as the Leafs fumbled to finish third, Mary Elizabeth Ballard married Allan MacLean, a junior executive with the Ford Motor Company in Oakville. Ballard gave away his daughter reluctantly, unimpressed with a relative stranger taking stewardship of a family possession. The family affair was later an embarrassing item in court documents. Investigators found an invoice "from Limousine Livery Toronto Limited in the amount of $60.00 . . . addressed to H. Ballard, Maple Leaf Gardens, Carlton and Church.

"The date is March 17, 1967, and the detail is livery services. Then a portion of the invoice has been obliterated and the words 'airport service' written above the obliteration — 3 limousines, 7:10 to 9:00 p.m., $20 each, $60.00. This invoice was paid by a cheque of Maple Leaf Gardens dated March, 29, 1967. . . . The invoice had the initials 'HEB' and was entered under 'Professional Hockey Expenses, travelling.'" The father of the bride had petted his company's petty cash.

The 1966–67 Leafs were a May-December blend, too much incompetent youth and too much aging competence. Punch Imlach, the manager-coach, collapsed near the end of an arduous schedule with a gall-bladder attack.

The deep thinking devolved to King Clancy, whose normal duties were to stay up late with Imlach and rip the leaves off calendars in the manager's office. He was the Leaf vice-president in charge of vice-presidents.

They were odd blocks of wood, Imlach and Clancy, temperamentally poles apart. Clancy was the original laughing boy with the built-in public relations of a Francis of Assisi. Imlach was a different saucepan of shad, perverse, profane, loyal, often a cussed martinet who refused to accept less from any player than his absolute best every day. There seldom seemed to be warm camaraderie between Imlach and his players.

The 1966–67 Leafs understood, most of them, that it didn't matter who their coach was. They understood, as professionals understand, that you play for yourself first because it is your approval that counts, not the approval of anyone else.

Even so, most people, including hockey players, are more favorably disposed towards men of peace than antagonists who harass, stirring up disorder, exposing us to ridicule. Guided by Clancy, while Imlach recuperated, the Leafs reeled off nine wins in eleven games to finish the schedule.

The Leafs fetched up in the first round of the 1966–67 playoffs against the Chicago Black Hawks, hockey's magnetic squad, attracting groupies as so many iron filings. Bobby Hull was their big commotion, freewheeling down left wing, scoring 54 goals, the first NHL shooter to smash the single-season barrier of 50.

Hull, most nights, was all slapshots and overdrive. He was better more often than Frank Mahovlich. NHL teams played each other fourteen times during the schedule, seven games at home, seven on the road. Hockey nights when Chicago came to Toronto were crackling nights. In Toronto, Hull would be on the ice more than the puck. He'd play regular shifts on left wing, on the point for power players, out to kill penalties when the Hawks were short a player.

He was photogenic and powerful, idling fluently, then surging into high gear as a chorus of sound came out of the crowd, the irrepressible reaction to a flashing superstar, rising with him in a long, drawn-out OOOHH! Hull's good manners with the press and public guaranteed his popularity wherever he played. My seat was beside Milt Dunnell's in the Gardens' press box and, when Hull was in Toronto, Milt would say, "I guess you feel the way I do. I hope the Leafs win 6–5, but that Hull gets all five Chicago goals."

Hull's associates were not as splashy, but impressive. Defencemen Pierre Pilote, centres Stan Mikita and Phil Esposito and goalie Glenn Hall were, like Hull, sailing towards the Hall of Fame. Hall, in Chicago, was called Mr. Goalie. The Leafs, against that roistering Chicago mob, were written off as losers. The writers reckoned without another incomparable goaltender, Terrance Gordon Sawchuk from East Kildonan in the north end of Winnipeg. He went back, in the spring of 1967, to the grandeur that was Sawchuk in the early fifties.

Sawchuk grew up dogged and determined, a chubby kid who wore his nickname Butch as a badge of juvenile toughness. There was uncommon persistence in his dedication towards a hockey career. He refused to attend movies as a child, lest the glare hurt his eyes; he avoided reading schoolbooks for the same reason.

My first wife attended Prince Edward Public School in East Kildonan with Sawchuk. "Terry was last in every subject," she said. "He refused to open any book."

Professional success came early. Sawchuk was rookie of the year in the United States Hockey League at 18, rookie of the year in the American League at 19, rookie of the year in the NHL at 21. In 1952, when the Detroit Red Wings swept the Stanley Cup in eight successive games, he achieved four shutouts and allowed five goals, a Scroogy average of .62 goals per game.

Sawchuk tended goal in the stand-up fashion admired by purists, seldom off his feet, almost never sprawled. To watch him make a save was to wonder who did the choreography: out the arm, over the stick, up the glove to catch the puck and throw it into the corner, swift and reflexive, a long padded blur.

Sawchuk's time seemed past in the spring of 1967. He had been signed to back up Johnny Bower, regarded by Punch Imlach as second string. He was 37 and he creaked from a back injury. He had battled infectious mononucleosis. He would not have played in the 1967 playoffs if Bower had not split an index finger in the last practice before facing Chicago.

The series seesawed, tied two games each entering the pivotal fifth game in Chicago on April 15, 1967, a memorable Saturday. Bower began the fifth game in goal, but was shaky. Sawchuk came off the bench to replace him with the score tied, 2–2. Terry was knocked down in the first 30 seconds of the second period when Bobby Hull drove a slapshot off his left shoulder.

Toronto trainer Bob Haggert skidded across the ice to aid the fallen netminder. The Hawks skated around in taunting circles, encouraged by 20,000 braying Chicago zealots. "Stay down, Terry," Pierre Pilote jeered. "Let 'em haul you off, Terry."

The trainer bent toward Sawchuk. "You okay, Ukey?" Haggert used the nickname Sawchuk went by in the dressing room.

"I'll be okay if you can get me up," Sawchuk said. "Get me up and I'll stone these bastards."

Up, angered, Sawchuk repelled the hottest shooters in hockey for 40 minutes. He made 37 saves in the last two periods, Jim Pappin and Pete Stemkowski counterpunched two goals, and the Leafs won 4–2. Punch Imlach, gum snapping, testified, "Sawchuk was like you writing guys say. He was Horatio at the bridge."

Imlach meant Horatius, the legendary hero of ancient Italy, who, with two companions, denied the hairy-legged

Etruscans access to a Roman bridge. Horatius, like Sawchuk, was outstanding, commanding and also pretty good.

Sawchuk sat off by himself in the cluttered Toronto dressing room after the game, smoking, answering questions from reporters he didn't always admire, taking ruminative sips from a paper cup containing Coca-Cola.

Everyone else had dressed and left before Sawchuk clumped off in clogs to shower. There was the merest hint of vanity in the last thing he said about subduing Chicago. "I'd like to leave hockey like that," he said. "In good style."

He did not leave, of course. The sixth game of the semifinal was scheduled in Toronto on April 18, 1967. Sawchuk played in it and won, 3–1.

Bobby Hull demonstrated, in a warm-up drill before the game, that hockey is hell, especially on non-combatants. He lofted a shot from one blueline that drifted over the protective glass at the end of the rink and shattered Ballard's spectacles. "I looked up," Harold said, "and I thought I'd come down with a severe fucking case of Halley's squint."

Harold was standing in his private pew, a sealed-off bunker for citizens designated as Very Important Targets. He was reading a program when Hull's shot struck him on the nose, and he did not read much for several days thereafter. Without his glasses, Harold cannot identify a bass drum in a phone booth.

Ballard's nose was broken, but the splintered right lens did not shatter into his eye. He was the Leafs' major casualty, and the only wounded millionaire in the Gardens' clinic. The Toronto chapter of the Hockey Writers Association decided not to hold a tag day.

Hull expressed regrets. "The shot wasn't a real rattler, but I guess it proved you can break a pane of glass from 70 feet."

Beating the Black Hawks qualified the Leafs for another Stanley Cup final, this time against the Canadiens, who had eliminated the New York Rangers in four inconsequential games. How the Leafs stifled the fire-engine flamboyance of the Canadiens, four games to two, is Toronto's last Stanley Cup story. I chronicled them daily for *The Globe and Mail* and, caring because they cared, was more cheerleader than is customary for me in print.

The 1967 Maple Leafs made the playoffs, which not every-

one expected, then advanced to the final round, as almost
nobody outside their dressing room thought possible. They
kept coming back with a defiance that made you appreciate
what they were. Before the sixth game against the Canadiens, I paused in the Leaf room to chat with Tim Horton.

"You know what they say," Horton said. "Goalkeeping is
like pitching." He gazed across the room where Sawchuk
was strapping on the bulky tools of his trade. "If Sawchuk is
Koufax tonight, we win. If he isn't" — a shrug punctuated the
simplicity of Horton's explanation — "well, as they say in
Montreal, c'est la guerre."

Games can be at least a small war: Sandy Koufax overpowering enemy batsmen when he was right and making the Los
Angeles Dodgers better than they were; or Sawchuk, in the
1967 playoffs, challenging the big shooters to drive the puck
past him, giving the Leafs the security that comes from near-
shutout goaltending.

"When Ukey charges out to cut down the angle," Bob
Baun said, "all you see to shoot at is a damn big goalie."

In the little war that followed, Sawchuk was the way Conn
Smythe described him gladitorially, "The leader of a bunch
of game guys who went over the top at Vimy in 1917!"

It was his last larcenous stand. Goals the Canadiens
scored in the first period weren't goals because Sawchuk got
there first, shutting off the daylight the shots were aimed at.
He robbed Montreal's best. Ron Ellis and Jim Pappin scored
for Toronto in the second period. Dick Duff closed the gap to
2–1 six minutes into the third period. It was testimony to
Toronto's relentless checking that the Canadiens never had a
good scoring chance in the last 14 minutes.

Captain George Armstrong released the last ounce of
pressure with 43 seconds left, his goal into an empty Montreal net winning the Stanley Cup 3–1. Terry Sawchuk's
ordeal was over. He seemed to sag, as though he was Sandy
Koufax and his last pitch had struck out the last batter in the
World Series. There has not since been a capering championship scene in the Gardens, no Stanley Cups since 1967.
There was noise and joy unconfined. You could have run a
fish net from Church and Carlton Streets 50 miles away to
Hamilton and not caught a single inhibition.

Sawchuk escaped to the dressing room, not waiting for the Cup presentation to Armstrong, finished. He sat for a long time, head down, hands cupped around a Coke, trying to absorb what had happened to him. He looked up after several silent minutes, eyes bloodshot, sweat coming off him. "My greatest thrill," he murmured. "Absolutely the greatest."

Comment came out of him heavily, the way it does when fatigue catches up and removes, even for victorious pros, the jubilation. Wet underwear hung on his gaunt frame.

"Jesus, but you were disciplined," a reporter said. "You gave Canadiens hardly a single rebound to pounce on."

"Discipline is hardly the word," Sawchuk said, smiling small. "I was scared every time they got near me. Scared shitless."

The last trace of getting up for major travail was gone, the last emotion wrung out of him. "I wouldn't want to play another game," he said, more to himself than to succeeding hordes of celebrators. "Not one."

Upstairs in the press box, typing to meet an insistent deadline, I reached the sum of what those Leafs were. "Statisticians can't employ their arithmetic to measure Terry Sawchuk and Red Kelly and Allan Stanley and Tim Horton and Marcel Pronovost and Bob Pulford and Dave Keon and the rest of the Leafs in these playoffs. They had loyalty to a hope that few outside the dressing room believed existed. Sawchuk certified that hope and last night, May 2, 1967, may be the last time he passed this way as a Leaf. We'll be talking about him a long time after he's gone."

It was Sawchuk's last game as a Leaf. He was lost to Toronto that summer in the expansion draft to stock six new NHL teams. He was gone forever in 1970, dead from complications in an operation to remove his gall bladder. Gone 19 years, and many of us who watched him in 1967 are still talking about him.

There was one last Stanley Cup party in Staff Smythe's house, in the mansion he had built with other people's money at 15 Ashley Park in Etobicoke. The property, high above the Humber River is, in fulsome real-estate terms, "spacious, panoramic, breathtaking, beautiful." Realtors never add, but should, "expensive."

The brazen swindle which Ballard insists was perpetrated by Staff Smythe started in the summer of 1965. The details were discussed by Judge Harry Deyman at Ballard's trial in August, 1972. By then Staff Smythe was dead, safely beyond the clutch of the courts.

"In August of 1965, Cloke Construction Company ... began to do certain work at Maple Leaf Gardens. This was by way of alteration to the interior to make provision for additional seats. On October 8, 1965 they also began to do certain renovations to Mr. Ballard's house at 6 Montgomery Road, Etobicoke, and almost concurrently they began to construct a house for Stafford Smythe at 15 Ashley Park, Etobicoke."

Invoices for all work done by Cloke Construction were sent to Maple Leaf Gardens. The invoices, for Gardens' bookkeeping purposes, were signed by old retainers. One of these was Donald (Shanty) MacKenzie, the building superintendent who had served with Conn Smythe in the Sportsmen's Battery. Another was Clarence Ivan James, the assistant building superintendent and maintenance foreman. James is called Jesse, as in Jesse James.

Judge Deyman's judgment was built on the bird-dogging by crown prosecutor Clay Morison Powell, son of Bert Powell, Ballard's old acquaintance from the Canadian National Exhibition.

The judge mentioned an invoice Cloke sent to the Gardens on August 31, 1966. "It is ... for carrying out work at Maple Leaf Gardens during July and August, 1966, $120,000. Written on it is 'alteration south end ... red seats, directors' rooms, concessions, rearranging north end seats' and this apparently has been written on the invoice by J. James, who also initials the invoice."

There was condemning coincidence in other invoices found in the Gardens. "An invoice from Cloke Construction, for Mr. H. Ballard of 6 Montgomery Road, for carrying out alterations as instructed, $16,500.00, and the detail is in Mr. James' handwriting '... for alterations south end, installation red seats, directors' room, concessions, H.E. Ballard and C.S. Smythe.'"

Another invoice concerned "Cloke Construction to C. Stafford Smythe, Ashley Park, Etobicoke ... carrying out work on new house as per plans, value to date $120,000 ... Detail written on it in J. James' handwriting is for 'progress south end alterations, pre-cast installation red seats, directors' rooms, concessions, rearranging north end seats, C.S. Smythe and H. Ballard' initialled by J. James and D. MacKenzie ..."

The court inferred, beyond the dispute of the Smythe-Ballard defence, that work allegedly done by Cloke Construction in the Gardens was actually done on the Smythe-Ballard dwellings, and paid for by Gardens' cheques. The defence, through almost four years, was led by John J. Robinette, a distinguished Canadian counsel.

"My God," I said to Ballard, when news of the scandal became public, "you only hire J.J. Robinette in this country if you're going to hang."

"We've got a chance to hang, all right," Pal Hal said.

In early June, the NHL expanded from six teams to twelve. The adroit R. Alan Eagleson, a Toronto lawyer, informed the NHL owners that an NHL Players Association was a fact. The first president of the association was an assistant Maple Leaf captain, durable Bob Pulford.

The historic NHL conclave opened on a muggy Monday in Montreal, the same day that the 1967 Arab-Israeli war began. The war ended in six days, before the NHL parley did. Broadcaster Joe Morgan said, "If Sandy Koufax had been pitching for the Israelis, the war would have been over in two days." Koufax, who threw bristling pitches, was a devout Jew who refused to play baseball on Yom Kippur, the Jewish day of atonement.

The six established NHL teams, in Montreal, Toronto, New York, Detroit, Boston and Chicago, admitted six suckers into the lodge, from Pittsburgh, Philadelphia, Minnesota, Los Angeles, San Francisco and St. Louis. The new boys were assessed an entry fee of $2 million each. Clarence Campbell, the NHL president, distributed the cheques to the old boys. Ballard and Staff Smythe were presented with Philadelphia's ticket for $2 million. That night, a pair of rover boys, Harold and Staff wandered into the press lounge in the Queen Elizabeth Hotel. Ballard showed the $2 million to those of us who didn't believe there was that much money in the galaxy.

"Okay," one of us said. "Get out the cards. Let's start a poker game. For starters, Harold, throw that $2 mil in the pot."

"Fuck you guys," Ballard said,. "This money pays off our mortgage on the Gardens." Then Mike and Ike, the Gold Dust Twins, wandered out of the hotel. Harold stuck the cheque, I noticed, in one of his back pockets.

Staff Smythe won more walking-around money on June 24, 1967, the day of the Centennial Queen's Plate at the Woodbine racecourse in uptown Rexdale, Ontario. His father's muscular filly, Jammed Lovely, won at lush odds of 11 to 1.

Jammed Lovely bounded down the Woodbine highway on a humid afternoon, ahead of 13 struggling rivals with 220 yards to run. A game colt named Pine Point came at her in a desperate drive on the outside, grabbing for the throat latch, still grabbing as they plunged under the wire, the filly first by the length of her comely neck.

There was champagne in the tack room at Smythe's barn and a stablehand named Wayne Delio was pouring the victory beverage into long-stemmed glasses. King Clancy and Joe Primeau were there from his old Maple Leaf winners. Mike Walton, a Maple Leaf married to Smythe's oldest granddaughter, represented the 1967 champions. Smythe's son, Dr. Hugh, was there, but his older son did not join the jubilation. Staff Smythe had wagered $100 to win on Jammed Lovely and, after she paid $24.90 for a $2-wager, he went away burdened with $1,242.00. Abrasive father and recalcitrant son were not speaking to each other in that golden high summer, the last winning year either would know.

The Leafs lost in 1967-68, the first season of modern NHL expansion. They missed the playoffs for the first time in 10 years, handicapped by no minor-pro farm teams. Ballard and Staff Smythe, grubbing money, sold the farm in Rochester, N.Y., to a Vancouver group for $400,000. The Leaf farm in Victoria was sold to a Phoenix syndicate for $500,000. Gar-

dens' profits went up, but the Leafs performance stayed
down.

"The pattern of fraud," as Judge Harry Deyman called it,
became apparent to the Gardens' treasurer on April 6, 1968,
a Saturday.

Leonard Charles Heath served with Major Smythe's
Sportsmen's Battery and had been the bookkeeper at the
Gardens for 22 years. He came late to the deceit of Ballard
and Staff Smythe.

Smythe, that Saturday, handed Heath a sheaf of invoices
from Cloke Construction. One invoice, for work done almost
two years earlier, carried Stafford's notation to the bookkeeper. "Len: This is apparently for work at my house but
nowhere near this work has been carried out. Apparently
Cloke are carrying the accounts on the same job number as
the Gardens. To avoid confusion at this time, have the Gardens pay these accounts and bill Harold and I for any outside
work after job is completed and invoices checked."

Len Heath inspected the invoices. He stared owlishly
through his glasses. His antennae of apprehension quivered.
"Stafford," he said finally, "there's no way I can pass these
invoices as Gardens' expenses."

Arrogance was on Staff Smythe, an insolent attitude of "I
can do no wrong." He looked at the man who had served his
father in a war, a faithful footman now refusing an order.

"If you can't pass those invoices as Gardens' expenses,
Len," Staff said, "you can quit."

Len Heath pondered ethics and responsibility and loyalty
to the Gardens for two days. Then, on April 8, 1968, he did
quit. Ballard asked him to reconsider his resignation, but he
refused. When Clay Powell came calling on behalf of the
Crown, he found Leonard Charles Heath an obliging witness against his former employers. Heath removed the cloak
from Cloke Construction.

Gumshoes from the Department of Internal Revenue
came calling at the Gardens in early October, 1968, accompanied by four Royal Canadian Mounted Policemen in plain
clothes. Ballard was attending to Gardens' business while
Staff Smythe was on vacation in Florida.

Ballard phoned Stafford while the government operatives

searched for incriminating documents. Ballard, out of earshot of the RCMP, said, "Stafford, we got some guys from the government in here nosing around."

Smythe maintained a brash front. "Fuck 'em," he told Harold. "The government is full of dummies. Throw 'em out."

Ballard was doubtful that the RCMP could be thrown out. "I tell you, Stafford, these guys don't look like they just fell off a load of hay. They ain't dummies. They know the filing cabinets they want to see. They're grabbing our confidential stuff."

Price Waterhouse, the Gardens' accountants, came from far behind on the fraud. Shareholders were at last informed: "The Department of National Revenue is making a special review of the company's income-tax returns for the past several years. . . ." A report for the financial year ending August 31, 1968, stated: "Incorrect invoices submitted by a construction company resulted in the inclusion in property additions for the years ended Aug. 31, 1966 and 1967, of amounts aggregating $212,800."

Staff Smythe, living in a dwelling paid for by shareholders, without their knowledge, vowed to fight the "tax people" in court. About then, in the autumn of 1968, sports writers began to contemplate the possibility of Smythe or Ballard or both going to jail.

Most of us agreed with Jim Coleman of the Southam papers. "Stafford will ride this out with his usual Smythe bluster," Coleman said. "Ballard's a big softy. He'll collapse."

Experts, once again, were not in doubt but widely in error. Smythe collapsed and Ballard rode out the embarrassment and punishment with the bravado of a defiant sea-flea driver.

Ballard said, "You never saw a guy cave in the way Stafford did. He'd come in the office with a quart of whisky around 10:00 a.m. Then he'd send a secretary out for a quart of milk. Both the whisky and the milk'd be gone by noon."

Caving in, trying to get his mind off his troubles, Stafford's motto was "Nothing in moderation." He spent more and more time in the penthouse apartment, S.H. Marlie. He had an insatiable appetite for oral sex. The maitre d'Hot Stove Lounge, Joey Faraco, provided pornographic films for the quirky gratification of the disintegrating Leaf president.

Disintegration was one word for the falling-apart social
fabric of North America in the late sixties. Assassins mur-
dered Robert Kennedy, a candidate for the U.S. presidency,
and Martin Luther King, who'd had an American dream.
Pierre Trudeau, wearing an ascot and sandals, rode Tru-
deaumania to federal power in Canada. Jackie Kennedy married a Greek shipping tycoon.

Staff Smythe, making mischief, threatened to fire Punch
Imlach in December, 1968, even though Imlach had two
years remaining on a contract to manage and coach the Leafs.
Imlach's reprieve was brief. Smythe did fire him on April 6,
1969, a few minutes after the Leafs had lost, on merit, to the
Boston Bruins in the first round of the Stanley Cup playoffs.

Imlach received $38,000 in severance pay, the money
owed from the year remaining on his Toronto contract. The
franchise has not since had a general manager to match the
Imlach of the 1959-69 years. He had an uncommonly agile
brain, a keen understanding of hockey tactics and politics,
absolute mastery of the gift of concentration and towering
confidence in his own gambling moves. A year later, in 1970,
he was the chairborne strategist of the Buffalo Sabres, an
expansion team. In five years, Imlach had the Sabres in the
Stanley Cup final, where they lost to the Philadelphia Flyers.

Dismissing Imlach was the last hockey decision of importance made by Staff Smythe. He replaced Punch with Jim
Gregory as manager and John McLellan as coach, both ele-
vated from similar jobs on the Leaf farm in Tulsa, Oklahoma.

The Ballard-Smythe scandal was the worst-kept secret in
Toronto. Their ally, John Bassett, began to slide away from
them, slipping along the sideline like one of his Argonaut
halfbacks escaping trouble. Bassett published the Toronto
Telegram and controlled CFTO, a television station. He did
not want the illegal acts of Ballard and Smythe to risk the TV
license granted to him by the federal government.

Other tinpot Caesars among the Gardens' directors began
to cringe. It was protect-my-own-ass time when Bassett, as
chairman of the brood, convened an extraordinary meeting
of the directors on June 26, 1969, a sodden Thursday. The
meeting was conducted away from the Gardens, in the Impe-

rial Oil Building in midtown Toronto. W.O. Twaits, the president of Imperial Oil, was a Gardens' director.

The sole business of the meeting was to dismiss Ballard and Smythe as chief officers of the Gardens. Fifteen of the twenty-one directors attended; the six absentees, essentially wimps, suddenly discovered they had business elsewhere. Ballard and Smythe, after rancorous debate, refused to resign.

Bassett, in the chair, decreed a secret ballot on the question: to throw Ballard and Smythe out, or not to throw them out? Bassett was surprised when he counted the ballots to find the vote tied, seven for retention, seven for dismissal. He cast the 8-7 ballot against the men whose company he coveted in 1961.

Ballard said afterwards, "Any help we got from our old buddy Bassett was debatable." Harold continued the bluff. "We got no problems. Staff and I are still in the Gardens at full pay. We'll operate the building and the club the same way. We'll feel our way along."

He added a plaintive postscript. "Maybe our partners don't like the way we promote. Hell, we've made them a zillion dollars." George Mara, a member of the Silver Seven and a former junior Marlboro, was appointed president of the Gardens. There was more finagling in creation of a new entity, the Maple Leaf Hockey Team. Smythe was picked president, Ballard as vice-president. Harold never missed a day's work at the Gardens.

The other shoe dropped on July 9, 1969. A headline in *The Toronto Star* summed up their plight: "STAFF SMYTHE, HAROLD BALLARD/CHARGED AS INCOME TAX EVADERS." They were summonsed on charges of evading income taxes and failure to report income. The charges involved $278,920 for Smythe and $134,685 for Ballard.

The *Star* reported:

> The information against Smythe alleges that between April, 1965 and March, 1968, he evaded income taxes as follows — a total of $208,166 appropriated by him from Maple Leaf Gardens in respect of the cost of construction and improving his residence.

The sum of $35,178 appropriated from the Gardens for personal and family expenses. The sum of $35,575 appropriated by him from monies payable to Maple Leaf Gardens in respect of the Marlboro Hockey Club. The other four counts allege that Smythe made false or deceptive statements in his tax returns for 1964, 1965, 1966 and 1967.

The Leafs won the Stanley Cup in 1964, to enhance profits, but the crown alleged "Smythe made a false statement by saying he had incurred a loss of $15,146, when he failed to report income of $4,910. In 1965, Smythe reported his income as $9,906, but failed to report income of $10,165.

"In 1966, the information said his return was falsified again when he reported income of $34,330. The crown claims he should have reported another $221,115. The 1967 return listed income of $38,323, which the crown said should have shown another $42,728."

The *Star* reported parallel allegations against Ballard.

The information alleges that Ballard appropriated $74,395 from the Gardens in respect of the cost of constructing and improving his residence.

It adds that he also appropriated $24,713 from the Gardens for personal and family expense and $35,575 from monies payable to the Gardens in respect of the Marlboro Hockey Club. The Marlboros are in the Ontario Hockey Association's Junior A League.

For the tax year 1964, the crown alleges Ballard made a false statement by stating his income was $65,628, but failed to report other income of $4,481. In 1965, it charges his reported income was $89,356, when in reality it was $13,717 higher.

In 1966, the crown alleges Ballard reported an income of $261,743, but failed to include another $41,686. Finally, for the tax year 1967, Ballard reported $68,113, but allegedly failed to show a further $74,798. . . .

One other event titillated Toronto and the world that summer. On July 20, 1969, a Sunday, two American astronauts landed on the moon. Buzz Aldrin looked for golfballs while

Neil Armstrong announced to a fascinated earth, "One small step for man ... one giant leap for mankind." Before the summer ended, miniskirts went up on a good leggy show.

It was Dorothy Ballard's last summer. A mastectomy did not check the malignancy gnawing at her. Harold took her to Europe and on one last journey to Jamaica. He sat with her in Wellesley Hospital, eight blocks from the Gardens. She comforted him as much as he comforted her.

Dr. Hugh Smythe would say, "Dorothy was strong and courageous. Harold never had such a stabilizing force." The force weakened, destabilized and died. Harold felt amputated; part of him died with her. She was buried from Kingsway-Lambton United Church, just west of the Humber River above Bloor, in early December, 1969.

Part of a sports columnist's responsibility, I think, is to express empathy. We are the caretakers of heirlooms. I wrote:

> There was bright sunshine on the cold morning of Dorothy Ballard's funeral. The church was packed to the vestibule, and those who could not find seats stood behind the rear pews to hear Rev. Harry Denning deliver a gentle eulogy ... It was a quiet service, restrained, composed of the most comforting passage in the New Testament.
>
> The Lord is my shepherd; I shall not want ... Yea, though I walk through the valley of the shadow of death, I will fear no evil. ...
>
> The mourners were a cross-section of the worlds Mrs. Ballard knew, and was part of, and delighted in. The big men of Toronto publishing and sports writing were there, and Mrs. Ballard would have appreciated that because her husband has been on the Toronto sports pages for 30 years.
>
> The Maple Leafs she applauded were there, her team, the blue and white with the big white leaf, and she would have felt at home with them. Maple Leaf Gardens was closed for the day, shut in respect for a graceful woman the employees enjoyed.
>
> One large wreath, yellow and white chrysanthemums, was signed "The ushers and gatemen of the Gardens." Mrs. Ballard would have liked that best of all.

I lift up mine eyes unto the hills, from whence cometh my help . . . The Lord shall preserve thy going out and thy coming in. . . .

The calm reading of the scripture moved on. The muted tones of an organ filled the background. In the pews, Mrs. Ballard's friends bowed their heads and prayed or remembered, each according to his fashion.

She had been sick a long time with a remorseless disease, unwilling to quit, going 15 rounds because she wanted to live for her husband, her daughter and two sons. "Dorothy was a beautiful woman physically," Rev. Denning said. "But more important, she had a beautiful spirit. In the dark days of her illness, she showed a courage that I rarely see in those so afflicted . . . We talked bluntly and roughly about her troubles . . . and her faith was undiminished."

The clergyman spoke as a friend, a dark-haired man gazing through glasses, economical with his words, reaching out with his voice. He quoted Tennyson: "Sunset and evening star/And one clear call for me!/And may there be no moaning of the bar/When I put out to sea."

It is there in the last book, Revelation, in almost the last chapter. "And I saw a new heaven and a new earth: for the first heaven and the first earth were passed away . . . And I, John, saw the holy city, new Jerusalem. . . . "

Slowly the church emptied. A file of limousines drew up to the curb, then drove away in the bright sunshine. Other cars followed, lights on for the last trip of a few blocks, through streets of tall bare trees to Park Lawn Cemetery.

There was thin snow on the rolling slopes and mourners moved up a knoll toward the grave where Harold Ballard stood with his children. Art Marshall took off his hat and said it for all the old Maple Leaf Gardens hands. "Such a lovely woman," he said.

Art Marshall spoke quietly to a friend, but his tone was like banners. . . .

CHAPTER 10

Our Falling Leafs

◆

A plain metal cross marks Dorothy Ballard's grave in Park Lawn Cemetery. The inscription on her headstone reads:

> Dorothy B. Higgs
> Beloved wife of
> Harold E. Ballard
> "Walked With God"
> Dec. 2, 1969
> Mother of Mary,
> William and Harold, Jr.
> "The Lord is Her Shepherd"

Her favorite gift from Harold, a necklace with a diamond-encrusted heart, was buried with her. "I buried a jewel with a jewel," he said. He returned to the big home he'd built for her as a bride, "Woodycrest 1941," and locked himself in the sun room where she spent quiet time during her cancer fight. Then he wept, uncontrollable sobs racking a rascal who went through life laughing. He subsided into self-pity, the most wasted of human emotions.

He came out of his gloom, not quickly. He began to talk about Dorothy as though she was a saint elsewhere. "God, she was wonderful," he'd say. "Best thing that ever happened to me. I see all the parasites and bums in society, giving nothing, sponging, and they just seem to coast right along. Then I remember Dorothy, that lovely woman who did only good and I feel like a goddamn big baby about to cry."

That, too, for some, is human. We bury our fireside cheering sections and lose the love they can no longer bestow upon us, the tenderness gone. Harold had lost the grace of the best friend he ever had.

The Maple Leafs lost, too, after NHL expansion, adding in the years after 1967 a new lacklustre to the term "big-leaguers." Maple Leafs equate with Maple Oops. Hogtown, in hockey, became Flogtown. Failure began when the NHL disallowed sponsorship of minor systems. The Leafs could no longer lock up NHL prospects on Toronto St. Mike's or Toronto Marlboros. All NHL prospects were subject to something called "the universal draft." All NHL teams – 21 now – have a chance at all NHL prospects. The teams draft the young meat in the reverse order of finish in the NHL standing, meaning the Leafs usually draft high.

The universal draft puts a premium on scouting, but hockey scouts discredit themselves with prejudice. Many have leather-jacketed minds, unsophisticated, burdened with gossip, humbug and ignorance. The 1969 draft, in Montreal, illustrated NHL numskullery.

One night in midwinter 1969, in the Gardens, I fell into conversation with Steve Brklacich, then a scout for the New York Rangers. (Bob Hesketh once mentioned, in the Toronto *Telegram*, that a lot seemed to be missing from the name Brklacich, such as vowels.) Steve had crisscrossed the country inspecting choice junior stock.

"So who," I asked Brklacich, "is the best kid in Canada?" Brklacich knocked the ash off his cigar. "Write it down," he said. "The kid's name is Clarke. Bobby Clarke of Flin Flon. Be sure you spell it right. It's Clarke, with an 'e' on the end. You're going to be writing his name a long time. Tough kid. Wicked. Hell of a prospect."

I checked with other scouts, all of whom endorsed Steve Brklacich's opinion. Robert Earle Clarke of the Flin Flon Bombers was the flossiest junior in Canada in the spring of 1969. One of them said, as an aside, "Clarke does have diabetes, but that should be no problem."

On the basis of what seemed sound information, I wrote a column in *The Globe and Mail* touting Clarke as the top draft choice in Canada. "He has diabetes," I wrote, "but that's been no barrier to athletic activity since 1922, when Frederick Banting and C.H. Best discovered insulin."

The hockey clans convened in Montreal in June to sort and choose the best available junior talent. I expected Clarke to be chosen high, too late for the Leafs, who were ninth in the drafting rotation. Bob Clarke was not taken in the first eight. Stafford Smythe, with new Leaf manager Jim Gregory, considered their selections at the Toronto table, bereft of Punch Imlach's shrewd influence for the first time in 11 years. "Toronto," Gregory said into the public address system, "takes Ernie Moser of the Estevan Bruins."

At the press table, I muttered, as Harold Ballard might, "Ernie fucking Who?"

The drafting went on until the Philadelphia Flyers, in the second round, took Clarke. He had gone seventeenth rather than first, where many scouts had ranked him. The Flyers first choice had been Bob Currier of the Cornwall Royals.

"How come you guys didn't grab Clarke?" I asked Stafford Smythe. "Everything I hear indicates he'll be another Ted Kennedy. Hard-nosed, implacable, mean, just what the Leafs need."

Smythe said, "We had good reports on Clarke, too. But we thought the diabetes he's got wouldn't make him strong enough to play a rugged NHL schedule."

I was exasperated. "Just because somebody's got diabetes is no reason to think they can't play NHL hockey. Hell, Stafford, four blocks from Maple Leaf Gardens is the Banting Institute. They invented stuff there more than 45 years ago that permits diabetics to play as hard as anybody."

"Yeah," Smythe said, "well, we still don't think Clarke is healthy enough to play in the NHL."

Never had a second guess of NHL stupidity been more warranted. Bob Clarke, a diabetic, was the dominant force driving the Philadelphia Flyers to back-to-back Stanley Cups, in 1974 and 1975. He was elected the most-valuable mercenary in the league three times. When the history of the NHL in the seventies is written, his will be a large chapter in it.

The junior the Flyers picked ahead of Clarke in 1969, Bob Currier, never helped them win anything. The junior the Leafs preferred ahead of Clarke, Ernie Moser, never helped Toronto dominate one second of one game anywhere. So much for the seventh sense of genius said to repose in hockey managers and owners. Punch Imlach, ever ready to ride a hunch, would have drafted Clarke the first time he had a chance. Imlach might not have known much about diabetes, but he knew a tough player when he saw one.

Off-ice jostling by Staff Smythe and Ballard took prece-
dence in 1970. They battled the federal government on the
income-tax issue with their counsel, J.J. Robinette, holding
the feds even. They battled John Bassett for control of
Gardens' stock, and won. They contrived to throw out their
detractors on the Gardens' directorate.

On June 20, 1970, Queen's Plate Day at the Woodbine
cavalry casino, I met John Turner in the walking ring. I'd
covered the Justice Minister as a cub reporter 20 years earlier
when he was Chick Turner, a sprinter just outside Olympic
calibre.

"So, Mr. Minister," I said, "what about Ballard and
Smythe? You've got them in a bind."

"It's not Ballard we're after," Canada's top cop said. "We
want the other guy."

John Turner's department did not get Staff Smythe. John
Robinette successfully argued that the Crown had no legal
right to proceed against Smythe by indictment, as authorized by Turner. Robinette claimed Smythe was being treated
"unequally before the law."

Bill Houston reported:

> If convicted by indictment, Smythe faced a prison term
> of two months to five years, a fine ranging from $25.00
> to $10,000 and a penalty of up to double the amount of
> taxes evaded. But, Robinette argued, the 1960 Bill of
> Rights entitled an individual to equality before the law,
> and the penalties under summary procedure – trial
> before a provincial judge – carried a jail term of only up
> to two years, not five. Judge Joseph Kelly of York County
> Court in Toronto agreed with Robinette and ruled that
> the relevant section of the Income Tax Act contravened
> the Bill of Rights. The charges were dismissed but the
> battle wasn't won. . . .

Turner, in response, told the House of Commons that the
Justice Department would ask the Ontario Supreme Court to
hold a trial on charges of tax evasion against Smythe in spite
of Judge Kelly's decision. The Supreme Court acceded to
Turner's request.

It was get-even time at the annual meeting of Gardens' shareholders on December 17, 1970. Staff Smythe and Ballard had enough stock and support to repudiate the directors who had removed them from top management 18 months earlier. John Bassett resigned as chairman of the board. Sixteen others refused to seek re-election. The Silver Seven, buoyant and loaded for fun in 1957, disintegrated. The directorate was whittled from twenty-one to eight.

The eight elected were oldtimer Dr. J.L. Hall; Douglas H. Roxborough, vice-president of Alleson Industries Ltd., whose father Henry wrote rah-rah cheerleading sports books; Paul McNamara, president of Northgate Hotel Ltd., son and nephew of two members of the Hockey Hall of Fame; Dr. Hugh Smythe; T.D. Jeffries, president of Viceroy Manufacturing Co. Ltd., and Staff Smythe's closest crony; Donald P. Giffin, president of Giffin Sheet Metals Ltd.; Staff Smythe and Ballard. Mike and Ike were back in total control. Don Giffin remains a close Ballard confident.

I covered the meeting for *The Globe and Mail* with Irv Lutzky from the paper's Report on Business section. Our dispatch made fascinating reading on December 18, 1970.

The annual meeting was not as cut and dried as a potato chip. George Mara, chairing the meeting as his last act as a retiring director, heard impertinent questions from a partner in the influential Toronto law firm of Blake, Cassels and Graydon.

The partner was Arthur Pattillo, a clone of John Diefenbaker, lean and spare, the same crinkly gray hair. He was past-president of the Canadian Bar Association and owned, he said, 100 shares of Gardens' stock. He commanded the room, austere and informed, a relentless cross-examiner.

Arthur Pattillo asked Chairman Mara: "I have heard disturbing rumors on the street that the new directors are linked in business and family affairs. Is this true?"

From the back of the room, Stafford Smythe interrupted and said he thought the question was out of order. "But I'll answer it," he said. "The new members are large shareholders and hockey fans."

Pattillo replied: "I won't accept that answer."

His next question was: "Has the chair any knowledge of benefits paid directly to any directors of Maple Leaf Gardens from the sale of the Rochester hockey club?"

Chairman Mara denied having any such knowledge.

Pattillo then asked: "Has Maple Leaf Gardens indemnified the Rochester hockey club for monies paid any directors of the Gardens for acting as directors of the Rochester club?"

Mara said he knew of no such money. (Pattillo was treading on sound ground; Ballard and Staff Smythe had been directors of the Rochester team when it was a Maple Leaf farm.)

Pattillo asked: "Did any directors benefit personally from the sale of what I shall call other farm teams? Were these monies disclosed?" Mara said no.

Pattillo then asked the retiring members of the board to explain why they were quitting. "Are these persons retiring because of lack of confidence in Ballard and Smythe?"

Mara said: "The ballot to remove these men in 1969 split ... I'm confident the Gardens can be run profitably and I own 3,000 shares to prove it."

W.O. Twaits, the president of Imperial Oil, which sponsored Maple Leaf telecasts, said: "Those of us retiring cannot guarantee the performance of the board from here in ... But I found I was frequently in conflict of interest as a director and as sponsor of Hockey Night in Canada. In the future the new board will try to get as much for the TV rights as they can and I'll be trying to pay as little as I can."

Charles Burns, horseman, stockbroker and an outgoing director, said: "I was uspet at various events and ... I think the board leaned over backward to keep from giving publicity to the legal problems of Ballard and Smythe."

Henry Borden, a director loyal to what Conn Smythe was, said: "We are ... bowing to the two biggest shareholders (Ballard and Staff Smythe) who can toss us out at any time."

Pattillo then asked questions about the business of the Marlboro junior hockey club. "What disclosures have been made to the board about relations of any director to the Marlboros? Was there any financial gain for Ballard and Smythe?"

Mara said: "While Conn Smythe was still president of the

Gardens the company took over the Marlboros. I know of no
financial benefit to the gentlemen you mention."

Pattillo said to Chairman Mara: "I address this to you, sir,
and to the company's chartered accountants. Is there any
significance to a bank account in the name of S.H. Marlie?"

Mara replied: "It would not be in the best interests of the
company to answer."

A representative of the chartered accountants, Clarkson
Gordon, said they could not find any S.H. Marlie account.

Pattillo then asked if Stafford Smythe had asked Maple
Leaf Gardens to pay expenses for the wedding of one of his
daughters. Mara replied that Smythe did ask the board to
pay such expenses, but the board refused.

Pattillo asked about the penthouse apartment, the
"Marlboro A.C." He asked, "Did the board authorize renting
any accommodation in the Village Green Apartments?"

Mara said: "The board did not make such authorization.
Maple Leaf Gardens had no financial commitment to, or
interest in renting any such apartment. . . . But there have
been designated club rooms in the City Park Apartments
back of here [the Gardens]. These club rooms have moved
to the Village Green . . . These premises were used for
such purposes as meeting the hockey committee and the
coach."

Arthur Pattillo looked around at the assembled shareholders, about 50. "In conclusion, ladies and gentlemen, I asked
these questions to comment on this whole enterprise and the
whole nature of the company."

Paul McNamara, standing at the back of the room,
shouted: "The problems of Smythe and Ballard have nothing
to do with the Maple Leaf Hockey Club!"

Pattillo's inquisition made page one of the Toronto newspapers. Staff Smythe had a stopped-dead smile on his face,
stunned. He began to crack under public ridicule.

One director said, "Staff tried to take his mind off his
problem with scotch and sex. We'd be sitting with our wives
at a game and he'd excuse himself. Then he'd go up to a
bunker high in the reds for a session with a secretary we used
to have around here. She was called Betty Blowjob."

One afternoon, a functionary in the hockey department

was called to Staff Smythe's office. He thought, "Oh, oh. Staff must want to trade a player or something." The man was repelled, when he walked into Smythe's office, to see the Leaf president lying flat on the desk with Betty Blowjob performing oral sex upon him. Any sex act is, strictly speaking, a non-spectator sport. The functionary fled while Smythe laughed.

Ballard was more sedate in dealing with his demons. He would take Joey Faraco, maître d'Hot Stove Lounge, on week-long trips to the Ballard cottage on Georgian Bay, across a narrow strait from the Christian Island of song and verse. They would talk and play cards and Ballard would swim. Faraco prepared meals with provender from the Hot Stove Lounge.

Faraco told Bill Houston: "I'd say 'Harold, I've got work to do in Toronto.' Harold would say, 'Fuck it. You've got the joint running okay.' It was 'fuck this, fuck that.'"

Faraco began to fear he might be investigated by plainclothes police baying after Ballard and Smythe. He was concerned that he would be held responsible for steaks, roasts and other food from lockers in the Hot Stove Lounge which landed in Ballard's cottage. He thought he could be charged with theft.

Faraco confided in another Gardens' director, who advised him to bill Ballard. It was Goodbye Joey when Ballard discovered Faraco had sought counsel from another director. Harold began to ignore his servant-friend. He called him, to other Lounge employees, a "fucking wop" and "goddamn banana peddler."

One afternoon, Faraco was in the lounge ordering supplies from a salesman. Ballard walked in the kitchen to make himself a sandwich. "Is that fucking dago bastard still here?" Harold said. "When's he going to fuck off?"

Faraco was incensed. When the salesman left, he challenged Ballard. "Here . . . here are the keys to the Lounge," Faraco said. "Take them and stick them up your fat ass." He walked out of the Gardens, finished forever with a man who once invited Faraco to be buried in the Ballard family plot.

Two Maple Leafs, not otherwise identified, had found out about the Federal Tax Department's raid on the Gardens' executive offices the day after it happened, in early October, 1968. The late Gardens' publicist, Stan Obodiac, told the two players about the raid. One of the players knew Clay Morrison Powell, a special prosecuter in the department of the Ontario Attorney General. The player told Powell, "Ballard and Smythe are going to try to make some deal with Government, or they're in big trouble."

The stocky, cocky Powell was the son of Ballard's contact at the Canadian National Exhibition, Bert Powell, the CNE's general manager. The younger Powell graduated from the University of Western Ontario to Osgoode Law School, an institution sometimes revered as the lizard in the downspout of Canadian jurisprudence. He worked nights and summers as a reporter at the Toronto *Telegram*, where he was called Butch Powell.

Powell remembered the tip from the players when the preliminary hearing was held on tax-evasion charges against Ballard and Smythe in 1970. He sat at the back of the courtroom for a day, listening. Then he went to his superior, the Attorney General.

Bill Bowman, director of public prosecutions, authorized Powell to supervise a special prosecutions branch "to do something about theft and fraud." Metro Toronto detectives Charlie Angus and Ray Creighton were assigned to Powell's fraud squad. Detective David Simser was recruited. They interviewed more than 180 people in an intensive investigation of Maple Leaf malfeasance.

There was misconduct with the junior Marlboros, under the fictitious S.H. Marlie. Powell's associates discovered that cheques intended for the Marlboros and, ergo, the Gardens were deposited from 1964 to 1969 into the bank account of S.H. Marlie, whose signing officers were Ballard and Smythe. The cheques were from the Ontario Hockey Association and the Canadian Amateur Hockey Association as the Marlboro share of collective playoff revenue.

Powell's pals checked Cloke construction work on Smythe's palatial spread on Ashley Park in Etobicoke. They determined that invoices for work on the Smythe house showed in Gardens' accounts as renovations to the arena.

Smythe's swindle extended to construction of a summer

cottage in the resort region of Muskoka Lakes, in central Ontario. Cloke carpenters did construction on Smythe's farm near Guelph, northwest of Toronto. Similar construction was done to Ballard's summer home near Thunder Beach on Georgian Bay, all of it charged to the Gardens.

Clay Powell's pursuit of Gardens' grafters took eight months. His detectives manually counted the seats in the Gardens to demonstrate that Cloke did not construct more pews. They went to Ashley Park to take a picture of Smythe's mansion, made a mistake and photographed the dwelling next door, then returned the next day for pictures of the correct place built by Gardens' shareholders. Powell assembled his evidence for the Ontario Attorney General, Allan Lawrence. Metro Toronto police were to snap the trap.

On June 17, 1971, Staff Smythe was arrested in Maple Leaf Gardens on charges of theft and fraud involving $395,000. Smythe was pale and rumpled when detectives hauled him to Metro Toronto police headquarters on Jarvis Street, six blocks from the Gardens. He was mugged and fingerprinted like any ordinary thief.

Smythe's lawyer, Colin Campbell, suggested in a brief court appearance that Smythe be released on his own recognizance. Provincial Judge P.J. Bolsby called the $50,000 bail recommended by Clay Powell "extremely moderate."

Released, Smythe shoved past reporters waiting for his comment. "See me later at the house," he barked. The Smythe party left the courthouse in an appropriate hockey scene. Clancy bodychecked a news cameraman. Tom Smythe, son of Staff, pushed another photographer. Then they rode off, steaming, in a red limousine.

Police searched for Ballard for half a day before locating him at his summer retreat. He heard on the radio that he was a wanted man and telephoned police to meet him at his Montgomery Road home. Detective Sergeant Charles Angus took Ballard for mugging and fingerprinting at Metro police headquarters.

Ballard rode out his arrest with smiling geniality. He walked out the back door of police headquarters and posed for photographers. He was asked if he had anything to say.

"Yes," Pal Hal said. "I'd just like to wish everyone a happy Father's Day."

Prosecutor Powell went after major roots in the Gardens. He interviewed Punch Imlach when George F. was still general-manager of the hockey team. Imlach had approved expenditures for hockey sticks which were actually spent on work and favors for Ballard and. Smythe. Imlach said to Powell, "You ask me anything and I'll tell you the truth, but I volunteer nothing." Old loyalties stuck, as jam to a blanket.

Powell had 73 witnesses scheduled to testify at Staff Smythe's trial in the fall of 1971. He might have called a 74th. He might have called Conn Smythe to testify about an errant son. Powell is a Maple Leaf fan, too; he was in a certain awe of the senior Smythe.

"Of course we approached Mr. Smythe with some respect," Powell said. "We talked to him and he started to cry. He was humiliated. He called Ballard 'a no-good rotten bastard' for leading his son astray. We didn't want to humiliate Mr. Smythe further. If Stafford had lived to stand trial, his dad wouldn't have testified."

Conn Smythe was 76 then, one of Toronto's icons, a stone eroded by obstinancy and sentiment. He was a philanthropist who blazed a wide path in supporting the rehabilitation of crippled children. He reflected old defiant Tory Toronto, notably in his gauche confrontations with Québécois.

During this period, in a presentation of NHL prizes in Montreal, the Major began a speech in the crudest way. "Gentlemen," he began, "and Frenchmen...." His rudeness was rapped, but not in Toronto. He had reached the stage of Grand Old Man who could get away with anything. We remembered what he had been in war, and in a war game with our team. Clay Powell was honoring what the Major had been.

There was feverish competition for control of the Gardens through 1971, Ballard and Staff Smythe versus John Bassett, old collaborators turned antagonists. Ballard, more ingratiating than the haughty Bassett, could call in more IOUs. He had done the most to increase the value of the stock while

Bassett sat collecting fat dividend cheques. His real passion
was football as played by the Toronto Argonauts.

The competition for control ended on September 1, 1971,
when Bassett abandoned the fight. Ballard was elated. "It
was the first battle Bassett ever lost in his life," he said. "He
couldn't believe it. But Staff and I got even for the way he quit
on us when we got in tax trouble."

Staff and Harold borrowed precisely $5,886,600 to pay for
exactly 196,200 shares dominated by Bassett, about $30 a
share. Then, Bassett, smoothly handing off cheques as a
quarterback dealing footballs, bought 99.45 per cent of the
Argonauts for about $2,312,800.

His Gardens' adventure, over 10 years, was gratifying for
Bassett. His original investment of $900,000 produced $5.8
million in the sale of shares to Ballard and Smythe, plus
dividends of $2 million, for a tidy profit approaching $7
million. The former city hall reporter for *The Globe and Mail*
could afford to buy city hall, or whatever he fancied.

Ballard and Smythe could not reach into a cookie jar for
the $5,886,600 needed to detach Bassett and his friends from
the Gardens. The benign interest of a friendly banker was
required. They nuzzled at the Canadian Imperial Bank of
Commerce but could not obtain what they considered an
"agreeable" interest rate. They were persuaded by a saga-
cious Gardens' director, Don Giffin, to contact the Toronto-
Dominion Bank.

Their contact was Allen T. Lambert, chairman and president of the T-D. "Let's talk," Lambert said. "I know you've got
tax problems and court cases, but you're the kind of good
promoters we like to do business with." The result was a
ceremony in Lambert's office on September 1, 1971, where
Ballard and Smythe signed to borrow $5,886,600 at what they
considered a "reasonable" interest rate of 6.5 per cent. The
interest on the principal was $1,048.28 a day.

The loan allowed Ballard and Smythe to autograph a series
of cheques to Bassett and his allies, all of whom Ballard
regarded as "encumbrances." The series included $8,250 to
John W.H. Bassett; $15,000 to Foster Hewitt Broadcasting;
$30,000 to Hewitt's sister, Mrs. C.A. Massey; $75,150 to John
Craig Eaton; $363,000 to Hewitt Dale Productions;

$1,045,200 to Baton Broadcasting; and $4,350,000 to the Telegram Publishing Company.

Bassett's modest cheque was for the small number of shares he owned privately. The bulk of his control extended through the *Telegram* and Baton Broadcasting colloquially known as CFTO, linchpin of the CTV network.

Foster Hewitt was involved in the sale as owner of CKFH, radio voice of the Maple Leafs. Hewitt Dale Productions, a Foster spin-off, is in the business of radio, television and recording sales. Hewitt was linked to Bassett in Baton Broadcasting and never saw a dollar bill he didn't want to warm his hands on. He, too, coveted control of the Gardens, but settled for the cash. "I'm quite pleased to take money from Ballard and Staff Smythe," he said. "Although I don't like Ballard much, anymore."

Their antipathy was mutual. Ballard interpreted Hewitt's allegiance to Bassett as disloyalty to himself. Harold took to calling Hewitt "cheap," which didn't quite define Foster's affinity for money. Foster was neither close nor tight, but he was fairly adjacent. As he lay dying, in the spring of 1985, Foster knew lucid moments from the Alzheimer's disease decaying his brain. A trusted friend, his financial adviser, sat with him near the end.

"Tell me," Foster said, "what am I really worth?"

The financial adviser mentioned that Hewitt's worth was in the multimillions. "Gee," said the voice that made "Hockey Night in Canada", "I wish I could take it with me."

Ballard felt a fresh challenge after buying out John Bassett and friends. "I'll have to promote like a son of a bitch now," he said. "Staff's falling apart and each of us is responsible for interest fucking payments of $524.14 a day."

I consoled Pal Hal this day in September, 1971. "Well," I said, "I just paid you more than the interest for one day. I just paid $554.40 for a pair of blue hockey tickets."

"You'll pay more," Ballard promised, and he was right. In 1988–89, the same tickets, now called golds, cost $2,494. "And you'll pay more yet," Ballard promised at the last annual meeting of Gardens' shareholders. Season-ticket subscribers make Toronto the best place for a pro hockey franchise on earth. The Leafs have not won since 1967 but, on a medium big night, they are the hottest entertainment ticket in town. Our collective name must be Sucker, not Tucker.

The fall of 1971 was fearful for the Smythe family. Conn had reconciled with Stafford, coming late with compassion for his fallen son. He sounded old when he told me, through gritted teeth, "I'm standing by my kid. Blood is thicker than your printer's ink."

The impending trial, scheduled for late October, plagued Stafford. He was corroded by shame, his only anesthetic shots of scotch. Pain in his stomach was constant and he vomited blood. He was admitted to Wellesley Hospital with a bleeding ulcer on October 6, 1971, as the Pittsburgh Pirates prepared to beat the Baltimore Orioles four games to three in the World Series.

Staff Smythe submitted to surgery and appeared to be recovering. Then, physically collapsing and perhaps not wanting to live, he began to bleed in the stomach vein and esophagus. Another operation was required to restrain a huge hemorrhage. Much of his stomach was removed. Conn Smythe visited his son through his travail. Stafford had given up. He opened his eyes and said, "See, Dad, I told you they wouldn't put a Smythe in jail." He died at 4:31 a.m. on October 13, 1971, a cool autumn Wednesday. The flawed heir to a hockey empire was 50.

Smythe's death prompted a certain consternation in the office of prosecutor Clay Powell, who would have relished facing Stafford in court. "We thought, briefly," Powell said, "that reports of Smythe's death were exaggerated. We thought about going up to the hospital and trying to get a set of his fingerprints."

The prosecutor's quarry had escaped in the most drastic way. Instead of going on trial on October 25, Staff Smythe's remains went to a mortuary on October 13. Ballard was shaken, but not to the point of inactivity.

From the Gardens, he issued a statement: "With great sorrow we announce the passing of our president, C. Stafford Smythe, who died this morning. The body will be resting at his home, 15 Ashley Park Road, in Etobicoke. Funeral services will be held in St. Paul's Anglican Church, Bloor and

Jarvis Streets, at 1 p.m., Thursday, Oct. 14. In lieu of flowers, kindly send donations to the charity of your choice."

Ghouls found irony in the fact that Smythe's body "rested" in the house he had built with money stolen from the Gardens. There was something ghoulish, too, in Ballard's watch of the coffin the night before the funeral. He, like prosecutor Powell, could scarcely believe Smythe was dead.

"I slept in fits and starts on a couch near the coffin," Ballard said. "I woke up several times and opened the coffin to make sure Staff was really dead."

There were ritualistic statements from survivors. John Bassett, who had strayed away from the troubled Smythe, piously said: "I am shocked by Stafford Smythe's death. He was a tough competitor who neither asked, nor gave quarter. He was, however, a true and loyal friend, and those of us who knew him well and got through the shell he built around himself to offset his shyness appreciated him. I will miss him very much indeed."

Jack Kent Cooke, sometimes called Jack Can't Cook when his Los Angeles Kings faltered, expressed shock from Southern California. "This is a terrible loss to hockey," Cooke said. "Stafford was one of the most intelligent sportsmen I've ever known, and he was one of my best friends, not only personally, but in hockey."

Stafford had been an adversary of Cooke's in several hockey matters, and would have been amused to hear Cooke conclude: "Really, this is a terrible shock and a terrible loss to hockey."

Ballard's tribute was genuine. His sense of loss was compounded; within two years he had lost the only woman he really loved, and a friend he had laughed with, conspired and caroused with.

"We were like flour and water," Ballard said. "We've been together more than 25 years and never had an argument that amounted to a hill of beans. He'd still be alive if he hadn't taken so much scotch in his milk."

King Clancy took umbrage at what he considered legal and press persecution. "I knew Staff since he was a stickboy," the loyalist of the Leafs said. "I feel terrible that he died. He took such a lot of punishment from people before anything was proved against him. I started with his old man, of course, but Staff was like his dad, a real class guy."

Smythe's pallbearers, that overcast October day, were his brother, Dr. Hugh Smythe, his son Tom, Ballard, George Mara and Terry Jeffries of the Maple Leaf directors, Leaf manager Jim Gregory, and Leaf players George Armstrong and Bob Baun.

Protestant funerals are not meant to be evil or callous, but there is an intrusive fiendishness in the finality of disposing of our dead. Many mourners, to the family of the deceased, seem like gawking buzzards. There was gawking at Conn Smythe, limping with a cane, his eyes glistening. Dorthea Smythe, the gentle widow, might have preferred a Catholic ceremony. She was supported at the funeral by her son Tom and daughters Victoria, Mary and Elizabeth. She had never been physically abused, as a wife, but mental anguish is more debasing torment. Except the scars don't show.

Smythe's funeral motivated Ballard to close the Gardens and postpone the opening of the NHL schedule against the Detroit Red Wings. It was the second time only that a death forced postponement of an NHL game in the Gardens. The first was the passing of the King of England, George VI, in 1952.

Smythe was buried in a private commitment in the grave-yard of Christ Anglican Church in Gregory, a village in the parish of Rosseau, Muskoka. "This is the place where he could get away from all the fights and pressures," Hugh Smythe said. "This is where he had real peace."

The grave is marked by a natural rock tombstone with a brass plate bearing a curious inscription:

> Here lies Conn Stafford Smythe, Lieut. RCNVR 1940–1944. He was dearly beloved of his wife, children and many friends. He was persecuted to death by his ene-mies. Now he sleeps in the quiet north country that loved him for the person he truly was. Born Toronto March 15, 1921. Died October 13, 1971.

There is much that is defensive in the inscription, as though Conn Smythe had written it. Staff's enemies, in his father's blunt view, were the press, the government lawyers and the cronies who led him from the rigid path of rightness. "Staff never needed much leading in the fuck-around department," Ballard said.

Conn Smythe quarrelled with Ballard a few hours after Stafford died. Conn demanded, on the phone, why Ballard closed the Gardens and postponed the Detroit game.

Conn said, "Ballard, you've got no guts, and you've never had any guts."

Ballard retorted, "Whaddya mean, no guts?"

"Stafford would have wanted the game to go on," Conn said. "Just like he was here."

"Well, Stafford's not here," Ballard said. "He was my buddy and now he's in a pine box. I'm closing the Gardens out of respect for him, and fuck you. Goodbye, Mr. Smythe."

For the first time, Ballard talked back to the despotic architect of the Gardens, aware he at last had the power of ownership. Smythe was seldom inclined to retreat, but he did in the face of Ballard's belligerence. "The old bastard phoned to pledge co-operation," Ballard said, "but I was damn sure I no longer needed the Smythes."

Ballard's court case had, like Staff Smythe's, been scheduled to start on October 25, 1971. The prosecution had concentrated on Smythe and sought an adjournment of Ballard's trial. Clay Powell, acting for the Ontario Attorney General, intended to press criminal charges against Ballard in 1972.

Ballard's accountant, Arthur Horning, took a political tangent two days after Smythe was in the Muskoka ground. He wrote a letter pleading for forgiveness to Alastair Gillespie, the Liberal Member of Parliament for Etobicoke, Ballard's home riding.

Horning wrote:

> . . . The subsequent result of the action by the Department of National Revenue is well known to not only the people of Canada but even the United States. An acquaintance of mine read about the charges in a Los Angeles newspaper. The tragic result had only become fully known in the past week. It becomes quite apparent that the Department of National Revenue has fulfilled its obligation to the fullest degree by "setting an exam-

ple" to the taxpayers of Canada of the consequences of
tax evasion even though the persons charged have not
been convicted.

When a taxpayer charged under the Income Tax Act is
agreeable to paying the unpaid taxes plus the usual
financial penalty, surely there is no further need for
persecution and discrimination which is so terribly
injurious to people that happen to be in the public eye.

One is inclined to wonder whether our elected representatives are so engrossed in their own problems and
their ambitions to advance in the political arena, that
they are unable to think or understand in depth the
effect of their conduct on taxpayers.

I appeal to you to exert what influence you can to
have the remaining charges dropped against the
deceased Smythe and Mr. Ballard, both longtime residents of Etobicoke, and heavy taxpayers at the municipal, provincial and federal levels. Surely, the tax liability,
whatever it may be, can be settled in an inconspicuous
and civilized manner before any further tragedies
occur. . . .

The accountant Horning was subtle as a crosscheck with
his suggestion that Ballard, if prosecuted, might follow Staff
Smythe to the boneyard. He was running a forlorn bluff;
Ballard was not about to rupture at any of his many seams.

Horning's appeal had all the impact of a wet flower dashed
against a window pane — shhhpot. The federal Liberals had
lost one corpus delecti, as it were, but Ballard would do as a
substitute for Smythe. Ballard's trial for theft and fraud was
booked for May, 1972, in Toronto.

Ballard was 69 in 1972, the year he gained absolute control
of The House that Conn Built. He had a fish tank in his office
containing piranhas, pesky voracious man-eating fish who
look at you as though you owe them money. Piranha Pal Hal
went after the Smythe family.

Tom Smythe, Staff's son, was 25 and desirous of maintain-
ing the family hockey dynasty. He was in charge of the junior
Marlboros and went to Ballard to find out what future he had
in the Gardens. Ballard, sounding gruff, said, "Don't bother

with this now. You ought to be consoling your mother. She is grief-stricken."

Ballard had the lever to buy out his late partner's shares, if he could get the money. The agreement struck by Ballard, Smythe and Bassett in their takeover of 1961 guaranteed that if one of the partners died, or wanted to sell, his shares must be first offered to his partners.

Dr. Hugh Smythe and Tom were prepared to conciliate immediately after Stafford died. Dr. Smythe nominated Ballard for president of the Gardens on October 21, 1971, with no opposition from other directors. The doctor maintained the Smythe presence as vice-president.

The warmth went only one way. Dorthea Smythe, the widow, told Bill Houston, "Harold changed drastically toward me. I'd meet him in a hall in the Gardens and say hello and never get an answer. I couldn't figure out what I'd done to him. We had once been so close."

Hugh Smythe was not surprised. "Harold remained the same guy. We were just seeing the other side. My father never liked Harold. They never really got along, and Harold had to eat that. So he had this resentment and inability to take direction from almost anybody except my brother. Most of the ones my father didn't like, he got rid of. But when the Marlboros fell under the direction of my brother, he protected Harold and Harold survived."

Tom Smythe, dapper, decent, third-generation, believed Ballard feared a return of the patriarch, Conn Smythe. "Harold's concern was wrong. Granddad wasn't coming back to the Gardens. Harold might have thought that if that happened, it would be a giant step backward for him. Harold felt he had paid his dues in the Gardens, and he was right."

Ballard said of Hugh Smythe, "I believe the doctor ought to stick to peddling his pills." Hugh is not exactly a pill-peddler. He is a rheumatism and arthritis specialist, attached to Wellesley Hospital.

The Smythes reckoned their only option to settle the rancor was to buy out Ballard. Ballard said, "Fuck that. Where are they going to get the money to buy me out?" The question, expressed in a belligerent tone, was pertinent. There were $6 million in liabilities against Staff Smythe's estate, $3 million of it part of the price to take out John Bassett and friends.

Hugh Smythe, feeling his way, approached wealthy friends of the Smythe family for financial backing. The friends were polite, but cool. Hugh did not know then that his father had contacted those friends and requested them to stay out of any fight with Ballard.

The doctor diagnosed the dilemma. "Here we were, battling Ballard and my father as well. I think father thought hockey had turned dirty and didn't want us to be part of it." There may have been a trace of jealousy. Conn Smythe did not want another Smythe surpassing him.

The dynamics of families are fascinating. "It wasn't my father's ego acting in any conscious way," Hugh said. "He was proud of Stafford for winning those four Stanley Cups. But he was a very dominant male. The closer you were within the family, the more dominance became part of what happened at every dinner-table conversation, at every golf game. This was friendly, usually, but in family situations, the younger members really couldn't compete equally with the older one. The sons' wives and the daughters' husbands also had a difficult time because they really weren't members of the family."

Dominant parents, Hugh was saying, cast long shadows. He had escaped into a sunshine of his own in the medical profession. Stafford, his benighted brother, had not escaped the shadow and was forever warped.

Ballard watched the Smythes' ineffectual moves to turf him out, then made his own move on February 4, 1972. He was an executor of Staff Smythe's will and simply sold Staff's shares to himself. He acquired a loan of $7,546,350 from the Toronto Dominion Bank to purchase the 251,545 Gardens' shares in Staff's estate. Ballard did not need to ask permission for the deal from the Smythes, nor did he. Tom Smythe heard about it on his car radio as he drove home.

Piranha Pal Hal had consumed the last morsel denying him absolute control. The Smythe family issued a statement of capitulation. "We're disappointed we didn't hear about it from Harold, instead of on the radio," Tom Smythe said. "But the most important thing is that my mother will be taken care of. We had tax payments on the estate due in two months, 50 per cent of everything we own, and . . . the estate could not afford to keep its shares."

Staff Smythe's will, when filed for probate, left $3,225,013 to his widow and four children. It cost less than half that amount to build the Maple Leaf Gardens in 1931. The major portion of Smythe's assets was stocks and bonds valued at $2,326,370. The controversial abode at 15 Ashley Place in Etobicoke was listed at $200,000.

Staff's summer home on Muskoka's Lake Joseph, no shack, was valued at $187,750. His farm in Puslinch Township, near Guelph, showed at $175,000. Another country home in Collingwood Township, a relative hovel, was pegged at $25,000. Material riches abounded for the ex-Maple Leaf stickboy and foreman in a gravel pit.

The widow, Mary Dorthea, was left the Etobicoke house and a Lincoln hardtop car worth $4,500 in 1971. The will provided her with life income of never less than $20,000 a year. The remainder of the estate was divided equally among the four children.

Harold Ballard, then close to his own three children, made plans to bring Bill and Harold Junior into the Maple Leaf firm. They had given him the gluttonous piranhas as an appropriate Christmas gift.

CHAPTER 11

Patriotism with Profit

◆

There was a piranhoid streak of ruthlessness in Ballard's conclusion of business with Hugh Smythe. Harold insisted, as part of the deal, that Smythe yield his season tickets. Hugh turned over the tickets, not without bitterness, and has been in the Gardens only once since 1972. That was after his father's death in November, 1980. Hugh returned briefly to the arena he treasured to pick up whatever belonged to Conn Smythe.

Ballard as boss became headline material, always available to reporters, seldom without a word for feature writers, who bought his stories retail. He told Earl McRae, now a trenchant columnist for the *Ottawa Citizen*, that he has blondes by the carload and brunettes by the platoon.

"Just like the players," Pal Hal said, "I've got broads in every city. And I can still handle 'em. The one in New York's a real beaut. When I'm real horny I fly down for a quickie. Then there's this one in L.A. I met last year. I was at the hotel and couldn't sleep, so I got up for a swim. It's about three in the morning. I'm approaching the pool when I hear splashing and here's this redhead swimming all alone. Gorgeous broad, about 26 and bare naked."

Harold claims he said to this delightful damsel, "Hi, honey. I see you're a real redhead, eh?" and invited himself to join her. Buck naked, he said, they swam and caressed. "Had a great time. See her whenever I'm on the west coast."

The ravishing redhead may simply have been a glorious figment of Harold's oversexed imagination. As when he said one day in the Hot Stove Lounge, during a raunchy conversation with a Maple Leaf scout, "You wouldn't believe the woman I had last night. Her cunt was as big as a washtub."

The scout, equally gallant, blurted, "Goddamn you, Ballard, you were fucking my wife!"

Ballard always needed a male sidekick, no matter how

factual or fictitious his female relationships were. He turned in 1972 to King Clancy, who had been everybody's pal since the Gardens opened. King had run with Charlie Conacher, Conn Smythe and Punch Imlach, sometimes to the derision of his old playmates.

Hap Day, close to Clancy as player and manager, said, "King was the biggest apple-polisher in the world. And why not? He was paid to do nothing by Staff Smythe and then by Ballard."

Clancy indeed rolled with every punch, or every Punch Imlach in the last 30 years in the Gardens. He had the Maple Leaf logo tattooed on his rear end, on both cheeks. He never challenged Ballard, and did what Ballard requested.

Ballard asked him late in the 1971–72 season to pinch-hit for Coach John McLellan, whose small intestine was ravaged by an ulcer. Clancy replaced McLellan for 15 games, not always to the satisfaction of the players.

"King was a lot of bullshit," one Leaf told Dan Proudfoot of *The Globe and Mail*. "We resent his two-faced tactics. He'd tell the defencemen that the forwards had cost us the loss. Then he'd go to the forwards and say the defencemen fucked up. He's a legend, but not to us."

The 1971–72 Leafs paused short of legendary status themselves, eliminated early from the Stanley Cup playoffs. Darryl Sittler from Kitchener was a rising Toronto star, but the team collectively would not shine for six more seasons. They regained a combative edge when Dave (Tiger) Williams arrived in 1974–75 from Weyburn, on the southern Saskatchewan plains. Williams was a delicious combatant whose nose had been so flattened, he could bite a wall.

The Crown, through the early summer of 1972, called witnesses who revealed in court the extent of fraud committed by Ballard and Staff Smythe. Judge Harry Deyman, gray-looking, seeming wise behind glasses, presided over the long deliberations. Deyman was regarded by defence lawyers as "a soft touch."

Howard Wise, co-owner of a plumbing firm, identified an invoice of $1,026.89 for work done at Ballard's cottage and sent to the Gardens. A landscape architect, Michael Nagy, said he sent a bill for $486 to the Gardens for repairs to a

sprinkling system when the work was for installation of an
underground sprinkler at Ballard's home.

The president of Cloke Construction, Arthur Wayling, testified that $74,000 of the $565,000 received for work at the
Gardens was for building at Ballard's home. The work
involved rebuilding concrete pathways and removing trees.
Other contractors testified to work done at Ballard's home
and cottage which was billled to the Gardens.

The business of the Marlboro team was laundered. The
juniors cost between $200,000 and $300,000 a year to operate,
administered by Ballard and Staff Smythe. Prosecutor Clay
Powell, pressing his case, accused Ballard and Smythe of
skimming money from the Marlboros for themselves. Bank
records revealed that $50,000 was withdrawn from the
Marlboro account on June 10, 1968. The same day, Ballard
and Smythe deposited $25,000 into each of their private
accounts.

Another Gardens' retainer, Buck Houle, was called to the
stand. Houle had been a manager of the Marlboros. He testified that chéques worth $65,942.45 to the Marlboros from the
Canadian Amateur Hockey Association were directed to Ballard and Smythe. Ballard never spoke to Houle again.

On August 15, 1972, a Tuesday, Judge Harry Deyman
rendered his verdict on Ballard's delinquency. A headline in
The Toronto Star said it all: BALLARD FOUND GUILTY OF FRAUD
AND THEFT.

Deyman, in a 112-page judgment, found "a clear pattern
of fraud" in six weeks of evidence. He convicted Ballard on 47
charges and acquitted him on two minor fraud charges
involving $196.75.

Deyman wrote: "I simply cannot understand a businessman of Mr. Ballard's stature seeing thousands of dollars
worth of improvements made to his home without making
sure he knew what the cost was."

Outside the courtroom, Ballard maintained his version of
innocence. "People think I should feel badly," he said. "I
don't feel badly because I still don't feel I did anything wrong.
I've never felt I was guilty and I still don't."

The County Court trial confirmed that Pal Hal and his late

partner, Staff Smythe, used Gardens' funds to pay for extensive repairs and alterations to their homes.

Ballard's defence, conducted by J.J. Robinette, was that he did not know the work done on his house and summer residence was being charged to the Gardens by altering invoices. Deyman said, "I find it completely incredible that a businessman of Mr. Ballard's acumen could have goods and services of such a variety and cost furnished to him to his knowledge without expecting to pay for them."

Deyman's words were damning. "I am driven to the inescapable conclusion that in the particulars set out against Ballard, he did have knowledge and in fact instigated most of them and I must find him guilty."

Deyman said the frauds were committed in three separate ways. "Invoices were falsified by suppliers, proper invoices from suppliers were falsified at the Gardens or composite invoices were made, totalling work done for Ballard and Smythe with Gardens' billings." The problem, as Deyman saw it, was "did Mr. Ballard know this was occurring and was he a party to it? In my view, the evidence is not open to any other rational conclusion but that he was."

Deyman's judgment was essentially a review of evidence in the case. He quoted extensively from the court transcript. He commented on the testimony of Clarence (Jesse) James, the assistant building superintendent at the Gardens.

James had testified about the manipulation of invoices for modifications to Ballard's home by Cloke Construction to make it appear to be work on the Gardens. Deyman said the changes made by James would have made it impossible for the Gardens' accountants to straighten out the accounts.

James' testimony convinced Deyman that Jesse had made up his story after changes to the invoices were made. The judge said, "There was no explanation for juggling the invoices. This confirms my view that there must be a conviction." Deyman referred to niggling items, the nickel-and-dime larceny involving motorbikes for Ballard's two sons and limousines for his daughter's first wedding.

"I'm convinced Mr. Ballard knew what was happening," Deyman said. "He was in touch on four occasions with

Brown's Cycle and Sports and received two cheques for $150 each for the resale of the two motorcycles involved. He also knew that he personally had never received any invoice for the cost of these motorcycles or their maintenance."

Then there was the count involving a trivial sum for transportation for the wedding. Deyman said, "Mr. Ballard alone seems to be involved in this matter. There is an obliteration in this invoice striking out the words 'for wedding' and inserting 'airport service.' The only person initialling the invoice is Mr. Ballard – 'OK H.E.B.'"

J.J. Robinette, a gray eminence among legal eagles, made a brief statement after judgment was rendered. He hoped, he told Deyman, that when sentence was passed "Your Lordship take into consideration Ballard's age, which is 69, and good reputation. Also, that restitution was made to the Gardens." Robinette said that before sentencing he would develop aspects of Ballard's good reputation. "There is no question," the lawyer said, "from a business standpoint that both Mr. Ballard and the late Mr. Smythe did an efficient job for the Gardens' shareholders over a 10-year period."

Prosecutor Clay Powell was satisfied with the decision favorable to the persistence and legwork of his staff. He thought Ballard would receive a jail sentence of 15 to 18 months. Then he took a telephone call from R. Alan Eagleson, beseeching on behalf of Ballard.

Eagleson said he was aware that Judge Deyman adjourned sentencing Ballard to September, but wondered if the adjournment might carry over to later in the fall after the Canada-Soviet series. Harold, Eagleson indicated, wanted to travel to Moscow as a chaperone of the Canadian team.

Powell said he warned Eagleson, "Phoning a judge about sentencing and adjournments is highly irregular. You can call Deyman at his home in Peterborough, if you like, but he might not like your intervention for Ballard's purposes."

Eagleson phoned Deyman, and Deyman did not like it. The judge, incensed, called Clay Powell. "Of course Ballard should not be allowed to leave the country," Deyman said. "But he can go to Russia. We'll adjourn sentencing until he returns. But he has just added a year to the sentence he is going to get."

"When Deyman said that," Powell said, "I knew he was really hot. I was certain then that Ballard would get at least three years. Deyman's wife bet that Ballard, being rich, would get to spend his time in a country club jail. I was prepared to bet that he wouldn't."

Sentencing was set for September 7, 1972, then postponed until after the Canada-Soviet series because permission was arranged for Ballard to travel to the Moscow portion of the adventure.

The hockey world, preoccupied with its own sweaty self, had nurtured the notion of a series at the summit between the elite players in the Western and Eastern hemispheres. Canadians devoutly believed that the NHL's best would devour the Soviet Union's best, and therefore restore Canada as the premier hockey power.

There was popular demand for the eight-game series, four games in Canada and four in downtown Russia. Many of us scoffed at the second-line Canadian players who annually lost the world championship to the Europeans, usually Russians. We had not won in world competition since the Trail Smoke Eaters conquered, in 1961.

R. Alan Eagleson was Canada's major promoter in organizing the Summit Series. He is a supple Toronto lawyer, 39 in 1972, one of those vital persons born to controversy. It is not necessary to know the man personally in order to hold strong opinions about him. He can be as slick as his smooth black haircut. Eagleson has an uncommonly agile brain, a harsh teamster's tongue, an absolute mastery of the gift of concentration, whether he is playing tennis, haggling with a general manager, or arguing a client's case. These qualities, together with his towering confidence in his own judgement, make him an exceptionally able executive director of the NHL Players Association.

Eagleson, who once played the poor man's game of lacrosse in the west Toronto town of Mimico, has become a multimillionaire out of hockey. Riches loomed when he became the agent for Robert Gordon Orr, a prodigy from Parry Sound, Ontario.

Orr, coming to the Boston Bruins from the junior Oshawa

Generals in 1966–67, vividly altered the way defencemen played. His way was to carry the puck out of his own end, showing the puck to players trying to check him, then bursting past them to lead the Bruins on constant power-play opportunities. Orr was the fast hub of Stanley Cup teams in 1970 and 1972, supported by a cast which included rangy Phil Esposito, goaltender Gerry Cheevers and Wayne Cashman, a left winger with psychopathic tendencies. Cashman could whack an opponent and feel no remorse.

Guiding Orr, the principal troglodyte in the game, Eagleson swayed power over players, owners, sports writers and politicians. He is still doing it. One of the gags in the NHL is that the best job in hockey is driving Eagleson's getaway car.

Ballard, embattled in court, threw his considerable girth on Eagleson's side. He authorized Hockey Canada to take any Maple Leaf desired for the Soviet series. He offered the Gardens free for the Hockey Canada training camp. He made the Gardens available on a non-profit basis for any of the four games played in Canada.

Skeptics, the Ballard backbiters, interpreted his largesse as a shrewd move to ingratiate himself with the government prosecutors. Ballard, indeed, wanted the government off his back, but had shown 40 years earlier that he enjoyed Canadian hockey teams travelling to Europe "to kick ass." If not a superpatriot, he was always ready to swipe an Olympic flag for Canada, or himself. He would, in years following the first Canada-Soviet series, carry an anti-Russia attitude to what he considered patriotic lengths.

MacLaren Advertising of Toronto, proprietor of Hockey Night in Canada, seemed the natural outfit to grab the advertising rights for the eight-game series. Eagleson, acting hastily for Bobby Orr, fused an alliance between Orr and Ballard. Then Orr-Ballard Enterprises, to Eagleson's unconcealed glee, outbid MacLaren, $750,000 to $500,000.

"Bullshit baffles brains," Ballard said during a June press conference to announce the coup. Eagleson estimated that advertising revenue would exceed $2 million. "We're hustlers," R. Alan said of himself and Ballard. "We'll have no trouble selling the advertising." Ballard, a patriot all the way, set aside his buccaneering instincts and said any profits would be dispatched to Hockey Canada and the NHL Players Association.

Ballard sent the Maple Leaf coach, John McLellan, and Maple Leaf scout Bob Davidson on a mission to Moscow. They scouted the Soviet side and, in a remarkable misjudgment, reported that the Russian goalminder, Vladislav Tretiak, had difficulty stopping a beach ball. Tretiak, in the spring of 1989, was nominated for election to the Hockey Hall of Fame.

Reaction to the September skirmish between Canadian pros and Russian pros was loud, and intense. Ballard described the confrontation "as the greatest sporting event in our history. How long have we been waiting for somebody to beat Russia? Twenty years? Now we got a chance."

That, I thought, was laying on the old horse manure a trifle thickly, even for such a grandiose spreader as Ballard. His carny imagination had visions of special concession booths in Maple Leaf Gardens when the Russians appeared for the second game of the series, on September 2, 1972.

"We'll have a special on salami sandwiches," Ballard announced. "And also bottles of beet borscht, with straws."

Several of Ballard's colleagues in the NHL were less enchanted by the notion of a super series. Weston Adams, president of the Boston Bruins, said: "There's no way I want any of our players involved. Can you imagine what our fans would say if we allowed Bobby Orr and Phil Esposito for Canada in such a series? Suppose they suffered an injury that might prevent them from playing with us for a year or more?" Orr and Esposito were Canadians owned by an American, and an American tightwad at that. It was said of Weston Adams, justifiably, that he was so generous he would give you a straw hat in a blizzard every time.

Sam Pollock, the savviest general manager of his time, spoke for hockey's superior team. Pollock said for the Montreal Canadiens: "The Canadiens are willing to allow any of our players to play for this Canadian team. At first it was only three Canadian teams – Toronto, Montreal and Vancouver – who had an obligation . . . but I am sure every player who is a Canadian citizen will be willing to play."

Not every Canadian citizen was immediately as willing as

Sam Pollock believed. Robert Marvin Hull, finishing his 15th season as a supershooter in Chicago, curbed his ecstasy.

"I don't think playing the Russians in September is such a hot idea," Hull said in the spring of 1972. "Such a series should be played under our rules in mid-season, or after the NHL season, when we are in top condition." Hull was a statesman among his kind, worth listening to. "There is no way we would be in top physical shape to play the Russians eight games in September," Hull warned. "Those Russians are never out of shape. They would be working constantly at hockey when we'd be engaged in our off-ice occupations. We have everything to lose, little to gain."

Brad Park of the New York Rangers, rated the second best defenceman in the NHL after Robert Gordon Orr, disagreed. "I'd jump at a chance to play the Russians," Park said. "The NHL pros should go with our best, and play like the Stanley Cup is at stake."

Vic Hadfield, the capacious captain of the Rangers who had scored 50 goals in 1971–72, expressed reluctance. "It would require a lot of thought on my part before making a decision to play the Russians," Hadfield said. "The Stanley Cup is more important to me than anything else."

Orr, the Wonderkid of the Bruins, was eager. "I'd be happy to play the Russians any time," Alan Eagleson's acolyte said. "They think they're the best hockey players in the world, but I think otherwise."

Phil Esposito expressed a few reservations. He was a large, opportunistic Boston centre with the brown soulful eyes of a Cuban bandit. "Sure, I'd like to play the Russians," Esposito said. "But first I'd have to have a lot of things set right. I'd have to be paid pretty good money for the series, and there would have to be some kind of an insurance policy in case I got hurt."

Esposito is one of the more realistic in a milieu where illusions are few. "I'm crazy," he said, "but I'm not that crazy to enter a Russian series without some protection." Such talk annoyed Alan Eagleson; before the series began, he called Esposito "a money-grubber."

The bickering and reservations annoyed Ballard, who deemed himself a godfather of the Canadian team. "The

Russians," he grumbled, "have got to be laughing at the way we're feuding among ourselves." He addressed himself to Hull and Esposito. "Already Espo is dancing the two-step, asking what's in it for him. Hull is saying it's lousy to schedule the series in September. Don't those guys remember they had the privilege of learning their hockey in Canada? Don't they owe a little bit to this country, especially to the kids?"

Weston Adams kept bitching in Boston. "What upsets me," the whining cub of the Bruins said, "is that Hockey Canada never consults us. I didn't know anything until I read it in the papers. I'm in favor of international play, but it's Hockey Canada's methods I object to. How does Hockey Canada speak for professional hockey? Its concern should be for amateur hockey. For God and country is wonderful, but these players are professionals."

Through all the wrangling, one character kept sticking and moving, boldly reaching for the main chance. Alan Eagleson shrewdly guessed before anyone else that the series could be a bonanza for the NHL Players Association and Hockey Canada.

"There'll be a series, all right," Eagleson kept saying in April, 1972. "And most or all the best NHL players'll be in it. Why? Because most of them are members of the Players Association, and most of them will listen to what I think is good for them."

Eagleson shut up the dissident American owners by devising a plan which hit them where they live, right in the pocketbook nerve. He wanted increased pension benefits for the players and contrived a formula which allowed the owners to contribute to the pension plan painlessly.

"Under our current pension plan," Eagleson announced, "a player gets $300 per month at age 45. We want that increased to $600. Television revenue from the Russian series can net $1 million, which I suggest be split equally: $500,000 to Hockey Canada, $500,000 to the players' pension fund."

The NHL owners, aware that the $500,000 that Eagleson promised from TV would be $500,000, agreed to the scheme. That was money they would not have to contribute to pensions. The eyes of an NHL owner are bloodshot with greed, but he can still see a windfall out of the corners of them.

Many of us, press attachés, were diverted in mid-winter to Sapporo on the northern island of Japan, to join the scratchy long-underwear set for the 1972 Winter Olympics. Canadian correspondents included the learned Jim Proudfoot of *The Toronto Star*, witty Jim Taylor of the *Vancouver Province* and irreverent Ted Blackman of the *Montreal Gazette*.

We did not have a Canadian hockey team to cover because Hockey Canada was boycotting the Olympics until Canada was permitted to enter professionals, as the Soviet Union and Czechoslovakia did. It was our view that, when it came to amateurs, the Russians and Czechoslovaks were as pure as the driven smog.

Russian hockey players in 1972 were, in fact, the most celebrated welfare recipients on earth. Gold medallists among them were installed in chateaus on the aromatic Volga River and paid .1 per cent of the national income weekly. On retirement, Russian hockey players are given a pension of 20,000 rubles a month, which is equivalent to many dollars, or $Many.00. On death, they are buried at public expense, and allowed to go on charging for vodka at government liquor stores.

There was time in Sapporo for Canadian sports writers to attend the comic press conference conducted by the coaches of the Soviet hockey team, the suave Arkady Chernychev and ebullient Anatoli Tarasov, who was sort of a burly Harold Ballard of the Bolsheviks.

The coaches responded to questions about a series between the Soviet Olympic champions and the NHL all-stars. "All for it, da," Chernychev said, showing his abundant bridgework in an iron smile. "Of course, such games as we would play with the Canadian pros would be of a friendly character, but not an official one." Sure, sure, Arkady, I thought. Such games would be friendly until some hairy-legged Canadian threw the first illegal crosscheck.

It was apparent in Sapporo that Soviet politicians, not Soviet coaches, would decide where the Russians played hockey, and against whom. The open-up era of glasnost was 16 years in the future. In 1972, Winston Chuchill's dictum on the Soviet Union applied: "It is a riddle wrapped in a mystery inside an enigma." At every Soviet press conference in

Japan, a gentleman in a fur hat stood behind either Tarasov or Chernychev. When he took the fur hat off, the press conference began. When he put it back on, the conference ended.

There was no accurate way of detecting how many Soviet politicians or security agents attended the Olympics in the guise of "correspondents." There seemed to be an uncommon number of Soviet sports writers, accredited to the press section in much the same way as several figure-skating mothers from Canada and the United States. The "correspondents," I suspect, were really nose-counters, there to make sure every Soviet hockey player returned on the back-to-Moscow express.

The Soviet Union won the Sapporo hockey tournament, the Americans were second, the Czechoslovaks third. Most Canadian observers, especially me, could not see the Russians with field glasses. Oh, there was passing reference to the three best prospects on display, all of them Russian. I wrote for *The Globe and Mail*, under a Sapporo dateline:

> The best hockey players here are goalkeeper Vladislav Tretiak, defenceman Vladimir Loutchenko and left winger Valery Kharlamov. The Russians have been rapped for their inferior goaltending, but that criticism no longer seems valid. Tretiak, rising 20, is the product of an intensive crash program to improve Soviet goalkeepers.
>
> Every team in the Soviet Union has a goalie coach, and Tretiak's force-feeding has included attendance at summer school in Sweden. Tretiak is as tall as Ken Dryden of Montreal Canadiens, agile in bulky fashion, and equipped with a fast hand for picking off either pucks or cherries.
>
> Loutchenko, 23, and Kharlamov, 24, are younger players on a Soviet team that seems in decline. Several of their national veterans, such as defenceman Rags Ragulin, are well over that old blueberryetski hill.

I should have been cautioned in my assessment of the Soviets by a conversation with Arkady Chernychev. "In non-organized hockey," the coach said, "we have 3 million boys on school and yard teams. Every year they play in our Prize

Gold Puck Tournament. At a higher level, from youth to adults, we have 1.5 million players from which to pick our national team."

I could not, however, project the Russian conquest of the 1972 Olympics as a threat to the supremacy of the NHL. I would, in an addled moment in August, pick the NHL stars to win eight consecutive games against their Soviet opponents. I did not, in that forecast, know a hole in the ground from the customary comparison.

CHAPTER 12

Only a Game

♦

The World Hockey Association challenged the NHL in 1972, impudent upstarts in Edmonton, Vancouver, Winnipeg, Quebec — in Canada — ready to raid the established league for players. The war was expensive for the owners, a boon for the players and the WHA ultimately flopped as the World Rocky Association.

In June, 1972, the WHA gained instant credibility by snatching Bobby Hull from the Chicago Black Hawks and installing him with the Winnipeg Jets. The contract seemed enormous, $2 million over 10 years, $1 million up front. For as long as the WHA lasted, Hull carried it on his back, a back as big as Asia.

Harry Sinden, coach of Boston's Stanley Cup champions in 1970, was chosen to lead the Canadians in the biggest hockey adventure in this country's history. His assistant was John Ferguson, who was the NHL's catch-as-catch-can dropkicking champion when he played for the Montreal Canadiens.

Irrespective of the pro war, Harry Sinden and John Ferguson picked the players they considered best in either the NHL or WHA. Their selections were announced on July 12, 1972, at a lavish reception in the Sutton Place, a modest inn in midtown Toronto where they charge you nothing for the coffee but soak you 75 cents for the cream.

Those selected are worth at least a footnote in hockey history. They were the first Canadians to play in the Super Bowlski for the hockey championship of civilization. In a summit series, as in sex, there is only one first time.

Any boob could pick the first 12 or 15 players, and several of us with bylines in Canadian newspapers did. A few experts honed in on the first 25 chosen by Sinden and Ferguson. The last 10 were the hardest because their selection wasn't based upon scoring statistics or all-star recognition.

Sinden said, "Balance was the deciding factor in our thinking. We could have written down the names of all the high-scoring players, but that wouldn't give us a team. We wanted the balance of a team like the Canadiens when they won five straight Stanley Cups between 1955 and 1960."

Suppose, Sinden said, the score is 3–2 in your favor and there's a face-off in your end of the rink. You have to have someone win that face-off for you.

And, he said, you must have specialists patrolling — the Paul Parise of Minnesota North Stars and Wayne Cashman kind of specialists. Neither score big, but they're great in corners. They muck in there for the puck, and dig and feed it to guys who can score.

Not to mention that boyish sprats on the order of Parise, Cashman and Bob Clarke were piece men. They wanted a piece of any opponent they faced. That is a peculiarity of hockey as developed in Canada. It dates back to March 6, 1907, when Owen (Bud) McCourt, playing for Cornwall in the Federal Amateur Hockey League, was clubbed to death by Charles Masson of the Ottawa Vics. Masson was charged with manslaughter and acquitted, on the grounds that he didn't mean it.

The balance among Team Canada defencemen was struck between shooters and puck-handlers, such as Brad Park, Bobby Orr and J.C. Tremblay, and shotstoppers of the order of Don Awrey, Jacques Laperriere and Bill White. That balance was destroyed when Orr could not play and Tremblay was barred from playing. Orr's recovery from an operation on his left knee in June was tardy. Tremblay would be blacklisted after he abandoned the Canadiens for the Quebec Nordiques of the WHA.

Sinden talked about striking a balance between smooth finesse and solid checking among the forwards; the finesse of Jean Ratelle, Phil Esposito, Frank Mahovlich and the checking of Bob Clarke, Ron Ellis and Peter Mahovlich.

Sinden was poetic on the balance between enthusiastic youth and tempered experience. "No matter, you must have youth. Their enthusiasm is so vital to a team that you sometimes go with lesser talent because of it."

There was acute interest in the players Sinden announced as the deliverers of hockey superiority back to Canada. A few, highly touted, did not deliver. Some could not catch the swift Soviets. One, Frank Mahovlich, psyched himself out of the series. A few never played as well before or later. Two, Phil Esposito and Bob Clarke, went to the Hall of Fame because of their extraordinary feats through 28 days in September, 1972.

The goalies selected were Tony Esposito, Chicago Black Hawks; Ken Dryden, Montreal Canadiens; Gerry Cheevers and Ed Johnston, Boston Bruins. The defencemen were Orr and Don Awrey, Boston; Park and Rod Seiling, New York Rangers; Tremblay, Laperriere, Guy Lapointe, Serge Savard, Montreal; Jocelyn Guevremont, Vancouver Canucks; Gary Bergman, Detroit Red Wings; Pat Stapleton and Bill White, Chicago.

Down centre the Canadians had Phil Esposito and Derek Sanderson, Boston; Gilbert Perreault, Buffalo Sabres; Marcel Dionne and Red Berenson, Detroit; Jean Ratelle, New York; and Clarke, Philadelphia Flyers.

The right wings were Rod Gilbert, New York; Yvan Cournoyer, Montreal; Ron Ellis, Toronto; Mickey Redmond, Detroit; and Bill Goldsworthy, Minnesota North Stars. Bobby Hull was the prize left wing, with his brother Dennis from Chicago, Peter and Frank Mahovlich, Montreal; Wayne Cashman, Boston; Paul Parise, Minnesota; Paul Henderson, Toronto; Vic Hadfield, New York; and Richard Martin, Buffalo.

Ballard might have been surprised that Dave Keon, his stylish captain, was not nominated. Keon could skate fluently, check relentlessly and he cared about the quality of the game enormously. He had managed, being his own person, to offend R. Alan Eagleson. He had not joined the NHL Players Association.

Petty hockey politics raised a scaly head as soon as Sinden announced his Canadian players. Clarence Campbell, really the general manager for the NHL owners rather than NHL president, claimed that no NHL player who defected to the WHA would be permitted to play. Campbell was talking

about J.C. Tremblay, Gerry Cheevers, Derek Sanderson and
Bobby Hull, all of whom jumped to the WHA for more
money than the pittance they were paid in the NHL.

It was then Canadians discovered that even King Pierre
the First had no power to prevent the NHL from banning the
jumpers from a team paid for by Canadian taxpayers.

Trudeau was deluged with protests about the NHL hec-
toring of Hull, probably the best left wing of all the years.
Cases could perhaps be made for other left wings, but not
many. What couldn't be argued was Hull's status among the
fans. He was the No. 1 box-office draw in the NHL.

Trudeau was nudged into addressing a telegram to
Clarence Campbell, Hockey Canada and R.A. Eagleson of
the NHL Players Association. "You are aware," Trudeau
wired, "of the intense concern which I share with millions of
Canadians in all parts of the country, that Canada should be
represented by its best players, including Bobby Hull and all
those named by Team Canada, in the forthcoming series
against the Soviet Union. On behalf of these Canadians, I
urge all of you to take whatever steps are necessary to make
this possible. In making whatever arrangements may be
called for, I would ask you to keep the best interests of Canada in mind and to make sure that they are fully respected
and served."

The prime-ministerial plea was scorned as a piffling
annoyance. The NHL would do business its own way, as it
always had, a cartel beyond the highest courts in Canada.
Alan Eagleson went along as a handmaiden for the NHL
owners.

It was a long, hot, controversial hockey summer. Senator
Keith Davey, one of the bigger jockstraps in the upper Canadian house, could not conceal his partisan Liberal politics.

"We're annoyed," Davey told me, "that U.S. bigshots
thumbed their noses at the Prime Minister. We're bothered
that we're being led by the nose by Al Eagleson, who's a big
deal in the Ontario Conservatives. But what can Trudeau do?
If he insists on Hull playing, the American owners could pull
out their players and the Russian series would be blown."

A few Canadians, I contended in *The Globe and Mail*, might

have agreed that blowing the series would have been worthwhile if it meant retrieving a bit of our hockey heritage from the United States. The majority of Canadians placidly assumed a round-heel position: Come seduce me, I'll make it easy. The toadying stance was best exhibited by Ballard, the only NHL owner who cared about the summit series.

When Hull was first banned, Ballard vowed to move heaven, earth and mainland China to get Hull reinstated. His motto seemed to be "To Russia with Hull." In the crunch, later, Pal Hal was among the Hockey Canada directors who said "To hell with Hull."

There were critiques, and Ballard protested against the editorial shafts hurled at his manly pelt. "You don't know how hard I worked to get Hull on the Canadian team," Ballard said, "even though he jumped the NHL. But I wound up voting against him because you can't fight city hall."

It was mentioned to Ballard that if Canada's hockey integrity means anything, it must sometimes mean having the guts to say NO to domineering, self-serving American promoters.

"But to have kept fighting for Hull," Ballard countered, "would have been disastrous. Everybody was worked up to play the Russians and Eagleson did a lot of work to line up the series. If we'd held out for Hull, the American owners would have withdrawn their Canadian players and left us with no team."

Only one objective conclusion could be drawn from the exclusion of Bobby Hull. The NHL would smash any player, even its reigning demigod, if any player defied the NHL. In repudiating Hull, the NHL condemned the one pro whose generosity with the public and consummate good manners put Clarence Campbell and Al Eagleson and Harold Ballard and anyone else who cares about hockey in a dress shirt.

Ballard explained the dynamics of the Canadian team. "At the start," he said, "Hockey Canada gave Harry Sinden, as coach, full authority to pick the team. That kept changing. I think if Eagleson had said Hull should play, he'd play. Eagle's the guy with player power."

It was no special secret that Hull and Eagleson were less

than cosy companions. "Any time Eagleson does something
for the players," Hull had said when he played in Chicago, "I
have the feeling that he's really doing it for Eagleson."

In Winnipeg, turning over his fresh WHA money with a
fork, Hull said, "It won't be Canada against the Russians. It's
the NHL against the Russians, not Canada. The team is
called Team Canada, but it's really Team NHL."

I cannot remember a summer, outside of wartime, when
Canadians seemed so caught up in a crusade. Or were we
only younger, in 1972? For reporters and fellow travellers, the
series became an excited confusion of planes quickly caught,
hotel reservations fiercely screwed up, of deadlines hurriedly
met.

Late-summer humidity lay like a damp cloak over Montreal's noisy enormity on the evening of September 2, 1972.
Crowds clogged St. Catherine Street outside the face-lifted
Forum for 90 minutes before the game, festive, expectant,
boisterous.

Inside, with nothing left except to wait, Coach Harry Sinden lounged outside the Canadian dressing room, caught up
in the national anticipation.

Sinden was telling me, "Whatever else this series does, it's
sure brought out some funny stuff in the writers. John
Robertson in the *Montreal Star* says the gourmet dinner on a
Russian aircraft is a roll of salami and an axe. You say Rags
Ragulin is over that old blueberryetski hill."

Oh, funny, all right. Funny as a rubber crutch. I had written in the *Globe*, on August 29, 1972: "So make it Canada, 8
games to 0. If the Russians win one game, I will eat this
column shredded at high noon in a bowl of borscht on the
front steps of the Russian embassy . . ."

King Pierre the First was in the Forum, and his comely
queen, who had not yet encountered the Rolling Stones.
There were 18,818 fans jammed in the seats, certain of a
Canadian conquest. We couldn't get the national anthems
played soon enough for Trudeau to drop the ceremonial first
puck and let the athletes take over.

The words were mouthed meaninglessly, if mouthed at
all, that first night. "O Canada, we stand on guard for thee,"
but against Russian hockey players, who needs guards?

The Soviet anthem was a long mournful pause, melancholy, steeped in the blood of ancient wrongs, of 900 days holding the line against the Nazis at Leningrad.

Then the series was on, and Gary Bergman threw the puck into the Russian zone and here were Frank Mahovlich and Phil Esposito poking at it in front of Vladislav Tretiak.

Goal! By Esposito, who skated around, arms lifted looking for somebody to congratulate. By God, it looked easy. Only 30 seconds had blinked off the time clock suspended above centre ice. Six minutes later, Bob Clarke scored, a low, quick shot from a face-off in the Russian zone, Canada up 2–0.

A young man running to suet, in a pink shirt and white trousers, bounced up in the seat in front of me in one end of the Forum. He moved as if in the final delights of orgasm whenever the Canadians made a move, and they made all the moves in the first 10 minutes.

"See that guy?" a French Canadian colleague said of the fellow in the pink shirt. "He gave three goals and bet $3,000 on Canada."

There was no reason for Pink Shirt, or any other Canadian bettor, to feel secure, even with a two-goal lead. The Russians righted themselves like a hogshead of vodka and, once settled on the truck, asserted a poise that tossed the Canadians into disarray. Eugeny Zimin, a stocky middleweight, shot the first Soviet goal at 11:40. He walked into the slot in front of Ken Dryden to accept a pass while Rod Gilbert, Rod Seiling and Guy Lapointe watched in admiration. Dryden was handcuffed by a quick, accurate shot.

Two Canadian power plays aborted, as though this was expansion shinny. Clarence Campbell was in his swivel chair, but all's not right in our toy world.

The Russians scored the only goals of the second period, two by Valery Kharlamov, who scooted between defencemen Rod Seiling and Don Awrey like a runaway waterbug. Kharlamov was a physical oddity among the Russians. Most of them had fair-haired Slavic countenances. Kharlamov was dark, reflecting his mother, who had been a refugee from the losing side in the Spanish Civil War and settled in the Soviet Union.

The most partisan Canadians, those in the NHL, felt

something slipping. Scotty Bowman, coach of the Montreal Canadiens, had wagered that Team NHL would win the eight-game series by 40 goals. Perspiration soaked through shirts and seeped into the armholes of jackets. Pink Shirt, in front of me, gasped like a gaffed fish. I kept thinking of the words I would eat, with no particular display of grace.

During the second intermission, at a soft-drink stand, I fell into stunned conversation with Jack Cahill, manager of *The Toronto Star's* bureau in Ottawa. He is an Australian with a snarly sense of pride in athletic achievement.

Cahill saw the looming rout of the Canadians as a portent of political doom. "You know what this could mean?" he said "It could cost Trudeau the next federal election. People will be so let down by Canada's hockey decay, their psyches so tattered, it could mean defeat for the Liberals."

In the desperate third period, Stan Mikita, who was not dressed for the game, came out of his seat to stand behind the Canadian bench and exhort his colleagues to rally, in vain.

Bob Clarke did close the gap to 4–3, deflecting a pass from Ron Ellis past Tretiak. Rod Gilbert almost tied it 4–4 on a shot which rang off a post.

The Russians rebounded in the last six minutes, momentum regained after a brief pause. Boris Mikhailov, wearing No. 13, made the moves of an erotic exotic dancer, in, out, in, to elude Seiling, then faking Dryden out of position before scoring on an audacious backhand shot.

Zimin was back for his second goal, uncovered in front of Dryden, juggling the puck before batting into the net. Rangy Aleksander Yakushev, all whipcord and whalebone, son of a Soviet air ace in the Second Great War, faked Dryden to the ice and lifted the puck high for the seventh Soviet goal.

The Canadian myth had been punctured, our fatheads deflated in a 7–3 defeat. The players subsided with a loss of grace. Good manners in international hockey include comradely handclasps at the end of the game, but the Canadians ignored the chummy ritual.

Prime Minister Trudeau, the red rose limp in his lapel, expressed annoyance to a sycophantic aide. "I do not like us not shaking hands," Trudeau said, mindful of the diplomatic accord he had established with the Soviet Union.

The Russians assembled at centre ice waited for the Canadians to return. Red Berenson and Ken Dryden, both of whom had played internationally, did return, but by then the Russians had skated to their quarters. There were no handshakes, only the derisive pounding of Russian sticks on the ice.

Many in the Canadian menagerie — "floaters," Phil Esposito called them — were shocked by the result, but not to the point of speechlessness. Clarence Campbell jumped off the Canadian bandwagon in such haste that he almost broke an ankle. The NHL general manager was critical of Coach Sinden's personnel switches, although Campbell had blackballed four of the personnel selected by Sinden, the four who dared leap to the WHA.

Harry Sinden admitted, "They outplayed us in every facet of the game. They were better everywhere, from goaltending to shooting, skating and passing. And, yes, they were in better condition than we were." Sinden spoke at a microphone set up on a makeshift stage in the dimly lit garage area of the Forum. "I was amazed," he said, "how well the Russians played at times. You play about as well as the other team permits you, and they didn't permit us to play very well."

Boris Kulagin, the well-upholstered assistant coach of the Soviets, responded for the other side. Jim Coleman of the Southam papers called him Chuckles Kulagin because his round, granite face never cracked the tiniest smirk. "Our players," Chuckles said, "proved we will never avoid any bodycheck." Harold Ballard, not chuckling either, announced he would pay $1 million for Valery Kharlamov, "if some son of a bitch can spring him out of Russia."

Ballard did not refrain from second guessing himself on how he was conned by Soviet agents who scouted the Team NHL training camp. He insisted that Arkady Chernychev and Chuckles Kulagin played a polite version of proletarian possum. "Was I ever led down the fucking garden path," Ballard said. "I did things for them, like arranging trips to

Niagara Falls and the Hockey Hall of Fame, and they kept saying, 'Oh, Mr. Ballard, against your NHL All-Stars we might be lucky to win one game.' Boy, was I fucking had."

Ballard had been so convinced of the NHL's superiority that he was prepared to be neighborly. "I thought we'd whip hell out of them," he said. "Then I'd make them a generous offer for some of their players to come to the NHL so we could teach them the fine points. Now we ought to make a deal in the other direction. I think some of our players should go to Russia and learn the fine points."

Alan Eagleson was not ready to concede any putts just yet. "I though we'd win eight straight," he said, "but I've got to revise that forecast. Now the series is best five games out of eight."

There was nothing left, after all the quotes were gathered, but to compose a mea culpa. My fault, my mistake, my goof. I decided the best means for getting off the hook was to report the 7–3 debacle with a half-boob air. Long after midnight, stripped down to underwear in the non-air conditioned Windsor Hotel, I composed at the typewriter:

> MONTREAL – All the grain is wormy on the Western Canadian plains, ravaged by a wheat-stem sawfly smuggled in from the Ukraine.
>
> Canadian back bacon has gone rancid on the hogs. All the maple sugar had vanished down the trees to become bitter-root. Sharpshooting agents from the Soviet Union's feared secret police have drilled holes in all those Smokey the Bear hats worn by the RCMP.
>
> All the Hudson's Bay blankets have moth holes. The Rocky Mountains are mere pebbles beside the towering Urals. Anne Murray can't carry a tune in a Kremlin coal scuttle.
>
> The North Pole is a lousy toothpick. The Northern Lights are dimmer than a mole's boudoir in a Siberian salt mine at midnight. All because the Borscht Belters beat Team NHL 7–3; suddenly Canada's national dish is crow. The Red Square, whose name is Chuckles Kulagin, is king of Parliament Hill.
>
> We laid 100 years of heritage on the line on Sept. 2,

Dorothy Ballard fell in love with Pal Hal in 1924 and married him in 1941. He lost his "greatest friend" when she died in 1969. (HOCKEY HALL OF FAME)

The Battling Ballards young: (left to right) Harold Jr., Mary Elizabeth and William. (HOCKEY HALL OF FAME)

Triumphant triumvirate of Harold Ballard, Stafford Smythe and John Bassett gained 60 per cent control of Maple Leaf Gardens for $2.3 million in 1961. (HOCKEY HALL OF FAME)

The Old Cashbox on Carlton Street was resplendent with Union Jack flying over Maple Leaf Gardens in 1950. (HOCKEY HALL OF FAME)

Master Blaster Charlie Conacher was Leaf scoring star with booming
shot 55 years ago. (HOCKEY HALL OF FAME)

Rollicking Babe Pratt won Hart
Trophy as the most valuable
mercenary in the National
Hockey League in 1944.
(HOCKEY HALL OF FAME)

"C'mon, Teeder!" was Leaf
rallying call when implacable
Ted Kennedy led Toronto to five
Stanley Cups. (HOCKEY HALL OF
FAME)

Dipsy Doo Max Bently came to the Maple Leafs from Chicago Black Hawks in 1947 in exchange for five players. Bently was as slick with the puck as Wayne Gretzky and the finest third-string centre in Leaf history. (HOCKEY HALL OF FAME)

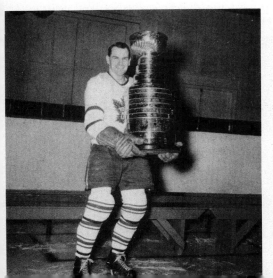

Stylish captain Syl Apps holds Stanley Cup won four times by the Maple Leafs in the five seasons between 1947 and 1951. (HOCKEY HALL OF FAME)

The most famous voice in hockey: "He Shoots! He Scores!" was the exciting shout of Foster Hewitt whenever a Maple Leaf performed a scoring dramatic. (HOCKEY HALL OF FAME)

Little pistol Conn Smythe fired up Leafs with stormy pep talks. He suffered serious back wounds in the Second Great War and wore a heavy windbreaker to stay warm when he watched the Leafs practice. (HOCKEY HALL OF FAME)

Punch Imlach wasn't always surpassingly bald, as revealed in 1938 photo of Imlach as a senior Toronto Marlboro. (HOCKEY HALL OF FAME)

Imlach trained to be a concert violinist but settled for being an NHL coach. (HOCKEY HALL OF FAME)

King Clancy was assistant coach and Punch Imlach's loyal subaltern when Leafs won four Stanley Cups in six seasons during the Sixties. (HOCKEY HALL OF FAME)

Ballard tells Golden Jet Bobby Hull that hockey is his game, too. (FRANK LENNON, TORONTO STAR)

Frank Mahovlich, on a big night, was the most vivid Maple Leaf who ever got the fans on their feet and cheering in Maple Leaf Gardens. (HOCKEY HALL OF FAME)

Number 7, Tim Horton, the strongest Leaf defenceman in history, listens to joke told by King Clancy, hockey's original good-humor man. (HOCKEY HALL OF FAME)

Bill Ballard shares Pal Hal's gloom with Father David Bauer after Team Canada loses first game in Russia in 1972. (FRANK LENNON, TORONTO STAR)

The most famous goal in hockey history was scored by Paul Henderson in 1972 when Team Canada rallied in downtown Russia to win the first hockey summit against the Soviet Union. (HOCKEY HALL OF FAME)

Fat Harold poses in Moscow in 1972 with NHL crony Bruce Norris, former owner of the Detroit Red Wings. (HOCKEY HALL OF FAME)

Bobby Orr, Wonderkid of the Boston Bruins, sandwiched between Alan Eagleson, boss of the NHL players' union, and Ballard in Moscow in 1972. (FRANK LENNON, TORONTO STAR)

Tiger Williams shot a bear with bow and arrow to make a rug for Ballard's office. (ROBERT SHAVER, TORONTO MAPLE LEAFS)

Pal Hal, flaunting Maple Leaf tie, regales NHL president John Ziegler. (HOCKEY HALL OF FAME)

Oops! Shortly after this publicity shot, Pal Hal shot down the Canadian tour of the Moscow Circus in 1983 after the Soviet Union shot down an unarmed Korean airliner. (FRANK LENNON, TORONTO STAR)

"Argos Suck!" Ballard agreed with Hamilton fans when Ticats beat Toronto in the Eastern football final in 1984. (FRANK LENNON, TORONTO STAR)

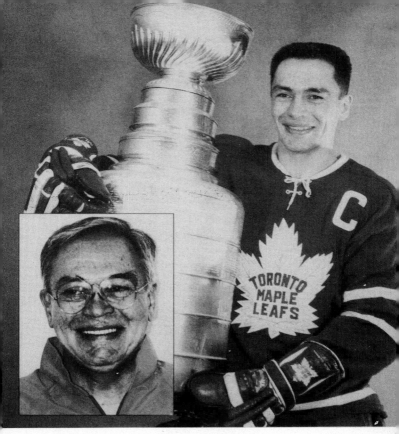

Former Maple Leaf coach George Armstrong with Stanley Cup won four times during his captaincy. The most reluctant coach in the NHL, George Armstrong was too nice a guy to tell Ballard he didn't want to coach the team. He was replaced anyway, by Doug Carpenter.(HOCKEY HALL OF FAME)

Gordon Stellick was the youngest general manager in the NHL when appointed to replace Gerry McNamara in 1988. (ROBERT SHAVER, TORONTO MAPLE LEAFS)

The boisterous Ballards, Harold Jr., Mary Elizabeth and Bill Ballard leave the courtroom in high spirits, September 1988.
(CRAIG ROBERTSON, TORONTO SUN)

Fun couple Yolanda and Harold at 1989 Queen's Plate, where octagenarian Ballard failed to meet octagenarian Queen Mother Elizabeth. Every time Yolanda steered Pal Hal near the Queen, Her Majesty strolled off to look at another horse.
(TIM MCKENNA, TORONTO SUN)

A solemn Pal Hal watches one of his last hockey games in the fall of 1989. (CANADA WIDE)

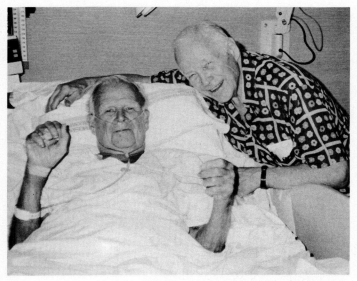

Old pal Allan Lamport visits Pal Hal a few weeks before Ballard's death. (CANADA WIDE)

Uninvited to the burial, Yolanda visits Ballard's gravesite accompanied by Denise Banks and Puck, April 18, 1990. (FRED THORNHILL, TORONTO SUN)

Toronto construction magnate Don Giffin, known as "Sheet Metal Giff," replaced Pal Hal as president of Maple Leaf Gardens. He is among the highest-paid Leafs at $300,000 a year. (NAYLOR PUBLICATIONS)

1972 and lost to plucky people who thought a net was for catching butterflies and fish until they took up hockey in 1946.

How would old Rudyard Cufflink have mourned:

> Far-call'd our pro stars fade away,
> Our hockey shine tarnishes to dull,
> Lo, all our pomp of yesterday
> Is gone with Howe and Bobby Hull.

How many autographs of Prime Minister Trudeau will you trade for one of Valery Kharlamov who, for one vivid night at least, was the best hockey player on the planet?

What price Conn Smythe's edict that a player should not get married during the season because a young man's fancy might turn away from thoughts of puck? Vladislav Tretiak, married for 10 days, is the best goaltender extant, at least pro tem.

Can the beaver remain our Canadian symbol? After Saturday he is nothing more than a buck-toothed rodent badly in need of an orthodontist.

We should have learned from Soviet tactics in other sports that they would not play this series if they were going to be muscled into embarrassing submission. When the Russians aim to be the best at something, they do not aim with their eyes shut. They won one for Boris Spassky, the disgraced chess master.

They wear shoddy skates that you'd be ashamed to throw into a Salvation Army hamper. When they leave an arena, they carry their own bags of soggy equipment. But they had the discipline to come from behind a two-goal disadvantage and romp against some of our highest-paid mercenaries.

Was their aim accomplished because they are in better physical shape, or, perish the thought, simply because they are better?

There may be other questions as the series shifts across the shrivelled ego of the country. Were some of us victims of a hoax? Should I run, not walk, to the nearest eye specialist? Has the National Hockey League perpetrated a fraud all these years by claiming to play the world's best hockey?

So the St. Lawrence Seaway is nothing but a leaky toilet in Omsk. Reporters like me were afflicted with Russian rinderpest, which is foot-in-mouth disease. And whatever did become of Bobby Hull?

CHAPTER 13

Mission to Moscow

◆

The sun rose the day after our hockey chauvinism was shaken, but reluctantly, I thought. The second game of the Super Bowlski series would be played at Maple Leaf Gardens, where Harold Ballard held corpulent sway.

Ballard held portly court in the Gardens on the morning of the second game, September 4, 1972, a Monday. The leader of the federal Conservatives, Robert Stanfield, may have been the best prime minister Canada never had, but always looked like he'd drop every football thrown to him.

Stanfield posed at centre ice with Ballard, who fitted the Tory captain with a jersey representing Team NHL. Frank Mahovlich, standing near the boards, smoking a furious cigar, watched Stanfield pose. "Damn politicians," Mahov grumbled. "Always climbing on the bandwagon as though this is just a game. Don't they know this is a war?"

Coach Harry Sinden switched goaltenders for the second battle of the war. He replaced the cerebral Ken Dryden with Tony Esposito, a Chicago Black Hawk with a catching hand faster than a pickpocket's. He became the savior of Canadian hockey, for the moment. I wrote:

> His name is Anthony James Esposito and he redeemed the national pastime by making big goalkeeping saves, particularly in the first period when the score was 0–0. . . .
>
> He stopped Kharlamov, Saturday's star. He blocked Eugeny Zimin from short range. He made, in sum, four saves in the first period that could have been Russian goals.
>
> Given that kind of vigilant goalkeeping, you've always got a chance. The Canadians came on with goals by Yvan (The Roadrunner) Cournoyer, Phil Esposito, Frank Mahovlich and an extravagant score by Peter

Mahovlich. The younger Mahov put the sort of moves
on the Soviet defencemen that you see in a Yonge Street
joint where the girls take their clothes off. Tip, tilt, oops,
deke and slip the puck behind goaler Vladislav Tretiak.
A great coital cry came out of 16,485 Canadian partisans.

Pete's goal, Canada's third, happened at 6:47 of the third
period on a pass from Phil Esposito. They were killing a
penalty assessed to Pat Stapleton when the sweating Esposito slipped Mahovlich the puck in the centre area.
Mahovlich weaved in, large and imposing, then fell into the
Russian net after scoring the third Canadian goal. It remains
the most famous shorthanded goal in hockey history.

Phil Esposito, after the 4–1 triumph, said it with simple
elegance. "You know how I felt when Pete scored? I felt just
like you do when you're having sex, just in that instant before
you come."

The Canadian myth had been restored. Steers capered on
the Cariboo ranches. Wheat sales soared. Silos swayed, beer
foamed in the Canadian breweries, and Niagara Falls was
more than a bathroom drip. The game of the people
belonged once more to the Canadian people who invented it.
Ballard barged around his Gardens, shaking hands like a
celebrating Shriner and booming, "Hoo and also fucking
RAY!"

Canadian hearts were light and gay for the first time in 48
hours. It was a bright new world and puck patriots cheered.
There was hope for this Canadian civilization, after all. Phil
Esposito hugged his brother Tony in a wet, ponderous
embrace. "Little brother," Phil said, "you sure came up with a
hell of a job to take the pressure off the rest of us."

The job was made easier by the rambunctious presence of
Wayne Cashman, a boyish ogre prepared to drink Russian
blood at body temperature, or near there. He was a tall chunk
of gristle who played left wing the best he knew how for the
Boston Bruins. The best he knew was learned on Canadian
rinks, where most of us learned the game. Most of us learned
very young that the best and most natural retort to make to

an adversary is a punch in the snoot. That was Cashman, elbows up, boisterously checking his Russian tormentors.

Tim Burke wrote admiringly in the *Montreal Gazette*, "There is nothing like a little Cash to get the free enterprise system going."

I had promised to eat my column in a bowl of borscht if the Russians won one game. The promise was kept, to the obscene delight of the Russian players. They flocked around chortling on the steps of their hotel in Toronto, the Hyatt House, as I struggled to prove that reporters do not live by bread alone. Sometimes we have to eat our words.

I therefore had a personal reason to be gratified by the Canadian victory in the second game. I got to regurgitate the wretched column I ate the day before.

There was time then, even on the sports pages, to ponder the Soviet Union. The squarest of Canadians reside in sports departments, most inclined toward the political right and especially in 1972, 16 years before Mikhail Gorbachev and perestroika.

Communism, or what passed for communism in the Soviet Union in 1972, is a grinding form of repression. The cultural revolution that Marxism entails is an unbearable impoverishment, a forfeiting of the intellectual's most cherished heritage. Germaine Greer wrote: "Yevtushenko, the poet, and Solzhenitsyn, the novelist, remind the intellectual horribly of the price that proletarian dictators must exact, in return for the least amelioration in the condition of the masses."

Many in the Canadian hockey contingent, Alan Eagleson prominent among them, regarded the summit encounter as more than a merely shinny showdown. The players, essentially unschooled in international politics, viewed the series as Us versus Them, White Hats against Black Hats, Good Guys confronting Bad Guys.

Frank Mahovlich fervently insisted that the series was more than a contest of cultures. To the Big M, it became a contentious crusade of Right battling Might. He thought harder than he played. Ballard is basically apolitical but had absorbed, apparently by osmosis, anti-Soviet sentiments. He had heard that to be Jewish in the Soviet Union was to be a non-person, "I'll be taking a bunch of bibles to Russia," he said. "I'll be giving them to Jews who want to escape."

On September 5, a Tuesday, the Canadians travelled to Winnipeg for the third game of the series. That day, Arab anarchists disrupted the Summer Olympics in Munich by killing 11 Israeli athletes. Mahovlich interpreted the bloody incident as a Russian plot.

On the bus ride to catch the plane for Winnipeg, Mahovlich spoke darkly of the Munich tragedy to Arthur Harnett, Eagleson's co-ordinator of the series' telecasts. "That's the Russians for you," Mahovlich told Harnett.

"Oh, no, Frank," Harnett protested. "Arabs were responsible for those killings." Mahovlich's attitude was ramrod rigid. "Don't tell me," he said, "that the orders for those killings didn't come from head office in Moscow."

The teams tied 4-4 in Winnipeg and flew to Vancouver for the fourth game, on September 8, 1972. Team NHL was bivouacked in the Bayshore Inn, an elegant flop at the entrance to Stanley Park, a glory of urban wilderness.

Mahovlich checked into room 1012 in the Bayshore and startled the bellhop by immediately tapping the walls and peering behind the drapes. His roomate was Serge Savard, who is more placid, politically speaking.

"Sshhh," Mahov whispered to Savard. "Don't say a word. This room may be bugged by Commie agents." Ted Blackman, documenting the Fears of Frank for the *Montreal Gazette*, could not contain his amusement. "It is," Blackman scoffed, "to laugh."

"It's no laughing matter," Mahovlich said. "I wouldn't be surprised at anything the Russians might do." His eyes scanned the twilight zone, somewhere beyond Ted Blackman's head. "No, sir. I wouldn't be surprised if they're training a football team at a secret army base. They'll beat the Dallas Cowboys next year."

Mahovlich told Savard, "What we should do in Moscow is camp outside in the hills beyond the city. We should sleep in tents."

"What the hell for?" Savard wondered.

Mahovlich said, "So we can get some sleep. Don't you

think the Russians will start a construction project outside our hotel at 4:00 a.m.? Just to ruin our sleep."

Savard tried to mock the preposterous notion with a joke. "But, Frank," he said, "most of our guys won't be in bed by 4:00 a.m."

"Don't laugh," Mahovlich said. "You don't realize what this series means to the Russians for propaganda purposes. They'll do anything. We should buy those tents."

The Canadians were slovenly in the fourth game, losers 5–3, to the vocal chagrin of 16,553 booing fans in the Vancouver Coliseum. Observers who had been around the block a time or two were not surprised. Vancouver fans do not devour their young, necessarily, but they do boo at funerals. The loss meant the series would revert to Moscow with the Soviet Selects leading, two wins, one loss, one tie.

Canadian players were dismayed at their reception in Vancouver. Ken Dryden, the goalkeeper, said, "Ridiculing us is unfair, but I think it's understandable. Canada had a party set up and the Russians are ruining it."

Phil Esposito, on national television, berated the Canadian public. "I'm disappointed some Canadians are against us," he said. He grabbed a fistful of his red sweater. "Damn it, we're all wearing the same color. The Canadian color. Most of us make our living in the States, but we love Canada. That's why we're playing Russia. The ridicule we're getting from some Canadian fans is below my dignity."

Esposito is rangy and voluble and those remarks certified him as the Canadian leader. Until then he had played in the shade of Bobby Orr in Boston and Bobby Hull in Chicago. Now Esposito was alone. Orr was injured and could not play in the Summit Series. Hull was ostracized by the spiteful NHL Establishment.

Esposito strode into the vacuum created by the absence of Orr and Hull and, trying harder, number two became number one. He emerged from the Canadian section of the series as the complete player nobody thought he was. He did it all, pass, shoot, forecheck, backcheck, continually lifting his associates, arguing.

Team NHL left Toronto for Europe on September 19, 1972, Ballard along as chaperone, an unlikely role for a truant facing a jail sentence. He travelled with his older son Bill, then 25. They were friends to such an extent that Harold named Bill a vice-president of Maple Leaf Gardens.

Canadian breweries have always horned in on hockey, Molson and Labatt and Carling-O'Keefe at logger heads over which brew controlled what NHL property. Operatives for Labatt got several members of Team NHL well oiled before the departure for Europe.

Labatt was large in the Canada-Russia series as the sponsor of one or two cars awarded to the outstanding Canadian players. "The way the Canadians played in the first four games," a critic in Vancouver grumbled, "the cars should be lousy Edsels."

Loaded, courtesy of Labatt, a few of the players behaved with sufficient boorishness to inspire John Robertson of the *Montreal Star* to label Team NHL as "Team Ugly."

Female passengers on the plane were insulted. At Frankfurt, after landing in Germany, Wayne Cashman of the Bruins made a diplomatic speech in the terminal.

"You fucking Germans better not start another world war," Cash declared. "Don't forget, you're 0-for-2 in this century." Later, pausing for two games against Swedish teams in Stockholm, a few Canadians ingratiated themselves with the peace-loving locals, "Where were you sons-a-bitching Swedes in the Second Great War? Hiding?" Harold Ballard, the chaperone guffawed.

Canadian comments were dutifully published in the Stockholm newspapers, to the considerable wrath of the Swedish players. One of them, in the first game, thrust six inches of his stick down Wayne Cashman's throat. The impetuous Bruin did not eat much solid food for the balance of the excursion.

Phil Esposito had been knifed by Alan Eagleson as "a money grubber," perhaps unpatriotic, but when Team NHL faltered in two messy exhibitions in Stockholm, Esposito took command of the dressing room. A few players grumbled when Coach Sinden did not pick them to play. Esposito grabbed one of them by the shirtfront. "Anybody who doesn't want to stand up for Canada," Esposito said, irascibility showing, "better take their fucking uniform off and go home. We don't want any goddamn quitters on this club."

While Team NHL paused in Sweden, about 2,700 Canadians, many prepared to party, caught flights to Moscow. Canada has not sent such a large chauvinistic contingent overseas, outside of a world war. Most of us experienced, for the first time, the strange foreign conditions of downtown Russia, drawn towards that silent mother who can devour.

It was difficult to realize, caught up in the shinny excitement in the benign sunshine of a Soviet September, that out there, beyond the broad city limits, is a boundless ocean of a country that tormented Napoleon and Hitler in their vain attempts to conquer Moscow.

The casual visitor, contemplating the mustard-colored Kremlin walls, could only report the small adventures of Canadian travellers. There was not enough time in September, 1972, to grasp the suffering soul of Russia, because a lifetime might not be enough time.

Mother Russia was not the female engaging the interest of many among Canadian yahoos boobishly ready to act like Grey Cup drunks. To be certain they wouldn't be shut out in a sexless socialist state, some of them imported girl friends.

The former general manager of a team in the Canadian Football League squired a tasty morsel said to be of Italian extraction. An old Toronto Argonaut went for the downs with a Dutch lady ready to catch all passes. Ballard, travelling with his son, seemed curiously sedate for a gentleman of his amorous appetites.

The organizers of Team NHL made certain the athletes would remain reasonably celibate in Moscow by flying over a shipment of the players' wives. I was between engagements, as it were, and my roommate in the Ukraine Hotel, on the banks of the Moscow River, was Brian Williams, the cordial host of CBC television sports.

The players arrived from Stockholm and, contrary to Frank Mahovlich's expectations, were not settled in the Moscow Hills. They were billeted in the Intourist Hotel, a bourgeois Holiday Inn known as the Moscow Hilton. They were greeted by noisy Canadian fans, some of them their wives.

Harold Ballard was the first to register in the Intourist. He was carrying two huge shopping bags from Dominion Stores. He spotted me across the crowded lobby and held up one of the bags.

"Rich," he yelled, "I got the Coke in! They said the Russkies wouldn't let me get it in, but I did." Ballard meant Coca-Cola, which, at least until 1972, was barred from sale in the Soviet Union.

Mahovlich was joined by Marie, his serene wife. She did not curb Frank's intense sense of paranoia. They had barely checked into their room when Frank began to search for the bug he was certain the Russian secret police install in every hotel room. Mahov spotted a suspicious-looking screw in the floor under the bed. "Found it," he muttered. He turned the screw, certain it was a bug, and pulled it out of the floor. The guests in the room immediately below the Mahovlichs' were alarmed to see their light fixture come crashing out of the ceiling. "Good God, Martha, head for the hills! This place is falling down!"

The impression of suspicious Canadians was that there was a Commie bogeyman under every bed. I was disabused of the notion by John Shaw, an old *Vancouver Sun* hand attached to *Time* magazine's Moscow bureau. "If the Commies have a bogeyman anywhere in your flat," Shaw said, "it won't be under the bed. It's likely to be in the form of an electronic device in the light fixtures, or the ashtray, or the wall."

The next morning, up early in the Intourist dining room, Ballard discovered that Russian cuisine, for him, wasn't "exactly fucking kosher." He was joined by Murray Dryden, another early riser and father of the goaltenders, Ken and Dave Dryden. A waitress brought a bowl of boiled eggs. Harold cracked one open and found it as soft as when the hen laid it. "For Christ's sake, waitress," he said, "bring me a straw so I can suck this egg up."

Then Ballard sampled the Moscow version of coffee. He dipped his spoon into what he took to be a sugar container and stirred two heaping spoonsful into his coffee, as he would in the Hot Stove Lounge. He drank from his cup, tasted the coffee and went "splat!" all over the tablecloth. He had dumped salt, not sugar, into his coffee.

"I tell you, Murray," Harold told Dryden, "these bastard Russians are trying to poison us."

Another day, at lunch with Toronto sports writers, Ballard picked up a lush hunk of sliced kolbassa, a red spicy sausage very good with beer. Harold held up the kolbassa and asked his companions, "You know what we'd use this crap for in Canada?"

Jim Hunt, the noted Toronto broadcaster and writer, said, "I'll bite, Harold. What would we use that kolbassa for in Canada?"

"For tire-patching," Ballard announced, triumphantly.

He reflected the attitude of many Canadian tourists, ever ready to compare the worst in Russian food with the best in Canada. Russian food is nourishing, although heavy and rarely varied. If you ask for a Canadian staple, steak, you make a mistake. The meat will come out as tough and fricasseed as a baked hockey puck. The food they do well in Moscow, the borscht and black bread and sour cream, is a gourmand's delight. Chicken Kiev would water the mouth of even old Kentucky-fried Colonel Sanders.

On his first morning in Moscow, after throwing up his coffee, Ballard opened his office to rescue Soviet Jews from tyranny. He lugged a small table from his room down to the Intourist lobby. He place 12 bibles on the table and scrawled a sign on a piece of cardboard: "Any Jews want a bible, come and see me."

Ballard was watched by the Intourist security, two hotel cops who resembled hotel cops all over the world. They all resemble defunct football tackles running to fat. Their uniform is universal, baggy brown three-piece suits with black shoes.

The Intourist cops beheld Ballard with arresting glances. A desk clerk who could read English explained to the Gulag gumshoes what Ballard's sign said. They moved towards Ballard's table. "Nyet," the bigger of them said. "No."

"Waddaya mean, nyet?" Ballard said. "You goddamn Commie fink."

"Goddamn Commie fink" must be a despicable phrase understood by the communist constabulary everywhere. One of the Intourist cops grabbed one of Ballard's arms and twisted it behind Harold's back, ungently. The other Intourist cop confiscated the bibles.

"But those goddamn bibles cost me money!" Ballard protested. The cops said "Nyet!" in unison, as though coached by the ghost of Joe Stalin. Ballard, up against Moscow muscle, abandoned his project to rescue Soviet Jews.

Harold felt, second-guessing himself, that he should have brought soap and towels and toilet tissue instead of bibles. The Soviet soap bits and towels were diminutive, suitable for use by stunted midgets. The toilet paper, in Ballard's assessment, had the tender texture of "goddamn sandpaper."

"Well," Jim Hunt said when Ballard complained of the Russian amenities, "you could have stayed home where the food's better and the toilet paper softer."

"But I had to come," Ballard said. "I'm preparing myself for the conditions I'll face in the Kingston can." It was his first admission that he thought he would get a purgatorial term for his Gardens' sins.

There was time, between games, to visit the Moscow circus, which has bears and seals trained better than most flunkies in a Canadian advertising office. It was mandatory to visit the Russian holy of holies, Lenin's Tomb. V.I. Lenin is revered as the pope of the proletariat, founder of the first Communist Party dictatorship.

Lenin's embalmed body lies in a glass-covered casket, protected on four sides by stainless steel railing. The corpse looks waxen, like nothing so much as a refugee from Madame Tussaud's museum.

It is hats-off time and lower your voice, please, in Lenin's Tomb, just as though you are genuflecting in Saint Peter's Church in Vatican City. I followed three irreverent cashews from the Ontario village of Bolton, all of us peering down at a bigger Soviet hero than Vlad Tretiak, the goaltender. One of the boys from Bolton reached into his pocket for a bumper sticker and surreptitiously stuck it on the railing around the sacred Lenin remains. The sticker suggested "COME TO THE BOLTON CENTENNIAL FALL FAIR, Oct. 14-15-16, 1972."

On the ice, the Canadian players began to coalesce as a team on the expansive ice surface of Luzhniki Sports Palace, 15 feet wider than conventional NHL surfaces. Luzhniki is a bright, well-lighted place, 20 minutes from Red Square on what must be the most efficient subway system in the world.

After two periods of the first game in Moscow, and the fifth in the series, Team NHL led 3–0. Jean-Paul Parise, Bob Clarke and Paul Henderson scored for Canada. Henderson and Ron Ellis, on a line with Clarke, skated with fast purpose on the wider ice, never better in their respective careers. Clarke did the checking, wicked with his stick, a whacker.

Ballard, after the first two periods, thought he knew why the Canadians played with such élan. "Our guys came alive when their wives arrived," the chaperone said. "The wives came with mattresses strapped to their backs and our guys got the fucking over fast and went to work."

In the third period of the fifth game, the Canadians subsided as though they were weary from too much activity on the mattress. They permitted the Russians to score five goals and lost the game, 5–4. With three games to play, the Russians seemed to have the series cinched with three wins, one loss and one tie. The Canadians needed to win the last three games to survive at the summit.

Harry Sinden, the coach, implored the players with a quotable speech. "Like I said in Sweden," Sinden said, "let's start rowing to shore, instead of hitting each other over the head with the paddles."

Four players heard Sinden, but did not listen. They abandoned the team because they weren't picked to play enough. Vic Hadfield, Richard Martin, Gilbert Perreault and Jocelyn Guevremont took it on the lam like Napoleon retreating from Moscow in the freezing winter of 1813. They flew home to Canada before the series ended.

"Cocksuckers!" Peter Mahovlich said. Phil Esposito told Sinden, "If you hadn't told those guys to go home, I would have. We don't need any quitters." Ballard said, "Goddamn deserters."

The desertions, more than anything else, turned the remaining players into a team. Without them, the Canadians assumed a mean-spirited myopia that shrank their world to the confines of Luzhniki Arena and welcomed few outsiders.

There are rules for hockey Canadian-style but the code is occasionally broken by cheerful galoots with wood in their hands. Canadian morality loosened in the second period of the sixth game, after Valery Kharlamov had zipped around, bewildering, a Bolshevik buzzsaw. The score was 0–0, but Soviet speed dominated.

Coach Harry Sinden usually gave the between-period instructions, but he turned this time to his tough-talking assistant, John Ferguson. The former rink rat from Vancouver has a prominent beak which looks as though it has been bent by the odd impious fist or two.

"Listen, guys," Ferguson said, "we got to get Kharlamov. Someone has to whack him. If we don't he'll kill us."

Most of the players were bent over, heads down, listening. Bob Clarke, the hard knocker from the hard-rock mining town of Flin Flon, heard words intended for him. "I looked around out of the corners of my eyes," Clarke related, long after. "There was Paul Henderson, I knew he wouldn't club anybody. There was Ron Ellis, hell of a checker but clean. I could see Rod Gilbert, who doesn't slug."

Sitting there in Moscow, three years in the NHL and a long way from Flin Flon, the avenging diabetic knew who John Ferguson was talking to. "I didn't look up," Clarke said, "but I knew Fergie was talking to me. If Kharlamov was to be knocked out, Fergie meant I must do the knocking."

Ferguson's instructions, immoral by even hockey's loose standards, were followed soon enough. Kharlamov came flashing on the big Soviet line, allied with slick Alexander Maltsev and malevolent Boris Mikhailov.

Kharlamov sailed through centre with the puck and here, on a baleful backcheck, came Clarke. He drew near the Soviet star, two hands on his stick and, crack, brought down the stick savagely on Kharlamov's right ankle. You see such vicious two-handers, sometimes, when a woodsman swings his axe against a harmless tree.

Clarke's infraction was obvious, even to the incompetent referees, Franz Baader and Joseph Kompalla. They assessed him a two-minute penalty for slashing. They tacked on another 10 minutes for mouthy misconduct when Clarke

profanely complained "Fuck you!" It is a compliment understood in all languages.

Clarke skated to the penalty box. Valery Kharlamov
limped off, grievously wounded, unable to play for the balance of the sixth game or in the seventh game. Canadian
fans, waving their Mike Pearson pennants, began to chant,
"Da, da, Can-a-da! Nyet, nyet, Sov-i-et!" They understood
chopping two-handers to the ankle.

Then the Canadians put it up to Paul Garnet Henderson, a
lean left wing from Lucknow in southwestern Ontario. Henderson scored his first of three game-winning goals and the
Canadians escaped with a 3–2 triumph.

Coach Sinden, smiling slyly, rebuffed notions that Clarke
intended to maim Kharlamov. "Clarke just gave him a little
toe-tickler," Sinden said, fairly straight-faced.

I addressed a statement to Clarke. He was 23 and he had
his dentures back in and he wore his fair hair long, as the
young did in 1972. "Geezus, Bob," I said, "that was a wicked
two-hander you laid on Kharlamov."

Clarke fixed me with a steady blue gaze. "Mr. Beddoes,"
he said, "if I hadn't learned once in a while to lay on a wicked
two-hander, as you put it, I'd never have got out of Flin Flon,
Manitoba." There would be ample reason, shortly down the
NHL road, to ponder Clarke's response. He would lead the
Philadelphia Flyers to back-to-back Stanley Cups, in 1974 and
1975, often leading by laying on the lumber.

There were two days between games, ample time for a
tourist to get in trouble if he had the opportunity. Opportunity did indeed present itself. The press room was on the
20th floor of the Intourist Hotel and, on an off night, a Canadian reporter was working at a typewriter near an open window. The drapes were open.

The telephone rang and the reporter picked it up.
"Hello?" On the other end, a woman's voice said, "Hello.
You Canadian tourist would like some fun?"

The reporter was surprised to hear a Russian speak such
passable English. The stirring in his loins suggested he
would like some fun. Strange town, strange woman, but the
same old familiar notion.

Still, the bold call seemed peculiar. How did she know

where to phone with her enticing offer of commercial companionship? "I live," she said, "in the apartment building across from your hotel. You can come to my place, or I can come to your place."

The reporter, remembering all the warnings about Soviet traps, even sexual traps, decided to be prudent. Suppose she was bugged, in more ways than one? He thoughtfully passed the information along to another jockstrap journalist who, less discriminating, made it with Naughty Nina.

It was at "her place," a small flat which she shared with her parents. She liked pantyhose as a gift, and a bottle of champagne "for to make whoopee." She suggested 20 rubles as the starting price for an assignation. At the Russian rip-off rate at one ruble for $1.30 Canadian, the price per assignation — per piece of assignation, as it were — was roughly $25. Since her parents had the only bedroom, the deed had to be consummated on the kitchen table. The comfort level, getting laid on a kitchen table, is not high.

The comfort level in the seventh game was higher for the Canadians. Minus Kharlamov's speed, the Russians were less imposing. Paul Henderson scored his second game-winning goal in a 4–3 conquest, and the series was tied.

It came snarled to the climactic eighth game, Canada three wins, Russia three wins, one game tied. Foster Hewitt would call Hockey Night in Minsk and he was never in crisper, firmer voice. It happened on September 28, 1972, a snowy Thursday night in Moscow. In Toronto, eight hours behind Moscow time, the telecast began at noon. The largest hockey audience in history, about 15 million in Canada alone, saw on television or heard on radio the epic insignificance.

Kharlamov returned to the Russian roster but, gimpy, he was not much help. Not that the Russians needed help in the first two periods as they rolled to a 5–3 lead. Before the third period, on CBC radio with the late Fred Scambati, I agreed with Howie Meeker that a tie would flatter the Canadians. Team NHL had come a long way, and played for a long time, but defeat loomed.

Early in the third period, in the TV booth, Foster Hewitt was telling Canadians at home: "Pete Mahovlich is going down left wing ... keeps on going into the corner ... is bumped back of the net ... centred in front ... here's Esposito getting it ... They score! Esposito! (Crowd roars) Esposito scores for Canada, from Peter Mahovlich! (Crowd still roaring) If you don't succeed the first time, try, try again!"

Hewitt had shucked objectivity, caught up as an electronic extension of a Canadian crusade. At 12:56 of the third period, Canada behind 5–4, Foster called: "Mishakov at centre knocked the puck back of the Canadian goal ... Park is trying to come out on the left side ... A long pass to Phil Esposito! Going in! He shoots! Oh, right in front of the net! Esposito banged at it! Here's another shot by Cournoyer ... He scores! Canada has tied it up!"

Hewitt looked at the replay on the TV monitor. "Esposito makes an incredible individual effort on this goal! I can't say enough ... Look at him fight for the puck ... and get it back in front of the net after having missed it once himself! ... I believe it's Yvan Cournoyer who gets the goal. ..."

Hewitt had difficulty pronouncing Cournoyer's name throughout the series. It is properly pronounced "Corn-why-aye." Foster called the Montreal road-runner "Ivan Corn-wire."

The score stayed tied 5–5 into the last two minutes. Canadian fans boiled with noise: "Da, da, Can-a-da! Nyet, nyet, Sov-i-et!" Team NHL untied it 6–5 with 34 seconds left in the summit series. Hewitt was on top of the frenzy:

> The Canadian team went into a huddle there, which seems a little unusual ... But they're really fighting ... The puck comes up at centre ice. Vasiliev carries it back into his zone, to Shadrin who missed it ... Peter Mahovlich is at centre, driving into the Soviet zone. Liapkin gets there first. Cornwire just touched it ... Savard, getting it at centre ice, clearing it off a skate ... It goes into the Canadian zone ... Yakushev, a dangerous player, is belted on that play. Cornwire rolled it out, Vasiliev going back to get it ... There's 1:02 left in the game.
>
> A cleared pass on the far side. Liapkin rolled one to

Savard ... Savard clears a pass to Stapleton ... He
cleared to the open wing to Cornwire. Here's a shot! ...
Henderson made a wild stab for it and fell ...

Here's another shot, right in front — they score! Henderson scores for Canada! And the fans and team are
going wild! ... Henderson, right in front of the Soviet
goal with 34 seconds left in the game!

Scott Young wrote it precisely right in *Hello Canada*, his
esteemed biography of Hewitt. Scott wrote, "That was
hockey when we were learning how good the Russians were,
and they were learning how good we were. It was also Foster,
calling that goal by Paul Henderson as it would be heard a
thousand times or more on radio and television specials to
come, a broadcast to remember him by."

Bedlam piled on bellowing in the Luzhniki loony bin.
Canadian imbeciles jeered the beaten Russians, "Da, da,
Can-a-da! Nyet, nyet, Sov-i-et!" The tourniquet of tension
was released. It seemed fitting to describe the chaotic scene
with a continuing half-boob air.

> The handle of the Hammer broke and the Sickle was
> a rusty old jack-knife. Lenin's Tomb trembled as though
> Richard Nixon was selling used Edsels in the Kremlin
> courtyard. All the Smirnoff vodka turned into rancid
> potato mash. All the garlic went greasy in the kolbassa.
> The KGB cops couldn't find the floor if they fell out of bed.
> Lennie Brezhnev's blood turned to cold beet borscht.
>
> All because Team Canada, alias Team NHL or Team
> Ugly, won a cozy little series at the summit in the last 34
> seconds of the last game, 6–5 in the most discussed and
> cussed tournament in hockey history. ...

Paul Henderson said in the carousing Canadian quarters,
"When I scored that final goal, I finally knew what democ-
racy was all about." His fervence would turn in another direction when his hockey career ended in 1980. He became
Reverend Paul Henderson, evangelist.

Phil Esposito, a heretic, was the soul of the Canadian
conquest. He clumped off the ice, sweat coming off his
sweater and face like a black Labrador sloshing out of the

water. He cooled out in the cluttered, jubilant room, posing for pictures, laughing, shaking hands, taking long gulps from a bottle of Coke.

"This was more emotional than winning the Stanley Cup," Esposito said. "A Stanley Cup's for your team and your city. Beating the Russians is for your country."

He reflected on the liveliest hockey adventure his generation will ever know. "What the hell," Esposito said. "We came together as a team, and as a team we had something to prove. We took a lot of booing in Vancouver and a lot of crap in the newspapers. So we just went out and proved how wrong people are about how pro hockey players feel about Canada. We care, some."

Then a Russian player thrust through the crowd elbowing around Esposito and handed Phil a bulky brown box. Viacheslav Anisin, a good young player, had come bearing a gift.

"For you," Anisin said. Esposito was incredulous. "For me?" Phil said. "A present for me? What is it? A Russian time bomb?" He got up, still wearing skates, and strode to a stick rack. "Here," he said, turning to Anisin. "For you, one of my sticks." They shook hands and Anisin left, and Esposito became an exuberant kid on Christmas morning.

"Let's open it," he said, and ripped brown paper off the big brown cardboard box. He reached inside and pulled out a gleaming samovar, the sort of souvenir every tourist wants to lug home from the Soviet Union. It resembed a miniature Stanley Cup.

"What the hell is it?" Esposito demanded. Ken Dryden, the erudite goaltender, told him, "It's a samovar. Excellent for heating hot water for tea. You ought to be proud to get a gift like that."

Esposito was moved up like a bettor who has just won a creamy daily double. "I can't believe it!" he said. "This is the first damn time I got a present from an opposing player! I feel like a chintzy bastard just giving him a stick."

Phil held the samovar, caressing it a little, and kept telling anyone who would listen, "I'll tell you what they call a game like that in Italian. They call it el heart attacko."

A late arrival asked Esposito what his gift was, and Phil

asked Dryden, "What did you say this damn teapot is?"
Dryden said, "A samovar."

"A smimovar," Canada's most valuable player said.

It had been, for all of us, an orgasmic experience, but,
reflecting, we could recall William Buckley's comment on the
nature of games. "If you win a basketball game by 50–30 or a
hockey game 7–3," the American reactionary wrote, "you are
the better team. If you win by a single point, what you have is
two evenly matched teams, one of which is lucky."

Team NHL had been lucky. Canada's hockey civilization
had been barely saved, pro tem. I asked Ballard how he felt,
now the great crusade was finished. "You feel relieved?" I
asked.

"No," Canada's chaperone said. "I feel let down. Now I've
got to go home and face the fucking music."

CHAPTER 14

Millhaven Motel

♦

Ballard appeared for sentencing on the fraud and theft charges in Toronto on October 20, 1972, a rainy fall Friday.

Judge Harry Deyman's courtroom was packed. Ballard, showman still, said, "Jesus, we should have sold tickets." Clerks brought chairs from nearby rooms and sat curious gawkers in every available space, including the jury box.

John J. Robinette, Ballard's counsel, had not called any witnesses for the defence during the trial. This day Robinette called several of Ballard's old friends to testify to his "good character." Ballard sat in the prisoner's dock, tears spilling out of him.

Ballard's advocates pleaded with Judge Deyman for compassion. Richard Meech, a retired lawyer, said, "If wrong has been done, there are so many good deeds in this man to right the record."

Harry Foster, Ballard's boating buddy from younger and happier Sea Flea times, said, "I'm proud to call Harold Ballard my friend." Then Foster wept.

Milt Dunnell, sports editor of *The Toronto Star*, perhaps the most respected Canadian reporter on the jock beat, talked of Ballard as a "soft touch." Dunnell said, "I have never encountered any person in all my years who is more involved in charities in this city. When there were children in hospital who wanted a souvenir, a signed hockey stick or something, there was never a case where you couldn't call Mr. Ballard and get a response."

Jim Coleman of the Southam newspapers, normally the funniest scribe on the beat, set aside laughter. "Ballard," Coleman testified, "does things compulsively for good."

Ballard was endorsed by Jack Dennett, whose remarkable voice resonated on "Hockey Night in Canada" and radio station CFRB. Dennett, on his newscasts at 8 o'clock in the morning, could make the storm clouds rolling up over Georgian Bay sound like the outbreak of a third world war.

Dennett was the only character witness who drew a comment from Crown Attorney Clay Powell, the prosecutor. It was a compliment. Powell said, "My day, Mr. Dennett, doesn't start until I hear you read the news."

Terry Kelly, a lawyer and superfan from Oshawa, recounted Ballard's generosity towards Chevrolet city, the Canadian home of General Motors. "Any time we in Oshawa wanted to raise money for crippled kids," Kelly said, "I'd phone Mr. Ballard and get him to bring the Maple Leafs out to play an exhibition game. We'd draw 4,000 fans and raise $15,000 and Mr. Ballard would say, 'You're not charging enough.'"

The consensus of the character witnesses, Terry Kelly said, was that "Ballard was above jail." Expressions on the faces of Ballard's old retainers were grim. King Clancy, who always seemed to smile, looked in constant pain. After the last witness was heard, Judge Deyman retired to his chambers for 30 minutes.

The judge returned and the 70 people in the cramped courtroom fell silent. Prosecutor Powell had asked for a minimum sentence of two years and a substantial fine. He knew Deyman resented Alan Eagleson interceding on Ballard's behalf so Pal Hal, under indictment, could travel to Russia.

Deyman began, "I'm impressed with the testimony of the character witnesses. I'm aware of Mr. Ballard's age, 69, and his previous good character. But" — the judge sounded grave, speaking to Ballard — "you were in a position of trust and you violated that trust."

J.J. Robinette had said, "A prison term for a man of Mr. Ballard's age is cruel and sadistic . . . Because Mr. Ballard is a man with not many years left . . . a penitentiary term should not be considered."

Judge Deyman disagreed. "Mr. Ballard's crime was not a spur-of-the-moment thing." He chided Ballard. "Your activity in the matter went on for some time. It involved persons under your control, Gardens' employees, and people who did business with the Gardens. . . . A penitentiary term is called for as a deterrent."

Ballard's sons, Bill and Harold Jr., listened intently. The courtroom was so quiet you could have heard a puck drop, "so quiet," Terry Kelly of Oshawa said, "it was like waiting for Arnold Palmer to putt."

Judge Deyman said, "You will be sentenced ... to three years in the Kingston Penitentiary ... three years for fraud ... and three years for theft ... both terms to run concurrently ..."

Ballard stood silently in the prisoner's dock as Judge Deyman pronounced sentence. Deyman neglected to say, as is usually said by judges at the conclusion of a case, "Remove the prisoner." A gray-haired sheriff, across the courtroom, waggled a finger at Ballard, "Come with me."

Ballard turned to his sons and shook their hands. "Take care," he said. Then he joined the sheriff and left for the cell where he was held before departing for, as he called it, "the Crowbar Motel" in Kingston. Bill Ballard, leaving, slammed the courtroom door, shocked that his father really was going to jail to serve, at least, one year of the three-year term.

Kingston is an antique town at the eastern end of Lake Ontario, a pressed rose in the Canadian history book. The morning sun slants across old rooftops and picks up the black barrels of cold cannon in the parks around.

The cannon are still ready but the men have gone. They left in 1758, after the British sacked the French outpost of Fort Frontenac and renamed it Kingston for George III of England. Some of the troops in the battle are still in plots of ground, resting. For a brief period, from 1841 to 1844, Kingston was the capital of Upper Canada. Its revered institutions are the International Hockey Hall of Fame, Queen's University, the Royal Military College and the forbidding federal pen, Crowbar Motel.

Ballard was driven to the pen by King Clancy on October 21, 1972, an unusual circumstance. Convicts, as a rule, are driven to Kingston by the van load. He was received by Gene McNeil, a muscular admittance officer. "Ballard got the same treatment from me as any other con," McNeil said. "I photographed him and took a set of his fingerprints. Then I asked him to take his clothes off and bend over."

"What the hell am I bending over for?" Ballard asked.

"Routine, routine," Gene McNeil said. "I've got to check if you've got anything up your backside that you shouldn't have up there." It was an indignity Ballard could not avoid.

He was transferred in a few weeks from Kingston to Millhaven, 16 miles west as the slapshot flies. Every week, King Clancy and Jim Gregory, manager of the Maple Leafs, drove 153 miles from Toronto for long visits. Often, late in the year, the Upper Canadian countryside is stark with December. The sky is frequently of dirty slate and the wind off Lake Ontario whips cold through dead trees and live wires.

A half mile beyond the village of Millhaven is the medium security prison on a rocky bluff overlooking the lake. Every room has a splendid view. A paved road curves through outcroppings of dark stone, remnants of the Canadian Shield, to a complex of squat one-story buildings. The complex is called The Annex.

Ballard was assigned, in The Annex, to the prison stores as an accountant. A guard solid as a tree trunk said, "Hi, Mr. Ballard. Remember me? I had a brief shot in the National Hockey League."

"No kidding," Ballard said.

"Not kidding," Joe Levandoski said. "I was with New York Rangers, 25 years ago."

There are those in the Canadian penal system who believe Ballard got a better break than most cons. One penal official told me, "I don't think Ballard did hard time at all. I hear he could send out for Chinese food and stuff like that when he wanted to."

Clay Powell, the prosecutor, does not believe Ballard was catered to. "It's absolute crap," Powell insists, "that stuff about Millhaven being a picnic resort. Nobody did harder time than Ballard."

It was hard in the sense that, for the first time in his hurly-burly life, he was restricted. Containment didn't completely curb his hearty clap-'em-on-the-back style. He tabulated equipment such as doors and windows in the Millhaven stores, and wondered about the irony of it all. "They got me doing accounting," Ballard said, "which they got me locked up for not doing properly at Maple Leaf Gardens."

Millhaven has rarely had a more celebrated inmate, with

the possible exceptions of the odd big-time stock thief or kidnapper. The other cons naturally wanted to know what is wrong with the Leafs under Ballard's supervision. "We don't have enough policemen," Ballard said, heh, heh. "And you guys know about policemen."

Visitors to Millhaven were screened through an assistant warden named Weaver, a husky middle-linebacker type, amicable but not especially helpful to the press. "You can visit Ballard as friend," Weaver told me. "But if you're operating as a newspaperman, and write something after you leave, we'd be most unhappy. We'd cancel your visiting privileges." Not long after I visited Pal Hal, late in 1972, an order came from penitentiary authorities that no journalists were allowed to see him.

A federal statute in Canada permits a prisoner "reasonable time to wind up his business affairs." This allowed Ballard to use the telephone for long-distance conversations with his colleagues in the Gardens, with his son Bill and King Clancy and general manager Jim Gregory.

The federal statute was not designed for winding up a multimillion-dollar operation such as the Gardens; it was meant for enterprises more on the order of hot-sausage stands outside the Gardens. Early in 1973, Ballard was denied easy access to the Millhaven telephone. Other cons were bitching about his "privileged treatment." Coach John McLellan steered the Leafs out of the playoffs in 1972–73 without Ballard's long-distance advice.

One prison official said, "Ballard's a real hot potato. He's up for parole in the fall of 1973, but that doesn't mean he'll be paroled then. The federal authorities in Ottawa aren't going to be in a position of being criticized because Ballard, a rich man, gets soft considerations. So far as we're concerned, he's to be treated like any other criminal."

Ballard was an expansive host when he had visitors. He showed friends around the tidy Millhaven quarters, somewhat more Spartan than his palatial office in the Gardens, which resembles an ostentatious vestige from "Ali Baba and the Forty Thieves."

"This," he'd say, "is the library. And next door, here, is the television room. We get the hockey games on color TV." He'd point out the swimming pool and say, a little wistfully, "And out there, just outside that window, we've got a pond which we're going to use for a hockey rink when it freezes over."

The Millhaven hockey team, he guessed, would not play any "away games," since freedom stops at the front door. Medium security still means security. Out of deference to the principal guest, in 1972–73, the prison team was called the Millhaven Maple Leafs. Harold said he was the icemaker.

Visitors would leave Ballard his favorite fruit, boxes of the creamiest chocolates, and depart down the curving road to Toronto. "Good luck," he'd say. "See you."

Ballard, at 69, received no female visitors. Other inmates were luckier; a visitor passing through the prison parlor noticed a couple in passionate embrace, oblivious to everything except the pelvic thrusts that remind a man of the sex he is missing on the outside.

Harold would sometimes slip a letter out with a friend, for delivery to someone in Toronto who might attempt "to get me sprung." There was no evidence that he was mistreated in Millhaven, but incarceration did not make him a fervent fan of the Canadian prison system. He believed he was "a tortured old man unable to conduct his business by phone."

"Incompetent" was Ballard's descriptive for the way he perceived the management of Millhaven, the sort of appraisal a wealthy private businessman can expect to give a government-operated clink. His entreaties to his friends in the Toronto media to "pull strings for me in Ottawa" failed to get him a reprieve through the end of 1972.

There was a terse statement from prison officials on December 11, 1972. "There is no way," the statement said, "that Mr. Ballard will be allowed out for Christmas." It was a blow, a jolting eight inches to the midsection of a man who always makes a big deal out of Christmas. After his wife died, he made a family habit of entertaining his sons and their friends on December 25, an ample chef cooking and carving turkey. Ballard would play Father Christmas by sending hampers to the Salvation Army. He lavished television sets and other presents upon reporters who had no regard for their self-respect.

Those who believed a TV set is too much to be a gift and

too little to be a bribe used to receive armloads of roses and poinsettias for their wives. The inscription on the cards always was, "God bless you – Harold."

Ballard rarely mentioned his dead hockey partner by name, but he was certain he was doing time for himself and Stafford Smythe. "All my troubles," he said, "were caused by The Other Guy."

He laughed when I told him, "Okay, we'll forget the 'Gold Dust Twins' as the title of the book you want written. We'll call your story 'Fat Harold and the Other Guy.'"

There was a sick sort of laughter in the joke prevalent in the Canadian sporting set as 1972 turned into 1973. Macabre wits were saying that the ideal Christmas gift for a man who has everything is a set of license plates made by Harold Ballard.

He received the occasional weekend pass and, on one of them, attended the graduation of Harold Jr. from Waterloo Lutheran University. He was photographed standing between Harold and his other son, Bill, all of them beaming. *The Toronto Star* noted that "Ballard had the photograph taken and distributed to the newspapers."

Harold was tight with his boys then, particularly with Bill, who seemed a chip off the old block, an "heir-head," in the felicitous phrase of Toronto writer Paul Kaihla. Bill studied law at Waterloo Lutheran University, now called Sir Wilfred Laurier. He was a BMOC (Big Man on Campus) as president of the students' council and centre on the football team. He completed a four-year honors' degree in three years.

Bill moved smoothly from Waterloo to Osgoode Hall Law School in Toronto, again a BMOC. He was captain of the football team at York University and top tongue on the Osgoode Hall debating team. He articled with the reputable law firm of Cassels, Brock and graduated magna cum laude from his bar examinations.

Bill said, in 1987, "Yes, I was sort of your all-Canadian boy. And then it all went to shit!" He said it in mock wonder to Paul Kaihla in *T.O. Magazine*, crackling, guffawing, a Ballard.

Bill was 25 when his father was sent to jail. He insisted, "The evidence was all circumstantial. My dad was given his holiday because he failed to pay the Caesar when the Caesar

wanted his money." Bill wept when sentence was pronounced, unable to reconcile the father he called "H.E." with
the word "criminal."

H.E. trusted Bill as a loyal family agent to guard Harold's
interests. "I was sent to the Gardens," Bill says, "to be vice-
president of corporate development. I was known to everyone whispering in the halls as 'the boss's son.'"

The boss made more news for the papers when he
received a pass from Millhaven to announce the signing of
the Leafs' top junior draftee, in the Hot Stove Lounge, on
July 3, 1973. The draftee was Lanny King McDonald from the
Alberta boonie of Hanna.

We didn't know then that McDonald would become what
cliché-ridden hockey scouts call "an impact player," or that
he would cultivate a lush mustache suitable for housing a
family of great horned owls. Sports writers were more interested in Ballard and life in the Crowbar Motel.

Harold did not disappoint. He put everybody on, as his
wont. "Boys," he said, "Millhaven is a country club. You
never saw such grub. Thick tenderloin steaks three or four
times a week. Luscious pork chops. Baked potatoes with
sour cream so thick you can dive into it. Apple pie à la mode,
all you want."

It was pure put-on and most of us, jock journalists aware
of Ballard's kidding, played the story as put-on. Editors of
The Toronto Star, the biggest boobs in Canada that day, missed
the joke. A *Star* headline on July 4, 1973, blared "Ballard Gets
Steak in Jail – Can't Wait To Get Back."

There was a certain amount of hell to pay when copies of
the *Star* landed on the desks of members of parliament in
Ottawa. Penal powers were asked embarrassing questions.
The National Parole Board hastily indicated Ballard would
not get an early release. He would have to wait until he was
eligible for parole, on October 20, 1973.

Ian Deans, a humorless New Democrat and wooly-haired
member of the Ontario Legislature, demanded that Ballard
be removed "from the Millhaven Correctional Institute and
transferred to the Kingston Penitentiary. Make it tougher for
him."

There were letters. The *Star* was full of expressions of

outrage in its Voice of the People on July 11, 1973. It was really April Fools' Day: the vox populi popped off, steaming, refusing to believe Ballard had been clowning.

One R.J. Doggett of Agincourt, Ontario, described by the *Star* as "Citizen," wrote: " . . . Rather than posing as a homecoming war hero, it would be more to Mr. Ballard's credit if he practiced a little humility . . . if he knows what the word means!"

Don Young of the old yuppie suburb of Don Mills wrote: " . . . Although crime doesn't pay, Ballard proves it provides a very luxurious living." Margaret Archibald of Gore's Landing, Ontario, was incensed. " . . . Harold Ballard's pleasures in the culinary and sportive arrangements provided him by government appal me. His incarceration on an indictment of outrageous fraud upon a gullible populace is represented as a rest cure few could ever achieve . . ."

Eric Carr of Toronto pounded the rich man-poor man theme. " . . . Harold Ballard is a thief – a convicted thief. But he did it big and he is a rich man. Let him do his time in luxury. Joe Blow stole a couple hundred bucks, but he's poor so he does his two years in the pen – no luxury. His crime – poverty."

Scott Young, in *The Globe and Mail*, wrote on July 12, 1973:

> I used to wonder who went around the country painting roadside rocks with the message: "Repent and ye shall be saved." Thank goodness now I know – Ian Deans of the NDP. Of course, he represented ethical paragons among all parties, letters-to-the-editor writers and editorialists (including *The Globe and Mail's*), when . . . he confessed himself maddened by Harold Ballard's apparent jollity during a recent day off from Millhaven. That's where Ballard is doing three years for fraud and theft.
>
> Deans has urged that Ballard be dispatched to Kingston, to make him whine a little. No lashes, though. Wonder why. I mean, if a guy's public manner in a time of intense distress is just too damn jaunty for the New Democrats, you'd think they wouldn't stop at merely having him transferred to another institution.

> . . . Has it ever occurred to, say, Ian Deans, that one of the world's easiest put-ons is for a person to act the way the world hopes and expects he will act? When he does that, no one questions whether penitence is only skin-deep. But when he endures his punishment and hides the scars with bravado, who is wise enough to see that could be a put-on, too?
>
> No, repent and ye shall be saved. Vengeance is mine, sayeth the Lord, and Ian Deans.

Shafted, the air let out of him, Ian Deans of the NDP was not heard to speak about Harold Ballard again.

The truth is that Ballard hated jail. Incarceration was impossible for a free-wheeling swashbuckler who had always been a law unto himself. Laughter merely masked how he felt.

A fellow inmate related how Ballard felt in a letter to Bill Ballard, written in Millhaven on July 9, 1973. Bill, looking for older friends that summer, shared the letter with me.

Leigh G. Simms wrote from the Millhaven Annex:

> I'm sure your Father would never tell you about the frustrations and tensions he goes through daily. Because of who he is and the constant publicity surrounding him, he gets few moments of peace. He could never miss a newspaper article mentioning him because someone will be sure to point it out, and go out of their way to do so. The same goes for news broadcasts. He is the most generous of people, and is taken advantage of outrageously. Even his modest attempts to make his quarters more comfortable are disrupted by inmates and staff alike.
>
> These things are merely the tip of the iceberg because the harassment is so constant that I marvel at his patience and fortitude. I would have gone around the bend long ago. I am an "old con" and I guess I have seen it all, which is a fact I'm not proud of. However, your Father has made me realize that there are after all real men left in this world, because this is a man.

The old con finished:

There are many more things I could tell you, Mr. Ballard, concerning the strength of your Dad, but it would be a book. What I want to say in a nutshell is that he is going through a private Hell with great courage. . . . Should you ever find him a little testy or depressed, understand that he is currently living a life that few men in his position could tolerate, and living it with honor. Outwardly he is still the same hearty, bluff and sometimes arrogant Harold Ballard of Maple Leaf Gardens, but inwardly he is often a hurt man, and he can't tell anybody.

Your Dad is not going to cry on anyone's shoulder, so I thought it was time to expose him for the basically fine man that he is. Despite everything he's going to make it through these next few months to parole. . . .

The letter was a decent expression of empathy with a fellow con, but Leigh Simms was something of a suckfish for Ballard, a sycophant. He was a cook and Harold spent time in the Millhaven kitchen. Paul Henry, a psychologist at Millhaven, remembers Simms as "Harold's personal cook. He looked after him unbelievably."

One of Ballard's charms is that he does not forget favors. When both returned to civilian status, Harold arranged for Simms to get a job in the kitchen of a Toronto hotel. Rehabilitation did not take; in short order the short-order cook messed up the job.

Harold was released on parole on October 19, 1973, transferred from Millhaven to Montgomery Centre, a halfway house in Toronto. He had served 364 days of penalty for himself and the ghost of his late partner. He refused to feel guilt. He told me, on his first day back running the Gardens, "Any infinitesimal guilt I felt disappeared when I signed the cheque paying back money to the Gardens."

I said, "There's only one thing I want to know. Were you really the icemaker for the Millhaven hockey team on that pond back of the jail?" Harold said, joshing "Yes, and I was a fucking good iceman."

I persisted, "So what did you do in the spring, when the ice in the pool melted?" Harold said, "You won't believe this, but they got a lot of fucking ducks and geese at Millhaven. When the ice melted, I took care of the ducks and geese."

Pal Hal had set me up for my own little joke. "Then," I said, "we've got a new title for the Ballard book. 'Bird Man of Millhaven.'" He laughed. "I'll kid a lot in the years I've got left. Everything fucking starts now. I cried a lot in the can, but I'm never gonna cry again."

He has not, but spinning out the last years of a life is hard for a man who cannot weep.

CHAPTER 15

The Locust Years

♦

Historians recall 1973 as the year when U.S. investigators found that Richard Nixon tried to steal a country. Secretariat, a mighty running chestnut, became the first thoroughbred to win the Triple Crown in 25 years, since Citation in 1948. Billie Jean King beat Bobby Riggs in a ballyhooed battle of the tennis sexes.

At Maple Leaf Gardens, the world swung on a lesser hinge. Harold Ballard was back and barging about his empire. One of his courtiers, publicist Stan Obodiac, issued a fulsome press release to herald the second coming of Harold.

Obodiac was a decent man, a Saskatchewan native hooked on the Maple Leaf dream, scorned and underpaid because he cared about the team as a patriotic patch on the Canadian fabric. Journalist Charles Davies told Bill Houston of the time he was interviewing Ballard for an article in *Executive* magazine. During the interview, Obodiac brought some papers for Ballard to sign.

"Hello, Stanley," Ballard said merrily. "What have you fucked up today?" Obodiac deflected the barb with a wan smile. "The day's not over yet, Mr. Ballard," he said.

Ballard chuckled right along. "Well," he said, "we'll give you a few more hours to see what you can do." Obodiac took the taunts and made excuses for the Leafs until he succumbed to cancer five years ago, driven forever to believe that the Leafs are Canada's dream team. They aren't any longer, but the dreams of Stan Obodiac's generation die hard.

Ballard is captive of a dream, too, still not realized, maybe never to be realized. He wants to win the Stanley Cup with himself listed as sole owner. He was part of four Cups in the sixties when he shared ownership with Staff Smythe and John Bassett. Just one time he'd like to own a Cup winner alone but, at 86, time is escaping him.

The Leafs have not won the Stanley Cup since 1967. Once

only under Ballard's imperial aegis have they made it to the
Final Four, in 1977–78.

Apart from 1977–78, Ballard's Leafs have spent their
hockey careers in foreplay, seemingly unaware that there is
no consummation until the Stanley Cup is won. In the 22
seasons since the NHL expanded, in 1967–68, Leaf teams
have missed the playoffs six times. Other seasons, with the
exception of 1977–78, could have been written off by Joel, a
minor prophet in the Old Testament, as "the years the locust
hath eaten." They made the play-offs those seasons, but were
eliminated early.

The fault was not entirely Ballard's. The fault was in the
men he hired, and he must take responsibility for hiring
them. He did interfere with the Leaf management, but there
were times when he did not interfere enough. He permitted
Punch Imlach, his general manager in 1979–80, to fire Lanny
McDonald in a spiteful trade. Ballard did not intrude, as he
should have, to keep a bonus right wing who pursued his
Maple Leaf dream with power and passion. Imlach wanted
to dispose of Darryl Sittler, the Leaf captain, but could not
because of a no-trade clause in Sittler's contract. Piqued,
Imlach got rid of McDonald, Sittler's best friend.

Jim Gregory generally managed the Leafs from 1969 for 10
years, up to the front office from the junior Marlboros, generally competent. He left the Leafs unwillingly in 1979, ultimately to become vice-president of hockey operations for the
NHL.

Ballard may have regarded Gregory as the stickboy Gregory used to be, but permitted him to make decisions damag-
ing to the long-range chances for the Toronto team. Harold
was at the Toronto table during the 1969 draft when Gregory,
advised by Staff Smythe and the Leaf scouts, ignored Bob
Clarke, the best junior player in Canada. All other NHL
teams passed on Clarke, too, because he is diabetic, but
Toronto fans care only about one NHL team, the Leafs. We
expect a team that has won 11 Stanley Cups to be more
sophisticated than the New-Jerseys-come-lately.

Passing on a Bob Clarke, as Jim Gregory did on behalf of
the Leafs in 1969, is equivalent to gambling with the rent
money. Ballard, also a diabetic, should have told his associ-

ates that Clarke, with care, could be as strong as any pro in the NHL. He did not, and the Leafs lost the most militant NHL pro of the seventies.

Gregory did draft wisely in other years. He took Darryl Sittler and Errol Thompson in 1970, George Ferguson in 1972, Lanny McDonald in 1973. His dice blew cold in the junior lottery of 1974. The best player available, several scouts agreed, was Bryan Trottier, an industrious centre from the Lethbridge Broncos. Gregory chose Jack Valiquette, who turned out to be inconsequential. Trottier became what hackneyed writers call "a franchise player," the pith of four consecutive Stanley Cups won by the New York Islanders.

The Leafs made a classic drafting goof in 1977. Mike Bossy was a flashy junior shooter from Montreal, responsible for 154 goals in his last two seasons with the Laval Nationals. The rap on Bossy was that he could not check, although a corollary of that deficiency is that a player does not have to check much if he has the puck as often as Bossy had it. The Leafs had two choices in the first round of 18. Bossy was still available when Gregory drafted left winger John Anderson, number 11, and defenceman Trevor Johanson, number 12. New York Islanders snared Bossy as number 15, the biggest steal since the Chicago Black Hawks won a trifling 14 games in 1937–38 and swiped the Stanley Cup from the Leafs, who won 24.

Bossy, playing right wing for Bryan Trottier, contributed conspicuously to the Islanders' four Stanley Cups. It is only slightly hyperbolic to say he outscored Anderson and Johanson, over his career, in one period.

In 1976 the Leafs had the wisdom to draft Randy Robert Carlyle, a smart cruising defenceman from Sudbury. Unwisely, in 1978, Gregory traded Carlyle and forward George Ferguson to the Pittsburgh Penguins for defenceman Dave Burrows. Carlyle became an all-star defenceman while Burrows' principal skill was to check hard, one-on-one, in the corners. He was never worth as much to the Leafs as Carlyle would have been.

Jim Gregory did not make these grievous decisions alone. He had counsel from King Clancy, the Toronto scouting staff and, perhaps, Ballard. There is no evidence that Ballard was

critical of Gregory's personnel moves; Conn Smythe might
have used Gregory's head as a bowling ball. Gregory was not
helped through the early seventies when Ballard was a dino-
saur thrashing around in the swamp in a war for players with
the bumptious World Hockey Association. Two big leagues
were good only for the players; the owners lost money and
the fans saw diluted talent masquerading as big league.
There was a premium on lunch-bucket mediocrities.

Ballard refused to pay to keep Bernard Marcel Parent from
Montreal, about to be visible in 1973 as the best goaltender on
earth. The Leafs were paying Parent $25,000 a year when the
Miami Screaming Eagles lured him to their Florida nest for
about $150,000 a year for five years.

Ballard was certain that Parent's lawyer, agile Howard Cas-
per of Philadelphia, was bluffing. Ballard told Casper, "If
Parent can get that kind of money elsewhere, let him go get it.
I won't hold him back. Fuck him."

Freed, Parent lammed to the World Hockey Association, to
the Miami Screaming Eagles, who died on the nest. He
landed in Philadelphia, where his disciplined stand-up
goalkeeping combined with Bob Clarke's pugnacity to
anchor Stanley cup teams for the Flyers in 1974 and 1975.

Ballard thumbed his nose at other Leaf defectors — at Jim
Harrison, Brad Selwood, Rick Ley and Paul Henderson — all
of whom earned more in the WHA than Pal Hal was prepared to pay in the NHL.

Harassed or not by the owner, goofs or not by himself,
Gregory assembled a reputable team for Red Kelly to coach.
Ballard was enamoured of the fastidious Kelly, who won four
Stanley Cups in Detroit as an all-star defenceman and four
more in Toronto as a diligent left wing and centre. No player
outside of the Montreal Canadiens won more than Kelly's
eight championship rings in 20 seasons.

By 1975–76 Jim Gregory had reconstructed the Leafs to
respectability. Sittler, Jack Valiquette and Stan Weir were
young down centre. Sittler formed a swift, high-scoring line
with Lanny McDonald and Errol Thompson, who produced
43 goals. Brian Glennie, Ian Turnbull, Bob (Waldo) Neely and
Borje Salming made an authentic defence. Tiger Williams
and Kurt Walker led the assault troops.

Ballard's opinions were sharply divided on the two Swedes on the Toronto roster, Salming and forward Inge Hammarstrom, a fast pacifist. Harold mentioned on the "Overtime" post-game program that he "would trade Salming for God."

"What about God and two draft choices?" murmured Dave Hodge, the host. "I'd consider it," Harold said. He despised Hammarstrom, whom he ridiculed as "a chicken Swede." He said, "You could send Hammarstrom into a corner with six eggs in his pocket and he wouldn't break any of them."

Tiger Williams revealed in his self-serving autobiography, *Tiger*, how to handle Ballard. The Leafs had lost a game and the warring Williams chewed his temper. Ballard said, "You're nothing but a godamned little stubble jumper from Saskatchewan." Tiger snapped back, "That's better than being a fat bastard from Ontario."

Williams said, "After I told Ballard off, we got along fine. If you put your tail between your legs, Ballard would be disgusted. You had to show him you had balls. If you didn't, he'd drive you out of Toronto and maybe even the league. He did that to Inge Hammarstrom."

Williams was cut from a piece of Ballard's carny heart. He shot bears for pastime, with a bow and arrow to give the bear a fighting chance. "I promised Harold the hide of the first bear I killed," Williams said. "He was delighted to put it in his office when I took it to the Gardens." Tiger's bear still lies in Harold's office, growling at strangers.

There was excitement in the spring of 1976 when the Leafs collided with the intimidating Cup defenders from Philadelphia. Those Flyers were called the Broad Street Bullies, as though they'd been weaned on knuckle-dusters on Philadephia's main street.

They bore the nicknames of terrorists — "The Hammer" Dave Schultz, "Killer" Don Saleski, "Mad Dog" Bob Kelly. "Travel in a straight line," Philadelphia coach Fred Shero advised them, "and arrive angry." Apprehensive players visiting the Flyer zoo, the Spectrum, were inclined to come down with what Ballard called "that fucking Philadelphia flu."

The Flyers, at home for the first two games of a best-of-

seven series, out-muscled the Leafs. In Toronto, the Leafs
muscled up themselves to win games three and four. Lumbering Curt Walker lowered his own hammer on The Hammer Schultz. Before they were parted, Walker spit derisively
and unsanitarily in Schultz's face.

Tiger Williams tangled with Jack McIlhargey, another "ver-
ray parfit gentil knight" who always mislaid his manners
when he put on his skates. Mel Bridgman beat up Borje
Salming. Maple Leaf fans, normally passive, pelted the team
with old rubbers and tennis balls.

Sleepy Roy McMurtry, Ontario's top cop as Attorney General, ordered common assault charges laid against Mad Dog
Kelly, Killer Saleski, Joe Watson and Mel Bridgman. Watson
was also charged with employing his hockey stick as a dangerous weapon against a Metro Toronto policeman.

Ed Snider, owner of the Philadelphia franchise, blamed
Ballard for McMurtry's intervention. Ballard scoffed, "That
just shows Snider knows fuck-all about a tough game." The
Leafs, after fighting back and tying the series in Toronto, then
lost the fifth game in Philadelphia.

It is a Flyer habit, in Philadelphia, to resurrect Kate Smith
to sing "God Bless America" before vital games. Coach Red
Kelly decided to match gimmick for gimmick before the sixth
game in Toronto.

Kelly hired a pyramid specialist from the University of
Toronto to build five pyramids and placed them under the
Leafs' players' bench. He lined them up with the magnetic
north. Then a bigger pyramid-shape was dangled from the
ceiling in the dressing room; if a player sat under it, he was
supposed to gain scoring strength. The entire caper cost
$25,000.

It seemed bucks well spent when captain Sittler sat under
the pyramid, absorbed strange waves of energy and went out
and scored five goals in an 8–5 upset of Philadelphia.

In the seventh and final game, in Philadelphia, pyramid
power was beaten by the powerful pipes of Kate Smith. It
was a moral victory for the Leafs to carry the fearsome Flyers
to the limit, but moral victories only put fur coats on bookmakers' wives.

Pyramid power could not save Red Kelly's job. Ballard

THE LOCUST YEARS 219

released him before the next season began. Tiger Williams said, "I'm not too sure what happened to the pyramids. I think we burned the bastards."

Bill Ballard remained a Gardens' vice-president when his father returned from Millhaven's post-graduate school. He defended the senior Ballard against Establishment figures who renounced Harold as a "loud crass act." Bill saw the monied maulies of the Eatons and Bassetts backing the clumsy attempt of the Smythes to buy Harold out of the Gardens in 1971-72.

Bill mentioned to writer Paul Kaihla, "H.E. said, 'Fuck this shit.' My Dad was not going to hand over the Gardens to the Upper Canada College set just because they had little crests on their jackets. Whose platoon would you rather be in: Harold Ballard's or John Craig Eaton's? I know where I'd go."

Bill strode in Pal Hal's platoon, but began to march to his own drummer. There has been some take-charge in him since he was nine years old and rescued a younger child from Mimico Creek, which meanders near the Ballard home in Etobicoke. Bill earned his first dollar for saving the toddler.

In the Gardens, Bill made his first overtures to gaining control of the rock music industry in Canada. He and a bright Gardens' accomplice, Peter Larson, made a deal with two equally adept youthful promoters, Michael Cohl and David Wolinsky.

Paul Kaihla reported on the merger: "Cohl and Wolinsky had an upstart company, Cymba Productions, running 30 concerts a year out of a two-room office above the China House Restaurant on Eglinton Avenue. In August, 1973, Concert Productions International [CPI] was formed as a Gardens' subsidiary with Bill Ballard as chairman, Larson, Cohl and Wolinsky as partners. The four bought CPI from the Gardens in 1974; Larson sold his share in 1977. Using the leverage Maple Leaf Gardens gave it, CPI soon signed a deal with CNE Stadium, formed an alliance with Montreal promoter Donald K. Donald and bought into Vancouver's Perryscope Productions. Now, if a major act wanted to tour Canada, they had to talk to Bill Ballard and Michael Cohl."

The Ballard grip on the Gardens gave CPI strength. Other

promoters were shut out from an arena that can hold 19,000
zonked-out zealots of the rock-is-cock persuasion.

Pal Hal scoffed at Bill establishing his own turf. He called
his first-born "a dope" and, in the presence of old-retainer
George Armstrong, "a stupid fucking asshole." Their family
feud erupted in the Hot Stove Lounge one winter midnight
in 1976.

Harold returned from a game in Detroit to find a reception
for horse-show riders shaking the chandeliers. He saw Bill
and came uncorked. He yelled, "What the hell are you doing
here, Bill? This isn't your reception. Get outta here!"

Bill was embarrassed. He burst out of the Hot Stove
Lounge, rushed up to his father's office, and began to trash it.
They quarrelled at the top of their voices. Bill resigned three
days later as vice-president in charge of corporate development in the Gardens.

The love-hate relationship did not extend to Harold heav-
ing Bill out of the Etobicoke home. Bill lived in Woodycrest
1941 with his wife, Dutch-born beauty Renee Belonje, and
their small daughter until the spring of 1989. Then, not
exactly slumming, Bill bought a mansion in Rosedale, a rich
Toronto enclave where the residents manage to job along on
several million soggy coconuts a year.

In the hockey department, in the spring of 1977, Red Kelly
kept hearing rumors that he would be replaced as Maple Leaf
coach by Roger Neilson, considered a genius among junior
hockey coaches.

Harold has difficulty firing people face to face, as though
tinged by remorse at dismissing someone he hired and
admired. Ballard's announcement sought to ease Kelly's
pain, and his own: "Red's been bothered by a bad back for
months. It's getting worse. I couldn't afford to take a chance if
he needed surgery and was out for three months. If he had
been in good health, I'd have rehired him. But his contract
was over and his health made the decision easier."

Within days, Roger Neilson confirmed the rumors. He
became the twelfth coach in Leaf history under peculiar circumstances. Manager Jim Gregory told him he'd be paid
about $40,000 a year and to "expect at least one crisis a week."
Gregory said, "Harold will blab to the papers about trades.

THE LOCUST YEARS   221

He'll ridicule the players. And don't mention to anyone you're going to coach the Leafs. Let Harold do it, when he gets back from out of town."

Neilson had been a high-school teacher and, for 10 years, coach of the Peterborough Petes in the junior Ontario Hockey League. Bill Houston wrote, "Neilson earned the reputation of being an innovator and motivator and of being a shrewd manipulator behind the bench. In the summer of 1976, the Leafs and Chicago Black Hawks hired him to coach their Central Hockey League affiliate, the Dallas Black Hawks. The Leafs told Neilson the chances of him moving up to the NHL, presumably with them, were very good."

Neilson privately agreed to join the Leafs in the early summer of 1977, then flew to Nigeria to join a friend, Al Dunford, for a vacation in northern Africa and Europe. Dunford was from Peterborough and had helped Neilson with statistics and videotapes when Neilson guided the Petes. Dunford had been teaching in Nigeria for two years.

They travelled through Nigeria and Egypt, then to Austria. Neilson wondered if his appointment as Leaf coach had been announced and, in Vienna, sought a Canadian newspaper.

In the June 29, 1977 edition of the *Globe*, Neilson saw a headline in the sports section: "Roger Neilson Takes On Leafs Coaching Task." Ballard had called the Toronto media a few days after Neilson left Canada.

The first paragraph of the *Globe* story was golly-gee-whiz adventurous: "The telephone jangled beside Harold Ballard at 7:45 yesterday morning. South Africa calling. At the very end of the line was a man who said he could coach Toronto Maple Leafs . . . From Johannesburg, Roger Neilson said yes to Ballard's job offer."

It was pure fantasy. In Western Canada, the yarn would be dismissed in a pungent prairie colloquialism, "Don't eat that, Elmer. That's horseshit." Neilson had been nowhere near Johannesburg. Neilson had not talked to anyone in the Leaf organization since he sealed his deal with Manager Jim Gregory.

Ballard peddled the same brand of bafflegab to *The Toronto Sun*. "I could hear Neilson as clearly as if he were in Cookstown," Harold marvelled. "He talked about a long-term contract and I told him he could have one for three, four or five years if he really wanted it. . . ."

The Toronto Star, according to Bill Houston, was set to cover the Neilson story in all-embracing *Star* fashion. The *Star* pondered sending hockey writer Frank Orr, presumably in a trench coat, to locate the Leaf coach in the deepest African bush. Orr would have said, "Roger Neilson, I presume?" Shades of Henry M. Stanley finding missionary David Livingstone in Ujiji on Lake Tanganyika on October 28, 1871.

Ballard's scam was harmless enough, in keeping with his credo that "bullshit baffles brains." He knew he could sell many members of the Toronto media all the cactus rights in Lake Ontario and they would buy his deal retail. A changing of the media guard would vary that when young terrier skeptics began to yap on the hockey beat.

Roger Neilson, returned from non-darkest Africa, provided Ballard with the best one-season coaching job Harold has had since assuming full control of the Gardens. Neilson used videotapes to show players where they played well and where they erred.

Toronto newspapers began calling Neilson "Captain Video." His assistant, Al Dunford, was assigned to handle details such as travel plans. Ballard dubbed Dunford "Cruise Commander" or, more often, "Fucking Cruise Commander."

The 1977–78 schedule moved briskly into December before Ballard had his first major rift with a prominent member in the Toronto hockey press, Frank Orr of the *Star*. They had been intimates on the road, the tall, weedy Orr often strolling miles with the peripatetic Ballard. Pal Hal chuckled at Orr's zinging one-line gags.

Then, on December 10, 1977, Orr wrote a column mildly deploring Ballard's intervention in the duties of Manager Jim Gregory. Orr wrote, in part " . . . Gregory is almost the forgotten man around Maple Leaf Gardens . . . surrounded on all sides by owner Harold Ballard, who's busy making Hall of Fame contributions to hockey, such as refusing to announce Gordie Howe's 1,000th career goal to the Gardens' fans."

Orr added, "When a man works for Ballard, he does his job with as little fuss as possible. Every day there's a crisis or a

hassle . . . Ballard's riding herd on the operation all the time
. . . and the public knocks he's delivered against some of the
team's athletes have made Gregory's job even more difficult."

Ballard's response was to cut Orr cruelly. He began telling
others that Orr was "a homosexual." He claimed Orr loitered
outside the St. Charles Tavern on Yonge Street "looking for
little boys." The St. Charles is a hangout for homosexuals on
the make for an all-male one-night stand.

Reporters and commentators are shamelessly used by promoters as conduits to brainwash the public. Those who balk
at being so used may find themselves excluded from off-the-
record briefings and subject to savage whispering campaign
attacks.

Ballard's attack did not harm Orr professionally; he
stepped up his criticism in the *Star* after he heard, second
hand, Ballard's slanders. It bothered Orr privately, and especially his wife because they are practicing heterosexuals.
Should Frank ever venture into the St. Charles Tavern, it will
be to buy a beer, not a boy.

I asked Orr, during the preparation of this memoir, if he
had the first paragraph in his head for Ballard's eventual
obituary. Frank said, "If it will get by the *Star* editors, my lead
on Ballard's obit will be something like, 'The fat is in the fire.'"
Meaning, of course, Harold will burn in hell.

Rex MacLeod, before retiring from the *Star* two years ago,
wrote the obituary held in files pending Ballard's death.
MacLeod's first paragraph on Ballard begins: "Now Harold
Ballard is in the red Hot Stove Lounge telling the Devil how
to put more seats in Hell without disturbing the Flames."

Orr, MacLeod and the rest of the Toronto hockey media
could appreciate Roger Neilson's Leafs of 1977–78. Mike
Palmateer, cocky and cherubic, arrived from the Dallas farm
club to play goal. Palmateer, full of himself, announced,
"Toronto's goaltending troubles are over."

Palmateer did provide the Leafs with their best goaltending since Bernie Parent escaped to Philadelphia. Darryl Sittler was a big grinder at centre, strong, rough, the captain
wearing Frank Mahovlich's grand old number, 27. Tiger Williams and Pat Boutette were aggressive let's-beat-their-ass-off
forwards. Lanny McDonald was an all-star on right wing.

Jimmy Jones, a defensive specialist, had played for Neilson in Peterborough. Ron Ellis was a steady veteran. Jerry Butler arrived from St. Louis with mean-mannered intent. Late in the season, the Leafs traded fleet Errol Thompson to Detroit for Dan Maloney, a left winger temperamentally equipped to fell any foe with his fists.

Neilson was exchanging finesse for fighters wanting to win the miserable little wars along the fences and in the corners. Most of Toronto's 11 Stanley cup champions had push-and-shove scufflers. The defence had three competent pros in Brian Glennie, Trevor Johansen and Ian Turnbull, and a marvel in Borje Salming, called "the noblest Swede of them all" by broadcaster Jim Hunt.

Noble or not, Salming had a smorgasbord of skills. He was a fast, fluid skater, adept at handling the puck, an accurate shot. A Maple Leaf scout, Gerald McNamara, mushing through Scandinavia in 1973, found Salming in the northern Swedish town of Kiruna. McNamara put a halter on the long-faced defenceman and led him to the Gardens. It was the best thing McNamara ever did for the Leafs and, some critics maintain, perhaps the only substantial thing.

Salming is not the best rearguard in Leaf history. Better arguments might be made for Tim Horton in the sixties or Gus Mortson in the forties or slam-bang Red Horner in the thirties. Comparisons aside, on any gauge in any year, Salming shone on the Toronto blueline. His one flaw is peculiar to many European imports. Many do not seem to realize that Canadian fans are not as interested in finishing first as much as winning the Stanley Cup in the spring.

Salming could have been Leaf captain, but he neither sought the captaincy from Ballard nor got it. He had an irresponsible streak which later got his name into the notebooks of narcotics officers on the Metro Toronto police force. He finally admitted to sampling cocaine when *Sports Illustrated* threatened to expose drug devotees in the NHL.

Cocaine is a nerve deadener. The addict withdraws into himself, not ideal behavior for a captain in a team game. As Robin Williams says, "Coke is the most selfish drug of all. The world becomes as big as your nostril."

The early Salming was a prime reason the Leafs of 1976–77

had their best finish since the early sixties. They won 41 games, lost 29 and tied 10, a resolute third in the Adams Division behind the Boston Bruins and Buffalo Sabres.

Those Leafs were not elegant. They were muscularly efficient in a fashion to gratify Tiger Williams, their boyish ogre. "By the spring of 1978," Williams wrote, "we were so close we could taste the Stanley Cup."

Tiger relived a brief high moment. "We rolled over Los Angeles Kings in the first round of the playoffs, then eliminated the New York Islanders four games to three. Against the Islanders, Roger Neilson gave a classic lesson on the value of a good coach. The team was perfectly prepared, mentally and physically. Neilson had me as a full-time checker, but I also got to work on the power play, a power play that had become the best in the league."

"Momentum" is an overworked word in the sports cliché bin, articulated to indicate how the balance of play switches from one team to another. Toronto momentum overtook the favored Islanders when Jerry Butler knocked Mike Bossy on his cazaza. Even so, the series went seven games, the last one on Long Island forced into overtime.

The teams were tied 1–1 and Lanny McDonald scored the winner with Williams steering the play. "Lanny took the puck off the end of my stick and drilled it past Chico Resch in the Islander net ... It showed how brilliant Roger Neilson's coaching was. Every period we came to play; every shift we gave the sons of bitches a little more pressure. . . ."

The Leafs were down to the Final Four, Ballard's best. "Against Montreal," Williams said, "it was obvious Neilson had taken us as far as we could go. They checked the crap out of us ... Canadiens had too many great players." The Canadiens swept the Leafs in four games and subdued Boston in six to win the Stanley Cup. Neilson was gone a year later, fired on television, because Harold found Neilson's defensive teams "boring."

Ballard could function on four hours sleep a night and he'd stay up nights "to make sure the sky didn't fall in." Restless, he decided he and King Clancy needed a summertime diversion. He focused on the Canadian Football League, which his Uncle George helped form in Hamilton in 1907.

Ballard's former confederate, John W.H. Bassett, owned the Toronto Argonauts in the early seventies. Harold attempted to buy them and was rebuffed. The response to his overture was "A Bassett will never sell to a Ballard." Then Harold tacked towards Uncle George's old port in Hamilton.

He tried in 1974 to buy the Tiger-Cats from Michael G. DeGroote, a Dutch immigrant who scored in trucking, school buses and garbage disposal. DeGroote did not score in football because of tightwad tendencies; he would not, in the argot of show business, give a worm to a blind robin.

DeGroote gladly yielded to Ballard's blandishments, in 1978, and sold the Ticats to Maple Leaf Gardens for $1.2 million. Harold and King Clancy had their summertime fun, expensive as it was. The Ticats under Ballard's sponsorship won the Eastern championship four times and the Grey Cup once, in 1986.

Before Ballard sold the Ticats, in midwinter 1988–89, they had cost him and the Gardens roughly $21 million. For 'Gardens' translate to read 'Ballard': he controls 80 per cent of the place. The millions needed to sustain the Ticats came from Pal Hal's pocket and minor shareholders in the Gardens.

Ballard was knocked by small-time Hamilton politicians, tinpot toads croaking beside a picayune pond, not one of whom had a dime invested in football. If "sportsman" is a word meaning someone who puts his money where his mouth is, Ballard fits the word. He was justifiably elected to the Canadian Football Hall of Fame for keeping the Ticats alive when not one of Hamilton's big spenders would.

He had the wisdom, in football, to interfere seldom with his Ticat general managers, first Ralph Sazio, then Joe Zuger. They assembled the teams, King Clancy led the applause and Ballard paid the bills. The CFL, desperate for dollars, could not afford to lose his generosity.

Ballard was less generous with his football foes. One of them was John Munro, once a cabinet member from Hamilton East in federal Liberal governments. Munro did not want Ballard to own the Ticats because of his "deplorable track record" with the Maple Leafs.

Ballard teed off in rebuttal. "Munro's comment," he said,

for publication, "is another in a never-ending series of moronic statements from one of Canada's supposed leaders ... Why's Munro shooting off his mouth in Hamilton anyway? Hell, he and those other barnacles and parasites should be in Ottawa straightening out the real problems."

Pal Hal does not talk in mush-mouthese. His comments, rude or crude, are forthright. John Ziegler, the NHL president, is fairly snug at five feet seven inches. Ballard has called him "the little Zed," "a know-nothing shrimp," and "little dictator." Ziegler, rolling with punches from one of his bosses, says, "Oh, that's Harold popping off."

One of Harold's partners in the NHL is less sanguine. Ed Snider of the Philadelphia Flyers says, "Ballard's not the kind of person I want to spend time with. What's he ever done except tear the Leafs down?"

Ballard has torn down Snider, in an immoderate manner of speaking. In June, 1979, during NHL deliberations in Montreal, a small fire broke out in the Queen Elizabeth Hotel, where the NHL owners met. "A fire, eh?" Ballard said to reporters. "Too bad that goddamn Snider wasn't thrown into it." Ballard's intemperate remarks sparked further animosity with John Bassett. On February 26, 1980, on the CBC program "The Fifth Estate," Harold uttered disparaging words about Bassett in a feature advertised as "What D'Ya Mean Ex-Con?" Bassett threatened to sue and Ballard, withdrawing, apologized on the CBC.

The Globe and Mail was Ballard's next platform for blasting Bassett. He had been interviewed by a perceptive feature writer, Judy Steed, and liked her. Steed's story, printed in the *Globe* on October 31, 1981, quoted Harold's slanders against Bassett. Bassett demanded a retraction from the *Globe*, and got it.

Bassett's lawyers pursued Ballard again, demanded an apology and got it. On November 14, 1981, in an advertisement Ballard paid for in the *Globe*, a headline on page four read "Harold Ballard Apologizes."

He ate these words, not with zest: "I apologize unreservedly ... and I sincerely regret any embarrassment the statements may have caused the Bassett family." I asked

Harold if he had paid any money to satisfy Bassett. "I think I settled out of court for $13,000," he said. "But for what I said, it was worth it."

Ballard did not permit his loathing for Bassett to die. He removed all pictures of Bassett from the walls of the Gardens. He altered the group picture of the 1967 champion Leafs by cutting off Bassett's head and replacing it with Bill Ballard's.

John Iaboni, a careful reporter from *The Toronto Sun*, asked Ballard about the pictorial alterations. "What d'you have against Bassett?" Iaboni wondered.

Ballard said, "The answer's easy enough. Bassett's picture doesn't deserve to be in the Gardens on account of all the things that happened in the past." The hatchet between them was buried, but in a shallow, well-marked grave. On December 2, 1981, *The Toronto Sun* published a front-page display of Ballard, grinning widely, burning a picture of Bassett. The title read, "Ballard goes bananas over Bassett."

"Going bananas" is a description for a gorilla in a zoo going berserk when he hears bananas are rationed. Maple Leaf fans were in a similar frustrated frenzy through the eighties. In the 10 seasons between 1979–80 and 1988–89, the Leafs missed the playoffs four times. At no time in that dismal decade did they advance in playoffs outside what telecaster Dave Hodge calls "the Porous Norris Divison."

In early May, 1989 the *Financial Post* listed the worst and best of the 106 professional sports teams in North America on the basis of wins and losses in the eighties. Statistician Murray Townsend ranked the Leafs 101st with 228 wins, 403 losses and 89 ties for a shrivelled success percentage of 0.378.

In the NHL, the New Jersey Devils were marginally messier: 102nd overall, 218 wins, 418 losses, 84 ties for a percentage of 0.361. The Edmonton Oilers, in contrast, were seventh: 418 wins, 211 losses, 91 ties for a percentage of 0.644 and four Stanley Cups. The Montreal Canadiens were 13th: 388 wins, 232 losses, 100 ties for a percentage of 0.608 and two Stanley Cups.

In the big picture, according to statistician Townsend, the Boston Celtics and Los Angeles Lakers of the National Basketball Association tied for the top. Each team won 531 games and lost 207 in the eighties for a triumphant percentage of 0.720. The Lakers won four NBA titles, the Celtics three.

Ballard chopped and changed through the eighties, coaches and managers parading through a revolving door. His general managers through that prostrate period were Punch Imlach, Gerald McNamara and Gordon Stellick. He went through coaches quicker than a kid can consume a box of Cracker Jack popcorn. Or, to be accurate, much quicker.

Since 1980, the Toronto coaches have been Floyd Smith, Dick Duff, Punch Imlach, Joe Crozier, Mike Nykoluk, Dan Maloney, John Brophy and George Armstrong. Garry Lariviere could be added to the list because, as the assistant coach in 1988–89, he ran the Leafs under Armstrong's supervision. The old joke applies when you're hired to coach the Leafs, don't sign any long-term leases.

Ballard romanced proved hockey people, but did not get beyond the necking stage. He nuzzled at Scotty Bowman, who coached teams to 1,276 wins in St. Louis, Montreal and Buffalo, plus five Stanley Cups with the Canadiens. Bowman was enticed but withdrew, uncertain of how much authority he would have in Toronto.

Ballard cuddled the shy, diffident Don Cherry, who wears shirt collars so high he cannot turn his neck. Cherry, a charmer, stoked up the Boston Bruins in the late seventies. He wandered off to coach the Colorado Rockies while Ballard dithered over a decision. When the Rockies became Schmockies, Cherry turned to television where he dissects games with a scholarly reserve.

In 1980, Ballard settled on a proved hockey person to manage the Leafs or, at least, someone who had fit that description in the past. Punch Imlach was fired as manager of the Buffalo Sabres, and landed on the first bounce back in the Gardens, where he had directed four Stanley Cup champions in the sixties. Bill Houston wrote, "In Imlach, Ballard finally got the tough hockey man he had been after for years. But, as it turned out, Punch was too tough and unyielding for the players and they quickly rebelled, marking the most turbulent period of the Ballard era. . . ."

Imlach had been gone a transient decade from the Leafs, but it was light-years in terms of player attitude. He could

and did underpay the Stanley Cup teams, champions composed of pros who won for their own self-respect no matter
how their employers welshed on wages.

The Leafs Ballard asked Imlach to manage in 1979–80 were
better paid, better advised, more aware of their rights; some
played for self rather than team.

Darryl Sittler controlled the 1980 dressing room by earned
right. On February 7, 1976, he scored six goals and achieved
four assists in an 11–4 slathering of the Boston Bruins. He
was the seventh player in NHL history to score six times in
one game, a feat not since matched. On September 15, 1976,
Sittler scored the winning goal in the Canada Cup tournament, 5–4 over the stubborn Czechoslovaks. Bob Clarke,
among Sittler's peers, ranked him the best centre in North
America.

Ballard, in the beginning, had similar sentiments. He presented Sittler and his wife, in recognition of the 10-point
night against Boston, with a silver tea service valued at
$8,500. Sittler seemed, on the surface, an all-Canadian boy
delighted to wear a Maple Leaf jersey.

Imlach and Ballard were to find a hard edge on their captain. Sittler had another side, as Bill Houston observed: "He
had a mean streak and could be as ruthless and cunning as
any street fighter when provoked." He was backed by his
agent, R. Alan Eagleson, who began breaking Imlach's geni-
tals in the sixties.

Imlach found that the Toronto press had changed in a
decade, as well. The writers on the Maple Leaf beat in 1979–
80 were younger, more skeptical, unfettered by appreciation
for Imlach's past accomplishments. Jim Kernaghan of the *Star*
said, "Our attitude was 'we know what you did in the sixties,
now show us what you can do now.' We weren't mesmerized
like Imlach's old friends in the media."

Globe reporters were particularly prepared to sandbag.
Houston, Jim Christie, Don Ramsay and Al Strachan
responded to the edict of Clark Davey, a *Globe* managing
editor who became publisher of *The Vancouver Sun* and later,
The Montreal Gazette. Davey's edict was, "If you see it or hear
it, write it." The *Globe* guys did, and still do, with vengeance,
not always fair, but pungent.

Recalcitrant players, a noisy owner, a recycled old-style manager, doubting reporters and cunning agents stirring the excrement made a muscles-and-media mix unparalleled in Leaf history. The stench remains.

Imlach was rebuffed the first time he challenged Darryl Sittler. He refused the right of Sittler and goalie Mike Palmateer to appear in "Showdown", a taped program of NHL players showing their skills in shooting, passing, scoring, saving. The program was inserted into telecasts of NHL games through the season.

Imlach was opposed to the Leafs' participation, ostensibly because the players might be hurt in a pre-season pantomime approved by the NHL and the NHL Players Association.

Imlach erred. He tried and failed to get a court injunction to prevent Sittler and Palmateer from appearing on "Showdown". He was suing the two Leafs he most needed, a glaring example of wretched in-house public relations. The players appeared on the program, staunchly steered by Alan Eagleson.

Ballard retaliated by refusing to allow "Showdown" to be shown in telecasts emanating from the Gardens. The producer of the program, deprived of the lucrative Leaf Market, went broke.

Punch was nothing if not perverse. He tried to trade away Sittler. He could not because Sittler had a protective clause in his contract which said, in essence, "I can't be traded unless I approve."

Punch persisted. He knew he could shed Lanny McDonald, Sittler's close friend and Toronto's best right wing since the last championship years. A trade was made with the Colorado Rockies, essentially McDonald for Wilf Paiement, who could play, but not with McDonald's caring for the Maple Leafs.

McDonald revealed his contempt for Imlach in *Lanny*, McDonald's autobiography produced with Steve Simmons, a candid columnist at *The Toronto Sun*. McDonald wrote:

> Punch Imlach stuck out his right hand and wished me luck. I refused to accept either the handshake or his good wishes.

> My only regret on Dec. 28, 1979, was that I didn't hit the general manager of the Leafs when I had the chance.

McDonald said he glared at Imlach, certain he was being fired from the one NHL team he had wanted to play for since he was an infant in Hanna, Alberta. His dream died.

"This is part of the game that hurts me the most," Punch began, and in his mind McDonald thought, "You lying son of a bitch."

McDonald asked, "Where am I going?" Imlach said, "We've traded you to Colorado."

McDonald wrote in *Lanny*: I couldn't believe what had just happened ... No one grows up wanting to play for the Colorado Rockies. ..."

Even the owners of the Rockies didn't want to play in Colorado. The franchise was subsequently shifted to New Jersey, where the Rockies were resurrected as the Devils. By that time, McDonald was in Calgary, where he has played in two Stanley Cup finals.

Ballard would later repudiate Imlach, but sustained him in 1980. The owner had his own problems with the intractable captain. Sittler led the Leafs against a Ballard charity.

It is one of Harold's charms that he does not boast about his contributions to the Charlie Conacher Fund for Cancer Research, the Ontario Society for Crippled Children, the Ontario Institute for the Deaf, the Salvation Army, and the Toronto Association for the Mentally Retarded.

"Let's talk about Ballard the giver," I once said to him on television. He said, "Knock that crap off, Richard. I want to be known as Ballard the rogue."

The rogue scheduled a charity exhibition in the Gardens between the Leafs and the Canadian Olympic team. The receipts were pledged to the Ronald McDonald House, a building with 21 beds designed to house families from outside Toronto when young cancer victims are treated in Metro hospitals. McDonald Restaurants supported the project. Alan Eagleson was a patron, Sittler the honorary chairman. Ballard supplied the Gardens. Harold arranged a midwinter date without consulting the Leafs. The players reneged because, counting the exhibition, they'd be playing four games in five nights. They consulted Eagleson.

The teamster boss suggested a trade-off which smacked of shakedown. The Leafs would not play in the charity match unless Ballard consented to an exhibition game the following season against a touring Soviet team. Ballard refused.

He had unilaterally broken diplomatic ties with the Soviet Union, even though he has a bust of V.I. Lenin, first Communist dictator in Russia, in his office. "Lenin had the right idea," Ballard says. "Help the starving masses. It's the fucking leaders who came later, like Stalin, that I hate."

There was no hockey entertainment for the McDonald charity, a guarantee of Ballard's enduring contempt for Sittler and Eagleson. He refused Eagleson's request to rent the Gardens for Canada Cup tournament games in 1981 and 1984. That meant cutting off Eagleson's nose to spite the shareholders, who would have profited from a cut of Canada Cup revenue.

Divided they stood, Eagleson-Sittler versus Ballard-Imlach. The dispute popped like a burst boil when Sittler, protesting Lanny McDonald's dismissal to Colorado, quit as Leaf captain. He cut the "C" off his sweater in a theatrical moment before a Saturday-night game.

Imlach countered by forbidding Sittler to appear on Saturday-night television, where he might have castigated the Leaf management. Ballard felt betrayed, but not to the point of reticence.

He said, "That's the maddest I've been in my goddamn life, when Sittler ripped the 'C' off his sweater. It was traitorous, like pissing on the flag of Canada. It was the act of a sulky, spoiled brat. I've told Punch Imlach to get Sittler's ass out of here as soon as we can make a deal."

A deal could not be made then, without Sittler's approval, and the Leafs continued in bumbling disarray. Eagleson, jerking Sittler as a Maple Leaf marionette, announced that Ballard could swap Sittler if he paid $500,000 for the player's permission. Ballard declined to have his pockets picked.

Anarchy was in the saddle; dressing-room dissidents shored up Sittler. Imlach sent a Sittler supporter, imprudent defenceman Dave Hutchinson, to the Chicago Black Hawks.

The day Hutchinson was traded, his friends held a jeering celebration in Delaney's bar, a gamey little salt lick near the Gardens.

Jim Kernaghan of the *Star* was invited to the party. He was invited on the condition that, if he wrote the story, the players were to be anonymous.

Kernaghan stayed. He saw the players tear a picture of Imlach out of the paper and throw darts at it. He heard them rap Imlach for trades he made to show he was boss. It was a hell of a yarn.

Imlach's media mates had a wrathful response. Milt Dunnell of the *Star* said, "If players don't have the guts to be identified, a paper shouldn't use their quotes." George Gross said in the *Sun*, "I hate players who hide behind anonymous quotes." Scott Young, in the *Globe*, awarded Kernaghan the "1980 National Newspaper Award for Cowardly Sportswriting."

Kernaghan argued that the players needed to be heard if they thought Imlach was destroying the team. Don Ramsay of the *Globe* agreed. Ramsay wrote anti-management stories based on quotes from anonymous Leafs. Coach Floyd Smith was shredded.

Darryl Sittler complained to Imlach about Smith's inability to coach. "He's no good," Sittler said. Imlach asked about Dick Duff, the assistant coach. Sittler made a cheap crack about Duff's alcoholic past. Imlach, loyal to players who had been loyal to him, was appalled. Duff had beaten booze and was a double letter winner, AA, from Alcoholics Anonymous. He had contributed impressively to two championships in Toronto and four more in Montreal. He won, in 18 seasons, six Stanley Cup rings; Sittler, in 15 seasons, had won none.

Imlach continued to play the muscle market. His best trade brought centre Bill Derlago and right winger Rick Vaive from Vancouver in exchange for forwards Jerry Butler and Tiger Williams.

Derlago and Vaive were perceived to be playboys but on the ice, where playing counted, they became the best Toronto attackers. Vaive scored 50 or more goals in three successive seasons, with Derlago feeding him his lines.

Williams did not depart for Vancouver before taking several oral punches at Imlach. They tangled in a bar in New York after a Sunday-night game against the Islanders.

Williams recalled the rumble in his autobiography, *Tiger*.

> I told Imlach I owed a debt to Ballard and King Clancy, old guys who counted on me . . . I told him the McDonald trade was garbage and that Sittler was one of the best leaders in the game . . . I said maybe Punch Imlach was once a great hockey man, but it had gone now. I leaned across the table and said, "Punch, you've lost it, boy."
>
> Imlach went crazy when I said those things. He started pounding the table. He said he had been the last guy to bring the Stanley Cup to Maple Leaf Gardens, and he was the only man in the world who could bring it back. He said the club and the players were nothing without him . . . It was going to be his way or the highway. I said he should take a real good look at the situation and get rid of all the bullshit or else make way for somebody who would. . . .

Ballard escalated the war with Sittler with the most dreaded word in the language. He called his ex-captain "a cancer." Various newspaper versions had Ballard saying "we've got to get that cancer out of the dressing room."

Don Ramsay, siding with Sittler in the *Globe*, wrote: "We are witnessing a sad soap opera about a cornerstone NHL franchise which in six short months has become the laughingstock of the league."

There was no laughing on March 14, 1980, when Floyd Smith was in a grievous traffic accident. Two people were killed and a third suffered a broken leg after his car crashed into another on the Queen Elizabeth Highway outside St. Catharines, Ontario. He was ultimately acquitted on charges of impaired driving and criminal negligence causing death. Ballard rallied to Smith and, following the trial, appointed him chief talent scout for the Leafs, a position Smith still retains.

There was urgent need for a coach to replace Smith for the ragged balance of the 1979–80 schedule and playoffs. Imlach named himself coach and picked a faithful Buffalo associate, Joe Crozier, to supervise the players from behind the bench. Crozier had been foreman of a Maple Leaf farm in New Brunswick.

In the playoffs, the Leafs lost two games of a best-of-five series against the Minnesota North Stars. Ballard accused them of malingering, "more interested in getting to the goddamn golf course than playing hockey."

Before the third game, in Toronto, Don Ramsay had a provocative story on the front page of the *Globe*. Ramsay quoted three anonymous Leafs to the effect that they were being outcoached. He added, "Imlach, through Joe Crozier, ordered all the players to check into a downtown Toronto hotel last night. One chuckled, 'They want to keep us off the booze. But haven't they heard of room service?'"

Scott Young was incensed over what he discerned as another Ramsay cheap shaft at Imlach. Scott resigned to protest the *Globe* publishing a diatribe based on the quotes of nameless poltroons. Scott's support of Imlach was admirable, and understandable. He had written one book with Punch, *Hockey Is a Battle*, and would write another, *Heaven and Hell in the NHL*.

The Leafs lost the third game of the Minnesota series and slovenly, disorganized, were eliminated. There has never been a more chaotic season in the team's jumbled history. We escaped, not soon enough, into the summer of 1980, bushed from too much exposure to the frowziness of the franchise.

CHAPTER 16

The Sunshine Boys

◆

"Overtime" was the title of a live, post-game hockey program on CHCH-TV after mid-week telecasts of Maple Leaf games. Dave Hodge, who sat under a thick clump of graying hair, was the urbane host, the best of the interlocutors in televised hockey. I, as CHCH's sports director, was a regular panelist on the program.

On December 13, 1978, one of the "Overtime" guests was Jim Hunt, a sports columnist for *The Toronto Sun* and sportscaster for CKEY, a Toronto radio station close to last in its league. Hunt is a congenial character who takes nothing in sport seriously, especially not himself and certainly not Harold Ballard as a hockey owner. Hunt regards Harold as hockey buffoon.

Hunt said, on "Overtime," that the Leafs were in constant competitive disgrace on a long-term basis "because Fat Harold can't even spell h-o-c-k-e-y. He ought to be ashamed."

I was not, in the circumstances, to be outdone in the denigration league. I chimed in, "And that Swede he's got on defence, that Borje Salming he's in love with, he's playing rancid. His name should be Salami. Borje Salami."

Ballard watched the program on a TV monitor in the Hot Stove Lounge. He was damned if he would allow any TV program produced in his building, knocking his team, to go unchallenged. He demanded equal time. Many of the poltroons who run television stations are timorous titmice who quaver when a bully roars. Ballard got equal time on CHCH, on December 20, 1978, a Wednesday night.

TV audiences for Maple Leaf games were big then, guaranteed to be huge this night because every schoolchild in the Ontario diocese was on Christmas vacation and likely allowed to stay up late to watch the end of the game. Ballard was a large, lumbering presence in the studio, an impertinent 75. Dave Hodge was perspiring through his makeup before the first insult was uttered.

Hodge said, "We are pleased tonight to have the owner of the Toronto Maple Leafs —"

Ballard blurted, "Oh, knock it off, Dave. You're not pleased at all. I'm here because I demanded to be here. I'm here to refute the remarks of a bastard you had on here last week. I don't want to mention who he is, but his last name begins with one of the first three letters of the alphabet."

Dave Hodge gamely said, "Oh, you mean Jim Bunt."

Ballard beamed. "By God, Dave, you're close. You miss by one letter. The letter C."

From there it was all downhill in the liveliest 25 minutes in the history of hockey commentary on Canadian television. The "Overtime" producers, to their credit, did not beep a single blasphemous word.

Ballard and I went orange head to comical hat. I said, "Jim Bunt is right. You shouldn't be running a hockey team. You should be guessing weights at the Canadian National Exhibition."

Ballard retorted, "And with all the funny clothes you wear, Beddoes, you should be a barker at a girlie show at the CNE!"

Hodge, as host, was relieved during a break for commercial messages. An attendant mopped Dave's sopping brow with a large white towel. On the second section of the show, because this was CHCH's Christmas program, we were joined by Santa Claus, portrayed by an ex-referee wearing the ridiculous red suit and white whiskers of the Yuletide jelly-belly.

A red light signalled that "Overtime" was back on the air and Dave Hodge, regaining equilibrium, said, "We're delighted, now, to be joined by Santa —"

Ballard butted in. He addressed Red Storey Santa Claus, "Hello, Santa, you old fart." A forbidden word, a four-letter word, had torn mercilessly into the fairyland of NHL hockey telecasts. To be sure, the word merely means the redolent wind expelled from the digestive system, but television producers were aghast. Members of the television crew, in the Gardens' studio, approved. They fell down laughing.

I could imagine the reaction Ballard was having in living rooms across Ontario. "Hey, Martha, turn up the volume!

Did you hear what Harold Ballard just said! Get up the sound!"

Dave Hodge was swooning as Ballard and I stood up, belly to belly, belaboring the unoffending air. The studio was loud with, "What do you know about hockey?" and, "Who the hell cares?"

At one half-sane juncture, I asked Red Storey Santa Claus, "Santa, what do you bring for a man like Harold Ballard, who has everything?"

Red Storey is a genuine Canadian comic. He reached into deep left field for an old gag, and found it. "For a man like Harold Ballard who's got everything," Storey said, looking square into the camera, "Santa brings penicillin."

After laughter in the studio subsided, I added, "I know some of Ballard's girl friends and he NEEDS penicillin." The ear-piece connecting Dave Hodge to the producer in the CHCH truck crackled, as though someone was squawking, "For God's sake, Dave, take control! Shut those bastards up!"

Hodge recovered long enough to get us off the air, not before we had shattered television tubes all over CHCH-TV-land. There were letters. There were telephone calls. A Protestant preacher in Niagara Falls, Ontario, sent in a copy of the New Testament with instructions that it be "force-fed, chapter by chapter, to Ballard and Beddoes. They are in immediate need of divine help."

Most fans seemed delighted by one of the rare occasions in hockey telecasting when the fun was unbridled, rude but real, unscripted and untamed, Ballard dropping verbal bombshells into the essentially phoney world of hockey comment on television.

A year or so ago, 10 years after Ballard's first appearance on "Overtime," I was walking down Yonge Street, not far from the Eaton Centre. I turned as car brakes squealed. Leaning out of a taxicab, impeding traffic, was a snickering driver. "Hey, Beddoes," he said. "Remember the night you had Ballard on TV and he called Santa Claus an old fart?" That is not fame; it is an instance when anyone can be, for 15 minutes, notorious.

Ballard made news again on March 1, 1979, a Thursday,

the night he fired the Maple Leaf coach on CHCH-TV. For
several weeks he had been loudly disenchanted with the
Leaf coach, Roger Neilson. The team under Neilson's pedantic guidance was, Harold said, boring.

Toronto newspapers, prompted by Ballard, speculated on
the date of Neilson's dismissal. It happened on March 1, after
the Leafs lost a tight test against the Canadiens in Montreal.
The game was carried on CHCH. Play had been intense and
fast, goaltender Paul Harrison keeping the Leafs in contention with vigilant acrobatics. Montreal won 2–1, but nothing
in the Leafs' deportment suggested that Neilson's coaching
was shabby.

I was certain, though, that Ballard would endorse the
rumors and fire Neilson after the game. I caught Ballard and
King Clancy in a corridor as they were leaving the Montreal
Forum. A top-rank CHCH cameraman, Harry Carson, had
the wit to follow us. He would record the first time that an
NHL coach was fired on television.

I asked, "Will you dump Neilson?"

"He's gone," Ballard said. "I don't care how good we
looked tonight, he's still gone."

Fans leaving the Forum stopped to gawk at Ballard being
interviewed on TV. Turn on a camera anywhere and you'll
draw a crowd, some to watch, many wanting to perform.

I asked Ballard, "So who will you replace Neilson with?"

"I don't know," Ballard said. "I'd like to get Ed Johnston,
who's coaching in Moncton for us and the Chicago Black
Hawks. If not him, maybe John McLellan, our assistant
general-manager."

I reiterated, to be sure, "But Roger Neilson's gone?"

"A gone goose," Ballard said.

His statements were repeated on "Overtime" within five
minutes, repeated and expanded upon by Dave Hodge. It
demonstrated that, with luck and legwork, even hockey telecasts can produce hard news rather than baseless views.

There was a postscript. Neilson was not gone, just then.
Ballard could not pry Ed Johnston loose from Moncton of the
American League, and John McLellan rejected Ballard's
request that he replace Neilson. The result was that Ballard
was stuck with Roger Neilson for the next Leaf game, on

March 3, 1979, a Saturday. He unfired Neilson, but could not resist a carny touch. He attempted to coax Neilson into wearing a brown paper bag over his head before the game, then discarding it after the first face-off. Neilson rebuffed the idea that he resemble the Masked Marvel of Maple Leaf Gardens. He finished the season as Leaf coach, but was gone after Toronto's early banishment from the Stanley Cup playoffs.

Barbara Frum is the doyenne of CBC radio and television, a skilful interviewer who can lift enough skin off a male antagonist that the poor chap is left sitting around in his skeleton. Frum crowded into Ballard's act on March 5, 1979, the Monday after Ballard had dismissed his coach on television.

She was the host of "As It Happens," the CBC's daily public-affairs program, the best forum of its kind in Canada. There was a sports feature once a week on "As It Happens," Jock Talk, which featured Frum, a guest, and me as resident know-it-all. We were linked by telephone.

Ballard would say that he didn't care for Frum "sticking her big bazoo into sports," but he never declined to appear on the program. Barbara said of him, "Harold was always a great talker, bold, blunt, outspoken. He was terrific at being chippy and strong-minded. He loved that role. But when we had him on for the Roger Neilson story, he was uptight from the beginning. Upset and uptight."

The Jock Talk segment of "As It Happens" began with announcer Alan Maitland, the ripest second banana in Canadian radio, giving the background: "Roger Neilson is back at the helm of the Toronto Maple Leafs — for the moment, anyway. Fired on Thursday night by Leaf owner Harold Ballard, Neilson was rehired on Saturday morning. Darryl Sittler impressed upon Ballard the players' loyalty to their coach. Neilson took his place behind the bench for Saturday night's game to a two-minute ovation from a sellout crowd. Both players and fans were telling Ballard he had made a mistake. We reached Pal Hal earlier today. Mr. Ballard joined our regular jock Dick Beddoes of *The Globe and Mail*."

Frum (pleasantly): Hi, Mr. Ballard.
Ballard (impatient, curt): How are ya?

Frum: How are you?

Ballard: Well, I'm all right.

Frum: You won a hockey game.

Ballard: Well, I won two on the weekend. Whatsamatter with your addition?

Beddoes: That's right, Harold. You won two . . .

Ballard: Why don't you get somebody on there who can handle the job, Dick? (Frum laughs.)

Frum (pleasant still): Listen, I just go for the hearts and flowers, so I'm there Saturday night . . .

Ballard: They shouldn't let females on the radio anyway. They're a joke.

Beddoes: They're a joke are they, Harold?

Ballard (angered): Yeah.

Beddoes: Well, Harold . . .

Ballard: You know where they're good . . .

Beddoes: That's what people are saying . . .

Ballard: You know where they're good doncha?

Beddoes: Well, I do know how women are best, I do . . .

Frum: Do you mind that millions of people are going to hear you say that?

Ballard (voice rising): You know where they're at their best doncha?

Beddoes: Yes, and I like it that way . . .

Ballard: So do I, and that's where they should stay. I let them out once in a while. I give them their shoes once in a while . . .

Beddoes: But talking about jokes, Harold, that's what some people are saying you pulled in respect to the rehiring after the firing of Mr. Neilson.

Ballard: Oh?

Beddoes: Is it a joke? Is it a hoax?

Ballard: Well, ah, no, not necessarily a hoax or a joke or anything else. I got what I wanted. I got the team winning, so you can't call it a joke.

Beddoes: Well, I'd hope to say I didn't think it was a joke when you and I talked in the Montreal Forum last Thursday night.

Ballard: That's right.

Beddoes: You said then — and certainly you were serious — that he was gone as your coach.

Ballard: That's right.

Beddoes: ... and you were going to have somebody else as soon as you could find somebody else.

Ballard: Ummm, hmmm.

Beddoes: And your problem probably was, Harold, you didn't have anybody you could grab immediately. If you could have grabbed Eddie Johnston from Moncton, I suspect you might have ...

Ballard: Well, I don't know. I'd have to give it a little more consideration. I mean to say, when you caught me coming out of the Montreal Forum, I mean to say, it was a very tense moment as far as I was concerned.

Beddoes: Yeah.

Ballard: When I came back, I called Roger and we sat down in the Hot Stove Lounge and had a little meeting and rehashed the whole thing. And it's quite simple: the reason Roger was axed, if you want to call it that, was the fact that the players let him down and they admitted that to me and I went to talk to them and they took full responsibility.

Frum: Dick? Would you describe the drama of Neilson's return on Saturday night? It was genuinely moving and, as Mr. Ballard so politely just said, I am something of a weak hockey fan.

Beddoes: Well, indeed, Barbara, it was one rare — rare ovation at Maple Leaf Gardens when the people — 17,000 of them — saw who was behind the bench.

Frum: It was a definite two-hanky scene, wouldn't you say?

Beddoes: Well, people were saying, "Hey! Something's happened! Hard-hearted Ballard has given in. And here we got back the guy we think should be coaching the hockey club and we're going to stand up and show how ..."

Ballard: Just a minute ...

Frum: And there's the godfather up in the window looking down benignly ...

Ballard: I'll tell you something. The night before, the
   Daily Star had an article saying the Leafs were the
   worst-coached team we've ever seen . . .

Beddoes: Harold, there's no question the Atlanta
   game . . .

Ballard: . . . and everybody — all you media guys, the
   whole bunch of you — "you should get rid of Roger
   Neilson" and the calls, and . . .

Beddoes: I beg your pardon, Harold. The news media
   did not say that.

Ballard (belligerently): They certainly did! I'll show you
   clippings out of the paper!

Beddoes: No, very few of the media . . .

Ballard: Now I'll start on you. There was a lot . . .

Beddoes: There was very few that I read . . .

Ballard: Of course I shouldn't pay any attention to you
   fellas because you don't know the difference between
   a puck and a ball. A baseball.

Frum (good naturedly): Well, lookit, Mr. Ballard. You
   did fire him . . .

Ballard (loudly irritated): I'm talking to Dick and you
   don't know the difference between them and why I
   should be taken in by a few dummies that don't know
   hockey — they don't write, they're critics!

Frum: Hang on now, Mr. Ballard . . .

Ballard: Would you keep quiet?

Frum: No. This is still my show.

Ballard: Well, it isn't . . .

Frum: I have another question for you . . .

Ballard: I'm not talking to you. I'm talking to Dick. So
   when you learn to mind your own business and let
   me talk to Dick, it'll be fine. Goodbye.

There was a large click in our ears. Pal Hal had hung up.
The line was dead. Frum and I were left talking to ourselves.

The next day, in Ottawa, there was hell to pay in Parliament.
Flora MacDonald, revered by John Diefenbaker as the
finest woman ever to walk the streets of Kingston, was
peeved at Ballard's implication on the CBC that the best

position for a woman is on her back. Nothing else happened in Ottawa.

We never interviewed Ballard again on Jock Talk. A few days after the offensive show, a noisy claque of Toronto harridans celebrated International Women's Day by marching outside the Gardens proclaiming "Down with Sexist Harold." There were outraged calls to the Gardens.

He told me, "You should have heard those feminist broads calling me after the Barbara Frum thing. I had all the calls put through to me. I'd say, 'Hi, honey, whatsamatter, can't you get a man today? Y'after my body? You want to get laid?'"

He fanned the feminist flames with gaseous bombast. "Boy, they went nuts. Loved it. Really loved it. Can't stand those feminist broads. Bunch of frustrated old maids."

Ballard kept attracting CBC attention after the debacle with Barbara Frum. The people's network sought more entertainment than news on what are designed to be news programs. "The Fifth Estate" hung microphones on Ballard and King Clancy during the 1979 football season, as they sat in their box seats in Hamilton's Ivor Wynne Stadium. They mixed up the identities of a few Ticat players.

Ballard asked, "Who's that? Kelly? Is he an Irishman?"

Clancy said, "Is he black?"

"No," Ballard said.

"Is he?" Clancy persisted.

"No," Ballard said. "He's white. You don't think there would be any niggers called Kelly, do you?"

"There's lots of them," Clancy said.

Ballard sounded incredulous. "No, King. Surely not."

Adrienne Clarkson, one reason "Fifth Estate" had a high estate, nailed Ballard on February 26, 1980, about what she considered his racism. He denied ill will towards any race, color, creed or sex.

> Clarkson: You're renowned for the outrageous things you say about women, about racial groups. Why do you say things like that?
>
> Ballard: Well, that's the way I think. And as I said before, I tell people what I think. I don't think one way and tell somebody else another way.

Clarkson: But you do have your prejudices. Come on, you're well known for calling people niggers, hebes. We have it on record. You do it.

Ballard: Oh, that's all right. I do that quite often. So do you. Everybody does. They get confused. They just get mad and that's the first thing. It's like swearing at somebody. You don't call somebody a goddamn fool and expect that they, uh, that you actually mean it.

Clarkson: Does it occur to you that they might be deeply offended by your referring to them . . .

Ballard: Oh, I don't think so. Listen, when you're in the sports business, you know, we have people in our club, we have French-Canadians and we have Polish guys. Johnny Bower, they often say, "you so-and-so Polack" or something like that. You want to get offended at that? It's stupid! If somebody says to me, I go to the States, "You Canadians, you're a bunch of Indians" and one thing and another, do I get offended? I don't care what they say. You know the old story, sticks and stones will break my bones but names will never hurt me.

He could, on one rollicking occasion on "Overtime," smear an entire civic administration. He was quarrelling with the local Hamilton government over the failure of the city to improve the falling-apart sardine can that is Ivor Wynne Stadium. One of the Hamilton aldermen had recently been charged with cultivating marijuana plants in his basement.

"What can you do about those clucks running Hamilton?" Harold said in a fine burst of rhetoric. "One guy's growing marijuana and the rest of them are smoking it."

What you get with Ballard, in the media, is what you hear. He is determined never to bore during his appearances on radio and television. We talked on CHCH-TV near Christmas, 1988, an interview conducted high in the red seats of the Gardens. What Carson McCullers called "the sinister glissando of the years" was playing out the string on Pal Hal. He'd had quintuple heart-bypass surgery, a world record, he said, for someone 85. There was no pressure on him to perform, but he always performs.

"I know you have domestic trouble," I said. "It's been in the papers, how your kids fight with your lover, Yolanda."

"I sometimes feel," he said, "that I'm surrounded by lunatics."

"Lunatics?"

"Her," Harold said, "and them."

Ballard and his three children controlled about 80 per cent of the stock in the Gardens. He controlled the voting shares. I wondered, when he died, how much each child would receive?

"They'll be multi-millionaires," he said. "Each'll get about $17 million."

I thought, "My God, $17 million for just being born a Ballard." I said, "Harold, quick, please adopt me."

He looked straight into the camera focused on him by my CHCH colleague, Phil LaChappelle. "Oh, hell," Harold said. "You're too old and ugly to adopt."

Ballard did, in effect, adopt King Clancy and their association had lunatic overtones.

Ballard and Clancy drifted together as bosom comrades after Staff Smythe died and Punch Imlach left Maple Leaf Gardens. Theirs became a friendship that ended only when Clancy died in November, 1986. Ballard called Clancy "Mike" and himself "Ike." Tom Murray caught their close, heckling, hilarious association in a definitive feature in *The Hockey News* of December 26, 1980.

Ballard had bought the Hamilton Tiger-Cats in 1978 "so Mike and me could have something to do in the summertime." He paid $1.5 million for the franchise and, keeping Hamilton alive in the Canadian Football League, spent almost $21 million on a team that could not draw flies to a garbage dump, which the Hamilton stadium is. Ballard sold the Ticats to the City of Hamilton for one dollar ($1.00) in the spring of 1989.

Murray met Ballard and Clancy in the Hot Stove Lounge one early morning of Grey Cup Week. Ballard lived in a studio apartment in the Gardens almost from the time he was released from the penitentiary, in 1973. He lumbered into the Hot Stove Lounge, 250 pounds of moribund porpoise with hair colored a lovely shade of apricot.

"Where the hell are the goddamned Greeks?" Harold demanded. In three seconds, three waiters in white jackets appeared with breakfast for their master. It was not the kind of meal necessarily recommended for a diabetic: a large bowl of cottage cheese sprinkled with too much salt, brown toast liberally spread with butter, and coffee sweetened with three packets of a sugar substitute. He was 77 and had been a widower for 11 years.

Mike's square name was Francis Michael Xavier Clancy, also 77, also a widower. They travelled with the Maple Leafs and Ticats, constantly together in arenas, stadiums, airports and press rooms. They were so close that Ballard insisted he caught his diabetes from Clancy.

"I call diabetes leprosy," he told Tom Murray. "There's no doubt I caught it from Clance. He had this chart in his office and I looked at it one day and, sure enough, I had a lot of those symptoms. I went to the doctor, and goddamn, I'd caught leprosy from the little bastard."

"We've been inseparable," Ballard said of King Clancy, "since his wife died several years ago. I knew she was going to die. She had a malignancy and the cancer ate her up. When she died, I had a limousine waiting for us at the cemetery. We got right into it, went out to the airport and flew to Las Vegas for 10 days. Clance'd gone nuts if I hadn't got him away from Toronto for a while."

Ballard checked his watch and looked towards the door of the Hot Stove Lounge. "Where is that little bastard anyway? He oughta be here by now." As though on command, Clancy arrived. He moved with a rapid rolling gait, gray, grinning, smaller than the Hall of Fame defenceman he used to be. Perhaps Clancy just seemed smaller beside Ballard's oval personage.

There were sartorial contrasts. Clancy always dressed his age in tidy dark suits, a natty parson out to greet his parishioners. Ballard's raiment was a bold blue-striped shirt, brown pants and a brown tie festooned with little yellow pigs. Each pig was marked in green capital letters "MCP" — male chauvinist pig, which Ballard can be.

"Where the hell ya been?" Ballard said, hearty as a trip-hammer.

Clancy pressed a few strands of old hair over his scalp. "I tell ya, Harold, I gotta call my doctor. All of a sudden, I can't hear a goddamn thing."

Ballard became solicitous. "Really, Mike? Sit down. I'll see if I can find out what's the matter. Go on! Sit down!"

"Fuck you," Clancy said. "I'll not be sitting down!"

"Sit down!" Ballard ordered. He stood up and pushed Clancy into a chair. He stuck his face near Clancy's. "Now then. Which ear is it?"

Clancy gestured to his left ear and Ballard pretended to peer into it. Then, with an enormous flourish, Ballard reached with his right hand and pulled down the zipper on his trousers. "Here ya go, Mike! This big syringe will clean 'er right out! Har! Har!"

Clancy jumped out of his chair. "You son of a bitch!" he yelled. "I don't need this! I gotta busy day! I'm the busiest son of a bitch in this place. I got a guy to clean out the gutters of my house and son of a bitch if he don't leave the broom up on the roof."

Ballard zipped up his fly. "That's good. Go up on the roof and get the broom yourself. Or sue him. All you goddamn Irishmen are cheap bastards anyway."

"Let me tell you something else," Clancy said. He reached for a cup of tea. "This girl drives me home last night and — "

Ballard interrupted. "Didja get lucky?"

"Kee-rrriiisst!" Clancy said. "Lucky! At my age! Are you nuts? Anyway, her car was parked outside my place. I drove her home after the game and she gets into her car and one of her goddamn tires is flatter than piss on a plate, So I gave her my car and now I don't have one and I'm very, very busy."

Ballard was unsympathetic. "Yeah," he said. "Didja get my office cleaned up?"

"Where the hell ya think I've been all morning?" Clancy said. He slammed his cup on the table. "What do ya know about that?" he said to a passing waiter. "I'm the vice-president and I clean up the president's fucking office! Every morning, when he's down here, I gotta go in and mop the whole goddamn place up. The shower's all fucked up and so's your goddamn sauna. . . ."

They would wrangle like that for an hour almost every morning, putting it on louder if they had an audience. Ballard would needle Clancy about religion. Harold's succinct view of the bible is that "it's a bigger fairy tale than *Alice in Wonderland*."

Clancy, a devout Catholic, took the needle. "I tell you, Clance," Ballard said, "that story about Noah is really something. Building an ark and taking every kind of animal on a sail for 90 days. They all wind up on a hill or some goddamn thing and start fucking. And that's how we got all the animals we got today. What crap!"

Then Ballard stood up, flung down his napkin, checked his watch and said, "C'mon, Mike. It's time to go to practice." The Leafs normally practice in the Gardens but, since the Gardens is booked for an ice show this week, they work in an alternate site in North York. Tom Murray of *The Hockey News* rides along with Ballard and Clancy.

Ballard is a tight squeeze behind the wheel of his dark blue Lincoln Continental, which bears a designer license plate, MLG - 1 — Maple Leaf Gardens Number 1. Clancy perches in the back seat, an elderly leprechaun.

Ballard on his way to hockey practice in 1980 is a vision in tackiness. He wears a bulky sheepskin coat suitable for climbing Mount Everest. The top half of the sheepskin is blue for Maple Leafs, the lower half yellow for Tiger-Cats. Under the coat he has a bulky blue-knit sweater with a maple leaf on the front. On his head is a blue-and-white Maple Leaf cap. He is talking about the Grey Cup parade, two days away in Toronto. The Tiger-Cats will play for the Canadian football championship against the Edmonton Eskimos, and lose.

"Ya should see the float I got for the parade," Ballard said. "Heh, heh, heh. I got this goddamn big tiger moving his jaws and eating up a Toronto Argonaut uniform. And I'm gonna — hey, Clance. Time for a pussy peek. Look at that one."

They notice an attractive woman in a mink coat getting out of a parked Mercedes-Benz. "Should we stop? You can go and shake hands with her."

"Not today, Harold," Clancy said. "She's not bad, though.

How'd you like to put Larry in her guardhouse? Geezus, I wish I could remember what I wanted to tell you."

Ballard kept talking about the Hamilton float in the Grey Cup parade. "Ya know *The Toronto Sun* sponsors the Argo Cheerleaders, doncha? They call 'em the Sunshine Girls. I got into some trouble a couple of years ago for saying they closed all the body shops on Yonge Street so they'd have no trouble getting cheerleaders for the Argos. Haw! Haw! They threatened to sue me for saying that."

Ballard, driving, can be a menace. He accelerated the car and moved into the right-hand lane without checking his rear-view mirror. "In this parade Saturday," he said, "I'm getting four of the biggest guys I know, put 'em in drag and have them sit on the tiger and go right through Toronto. Heh, heh, heh. That'll piss a few people off, eh, Mike?"

"You're goddamn right, Harold," Clancy said, leaning over the front seat. "I just remembered what I want to talk to you about. There's a lady that called your secretary and ordered two tickets for last night's game. Gold tickets. But she never picked them up."

"So what?" Ballard said. "No business of mine." He switched lanes again, not checking either side.

"So what?" Clancy said. "Whaddya mean so what? I had to pay 31 beans for those tickets she didn't pick up."

Ballard grinned. "You little bastard. You've got some nerve trying to tell me you never met that broad. You been humping her."

"Whaddya mean?" Clancy said. His fingers gripped the front seat tighter.

"You know what I mean," Ballard said. "You been fooling around her for a month. And now you're trying to tell me to pay for your broads. It's your love life. I'm not falling for it. Haw, haw, haw!"

Clancy said, "Now wait a goddamn minute. I —"

Ballard interrupted. "I don't jump the broad! You do! So you pay for her. Har, har, har!"

Ballard slammed his brakes, barely in time to avoid hitting a car moving up on his right as he was changing lanes. The driver of the car waves his hand, shakes his fist and utters coarse language.

Ballard laughs, his hide thick as a rhino's. "Get over, ya bastard!" The other driver, a dark chap with a mustache, shakes his fist through his closed window.

Clancy plays co-pilot. "Look out, Harold. He's gonna try and sneak in on the right. God damn it! We nearly gave him a kiss."

An urchin's glee is upon Ballard. "That's all right. It looks good on him. C'mon, you motherfucker. Move your ass."

The other driver darts in front of Ballard's car and retaliates. He speeds up, then stops short, all the time shaking his fist at Ballard through his rear-view mirror.

Ballard pulled out and into position on the right of his tormentor. He honked his horn and, when the other man turned, thumbed his nose at him. "Kiss my ass!" Harold said.

Clancy shouted, "Go fuck yourself!" as Ballard drove off. "I think he wanted to fight us, Harold. Swell chance he'd a had with us. You could hold him down and then I'd kick him in the cubes."

The North York Arena is cold and dank, and Clancy turtles down in his overcoat. He talks about Ballard, who is off advising the Maple Leaf coach.

"When I lost my wife," Clancy said softly, "Harold was a great soother. I buried her at 10 in the morning and at 11 he's got me on my way to Vegas. He said the best thing I could do is forget it. He'd been through it when his own wife died. Harold really gave me a big lift."

"The pair of you," Tom Murray of *The Hockey News* said, "are peas in a pod. Inseparable."

Clancy agreed. "Inseparable is right. We go most places together. All the games, the NHL meetings . . . I used to have a lot of friends, but you get to be 77 and a lot of them have passed away. I got a few girl-friends now my wife's gone, but nothing serious. There's nobody could take my wife's place, no way. I had too much of a free hand when I was married. And Harold's the same way. Neither of us will ever get married again."

Clancy's wife's name was Rachel, he called her Rae, and she was like Ballard's Dorothy. Always there, always parenting two Clancy sons and two Clancy daughters. King would be away refereeing a game in Chicago or somewhere on Christmas Day and he would get on the phone to Rae and their children and they'd all be bawling. Hockey Night in Canada, for the participants, wasn't always Christmas Day in Canada.

"I've had a hell of a life," Clancy said. He shivered in the clammy air of the arena. "That's what life's about, having fun. What in heaven's name is the use of getting down. You've got to roll with the punches. Everything isn't apple pie. You got to expect to get knocked down once in a while. I just enjoy life and I thank God He's taken care of me so far. And I don't know where I'd be if it wasn't for laughing with Harold. Probably dead."

Two days later, on a cold November Saturday in 1980, Ballard and Clancy are in the Grey Cup parade. Bandsmen strut. Goose bumps grow on the uncovered pelts of cheerleaders. There is noise, especially around Ballard's Ticat float. A huge tiger, 25 feet long, dominates the float. A dummy dressed in the blue colors of the Toronto Argos hangs from the tiger's jaws. "Yeah, Argos." Ballard hated the Argos, who were once owned by John Bassett, his old backsliding friend.

Four of the largest, ugliest women in Toronto stand beside the Hamilton Tiger. They are guzzling beer as though all the breweries have gone dry. They are really four hairy-legged undergraduates recruited by Ballard from the University of Toronto. They wear blue tights, construction boots, padded brassieres, wigs and lipstick. Each has a bright yellow sweatshirt bearing the words "Moonshine Girls." Take that, whap, you *Toronto Sun* sponsors of the Argo Sunshine Girls.

Ballard stands behind the tiger in a thick black overcoat, and a Ticat hat and a yellow scarf. His lapel button proclaims, "Luv Ya, Black And Gold."

He'd wanted to go rude all the way. "I wanted to have a pair of Argo socks hanging out of the tiger's ass," Harold said. "But they talked me out of that. Said it'd be going too far, even for a Grey Cup parade. Maybe we can get some exhaust fumes from the car pulling our float to come out of the tiger's ass. ...."

King Clancy pops on the scene. He wears a Ticat toque on his head and palms an inflated football. He wags a thumb at the golf cart parked behind the tiger. "Hey, Harold, are we gonna ride this goddamn cart?"

Ballard goes "Heh, heh, heh. I don't know. Some of these bastards on the parade route might have a bushel basket full of tomatoes, just waiting for me to pass by."

Clancy pounds the football in his hands. "Fuck 'em! The first son of a bitch throws a tomato, I'm off after him!"

A gaggle of Hamilton cheerleaders prance into prominence in black tights and yellow windbreakers. They wave yellow pom-poms and generally act idiotically.

The Hamilton cheering claque is led by Pigskin Pete, who wears a black derby hat, a black-and-yellow striped sweater and a coonskin coat. When he flaps the arms of the coonskin coat, a clothes moth escapes.

The girls surround Ballard and Clancy, squealing as though goosed. "Mr. Ballard! Mr. Clancy! Oh, Mr. Ballard, can we have our picture taken with you? Please! Please!"

Ballard obliges. "Heh, heh, heh. Sure girls. Come to poppa." He spreads his big arms to embrace everybody. "Everybody jump in. Nobody goes home unhappy. Clance! You get in this goddamn picture, too!"

A photographer clicks off several pictures. Pigskin Pete, a perennial sophomore, jumps up and begins to lead the Hamilton contingent in the Ticat cheer. Ballard and Clancy join in.

Pigskin Pete hunkers down. He shouts, "OSKEE WEE WEE!" He capers around waving his derby. "OSKEE WAH WAH!" He screams as a runaway from a booby hatch. "HOLY MACKINAW! TIGERS! TIGERS! TIGERS! EAT 'EM RAW!!!!!"

Ballard chuckles. "Har, har, har. Isn't this a load of bullshit?" He wanders across the street to a jammed parking lot looking for a spot to urinate. "Geezus! I got to go to the can so bad my back teeth are floating!"

He moves towards a house just off the parade route. "Looks like there's no one there." Something is there, a belligerent dog locked up by its owner. The dog begins to bark when Ballard begins to urinate. "Shut up!" Ballard says.

The dog keeps barking. "Heh, heh, heh," Ballard says. "This goddamn pooch knows a good thing when he sees it. The son of a bitch is licking his lips. He must be homosexual. Say, pooch, are you homosexual?"

The dog's response is more angry barking. "Har, har, har," Ballard says. "I think his answer is yes." He walks back across the street to the Ticat float. A kid on the other side of University Avenue recognizes him. "Hey, Harold!" the kid jeers. "You're a horse's ass!"

Harold is not insulted. He has been called worse. "Wonderful!" he yells back. "And how are you doing today? Har, har, har!"

A group of fans picks up the chant. "Harold Is a Horse's Ass! Harold Is a Horse's Ass!" Ballard is too preoccupied to notice. He's making a dash for the car carrying Miss Hamilton Ticat. Clancy rushes along with him. Ballard jogs alongside the open car until he is close to Miss Ticat. Then he grabs her and kisses her with MCP vigor on the mouth. The crowd boos as he backs off. "Harold Is a Horse's Ass!"

Ballard and Clancy retreat to the Ticat float as the parade moves out. "Wow," he tells Clancy, who is tossing the silly football. "Didja see the one in front with the big boobs? I'd take her in a second. Har, har, har."

They jump on the golf cart behind the Hamilton float. Clancy sits in the back on a pile of empty six-packs. Ballard sits beside the driver, riding shotgun. He fends off a drunken Moonshine Girl who wanted his picture taken with Ballard.

"This is okay, I guess," Ballard says. "But I still wish I'd put those goddamn Argo uniforms coming out of the tiger's ass. That would really have pissed the parade organizers off. Heh, heh, heh."

The next morning, a chilly Sunday, Ballard and Clancy get into Harold's car at the Gardens and wheel down Yonge Street. They are quiet until Harold notices what he takes to be Western Canadians, yokels in cowboy boots and rodeo hats.

Harold rolls down his window. "Hey," he hollers at the window shoppers. "Why don't you all go back to Edmonton where you belong? I can smell the cowshit on your boots from here. Har, har, har!"

He speeds off towards the expressway to the CNE Stadium, where the Grey Cup game is scheduled. The car stops for a red light. Clancy says, "This is a nice corner."

"Oh, yeah," Ballard says. "Why the hell's that?"

"Because of that church over there," Clancy says. "There should be a church on every corner in the city."

"Balls!" Ballard says. "They're a bunch of goddamn thieves. I never saw a skinny priest."

Clancy retorts, "I seen lots."

Ballard presses his anti-clerical needle. "And," he says, "those bastards don't have to pay any taxes, either."

Clancy protests, "And why should they?"

The light changes to green and the Lincoln Continental slides forward. "You goddamn Irishmen are all the same," Harold says. "All you do is give, give, give. All you're doing is keeping those fat old priests in booze and broads."

They gun along the Gardiner Expressway, almost missing an exit ramp to the CNE grounds. "Hey, Harold! Where the hell are ya going?"

"No idea," Harold says. "I never drove this fucking way before." He applies brakes and the Lincoln slows grudgingly, enough to make the exit.

Clancy relaxes. "No question with the cops if they stop us. I'll tell them we gotta make the game to blow up the footballs."

Ballard, in the parking lot reserved for football owners, is surrounded by fans seeking autographs. He signs every program offered to him. He signs more autographs than any athlete he has ever employed. "When the fans stop asking me," he says, "I'll know it's time to retire."

They amble through the crowd to the CNE elevator which will take them to the press box on the top floor of the Stadium. They intend to watch most of the Grey Cup game before driving to Pearson International Airport for a flight to Boston. They will watch the Maple Leafs play the Bruins this night.

Tom Murray of *The Hockey News* asks, "Suppose your team wins the Grey Cup. Won't you stay for the presentation? Will you still go to Boston?"

"Sure," Ballard says. "Why the hell not? Whatever happens here this afternoon will be history by the time we're on that plane to Boston. We gotta keep moving forward, Mike and me."

The elevator stops, the doors open, and Ballard moves swiftly across the roof to the press box, Clancy trotting in pursuit. They are surrounded by reporters, all clamoring for a word with the Sunshine Twins. "Fuck you!" Ballard yaps at Jim Hunt, who has picked the Eskimos to drub Hamilton.

"You tell us, Fat Harold!" Hunt yaps back.

Ballard and Clancy shift down to the far end of the press box to join Ralph Sazio, then the general-manager of the Ticats. Ballard looks across the field, off towards Lake Ontario churning in the distance. "I gave up seats on the 55-yard line," he says, "to sit up here with my boys."

Clancy chimes in, "Damn right. We could have been sitting down there with a bunch of dignitaries."

"I'd feel uncomfortable sitting with those bastards," Ballard says. "I mean, you call somebody a cocksucker and everybody turns around and says 'Ooooo, what's that?' Ya know what I mean? Har, har, har!"

Below, the Western champions are warming up. Clancy leans over the railing of the open-air box to shout insults. "Hey, ya goddamn fruits! Ya big goddamn fruits!"

One Eskimo looks up, notices Clancy and waves. Clancy shakes his fist and hoots, "Hey, ya big prick, go fuck yourself! A good think won't hurt ya!"

Ballard wallows in the fun, musing on it. "It's like this 365 days a year, Clance and me. No two days are ever the same. I'm having the time of my life. I have more fun than anyone in the whole fucking world."

Clancy is still addressing sweet forget-me-nots to the Eskimos. One of them dropped a pass. "Hey, ya big faggot! Ya sure looked good on that one!"

A band plays "O Canada" before the kickoff. Harold thinks Hamilton is kicking off to Edmonton. "C'mon now, Rudy," Ballard shouts, big hands cupped around his mouth. "Kick the living shit out of that ball!"

Clancy is bewildered. "Harold," he says. "We're not kicking off. We're receiving the ball."

"That's okay," Ballard says as the ball sails into the arms of

a waiting Ticat. Then, rumbling, "MURDER THE COCK-
SUCKERS!!!"

The 1980 Grey Cup game was murder all right, advantage
Edmonton. The Eskimos led 23–6 at half time and 47–10
when Ballard decided it was time to leave. "C'mon, Mike,
let's beat the crowd or we'll never catch that plane."

Clancy doesn't want to depart. "Hell, Harold, we have lots
of time."

"Bullshit," Ballard says. "This game's history. It's time to
do something else. We got another game to see in Boston and
I don't want to miss that plane."

They leave, Clancy following Ballard, into the elevator and
out of the CNE Stadium. They listen to the remainder of the
game on the car radio, the Eskimos slathering the Ticats, 48–
10. Ballard hurries the big car to the top floor of the airport
parking terminal.

"What's the rush, Harold?" Clancy says. "We're in lots of
time."

"Knock it off, Mike," Harold says. "You run ahead and
grab the elevator. I want to take off some of these heavy
football clothes."

Ballard was 77, but acted 50. He peels off layers of clothing
and heaves the stuff into the car trunk. He sprints over to the
elevator in time to see Clancy watching the doors of a
crowded elevator about to close.

"What the fuck are you doing?" Ballard says.

"Fuck it, Harold," Clancy says. "It's full. We'll get the next
elevator."

"Bullshit," Ballard says, and thrusts one arm between the
elevator doors. The doors spring open and they step inside,
cursing each other. Ballard looks around at the other passengers, all dark-complexioned and brown-eyed, apparently
Arabs.

"Balls," Clancy says. Ballard can't find a familiar face in the
crowded elevator, but that doesn't stop him from being familiar. Just before they reach the Departures level, Ballard
nudges the Arab standing next to him.

"Say," Harold says to the Arab in a confidential tone, "how
the hell are ya! You haven't seen a couple of guys riding a

camel through this airport, have you?" Clancy and Ballard get off, laughing.

They flew to Boston, in time to see the Leafs tie the Bruins 5–5. They flew back with the Toronto team at 3 o'clock in the morning. A few hours later, they were drinking coffee in the Hot Stove Lounge and amiably insulting each other. It was business as usual, a lot of monkey business. They had more fun than monkeys or people.

CHAPTER 17

Saints and Sinners

◆

God was popular in Toronto in the high summer of 1980. Conventioneers for Christ spoke in a confusion of language, as reported in the Book of Genesis.

The Lord destroyed the Tower of Babel, on the arid Plain of Shinar, as a lesson in humility. "Come," this Mighty Voice spake, "let us go down, and there confuse their language, that they may not understand one another's speech."

Godded up, 20,000 Baptists throbbed and thronged through Maple Leaf Gardens in a world assembly of scrambled language, much of it gibberish. They were resplendent in wash-and-wear seersucker and polyester, tacky as tourists from America's Deep South hookworm belt.

I wandered into the Old Chapel on Church Street, somewhat seedy myself as a reporter on the bible beat for the *Globe*. I was greeted by Shanty MacKenzie, the building manager and a devout parson of the puck.

"Welcome," Deacon MacKenzie said, "to Ballard Cathedral." Heretical Harold was not far away, gleefully looking like a brat on his first trip to Sunday School.

Of a sudden, on this steaming early afternoon, a shiny black limousine eased up in its grease outside the Gardens. There was a bustle of bodies as six outriders, all young and brushed and clean as a squeak, convoyed the afternoon's main attraction to the convention floor.

The attraction was the Reverend Billy Graham, the boy wonder of the Baptists grown older. He wore a three-piece raiment of robin's-egg blue and enough pancake makeup to be a TV anchorman or the centrepiece at his own funeral. He had played the Gardens before, once with the Reverend Charles Templeton, now a renowned agnostic.

Reverend Graham smiled this way and that and seemed to nod towards Ballard. The Mammon of the Maple Leafs moved in, excusing himself as he plunged through Graham's outriders. "Pardon me, fellas," he said. "I own this joint and want to meet your leader."

Ballard stuck out a meaty paw and Graham, somewhat alarmed, shook it. "Put 'er there, Preacher," Ballard said, beaming, mischievous. "Geez, Preacher, would I like to have part of your racket. All cash and no invoices."

Harold was kidding, barely. Too many improper invoices was why he went to jail. Graham was uncomfortable in the presence of such a hearty heathen. His outriders nervously veered their leader out of the foyer inside the Gardens, towards the pulpit.

Ballard kept grinning as the group shuffled off. "Bless you," Billy Graham mumbled. Ballard said, "Bless you, too, Preacher."

Ballard turned to me and said, "You notice that preacher when I grabbed his hand? He was so surprised, he didn't know whether to shit or wind his watch."

During the week-long Baptist convention, Ballard stopped at a concession stand to ask how the soda-pop sales were going.

"We're not selling much pop, Mr. Ballard," the concessionaire said. "These Baptists keep asking for water."

"Water, eh?" Ballard said. "Okay, charge 'em 75 cents a cup." Then, turning to Shanty MacKenzie, Harold rubbed his meaty hands with the mirth of an avaricious Shylock. "I just lu-u-v Baptists," he said.

Harold had been raised a nominal Protestant, but his exposure to the bible convinced him "it's just a pack of fairy tales." He would say to King Clancy, an avowed Catholic, "We're supposed to get a lot of years in heaven, Clance. I'll trade you all mine up there for more of your years down here."

About then, in the late summer of 1980, Pal Hal decided to take total charge of his hockey team. The result could be summed up in the title of the autobiography of Hugh Garner, a flinty Toronto writer, *One Damn Thing after Another!* Ballard could be as maladroit as Garner was.

He began undercutting his general manager, Punch

Imlach. He made up with his ex-captain, Darryl Sittler. He was 77 and had his hair rinsed to a shiny shade of pumpkin. No senior citizen blustered with more junior ginger.

Imlach's control of the Maple Leafs faded in a contract collision with Borje Salming, Ballard's idea of God. Salming wanted $400,000 a year; Imlach correctly assessed the Swede's worth at $250,000. Then Imlach was struck with two heart attacks. While he recuperated, Ballard gave Salming a contract for more than $300,000 a year.

Imlach has been dead since 1987 but the current general manager, 32-year-old Gordon Stellick, is burdened with the Salming cross. Ballard was ready in 1989 to pay almost $400,000 a year to the 38-year-old defenceman with eroded skills, his good games further and further apart. Salming abandoned Ballard for $425,000 U.S., offered by the Detroit Red Wings.

As he aged, Salming was more accessible to the press and public. He was typical of eldering athletes who become more agreeable as they attempt to cling to what they were. He was learning to say hello when it was time to say goodbye.

Imlach's heart attacks, in the fall of 1980, provided Ballard the excuse to regain dominance in the hockey office. He restored Darryl Sittler as captain. He said of the recuperating Imlach, "Punch is still general manager, but I don't want to overwork him. I don't want to be the one to put him in a pine box."

Lurking off there in the Toronto hockey office was DOBS, Gerald McNamara, the Discoverer Of Borje Salming. McNamara became the ad hoc general manager in Imlach's absence. That meant he got to genuflect a lot to Ballard.

McNamara had been a hulking goaltender, hooked to a Maple Leaf hope that aborted. He played 323 minutes for the Leafs in the sixties, fewer than six games, his journeyman skills suited more to senior amateur hockey. He is a dour, devout Catholic, fearing only his God and, when he worked for the Leafs, Ballard. He did not utter dirty words as Leaf manager but volunteered dirty opinions.

Bill Houston began walking the Leaf hockey beat for the *Globe* in 1980 and, the first day the they met, heard McNamara's opinion of the newspaper. "Let's get something straight," McNamara apprised Houston. "Your newspaper writes lies."

McNamara dissected Houston's *Globe* colleagues. Don Ramsay "is a snake," Al Strachan "an armpit," Marty York "a liar." McNamara extended his vituperation to Lawrence Martin, who had left the *Globe* sports department to serve with distinction as a foreign correspondent in Washington and Moscow. Martin, in McNamara's bad mouth, was also "a liar."

McNamara suffered from newspaper paranoia, a disorder characterized by delusions ascribed to the supposed hostility of sports writers. One memorable night, he chased Don Ramsay out of the Toronto press box to protest some published slight in the *Globe*. It was the most resolute rush the Leafs made that season.

McNamara's paranoia was catching. Mike Nykoluk, one of the Leaf coaches, contracted a particularly virulent form of the mind malady. Nykoluk characterized two yammering telecasters at CFTO, Ferguson Oliver and Patrick Marsden, as "scum" and "hypocritical jerks."

Nykoluk had a wild aversion to the editorial barbs thrust into his indifferent coaching by Al Strachan of the *Globe*. After one game, Nykoluk grabbed Strachan and shoved him from the Leaf dressing room. "You start running me down, you son of a bitch," Nykoluk said, "and I don't want you in here. Now get the fuck out 'cause you're no goddamn sports writer!"

A *Globe* cameraman, Jim Lewcun, snapped pictures of Strachan's forceful expulsion from Coach Nykoluk's press conference. Assistant coach Dan Maloney, striding by, told Lewcun, "Come around here again and I'll smash that camera over your head." The contretemps seemed contrived by the *Globe*. If a reporter suspects he'll have trouble on an assignment, it is always wise to have a photographer handy to record the manhandling.

Unlike his bootlickers, Ballard never suffers from newspaper paranoia. He cultivates a few reporters, and is congenial with those he has known for years. The rest, when they write items offensive to Ballard, are dismissed with a curt "Fuck 'em!"

Infighting, the Media vs. the Maple Leaf management, made more news than the Maple Leaf players. If the management had spent more energy mustering a more competitive team, the media would have been less inclined to sneer. Modest achievements, diligently earned, receive ornate raves in the Toronto sporting press.

One Damn Thing after Another, indeed. Punch Imlach found he'd been phased out as Leaf manager when, returning to the Gardens after heart surgery, he discovered somebody else's car in his parking spot. Imlach said, before he died in 1987, "Coming back to the Leafs was the worst decision I ever made."

In 1982, Ballard discarded Toronto's top junior draftee in 1979, Laurie Boschman of Major, Saskatchewan. Boschman converted to born-again Christianity which, Ballard believed, softened the husky centre into a pacifist. A bout of infectious mononucleosis may have done the softening.

Boschman got better after he was traded to the Edmonton Oilers. He is still in the NHL, not notably pacific, administering bible punches on behalf of the Winnipeg Jets.

Ballard's off-again, on-again relationship with Darryl Sittler was off forever when the captain demanded a salary increase from $175,000 a year to about $280,000. Ballard refused. Sittler abandoned the Leafs on a road trip and agreed to be traded to the Philadelphia Flyers. It was, as Conn Smythe might have said, a case of crass before class. Bona fide pros do not quit on their teammates as Sittler did.

Ballard took his controversial show on the road on February 9, 1982, to the White House and the best known address in the Western world — 1600 Pennsylvania Ave., Washington, D.C., U.S.A.

The 1982 NHL all-star game was played in the home of the Washington Capitals, an arena tucked in the Maryland thickets around Landover. The Washington owner, Abe Pollin, had enough political muscle to pry an invitation to lunch with Ronald Duck, a former Hollywood actor who impersonated the U.S. President for eight years.

The President was a slightly reformed sports announcer known as Dutch Reagan 52 years ago when he broadcast baseball games played by the Chicago Cubs. A Follywood flack changed the pronunciation from Ree-gin to Ray-gun when the sports announcer landed in moving pictures.

Reagan played football player George Gipp, a Notre Dame luminary who died in his senior year. He played a hockey coach in *Hell's Kitchen*. He was the baby sitter for a monkey in another forgettable film, *Bedtime for Bonzo*.

Reagan greeted NHL stars in the gleaming East Room on the first floor of the White House. They browsed on crab bisque, roast beef and chocolate cake, a reasonable repast considering that White House chefs are not culinary hall-of-famers.

Hall-of-famers from various branches of show business sat with the President. Gordon Howe, Wayne Gretzky and Phil Esposito represented hockey, all with more impressive credentials in their game than Reagan in his. Comedian Bob Hope, Speaker Tip O'Neill of the U.S. House of Representatives and Canadian ambassador to Washington, Alan Gotlieb, dined with them.

Reagan was at home with a jock crowd, where thinking isn't mandatory. He had fun with the venerable Howe when he got up on his hind legs to speak. Howe played 32 seasons as a pro, his hockey abundance rolling up until he was 51.

"It's a real thrill for me to see Gordie Howe," Reagan said. "I remember my mother used to take me by the hand . . ." The crowd laughed, and Reagan added, "Gordie, would you believe, I was once a teenager." The President was then 71.

Reagan described hockey as "majestic," a laudatory term never used by even the loudest NHL tub-thumper. He mentioned his role as coach in *Hell's Kitchen*, where he supervised a gang of hockey cement-heads from the New York borough of the Bronx.

"Keeping a bunch of hockey players in line is no easy job," Reagan said. "I have a deepest appreciation of how hard it is to keep peace on the ice." Howe could have told him that hockey peace is kept by skating hard and wielding a big stick, as an earlier U.S. president, Theodore Roosevelt, more or less said.

After lunch, the leader of the Western world posed for pictures with Ballard and other NHL dignitaries. The Mahatma of the Maple Leafs, an old mummer himself, felt chummy beside the presidential hamborie who, in an X-rated movie, played second banana to a baboon. The X stood for "Excuse me."

Reagan's eyes glazed over as Ballard threw an arm around the President's shoulders and asked, confidentially, "Tell me, Ron, what d'you hear from Bonzo? Haw, haw, haw."

A large color picture of their meeting hangs in the Gardens. Stan Obodiac, the late publicist, put a swanky tag under the picture proclaiming "President Meets President."

Ballard's next excursion into international affairs occurred in the late summer of 1983 when a Russian SU-15 fighter plane shot down a Boeing 747 airliner, Korean Air Lines flight 007, over the Sea of Japan. All 269 people aboard were killed.

The Korean aircraft had violated Soviet air space over Sakhalin Island on the route from Anchorage, Alaska, to Seoul, South Korea. The Soviet despot, Yuri V. Andropov, refused to express remorse; he claimed the airliner had been spying over restricted territory.

When the airliner was obliterated on September 1, 1983, the fascinating Moscow Circus was about to begin a Canadian tour in Halifax. Appearances were scheduled in the Montreal Forum and Maple Leaf Gardens. Ballard, who often seemed apolitical, scuttled the circus.

He told me on CHCH-TV, via ship-to-shore radio from his boat in Georgian Bay, "You don't have to hit me with a bag of horse manure to make things move. I will not permit the representatives of Russian murderers to infest the Gardens. I'm cancelling the circus."

The Moscow carnival was booked for a week in the Gardens. Ballard's cancellation cost him and other shareholders a minimum of $500,000, but he called it "money well spent. The only way to make the Russians behave, short of shooting lead at them, is to put restrictions on them touring Canada. There are lots of good Russians, but their leaders want to rule the goddamn world. It's another Hitler situation."

The acrobats, dancing bears and trained seals returned to Moscow without performing a single somersault in Canada. The Gardens was stuck with scores of posters printed to advertise the circus, but the canny treasurer, Don Crump, is not inclined to leave any asset uncashed.

"What the hell, Duck, are we going to do with these posters?" Ballard asked. He always plays the nickname game. He calls Crump "Duck" as he called his wife "Jiggs" and King Clancy "Clance."

Duck Crump said, "You autograph these posters, Harold, and we'll sell them. The money we make you can turn over to charity." The posters were signed by Ballard, and sold, and the receipts sent to a fund for Jewish relief in the Soviet Union. A grateful B'nai B'rith lodge in Toronto named Ballard its man-of-the-year for 1983.

There was a postscript to Ballard's crusade on behalf of the proletariat. Yuri Andropov died on February 9, 1984, and was replaced by another walking dead man, Konstantin U. Chernenko. He died on March 10, 1985, after 13 months as Soviet dictator.

Duck Crump mentioned to Ballard, "You've been to Moscow, Harold . . ." Ballard interrupted, "And hated every minute of it. But I got a hell of a kick seeing old Lenin snoozing in his tomb." Crump continued, "So why don't we send condolences to the Kremlin. Want me to send a wire?"

"Splendid fucking idea, Duck," Ballard said. "Get on it." The telegram, expedited over Ballard's name to the Politburo of the Soviet Central Committee, read: "Wish to express sympathy on death of Comrade Chernenko. In his name, Maple Leaf Gardens is sending money to help Jewish refugees escape U.S.S.R. Chernenko's death couldn't have happened to nicer guy."

His wire to the Kremlin was proof, if further proof was needed, that Ballard keeps fueling his feuds. On the home front, for example, he settled with Foster Hewitt, who linked with John Bassett in sidestepping Ballard before he was sent to vacation for a year in the Millhaven Motel.

In 1978, Ballard removed the radio rights from Hewitt's station, CKFH, the voice of the Leafs for more than 25 years.

Ballard said, "Hell, I finally wanted to hear the goddamn games. You couldn't hear 'FH up at Yonge and Wellesley, unless there was a hell of a tail wind." Wellesley Street was four blocks north of CKFH on Yonge, about as far as Eddie Shack could drive a puck.

Ballard awarded the radio rights instead to CKO, a Toronto

station on FM band. He received the same amount of money, but cut off many hockey listeners to spite Hewitt. CKFH, with an AM signal, reached a wider audience than CKO, even without a tail wind.

Rick Boulton is a free-lance Toronto writer and, in 1979, one of his jobs was editing the Maple Leaf hockey program. Boulton walked into the Gardens one day in September, looked up and noticed that the most famous piece of memorabilia in the Cash Box was missing. The gondola was gone.

The long, narrow gondola hung down from the roof, out over the ice surface, the best seat in the house. Hewitt had broadcast Leaf games from the gondola since the Gardens opened, in 1931. It was the first furniture visitors wanted to see on their first trip to the Gardens.

Rick Boulton checked around and discovered that the gondola had been destroyed. The steel was stockpiled, the wood tossed into the Gardens' incinerator. Boulton sold the story to *The Toronto Star* and, after publication, was fired as editor of the Gardens' program.

The *Star* streamed the details across the front page, under the headline "Oh no! Ballard's trashed Hewitt's gondola." NHL president Clarence Campbell was quoted as sounding incensed. "The gondola represents one of the most significant things in Canadian history. It is a worthy historical site. It should have been preserved for people to visit in the Hockey Hall of Fame."

Maurice (Lefty) Reid, curator of the Hall of Fame, expressed dismay. "Why wasn't I called?" Reid said. "Of course I wanted the gondola, when we have space for it." The space needed would have been 60 feet long and 10 feet wide.

Hewitt said, "I can't believe it. The gondola was home for me. It's typical of Ballard. He has no respect for memories or nostalgia." Sports pundits asked, "How could this happen?"

It happened because the chap with the orange hair who owns the place made it happen. Ballard said, "We're installing private boxes up under the roof and the gondola gets in the way of seeing the ice surface. The gondola had to go."

The *Star* was pro-Hewitt since Foster started his broadcasting career for a prehistoric *Star* station. The paper followed

Rick Boulton's report by asking Ballard if he'd pay to have the gondola rebuilt and sent to the Hall of Fame.

"No," Ballard said. "I'd like to see Foster pay. Let him pay for the rebuilding." Harold added, "Hell, I'll even pay for the nails."

Bill Houston of the *Globe* mused on the bashing of the broadcast booth. "Whether the gondola was worth saving is debatable," Houston wrote. "Those who know Ballard say there was no malice in his decision to trash it. Not one to miss a chance for a little more publicity, Ballard announced a few days later that Hewitt's gondola chair had been saved."

That was a bit more of Ballard's carny proclivity. He had the Gardens' maintenance crew find scores of old kitchen chairs, paint them red, and label them "Foster's Chair." Harold insisted he sold 100 bogus chairs at $5.00 each.

Foster didn't care for the joke. "When I lost the gondola," he said, "I lost a piece of my life." And yet, and yet, old allegiances can transcend animosities. Harold had helped Hewitt's father manage the Canadian gold-medalists in the 1928 Olympic tournament, and Foster remembered.

In 1981, on the 50th anniversary of the opening of the Gardens, Ballard asked Hewitt to join in a ceremony at centre ice. Foster did, glad to be there with King Clancy and other vintage remnants of the 1931–32 Stanley Cup team. The older we become, most of us, the more excessive our loyalty to the past.

Clancy and Ballard moved through the eighties, both slowed by diabetes. Too many chocolates and sugar-packed ice cream sundaes clogged the blood vessels in Harold's legs. Clancy was rising 84 in November, 1986 when a gall-bladder attack struck him down. The organ was removed in Wellesley Hospital but he did not recover from the operation. His two daughters and two sons and the Clancy Irregulars – bookmakers, ticket scalpers, sports writers, old playmates – kept watch, more solemn than King ever was. The vigil ended when he died, on November 10.

Ballard took charge of his closest friend's funeral, perhaps with more grace and muted respect than Clancy's family thought possible. He decreed that King's remains be placed in the directors' room in the Gardens to permit hockey fans to tender last regards. They came in off Carlton Street in steady hesitant numbers, aware that if anyone should lie in state in the Gardens, it should be a player who had sweated, for not much money, to pay the mortgage on the building.

Clancy was a horse bettor, not heavy but steady. You'd see him in the betting lines in the warm Toronto summers at Woodbine. He'd be there with Ballard or, more often, with a devoted companion named Joan.

That last morning, in his coffin in the Gardens, Clancy looked as though he was about to open his eyes and declare, "C'mon, Harold. Let's get going. First post's at 1:30 and I want to play the daily double."

Ballard had a Racing Form and he tucked it beside King in the coffin. I reached into my wallet for a two-dollar bill and gave it to Harold. "Put this in King's pocket," I said. "There may be horses running where he's going."

Clancy was buried from St. Michael's Cathedral in Toronto and a mourner, kneeling, could reflect what his passing meant to the hockey clans. There is never enough laughter, even in games, and now a big irreplaceable chunk of it was lost. Some of our dreams went into Clancy's casket forever.

CHAPTER 18

The Battling Ballards

♦

Male bonding is central to Ballard's existence, a buddy system based through the years on mutual reliance in speed boats, hockey teams and similar rowdy business. Red Foster, Hap Day, Staff Smythe and King Clancy were Harold's pals-old-pals, but he has connected with an assortment of other cronies to sit around and tell ribald lies.

There is some small boy in his bonding, a tree house where the guys can escape the girls. Ballard's tree house is the bunker where he sits for hockey games in the Gardens, an exclusive domain for himself and favored male companions — one of his hockey scouts, the father of one of his players, another NHL owner, a sports writer. No women need apply.

The loss of King Clancy deprived Harold of his last great friend. He has discovered, at 86, that most of his contemporaries have hobbled through what Robert Lowell called "the grizzled grass." He finds it convenient to have a black necktie handy in case of a sudden funeral.

Ballard had his best moment as a team owner three weeks after King Clancy died. His Hamilton Ticats, maligned in pregame predictions, roared football defiance and trounced the Edmonton Eskimos 39–15 to win the Grey Cup, in Vancouver, on November 30, 1986. Coach Al Bruno and the Cats ate 'em, as they holler in Hamilton, "Raw, raw, RAW!"

Harold, hugging the Cup, was more reflective than exultant. "It's humanly impossible to say how I feel," he said. "It's something I've never had happen in a long series of defeats with the hockey club."

He seldom permits sentiment to show, but his guard came down on his Grey Cup Day. "I'm so sorry King couldn't be here to share this prize," he said. "But you can be sure that wherever Clance is, he was watching and playing a part in every play."

Ballard can, in contrast to his affection for Clancy, dismiss a friend with cavalier disdain, often for long periods or forever.

Munson Campbell owned the Colorado Rockies before that funny franchise was switched to New Jersey. Campbell was a constant companion in Ballard's bunker, instrumental, he says, in getting Harold elected to the Hockey Hall of Fame in 1977. Campbell and Ballard quarrelled a few years ago after Ballard failed to attend the funeral of a mutual friend, Bruce Norris, at one time the remote, chilly owner of the Detroit Red Wings. Campbell and Norris were classmates at Yale University; Harold and Norris had cut up jackpots for 25 years in the NHL. Campbell complained to Harold about missing the Norris farewell; Harold told Campbell "to go to hell."

Jean Sonmor, a sensitive sports writer, interviewed Campbell in November, 1988, on the complexities of Pal Hal.

Campbell was detached, but generous in his assessment. "You have to admire Ballard's indomitable chemistry," Campbell said. "He's got an excellent business mind." He added, less generously, "But Harold's letting Yolanda make a jackass of him."

The name Yolanda appeared as well in litigation involving Ballard and Michael J. Gobuty, a heavy Winnipeg promoter with several chins clacking up towards his jawbone. Gobuty snuggled up to Ballard after King Clancy died, adopting the role of favorite son anxious to have Ballard back "a friendly takeover for the Gardens."

Ballard signed loan guarantees to Gobuty, apparently unaware the money would be used to pay off outstanding Gobuty debts. The pre-trial examination for discovery revealed that in September 1987, Gobuty sent "Yolanda Ballard" a certified cheque for $75,000. Acountants at the Gardens, anti-Yolanda, claim the $75,000 was a finder's fee for Yolanda introducing Gobuty to Ballard. Yolanda informed me that the $75,000 was "for jewelry Gobuty wanted from me."

Yolanda Ballard is the lady's legal name, not her married one. An action in the Supreme Court of Ontario, dated Sep-

tember 19, 1986, resulted in a name change from Yolanda
Anna MacMillan to Yolanda Anna Ballard.

Ballard made no apparent fuss about his lover altering her
name to his. Ballard mentioned to Don Giffen, his closest
colleague on the Gardens' directorate, "I wouldn't pick
Yolanda as someone to marry, but she is nice to me."

Their affair, Harold and Yo's, is titillating soap opera, the
slobbering stuff of "Dallas" or "Dynasty". The Battling Ballards is played out in the Toronto media, private lives as
public property, the buzzards of Bay Street circling his bed
every time he goes to hospital, scandalmongers besieging
her in her vehement struggle with the three Ballard children.

She entered their lives in 1983 as Yolanda Babik MacMillan, divorced, short, white blond hair above an attractive,
knowing face that can smile or scowl. She can cross herself
dramatically, murmur, "Holy Mary, Mother of God," or call
homosexual men "bum whackers."

She has been used by men, and knows how to use them
and, by 1983, was as demure as an iron foundry. Ballard
would be 80 on July 30, 1983, and Yolanda MacMillan, at
loose ends, bankrupt, decided to deliver him a birthday cake.
There may have been deliveries of several birthday cakes
before she caught him in the Gardens.

The day she caught him, in the executive offices, she is
supposed to have offered him the cake and he is supposed to
have asked what he could do for her. Harold may be sexist,
but he will oblige most women he considers sexy.

Yolanda asked if they could talk alone and Harold, gallantry unlimited, invited her into his private sanctum. Again
he asked what he could do for her, and she said, "Mr. Ballard, I had the same problem you had."

He said, "What could that be, my dear?" and she said,
"I've also been to jail like you." From that bizarre beginning,
their tempestuous union has been one damn thing after
another, frequently on the front page, figuratively surrounded by a picket fence of exclamation marks.

Yolanda Babik was 20 and saucy when she kicked her
heels out of the grain-elevator jerkwater of Thunder Bay in
1953 and landed in Toronto chasing a rainbow of big bucks
well spent. Her first job was as an operator for Bell Tele-

phones, but her extravagant ambitions weren't gratified by saying "Number, please?" into a mouthpiece.

She met a younger lawyer purposefully on the rise, William MacMillan, and married him on January 12, 1957. That year, they moved to MacMillan's hometown of Windsor, where he opted to practise law.

The details of their crumbling marriage were made public in a report on Yolanda MacMillan prepared for the Ontario Ministry of Correctional Services before she was sentenced in 1981 on charges of committing perjury and conspiracy to commit fraud. The trial, before the Honorable Mr. Justice Trainor of the Supreme Court of Ontario, was held in the western Ontario community of Chatham.

The pre-sentencing report had all the surface facts.

The MacMillans' first child, a son, was born on March 2, 1958, and a daughter was born on Feb. 22, 1963. It was at this time the offender (Yolanda) became acquainted with Mr. Donald Lloyd, a Chatham businessman who owned property, which included houses and apartments. The offender was invited to act as his agent in renting and managing the properties.

According to the accused, in 1961–1962 she became aware of property located at 810 Devonshire Road, 819 Argyle Road and 2030 Catarquara Way in Windsor, which was occupied by a religious order of Maltese priests who were interested in selling the property. The property was located in an exclusive residential area of Old Walkerville, according to the accused, and there was no problem in renting the apartments. The money for the down payment on this property was borrowed from her parents but the property was listed in the names of both the accused and her husband.

In 1966, the accused's marriage began to flounder and her husband left her in 1967. According to the subject, her husband was "fooling around" with other women. Her husband sought a divorce but the accused did not agree, and this resulted in an acrimonious divorce action which attracted considerable publicity at the time.

The accused maintains that she did not want a divorce and said that "I chased him halfway around the world" in an attempt to effect a reconciliation, without success, however.

In 1967, the accused and her two children moved to Toronto, without, according to Mr. W. MacMillan, conferring with him. Both children were enrolled in private schools. The daughter was in residence at Bishop Strachan School, where the annual fees were approximately $8,000.00. The son attended St. Andrew's College in Aurora, Ont. . . .

A transcript from the Supreme Court of Ontario documents the case of "Her Majesty the Queen, respondent, and Yolanda MacMillan, appellant."

THE FACTS: 1. The Appellant entered pleas of guilty at Chatham before the Honorable Mr. Justice Trainor on Nov. 9, 1981 to two counts of indictment charging that Robert Irwin and she . . . between the 1st day of June, 1977 and the 31st of October, 1979, inclusive, at the Town of Wallaceburg and at the City of Chatham, in the County of Kent, and in the Province of Ontario and elsewhere, did conspire together with Louis Puscas and Marion Lloyd, each with one or more of the others . . . to commit the indictable offence of fraud, to wit:

By deceit, falsehood or other fradulent means to defraud (by means of a forged Will dated the 8th day of October, 1977), Gary Lloyd, Neville Lloyd and Noran Deane, said persons being the beneficiaries of the estate of the late William Donald Lloyd, of property, money or valuable securities having a value of approximately $3,000,000.00, contrary to Section 423(1)(d) of the Criminal Code of Canada.

And further that she . . . with intent to mislead, gave false evidence that on the 8th day of October, 1977, she was present and witnessed the late William Donald Lloyd sign his signature, as testator, to a Will dated October 8, 1977, which instrument was alleged to have been the last Will and testament of the said late William Donald Lloyd, knowing such evidence to be false and did therefore commit perjury, contrary to Section 121 of the Criminal Code of Canada.

2. The Appellant was sentenced on December 18, 1981, to imprisonment for a period of three years on each charge concurrent.

3. Pursuant to the Order of the Honorable Mr. Justice Arnup dated April 8, 1982, the Appellant was released pending the determination of her appeal, following one hundred and thirteen days of incarceration. . . .

Yolanda Ballard, in the argot of the law, cops a plea on the case against her. She maintains she had no other option; according to Jean Sonmor in *The Toronto Sun*, "she didn't have the $50,000 Eddie Greenspan wanted to defend her."

Greenspan is a prominent Toronto defence counsel, accustomed to charging high fees for high-profile clients. It is debatable if any noted counsel could have rid Yolanda of what she calls "my legal problem." She pleads for forgiveness, and forgetting. "I've paid with tears and suffering and heartache."

There is no forgiving or forgetting in the court documents.

THE FACTS UPON THE PLEA OF GUILTY: On November 9, 1981, prior to endorsing the indictment with the acceptance of the Appellant's pleas of guilty, the following facts were adduced by Crown counsel:

On March 11, 1978, William Donald Lloyd, of Chatham, Ontario, died after a brief illness of a month. He was a manufacturer and owner of the Lloyd Bag Corporation in Chatham and Donald Lloyd Enterprises in Windsor. Lloyd left an estate valued at over $3,000,000.00.

During his life he had two marriages. The first in 1936 to Noran Isabelle Skellet, the mother of his only child, Dr. Gary Lloyd, who is currently a plastic surgeon in Oakville, Ontario. His second marriage was to Marion Semenyn in 1965, with whom he was living at the time of his death and who will be referred to in this case as Marion Lloyd, his widow. . . .

The accused Irwin was a lawyer . . . and practiced in Wallaceburg with the law firm Burgess and Irwin at the time he acted for the late Donald Lloyd on occasion and knew him socially.

Both the accused Irwin and MacMillan of Toronto have been lovers and associates for a number of years and were in that capacity during the time frame of this indictment, and still are. . . .

The four co-conspirators in the scheme were the lovers Robert Irwin and MacMillan, the widow Lloyd, and Louis Puscas, described as "a friend and client of Irwin's who had done business with the late Donald Lloyd and also was a friend of his."

The dead man, Lloyd, was another client of the accused lawyer, Irwin. In 1971, on Lloyd's instructions, Irwin drafted and executed a will for him. The will provided for an annual income of $20,000 a year for each of the first and second wives. The bulk of the estate was left to Lloyd's only child, Dr. Gary Lloyd, the principal beneficiary and executor of the will.

Dr. Lloyd assumed management of his father's company when his father became ill and incapacitated in February, 1978. Prudently, Dr. Lloyd removed his father's will from the company safe in Chatham and gave it to his own lawyer in Oakville for safekeeping.

Donald Lloyd died on March 11, 1978, and was buried three days later. Robert Irwin, a lawyer engineering the plot, contacted Robert Savage, a lawyer, and Dr. Lloyd, on the day of the funeral.

Irwin, impelled by urgency, asked Savage to meet him in Toronto on the evening of the funeral to discuss the Lloyd estate. They agreed to meet in the Sutton Place, a midtown hostelry on Bay Street.

The Crown established that "Savage met both Irwin and MacMillan that evening, March 14, 1978, for dinner at that place. Irwin introduced MacMillan as his client and he offered, in MacMillan's absence, to not contest the estate or the 1971 Will if Marion Lloyd be given $900,000.00 or the Windsor properties which were valued at approximately that amount. . . . At no time did either Irwin or MacMillan ever mention any knowledge of a supposed 1977 Will, even though later Irwin's close associate and lover, MacMillan, would allege and testify under oath that she was an attesting witness to an alleged Will dated October 8, 1977, allegedly on that date in Las Vegas, Nevada."

The Crown underscored why the four co-conspirators arranged a fake will. "Prior to Lloyd's death, both Irwin and MacMillan were in financial distress, Puscas liked to go to Las Vegas to gamble; while Marion Lloyd was not, or course, the principal beneficiary of the estate valued at approximately $3,000,000.00" Their collective motive was greed, in Yolanda's case, desperate greed.

In late June, 1978, Louis Puscas was asked by Robert Irwin if he, Puscas, would be interested in signing a document in exchange for $50,000 in U.S. funds. Puscas agreed. "A few days later Irwin had Puscas . . . sign as an attesting witness to a forged Will dated October 8, 1977. The forged signature of the late Donald Lloyd was already on the Will at the time . . . MacMillan was there at the same time and Puscas saw her affixing her signature as attesting witness to the same phony Will dated October 8, 1977."

The Chatham Police Department, in mid-July, 1979, requested the assistance of the Racket Branch of the Ontario Provincial Police in investigating the forgery. A search of Robert Irwin's law office produced incriminating evidence.

> The most significant document was a piece of tracing paper that was found in a plastic envelope in Irwin's desk in his law office, and a file, and it bore a simulated signature of the late Donald Lloyd, similar to the one on the forged will dated October 8, 1977. This signature on the tracing paper was a forgery.
>
> In January of 1980, all four co-conspirators in this matter . . . were arrested and charged by the Racket Branch of the Ontario Provincial Police in Toronto . . . Counsel for MacMillan admitted, quite clearly, that MacMillan witnessed a signature on a Will after Donald Lloyd was dead, knowing he was dead, and that she then conspired . . . to carry that Will forward as a valid Will. . . .

Yolanda, sentenced to three years imprisonment, served a

few days short of four months in the reformatory for women at Brampton, Ontario.

The architect of the swindle, lawyer Irwin, was jailed for four years and disbarred by the Law Society of Upper Canada. A communiqué from the Law Society on January 21, 1982, announced: "ROBERT LEROY IRWIN of Wallaceburg was disbarred. He improperly borrowed from two clients who had lost more than $55,000 and then attempted to conceal the borrowings from the Society by giving false information to the Society's auditor."

Irwin was 50 in 1982 and had practised law for 24 years after being called to the Ontario bar in 1958. He claimed to be a past president of the County of Kent Law Association and former president of the Wallaceburg Chamber of Commerce.

The details of the disbarment indicated that Irwin and Yolanda MacMillan were bonded in both business and boudoir. Researchers for the Law Society, checking registries at the Ontario Ministry of Consumer and Commercial Relations, found a numbered company, 383242 Ontario Ltd. According to the Law Society, "The searches revealed that the head office of the company was Wallaceburg, Ont.; that Robert Irwin was a Director and President and that Yolanda MacMillan was Vice-President.

"In their testimony, both Mrs. MacMillan and the solicitor indicated that at the time of incorporation and the time of these borrowings, the solicitor had a 20 per cent interest in the company, the remaining 80 per cent being held by Mrs. MacMillan. ..."

One of the two men who were fleeced of $55,000 testified "that he was advised by the solicitor (Irwin) that if he assisted the Law Society he would not get his money back." Irwin defended himself and lost, again proof of the legal adage that a lawyer who defends himself has a fool for a client.

Irwin is seen occasionally in Toronto, sometimes a few blocks north of Maple Leaf Gardens, on shady Dundonald Street, not far from the fashionable townhouse formerly occupied by the adult son and daughter of Yolanda Babik MacMillan Ballard.

Yolanda stirred a variety of opinions when she lived in the Windsor-Wallaceburg area, the opinions all black or white, never bland indifferent. The pre-sentence report prepared by a Probation and Parole Officer for the Ministry of Correctional Services portrayed "The offender as a person."

"The offender was described by her former husband, William MacMillan, as being as a compulsive liar, who was adept at deception. She would use exaggeration, promises and evasions to achieve her objective. He described her as being very persuasive with manipulative skills, enabling her to convince all kinds of people."

The picture emerged of a disenchanted ex-husband discussing an ex-wife with candor steeped in bile. "Mr. MacMillan described her as being overly concerned with receiving recognition from the 'high society' of Windsor . . . and with strenuous efforts at entertaining to obtain acceptance . . . and achieve the status she desired."

She was bitten by a gnawing ambition to be somebody somewhere with money to be flung as the materialistic measure of success. She is not unique, but gaudy.

"Mr. MacMillan said that he remonstrated with his wife when she entertained lavishly on a scale that was inappropriate for a young lawyer. He added that the accused could be extremely generous and gave flowers and gifts to friends and acquaintances. Alternately, she could be mean and cheat local tradespeople out of small amounts of money."

Angus MacMillan Jr., brother of Yolanda's former husband, expressed prejudice against her. "He said . . . she was unable to appreciate the necessity of telling the truth, was an extrovert and capable of behaving in an entertaining and spectacular way to persuade others to her point of view."

Yolanda's affairs, tangled in her relationship with Robert Irwin, involved a golf club.

> In 1977, the accused and R. Irwin purchased the St. Clair Golf and Country Club at Wallaceburg, the previous owners having failed in operating the golf club.
>
> The accused said she worked hard to try and renovate the clubhouse and make it into a paying proposition. The golf club failed, however, and closed on Sept. 20, 1980.
>
> The accused claims she has obtained mortgage funds

through good friends enabling the St. Clair Golf and Country Club to commence operating as a Health Retreat. An Ontario Development Loan has been extended to cover the new business venture, now called the Country Club Total Health Retreat. This will provide accommodation and treatment for a maximum of thirty clients.

The properties owned by the accused are estimated by her to be valued as follows: 810 Devonshire Road at $650–750,000; the St. Clair Golf and Country Club at $700–750,000; and a Wallaceburg office building at $90,000. She also claims a collateral worth of $400,000.

The report for the Ministry of Correctional Services concluded:

The offender is a remarkable woman of determination and ambition. She is both manipulative and persistent and able to employ an assortment of tactics including domination and flattery as the situation dictates. . . .

She admits to having been described as "theatrical" in her behavior, where she calculated it might prove profitable. She proudly asserts that she is an emotional person and is prone to weep when describing a touching or sad scene or event. . . .

The probation and parole officer found no remorse in Yolanda over the dumbbell crime of forging a spurious will. "She is not embarrassed at the situation she finds herself in and does not consider telling falsehoods a breach of business ethics. . . .

"She admits freely her guilt but claims she was led astray, insisting she didn't read the document, that she lied to help another person and that she was taken for a 'true blue sucker.' She accepts no feeling of guilt or remorse for the part she played in the offence but asserts that she was naive, and in her offer to help she was taken advantage of. . . . "

Yolanda served a brief penalty but paid a greater price in trying to leap from a bottom-dog background to upper-class wealth. The Ontario Development Corporation seized and sold her Wallaceburg golf course. A second mortgagee took control of her Devonshire Road property in Windsor. The Toronto-Dominion Bank seized and sold her office building in Wallaceburg.

Another indignity was the loss of her penthouse suite in a condominium building, the Palace Pier, which sits on the south-east toe of Etobicoke, west of the Humber River. Sheriff officers acting on behalf of the condominium corporation evicted Yolanda and seized her belongings. The eviction followed her failure to pay condominium fees.

On August 31, 1983, filing for bankruptcy in Toronto, she signed a form declaring that she was "unemployed, had nil income and was being supported by friends." The statement of her liabilities showed a "grand total of $592,500.00." Her creditors ranged from Bell Telephone ($500.00) to lawyer E.L. Greenspan ($6,000.00) to the Toronto-Dominion Bank ($60,000.00) and the Royal Bank of Canada ($330,000.00).

Her statement of assets ranged from cash on hand (nil) to furniture (nil) to real property (nil) to stocks and bonds (nil) to motorized vehicles (nil) for a grand total of NIL. On April 27, 1984, she received an "absolute order of discharge of bankrupt" in the Supreme Court of Ontario. She was 51 and still aspiring to be what she couldn't afford. Her creditors qualified for a word employed profanely by horse bettors who blow their bankroll on beaten favorites. They were "stiffed."

The seamy details were of intense interest to Ballard's three children when Yolanda began to nest with Harold in the studio apartment on the second floor of the Gardens. She brought along a great, white, curly-haired joyous brute of a Bouvier dog. Harold, with his fondness for nicknames, called her "Yo" and the massive mutt "T.C. Puck." The T.C. stands for Tiger-Cats, the Puck for Maple Leafs.

T.C. Puck is not the sort of pet you'd keep around unless you wanted to sic him on some intruder on the lawn. He is the Al Iafrate of Toronto dogs, big, willing, eager and not precisely certain what big feet are for. Iafrate is a Toronto defenceman who has everything for stardom if he could focus intently on every shift in every game.

Harold may not have wanted to keep Yolanda, bold and

smiling, when she walked in on him with a birthday cake that summer day in 1983. He did not, to his children's chagrin, ask her to leave. "She got to be such a nice little thing," Pal Hal said. "Cuddly-like." Ballard's offspring couldn't stand the cuddling when they discovered her involvement in the faked-will scam. It could happen, they reasoned, to their father's real will, which was drafted to leave them multimillionaires.

Mary Elizabeth, married a second time, has the good looks of her mother and the stay-up-all-night vigor her father used to have. She says of herself and her two brothers, "We're the Battling Ballards and we stick together."

Bill Ballard, who is not offended when the Toronto newspapers describe him as "boyishly handsome," inherited his father's excessive overdrive. He is president of Concert Productions International, a gadfly who buzzes in other directions.

Bill, in concert with Michael Gobuty, attempted to buy the St. Louis Blues of the NHL in the mid-1980s, when the team was owned by Harry Ornest. "They offered me a cashier's cheque for $3 million to move the Blues to Hamilton," Ornest said. "Nothing happened."

The background strokes are quickly sketched. Ornest grew up scuffling in Edmonton 55 years ago, a Depression kid peddling newspapers, scraping ice rinks, hustling to escape the economic ghetto imprisoning his parents, impoverished Jews from Poland. He succeeded and, in 1983, purchased a dilapidated St. Louis franchise then on its lowest Blues note.

Ornest saved the game in St. Louis, or, more precisely, preserved the team from being moved to Saskatoon. Harold Ballard was among the NHL owners who supported Ornest's bid in St. Louis, for perverse reasons. "Who the hell wants to go to Saskatoon?" Harold demanded. "We'd have to get in there by dog team for the games. Big planes can't fly into Saskatoon." We were gabbing on television when the St. Louis shift to Saskatoon was a lively topic. "I'm goddamn against it," Pal Hal said. "Saskatoon can't handle a big plane. Why, just the other day, a great horned owl tried to land in Saskatoon and overshot the goddamned runway."

Bill Ballard's efforts to transfer the St. Louis team to Hamilton was a laudable idea. Hamilton has, in Copps Coliseum, a big-league arena with a capacity for 17,000 spectators. It has a constituency of hockey fans to fill it. Under the arbitrary NHL law, Harold Ballard owns Hamilton for NHL purposes because the Steel City is within a 75-mile radius from Maple Leaf Gardens. Any promoter of an NHL team in Hamilton must indemnify Ballard for the territory.

Harold pledged, "No problem. I'd give up my NHL rights in Hamilton for a buck if the Hamilton city council would renovate the damn inadequate stadium where my Ticats play." He meant Ivor Wynne Stadium where, in the words of a ballad from the Second Great War, "There are rats, rats, big as al-ley cats/ In the park/ In the park/ There are rats, rats, big as al-ley cats/ In the Ticat football park. . . ."

None of the above happened. Harry Ornest stayed in St. Louis, ultimately selling the Blues for a satisfactory profit. Ballard sold the Ticats to hopeful Hamilton buyers who will be lucky to survive in Canadian football.

Ornest, sticking and moving with a shrewd promoter's instinct, bought the money-losing Toronto Argonauts, but they are not the Toronto team he wants. He wants the money-making Maple Leafs, and not merely because they make money. He, too, shivered with delight on those winter Saturday nights when Foster Hewitt hollered, "He shoots, he scores!"

The Ballard children, Mary Elizabeth, Bill and Harold Jr., may have thought Yolanda might own the Gardens upon the death of Harold Sr. She won't. There was a time when the senior Harold thought Bill could run the Gardens, but he hasn't thought so in recent years. He told Jean Sonmor of *The Toronto Sun*, "Bill has no brains. He'd still be eating out of garbage cans if it weren't for his partner, Michael Cohl."

Bill and Cohl, in tight circumstances five years ago, borrowed $5 million from Harold to keep CPI solvent. The money was repaid, with substantial interest. The Labatt brewers later bought 49 per cent of CPI, for a reported $15 million, but Labatt didn't buy a rock-concert outfit without having one large, crafty, corporate eye on the Gardens.

The cool scheming eye of Yolanda Ballard is the one that

concerns Bill Ballard, a graduate lawyer with a virulent and unyielding hatred for his father's nurse, lover and chatelaine. He has kept track of the time he has had suspicions about her, almost from the day she entered their lives. He said to me on September 23, 1988, "I've been trying to get Yolanda for five years, eight months and 21 days. I like to fish and, in her case, I'm going for a big one."

In 1982 Yolanda MacMillan sought the friendship of Stephen Boleslav Roman, a chunky Slovak immigrant grown rich from a uranium deposit in northern Ontario which became the base for Denison Mines, Ltd. Roman became, before his death in 1987, the patron saint of Ontario Slovaks, a constituency which included Yolanda Babik's parents in Thunder Bay. He also presided over the World Slovak Congress.

Brian O'Malley directs Standard Trust, a Toronto company founded by Roman, and O'Malley recalls an overture Yolanda Babik made towards Roman. "She was complex," he said. "She had some sort of deal she wanted to sell Roman, in return for his financial help."

Yolanda didn't get any help from that source, although Roman may have known her father. Her next stop was Maple Leaf Gardens, to the delight of Harold and the distress of his children. Yolanda was prepared, when the affair began, to reach detente with Harold's family. She arranged a birthday party for Harold in 1985 in Mary Elizabeth's home in the gilt-edged Toronto enclave of Forest Hill. "I've tried," Yolanda insists, "to get the Ballard family together."

Harold asks her, when she refers to his family, to "knock off that bullshit. You shouldn't say anything about my kids the way they talk about you, calling you an old whore and everything." Not that Harold's terms for Yolanda are entirely endearing. He has talked too harshly about too many people for too long to ease up even on this most intimate roommate. He has called her "a bloody nuisance and a real bawl baby. If she was a boat, she'd have sunk long ago."

Once, feeling trapped, he said to me, "I'm surrounded by lunatics." I said, "Who?" and he said, "Her and them," meaning Yolanda and his progeny.

There are other times, when Harold's alone and ailing in

hospital, when he leans on her physical support and company. She can be a vision in pink, her favorite color, wearing gold ornamental fabric boots too young for her years, as she comes bouncing into the hospital room to light up his night. Those times, tender times, he'll call her "sweetheart" and "princess."

Many of Harold's confidants have difficulty describing Yolanda in endearing terms. The late Robert Sedgwick, Ballard's lawyer and alternate Toronto governor in the NHL, controlled his affection for her with a firm, tight hold. One day, playing golf, Sedgewick teed up his ball and said to his partner, Manager Frank Bonello of the Marlboros, "She is a wicked woman." Ballard relishes that wickedness.

Bill Ballard chimes in, "My sentiments exactly." Bill threatened to dig up his mother's coffin in Park Lawn Cemetery and remove it to a location unknown to his dad. He said, "I don't want that bitch Yolanda tramping over my mother's grave with flowers."

Bill and his brother Harold Jr., or Bobby, contained their loathing for Yolanda long enough to attend the 84th birthday party she arranged for Pal Hal on July 30, 1987. It was a day of high sun and good humor on the lawn of his Thunder Beach summer home, built on a bluff above the merry tossing blue-dark waters of Georgian Bay. Yolanda padded around in slacks, wanting everyone to enjoy the day. A nice man from the Hot Stove Lounge barbecued steak and boiled ears of corn and served enormous wedges of strawberry cheesecake. City guests ambled about inhaling the fresh, nippy air and dipping their beaks into assorted beverages and grinning at each other and saying contented "Aaahs. How the hell long have people been living like this?"

Ballard sat sunning himself like a king walrus, in white shorts and brown loafers and a large white planter's straw hat about as far around as a six-furlong racetrack. He was at home with people who brought presents for a man who has everything. Somebody gave him a silver-plated navel lint remover. Steve Stavro, a Gardens' director and influential farmer from the Knob Hills, brought a goose and a gander with ribbons on their necks identifying one as "Yolanda" and the other as "Harold." Bob Morrow, the lanky mayor of Hamilton, brought a plaque saluting Ballard as "a fine upstanding citizen for keeping football alive in Hamilton."

"I can hardly wait, Your Worship," Harold said, "for the McTamney pawnbrokers to open tomorrow so I can see what I can hock this plaque for. Haw, haw, haw!"

Dick Duff, the quick Leaf sniper, was there with John Brophy, the former rough-edged Leaf coach whom Ballard liked. They were interesting contrasts, owner and coach. Harold had tangerine-colored hair; he was 84 but his hair was 36. Brophy was 54, so gray his hair is older than he is.

Bobby Ballard got a little drunk and forgot his usual good manners. Across the yard, he noticed Yolanda who, in slacks, is put together in bunches, like grapes. "There goes my dad's lover," Bobby jeered. "Tugboat Annie." Somebody who had sampled Yolanda's hospitality said, "Aw, shuddup."

The party was an epic insignificance of the pleasant life, an escape from the banal daily treadmill. A sunny afternoon drifted into a tranquil evening, the wind subsiding until only wavelets chopped Georgian Bay. Stars appeared, fistfuls of confetti dotting the night sky.

Guests departed but Harold didn't want a good day to end. "Stick around," he said to me. "We got some more corn Yolanda'll heat up. I'd like to talk."

He said of the Gardens, looking ahead, "It won't be left to my kids. But what the hell do they care? They're each going to wind up with about $18 million."

I said I thought his son Bill could run the Gardens and the hockey team, but Ballard said, "I don't think he could run it well. Bill's trying to out-Harold Harold. Too much bragging."

He said he'd like to leave the Gardens to charity, "to the Cancer Society, maybe." He reflected on his late partner, Stafford Smythe, dead for 16 years. "Staff used to say 'You keep making the money, Harold, and I'll keep spending it.'"

He reiterated his thought on immortality. "I don't know about heaven. A man says to me, 'You can live forever in heaven,' and I told him, 'I'll give you all my years in heaven if you'll give me all yours here on earth.'"

King Clancy had been dead for nine months and Ballard reflected on his friend's passing. "Clance just goddamn stopped moving. Slowed down, didn't travel anymore.

That's not going to happen to me. I'll get in the big car and drive like hell and death's going to have to bear down to catch me." Death did bear down, a year later, and didn't catch him.

We said goodbye on the porch, two public clowns, I suppose, with no need to show off because we didn't have an audience. "Yolanda," Harold said, "walk Beddoes to his car."

The path to the road where my car was parked led across a bridge over a flowered ravine. You could hear, in the velvet night, water trickling over rocks below the bridge.

I complimented her on a pleasant party, a decent thing to do for Harold. She was in a reflective mood, too, all her guards down. She said, "I suppose I'll only get crumbs from the Ballards' table." I said, "Harold likes you. You're in at least for a whole loaf."

She turned back at the gate to the road, back to where Harold was silhouetted on the porch light beaming through the kitchen door. She called to him, "Where did you put the geese, Harold and Yolanda?"

He called back, "I put them in the ravine." She said, "D'you think the fox might get them down there?" Harold's reply was full of practicality. "If those goddamn geese don't know enough to get in the water," he said, "the fox deserves to get them."

CHAPTER 19

Hospital Follies

◆

His 84th birthday party was one of the few last good days that Ballard has known. He had slowed to the pace of a moribund porpoise, burdened with diabetes, locomotion trouble and a slightly frayed heart. Then, in mid-August, 1987, a fat man on the make breached his alleged father-son friendship with Harold.

Michael J. Gobuty and one of his solicitors visited Ballard at his summer residence on or about August 18, 1987. According to documents from the Supreme Court of Ontario, " ... Gobuty provided Ballard with a standard form guarantee from Lloyd's Bank in an amount of $5 million guaranteeing the indebtedness of Gobuty to Lloyd's ... Ballard signed the guarantee because of his trust of Gobuty, in reliance upon his friendship and because he believed Gobuty had substantial means and only needed temporary assistance."

Gobuty once owned a piece of the Winnipeg Jets of the World Hockey Association and, later, the National Hockey League. He was in the fashion business in Winnipeg with a company identified as Victoria Leather.

The Statements of Defence and Counter-claim in a Supreme Court of Ontario action in January, 1988, between the National Bank of Canada (plaintiff) and Michael J. Gobuty and Harold Ballard (defendants) showed Gobuty " ... the principal in a number of corporations including Canus Containers Ltd. (Canus), a corporation engaged in the garbage container business (in Etobicoke, Ont.); Winnipeg Beach Properties Ltd. (Winnipeg Beach), a corporation engaged in real estate development; and Gobuty & Sons Ltd., a corporation engaged in the fashion industry. ... "

Ballard relied for financial advice on the Gardens' controller, Don (Duck) Crump. Gobuty had informed Crump that his net worth exceeded $8 million. Crump discovered, with considerable chagrin, that "Gobuty was hopelessly insolvent. His assets were grossly overvalued or owned by others."

Banks were squeezing Gobuty. The same documents alleged that he owed the Standard Chartered Bank of Canada $2.3 million and Standard, fearing loss on its loans to Gobuty, "pressured Gobuty to utilize his friendship and influence with Ballard to obtain a guarantee so as to secure funds to pay down his indebtedness to Standard Chartered. Gobuty succumbed to this pressure and procured the Lloyd's guarantee for this purpose."

Lloyd's bankers became aware that the guarantee for $5 million signed by Ballard to back Gobuty was "potentially unenforceable." Lloyd's leaped at Gobuty and pressured him for repayment. Nimble as a song-and-dance man, Gobuty jumped to another bank, juggling financial balls. He kept trading on his palship with Pal Hal.

Gobuty put on a minstrel show for the National Bank of Canada with an outlandish promise of taking over the Gardens. According to the Statements of Defence and Counterclaim:

> On or about Oct. 8, 1987, National agreed to provide financing to Gobuty for the purpose of paying the indebtedness to Lloyd's Bank. A material factor in National's agreement was Gobuty's representation that a take-over of Maple Leaf Gardens arranged by Gobuty as a result of his close friendship with Ballard would soon take place and that National would be part of the take-over. A condition of the loan was that Ballard sign the guarantee. National at all times knew or ought to have known that Gobuty had no ability to personally repay the amount of the proposed loan and only agreed to fund Gobuty as a means of advancing its own goal to participate as a lead banker or equity participant in an MLG take-over.
>
> On or about Oct. 9, 1987, Mr. Tom Reber, a senior officer of National attended with Gobuty upon Ballard. At that time, Reber presented Ballard with a guarantee (the National Guarantee) and Ballard signed it. Ballard signed the guarantee because of his relationship with

Gobuty because he believed Gobuty's statement that
Gobuty had substantial assets and only needed tempo-
rary assistance.

Gobuty and Reber of the National Bank attended upon
Ballard in the Gardens, high in the red seats, where Harold
was watching the Leafs train for the opening of the 1987–88
hockey schedule. The conditions were not as confidential as
bankers prefer when loaning large sums.

Reber of the National, a vice-president, therefore wrote
Ballard a private and confidential and unctuous letter on
October 14, 1987, oil oozing out of every paragraph.

Dear Mr. Ballard:

It was a real pleasure to meet you last Friday! I must
thank Mike Gobuty for introducing me to *the* legend of
NHL owners!
Enclosed is your copy of the Cdn. $5,000,000 Guarantee
you signed supporting Mike's obligations to the
National Bank of Canada. We will be providing him
with a Cdn. $2,500,000 facility.
Due to the fact that we met in the arena with other
people present, I was concerned about the confidential-
ity of this transaction and, therefore, did not discuss any
of the details of the Guarantee.
I would very much appreciate your confirmation now
that you have read and understood your obligations
under the Guarantee.
In the short time I have known Mike and his son Mark, I
have been impressed with both their sincerity and over-
riding concern that any deal made will be one that you
are entirely comfortable with.
I would appreciate your signing and returning the
enclosed copy of this letter to confirm that you have
reviewed and understood the Guarantee.

Your truly,

Thomas E. Reber
Vice-president

Ballard didn't know that National advanced $1.96 million to Gobuty on October 13, 1987, to reduce Gobuty's debts. Ballard began to balk when the Gardens' treasurer, Don Crump, advised him that the National Guarantee he signed for $5 million was not being used, as he thought, to lead "a friendly take-over of the Gardens." It was being used to bail Gobuty out from a morass of debts.

Ballard's intransigence prompted the National Bank to demand repayment of the loan. Harold refused to pay and Gobuty couldn't. Their fellowship ended abruptly. The bank began a lawsuit, still pending, against Gobuty and Ballard.

A man in the executive suite of the Gardens said, "I think Gobuty got to Ballard through Yolanda. Gobuty came on too nice, too smooth. He came to be looked on as a favorite son. After Clancy died, Harold needed someone to sit with him in the bunker for hockey games. Gobuty was polished and Harold welcomed him. He drove Harold to football games in Hamilton. He filled the void Clancy left."

Gobuty offered, in writing in the fall of 1987, to buy Maple Leaf Gardens Ltd. from Ballard for $35.00 a share, about $105 million. Gobuty was lubricious, insisting that Ballard "guide me as your protégé in running the facility, sign all the cheques, and the Russians will NOT play in Maple Leaf Gardens for as long as I, Gobuty, am involved."

Gobuty's toadying towards Ballard received short shrift and shredding by Harold, many months later, at the pre-trial examinations for discovery. Ballard, asked how long he'd known Gobuty, said, "I would say a year. I have known him more but I would say a year personally." He was asked if he knew Gobuty in October, 1986. Harold said, "I probably met him, but just to say hello."

The answer seemed peculiar because Ballard had signed a guarantee to the Standard Chartered Bank of $1 million on behalf of Gobuty on October 18, 1986. Harold told the examiner he couldn't remember signing it.

Ballard was asked, "Do you remember signing any guarantees for Mr. Gobuty for his indebtedness?" He answered, "Well, I signed . . . whether they represented a guarantee or not I don't know. He just asked me to sign papers for him."

The examiner showed Ballard another guarantee he

signed, with Lloyd's Bank, regarding Gobuty's indebtedness. Question: "Do you recollect signing this document,
Mr. Ballard?" Answer: "No. I don't remember signing it, but
that is my signature."

Another question: "Has Mrs. MacMillan ever witnessed
your signing of these guarantees?" Answer: "No." Q.: "Just
for the record, Mrs. MacMillan is your long-time companion,
Mr. Ballard?" A.: "That's right."

The examiner was attempting to show that Ballard, at 85,
was not "a sophisticated business person." Lawyer John J.
Chapman, acting for Ballard, fended off such speculation.

In the examination of Gobuty, John Chapman pursued
references to Yolanda Babik MacMillan. Q.: "I'm showing
Mr. Gobuty a copy of a certified cheque produced to us by
Lloyd's Bank payable in the amount of $75,000.00 to Mrs.
Yolanda MacMillan dated Sept. 11, '87 ... Mr. Gobuty, was
this money paid to Mrs. MacMillan in return for her assistance in helping you get these guarantees?"

Gobuty's representative instructed him not to answer.
Chapman asked, "Did you pay any further monies to her?
... Did you pay any monies at her request?" Gobuty was
instructed not to answer.

Chapman persisted. "Why did you pay her the
$75,000.00?" No answer. Q.: "Was Lloyd's Bank aware that
Mrs. MacMillan was Mr. Ballard's close, personal companion?" No answer from Gobuty.

Q.: "Did you indicate to Mr. Ballard that you were going to
be paying Mrs. MacMillan $75,000.00?" No answer. Q.: "Did
you indicate to Lloyd's?" No answer. Q.: "The loan was for
particular purposes and this $75,000.00 isn't for one of those
purposes?" Michael J. Gobuty finally answered.

"I wrote the cheque," he admitted. "It was cashed." The
cheque was cashed, Yolanda said later, in exchange for jewelry she possessed. She wears an abundance of sapphires
and diamonds, among the gems a nine-carat pear-shaped
diamond worth more than $100,000 gleaming on one finger.

Ballard prefers his paramour to dazzle. "When she gets
shined up," he says gallantly, "she's not a bad looking chick."

Ray Houlihan, the Crown Prosecutor against Yolanda in
the case of the phony will, describes her as "tough and

worldly." Ballard's lawyer, John J. Chapman, seemed to think she was the loan arranger in negotiations with Michael Gobuty.

For all his legal and health troubles, Ballard entered 1988 with his face full of jovial sunlight. He rode into the new year on a stationary bike in the Gardens' gymnasium, accompanied by his favorite columnist, spry Milt Dunnell of the *Star*, another octogenarian.

Ballard had made a New Year's resolution, he told Dunnell. "I'm giving up trying to be the most miserable old bastard in the country. That's the image I've tried to create. I've failed. Everywhere I go, people ask for my autograph. My mail and the messages I get indicate the whole damn thing has been a total failure. I'm more popular than I ever was."

His popularity did not extend to his children when they read his New Year's greetings in the *Star*. "People ask if I'll leave the Gardens to my kids," he said. "The answer is no. The worst thing that could happen would be for my three kids to take over. It just wouldn't work."

He expressed a turbulent dislike for his eldest child and only daughter, Mary Elizabeth Flynn. "My three," Harold said, "have fought among themselves ever since they were kids. My daughter is the worst." That is a latter-day reaction towards Mary Elizabeth; she has particular distaste for Yolanda as the replacement for her mother.

Harold had a pungent response to Dunnell's question about where the Gardens will go when Ballard goes. "I'm not going anywhere," he said, "except maybe to Hartford or Chicago when we play there. I'm looking to be 95 and beyond."

But he has, he said, given thought to leaving the Gardens to charity. "The Gardens and the hockey club will be run by a trust that represents charities, some of which are already damn important to me. It will be up to each charity to name a trustee ... I'm not gonna name the charities now, but you can bet the Cancer Society will be one of them. My parents died of cancer. My wife died of cancer. Lawyers are working on the arrangements."

The arrangements, casually announced on the front page

of Canada's largest newspaper, was indeed news to Ballard's youngest child, Harold Jr., then 40. *Star* reporter John Temple found him in the approximation of a garret in North York, a Toronto satellite city that fancies itself with "a heart."

Reporter Temple wrote: "Sitting in the barren living room of his North York apartment, Ballard Jr. fought back emotion as he discussed his often rocky relationship with his father. A single, bare bulb lit the room of the man who claimed to be worth $5 million to $30 million. The only furniture was an armchair and a television."

The junior Harold, or Bobby, disputed his father's right to leave the Gardens to charity. "He can't do what he says he's going to do. I know he can't. This is just an old guy trying to have some fun. He likes to throw a curve every once in a while. He can say anything he wants and he can do anything he wants. It's just that he can't touch what's mine."

Bobby Ballard's point is instructive. His parents established H.E. Ballard Ltd. as three nest eggs for Bobby and his two siblings. He had one-third interest in the holding company which owns 71 per cent of the Gardens. Harold Sr. maintains control through his separate preferred voting shares.

H.E. Ballard Ltd. has paid no dividends and the children have no power in the company. Bobby said, "I own a third, but I don't have anything to do with it. I've been effectively left out in the ozone." He had not, however, been bereft of assistance from his father. He was given a job in the ticket office in the Gardens and did not keep it. He was a salesman for Davis Printing, a company owned by the Gardens in Mississauga, and quit. He was kept on the payroll at Davis Printing until early in 1989 when his father ordered his name expunged from the Davis records. The order followed Bobby's comments on CBC radio about the Battling Ballards.

Bobby is tall and personable and, in a stylish double-breasted suit, looks as though he just stepped out of *Gentleman's Quarterly*. He differs from his brother and sister, with less of a cutting edge, gentler, more akin to his mother. He is a competent painter who could be a commercial artist.

It was news to Bobby, in early 1988, that he and his brother and sister bicker and hurl Ballard billingsgate at each other.

"It's simply not true," he said, "that we hate each other. It's Yolanda MacMillan who incites all this."

He is offended that Yolanda "wears my dad's wedding ring. I don't like her calling herself Mrs. Ballard. I sure don't like her asking me to show my share certificates to her."

His relationship with his father has the combustible qualities that keep guttersnipe gossip papers in supermarkets catering to sleaze. He was married to a lovely Lebanese, a divorcee with two children, but his father never acknowledged the inter-racial marriage. He was, at one time, offended enough by his father's anti-Jewish remarks to stop referring to himself as "Harold Ballard, Jr." He called himself "Harold Garner," Garner being his middle name.

Bobby's attitude was changed when he spoke to John Temple of the *Star*. "No matter what my dad says or does," he said, "it can't deter what I feel about him. I love him."

Harold Sr. was less charitable when he read that his youngest child was living in an unfurnished flat lit by one bulb. "Now I got another nickname," Pal Hal said. "I called his mother Jiggs. Now I call him Lightbulb Harold."

Ballard promised to leave the Gardens and the Maple Leafs to charity, unaware that some charities might not take the Leafs, given their slovenly hockey record. They were in a prolonged slump in January, 1988, capable of beating only the Rotary Club. Harold's idea of leaving the Cashbox to a trust representing charities was, at the very least, uncommon. It would be more customary to sell the Gardens and funnel the money to various charities.

The Ontario law regulating charitable donations forbids any charity from owning more than 10 per cent of a business. To bequeath the Gardens to charity would mean naming 10 or more charitable foundations as beneficiaries. In Pal Hal's case, he could endow the Cancer Society and nine other institutions, unwieldy as that might be.

He dropped his charity bomb mot and left Toronto before the fallout hit the ground. He and Yolanda were scheduled to take the Florida sun in Palm Beach with Steven Stavro, the famous farmer from the Knob Hills. Palm Beach is a Gold Coast lined with mansions and millionaires, most of them old, fencing themselves off from reality, living in a gilded garbage-disposal unit with money.

Ballard and Yo-Yo arrived in Palm Beach on January 3, 1988. He began to have chest pains and shortness of breath. Yolanda insisted he be checked into the Good Samaritan Hospital in Palm Beach. He had suffered a heart attack, his first. He was transferred a week later to the Heart Institute in Miami.

The condition of Pal Hal's heart roused the pulse of stock in the Gardens. Shares began trading at $30.50 on the Toronto Stock Exchange on January 12, 1988, and rose to $33.00 before the session ended. One shareholder wanted to sell his holdings for $50.00 a share. Investors believe a change of ownership would significantly increase the value of the Gardens, perhaps by demolishing the Maple Leaf Mint and replacing it with a high-rise office tower. The Buzzards of Bay Street hovered over Harold's hospital bed.

In Miami, Yolanda rode rugged herd on reporters and visitors who wanted to see the patient she calls "My Harold." Ballard announced he would give interviews only if the interviewer paid $25,000 to charity. Bill Ballard, there to see his father, clashed with Yolanda.

Bill barked at her, "I'll run you to the River Styx and chase you into hell." Yolanda knew about hell, having been through some of it in a courtroom, but the Styx may not have been part of the geography she learned in school in Thunder Bay, Ontario. Bill Ballard, being a college man, knows that, according to classical mythology, the Styx is a river flowing seven times round the infernal regions where the eternal furnace is forever stoked high. Bill spoke in less classical terms in describing one of the fates he hopes awaits Yolanda. Kidding, I think, he said, "I have a standing offer to Wendel Clark. I'll pay him $10,000 if he'll hit Yolanda with the puck."

Clark is a daring left wing possessing a wicked shot. He can be the guts of the Maple Leafs, as Ted Kennedy and Bert Olmstead were in their combative primes, if a chronic back ailment permits him to play with pugnacious abandon.

Ballard kept issuing bulletins by telephone from his hospital room. He again sounded like the Mount St. Helen of hockey, always blowing his top. "When I get back," he promised, "the shit will hit the fan. Beginning with the manager."

He recovered faster than the 1988 Leafs who, between December 23, 1987 and January 27, 1988, limped through 15 games without winning, the longest fling of failure in the team's history, eleven losses and four ties. The coach was John Brophy, silver-haired, coarse-tongued, once the scourge of the rough and ruffian Eastern League as playing coach of the Long Island Ducks. He served 3,593 minutes in penalties for hockey sins, seven minutes short of 60 complete games, almost an entire season. One night, an enraged fan in the Connecticut burg of New Haven fired a bullet at Brophy through a dressing-room window. He missed, but not by much. Brophy was known thereafter as the Grey Ghost.

The king of Ballard's managerial hill was Gerald McNamara, but it was not a very high hill. McNamara came across as a dorky essence-of-busher chap afflicted with puck paranoia. He behaved as though he thought the media was always about to massacre him. Some in the media did, with reason. The Leaf teams McNamara recruited in the six years he served as Ballard's second-in-command gave him the lowest percentage of games won of any general manager since the NHL began on November 22, 1917.

There were three Toronto coaches during McNamara's tenure as manager, Mike Nykoluk, Dan Maloney and Brophy, all of them Ballard's choices, not McNamara's. The team had shown modest playoff improvement under the truculent Maloney, who quit in 1986 when McNamara didn't help him secure a modest raise in salary. McNamara wanted to fire Brophy in 1987, but Ballard said nuts to that noise. Brophy was the roughneck Pal Hal fancied himself to be.

From 1982 to 1988, McNamara was involved in the Maple Leafs drafting a handful of handy professionals — Gary Leeman and Ken Wregget in 1982, Russ Courtnall and Allan Bester in 1983, Al Iafrate, Todd Gill and Jeff Reese in 1984, Wendel Clark in 1985, Vince Damphousse and Darryl Shannon in 1986, Luke Richardson and Daniel Marois in 1987.

Leeman, the fleet son of a Toronto fireman, can start offensive blazes. He has what are known in the hockey trade as "soft hands," so accomplished a pickpocket that he is one of the few players in the NHL who can lift a goaltender's wallet while wearing hockey gloves. Leeman and Clark are the modern Leafs most coveted by other NHL teams, Clark only if his ailing back allows him to play 65–80 games a year.

McNamara did arrange a few useful trades. He acquired tall Tom Fergus, Toronto's most proficient winner of the puck on face-offs since 1985. He obtained the agile Ed Olczyk from Chicago, but gave away rocket-shooting Rick Vaive and unflinching Steve Thomas, who grew up in Toronto with an intangible which cannot be measured in money. He wanted, above anything else in his life, to be a Maple Leaf.

On balance, McNamara made glaring errors of commission and omission. He ventured on a cloak-and-dagger sortie to Czechoslovakia in 1985–86 to heist Miroslav Ihnacack, touted to be the finest left winger behind the Iron Curtain. McNamara and Ihnacack escaped through a chink in the Curtain, at the ultimate cost of $1 million to the Leafs.

Ballard's indignation was loudly profane after Ihnacack turned out to be a person displaced on the Toronto roster. He scored eight goals for the Leafs before being excused from the organization in 1988.

"Cost me a million listening to McNamara on that Czech deal," Ballard said. "Gerry sold me a goddamn bill of goods. I don't know if he and IH-nuh-chehk escaped out of Czechoslovakia in a used Volkswagen or not. Anyway, I got stung. I wish I could find the fucking Volkswagen and ship McNamara and IN-nuh-chehk in it back to Czechoslovakia, one way."

McNamara, cautious as a virgin on the verge, omitted to make trades that were possible. He could have obtained Brad McCrimmon, one of the NHL's proficient defencemen, from Philadelphia and did not. McCrimmon went to Calgary instead and helped win the Stanley Cup through the exciting spring of 1989.

A stark McNamara omission was his failure to bid for Paul Coffey when that Hall-of-Fame defenceman abandoned the Edmonton Oilers in the late fall of 1987. Coffey is a downtown Weston boy, a few miles from Maple Leaf Gardens, where he had a yearning to play. The Oilers, aware the all-star rearguard refused to return to Edmonton, shopped Cof-

fey around the NHL. They would accept the best deal they
could make. There is no evidence that McNamara contem-
plated assembling a package of Toronto players that Edmonton would accept for Coffey. The Oilers finally swapped
Coffey to Pittsburgh, where he and dexterous Mario
Lemieux have stimulated the Penguins to playoff prominence.

Ballard had, in sum, a general manager reluctant to gamble, afraid to rattle-and-roll in the NHL crapshoot. Harold
had ample reason to fire the brooding McNamara much
before he did, on February 7, 1988. Coffey would have cost
Ballard about $750,000 a year, but, as Pal Hal properly
snorted, "Hell, he'd have given us a couple of playoff games
that would have more than paid for his salary."

Ballard fired McNamara by telephone, long-distance from
Toronto to Hartford, where the Leafs played a Sunday game.
"Gerry," he said, "I've been trying to get hold of you and tell
you to resign, on account of I'm gonna make a change. You
could say you don't want to work for that old son of a bitch
Ballard any more. Lots of people would give you credit for
that."

McNamara confirmed the phone call for Milt Dunnell in
the *Star.* "Mr. Ballard called me and said he was going to
relieve me of my duties," McNamara said. "He did suggest I
resign, but I refused. I never quit on anything in my life. Why
should I start now? I told him he would have to fire me. He
did."

McNamara echoed complaints of his predecessors that
Ballard emasculates his general managers. Big Mac said,
"I've heard it said that the team which McNamara is trying to
build is not the one John Brophy wants to coach. Did I want
to fire Brophy? Yes, I did. But I didn't have the authority. I was
trying to operate the team with handcuffs on."

McNamara's rationalizing prompts a thought about com-
promising one's self-respect. If McNamara was handcuffed
by Ballard, he could have broken the managerial manacles by
quitting long before he was fired. But he represents every
man striving to be somebody who risks giving away pieces of
himself to achieve his ambition. A guy comes up through the

system of an NHL team selling his pride, yielding 50 cents of himself at one point, a dollar at another point.

At the end, such a person is a piece of goods marked down to $1.49 on a high shelf in a bargain basement, a piece of marked-down goods afraid of height. Organization men, with their delusions of adequacy, forget that saving their own cussedness is more important than a good position at the feed trough.

McNamara left the Leafs with 18 months to go on a contract which Ballard honored, his place at the trough assured. He surfaced in the 1988–89 season as a scout for the Calgary Flames, the Stanley Cup champions, still part, however remote, of the National Hacking League.

Ballard replaced McNamara with a rump parliament consisting of Leaf scout Dick Duff, coach John Brophy and assistant manager Gordon Stellick. Ballard dissolved the rump on April 28, 1988, and anointed Stellick as his latest general manager. Stellick was 30, the youngest G.M. in NHL history, up in 14 years from press-box assistant to headship of a ragged franchise in the best city for pro hockey in the world. Toronto fans keep buying tickets, oblivious to the fact that the Leaf emperors seldom wear winning clothes, or any clothes.

The Leafs qualified, barely, for the 1987–88 playoffs because they were marginally superior to the abysmal Minnesota North Stars. They were eliminated in six games by Detroit Red Wings, vanquished 8–0 in one grubby game, on April 10, 1988.

Toronto fans habitually exhibit the lowest yahoo content among crowds in the NHL. They can be sullen, not mutinous. They lost their forbearance in the third period of the 8–0 demolition. They pelted the playing surface with pucks, tennis balls, paper cups, programs and pennies. Three disillusioned witnesses wrapped up expensive Leaf sweaters they had purchased at a concession stand and hurled the bundles to the ice. It was the ultimate gesture of disgust in the Mother Temple where a Leaf jersey is revered as the vestment for a demigod.

Coach Brophy uttered a hot streak of "Fuck its!" and added, "When the wheels fall off, how the hell can you

move?" Gary Leeman, one of Toronto's very few professionals, said, "We have no system and no power play. Brophy
should be crucified."

"Leafs were truly a disgrace," Jim Proudfoot wrote in the
Star. "It's too bad Boss Harold didn't stay to watch the end.
As the catcalls and garbage rained down, he might have
picked up an ominous message ... 'We're mad as hell and
we won't take it much longer.'"

Gordon Stellick, putting himself under Ballard's gun, was
candid. "We've got a talented team," he said, "but it's an
underachieving team. The management structure's clouded.
There's internal friction. The competition for the entertainment dollar in Toronto is the toughest ever."

Yet Stellick, too, like so many of us with a romantic vein, is
a captive of the Leaf dream. He was nine years old and living
with his family in the Toronto suburb of Willowdale the last
time the Leafs won the Stanley Cup. He pleaded with his
parents to let him stay up to watch the sixth game of the Cup
final between the Leafs and Canadiens on May 2, 1967, a
Tuesday. He lay on the living-room carpet and watched the
Leafs win 3–1 on television. He stared, fulfilled, as captain
George Armstrong skated exuberantly around the Gardens,
Lord Stanley's old birdbath held high. Where else would a
Toronto kid of that palmy period rather be than the Gardens?

Now, as manager, Stellick is the nominal boss of George
Armstrong, a reluctant coach doing Ballard's bidding. Stellick is the precocious grandson Harold never had, but he told
me on television, "If Mr. B. overrules too many of my decisions, I'll resign."

Ballard was resigned, in the spring of 1988, to paying off
substantial hospital bills incurred during his month of recovery from his heart attack in Florida. "Goddamn," he said,
"American doctors carve you up in more ways than one. They
charge $1,000 just to put a stethoscope on your heart." He
insisted, "There's not a damn thing wrong with my heart. It's
the fucking diabetes that's slowing me down." It was a bit like
whistling past his own graveyard; by July, the clogged vessels
around his heart slowed him down to sluggish.

Harold's long, hot summer began in Hamilton on July 16,

a stifling Saturday. He was in dilapidated Ivor Wynne Stadium where, he has said, you sit very carefully "so you don't get slivers in your ass." He hobbled along slowly and met Jim Hunt, an old sparring partner from *The Toronto Sun*. "Hunt," Ballard said, "aren't you dead yet?" Hunt said, equally derisive, "Harold, I'm like you. I'm too miserable to die."

Ballard's circulatory ailments prevented him from walking up to his seat at the top of the stands. A crane described as a cherry picker plucked him up and carried him to his private perch.

The Tiger-Cats, against the betting line, beat the visiting Toronto Argos, to Ballard's obscene delight. He kept saying, "Give it to the fuckers." When the game ended, the crane lifted him down to the big blue chauffeured Lincoln for his return to Toronto.

At home, in the Hot Stove Lounge, Ballard went on a sugar binge to celebrate his Ticat triumph. He heaped up a quart of ice cream with a sumptuous sauce topping of chocolate and marshmallow, then wallowed in the sticky lot. The next day, Sunday, Ballard paid for pigging out. He struggled out of the canopied bed he shares with Yolanda, pale, sick and muttering, "Christ, I feel lousy." She checked him into the Wellesley Hospital, one of the institutions on his list of charities.

He was transferred a few days later to Toronto General Hospital, knocked flat by diabetes and his laboring heart. The General described his condition as "serious." Yolanda, bustling nervously, moved into a room in the hospital as "Mrs. Ballard."

Ballard said in the following weeks, "I didn't know how the hell sick I was until the doctors started talking about cutting around my heart. Said I needed bypass surgery to survive. I asked one of them what my chances were and he said bleak without an operation. I said, 'Doc, cut me.'"

Ballard was cut by Dr. Tirone David, the chief of cardiovascular surgery for The Toronto Hospital, a merging of Toronto General and Toronto Western hospitals. Dr. David is tall and debonair, sort of a Cary Grant of cardiology.

In a generation, pharmaceutical companies have made living better for heart patients through chemistry. Nitroglycerin is now augmented by beta blockers, calcium blockers, enzyme inhibitors, even aspirin. The most dramatic treatment of all is coronary artery bypass graft surgery, the rerouting of blood around the blocked supply lines to the heart. The grafting procedure uses transplanted veins from the patient's own leg.

Ballard's operation, on July 22, a torrid Friday, required more than three hours. Rumors swept through Toronto that he had died on the operating table.

The rumors jolted the Toronto Stock Exchange. The price of Gardens' stock jumped $2.50 a share to $42 on more than 30,000 shares traded. The Saturday *Star* ran a headline on the front page on July 23: "Ballard critical after mystery surgery."

Paul McNamara, chairman of the Gardens' directors, quelled the rumors with a statement: "Dr. Tirone David related that he performed a quintuple coronary bypass and explored the aortic valve on Mr. Ballard. The doctor advised that Mr. Ballard . . . is progressing most favorably and in his opinion, barring unforeseen complications, Mr. Ballard will be going home within 10 days." Pal Hal was listed in serious shape under intensive care, but stable. He was conscious, unable to issue his own statement because of an assortment of tubes jammed into his mouth.

On July 26, in *The Globe and Mail*, Jim Christie wrote, "Ballard played Fool the Ghouls again . . . as his condition improved, share prices tumbled four dollars, from $42 to $38."

Yolanda Ballard hovered around the intensive-care unit, fussing and tearful, sitting with Harold, holding his hand. She was the first person he noticed when he was taken off the respirators, three days after the operation. He sounded gentle for one so bombastic. "I love you, Madame Queen," he said.

Yolanda can well up with tears in sentimental moments, and turn off the tap in tougher moods. "You've been reading about the vultures watching the Gardens' stock?" she said. "They're just a bunch of maggots who want to live off my Harold's flesh."

She was adamant about his recovery. "My Harold fooled them all. He'll outlive all the greedy ones. He played the biggest role of his life on that operating table, and came through with flying colors. He's going to live to be 102, plus, plus, plus."

"You've got it wrong, Madame Queen," Harold said. "If it's true that only the good die young, I'll live to be 203."

Yolanda monitored the visitors when Harold was moved to the heart ward at Toronto General, vigilant, approving few. She had been similarly selective when Ballard was in the Miami Heart Institute in January. She had hung a sign on the door to Harold's private room: "Admittance refused to all except wife and daughter-in-law." Bill Ballard ripped off the sign in Florida and was similarly contemptuous of Yolanda in the General.

Harold's convalescence made it impossible for him to attend his 85th birthday party in the Royal York Hotel on July 28, 1988. The event was pure jockstrappery, 1,200 athletes, businessmen and politicians behaving like sophomores, mostly there to tell dirty racist and sexist jokes. They raised $250,000 for the cancer research fund named for Charlie Conacher, a vintage Leaf with a booming shot who succumbed to throat malignancy in his 59th year.

Lieutenant-Governor Lincoln Alexander, who prefers to be called King Linc of Ontario, told the assemblage, "Thanks for your help in funding cancer research. My Pal Hal will be very proud."

NHL president John Ziegler, the Little Zed, lowered the microphone to his level and presented Ballard, in absentia, with a sterling silver tray engraved with the logos of the league's 21 teams " . . . with gratitude for Harold's long service to hockey."

The Toronto mayor, Arthur (Eggs) Eggleton, proclaimed July 28, 1988 " . . . Harold Ballard Day." Hizzoner's nickname is Eggs because his shapely skull is Grade A large. Ballard, watching a videotape of the festivities, said, "I appreciate having a day declared for me, but I wish the mayor had got the goddamn date right. I was born on July 30, not the 28th."

Yolanda screened Ballard's younger son from the small birthday party she staged in his hospital room on July 30. She stopped Harold Jr. from seeing his father early in the afternoon on the pretext that the senior Harold was asleep. "Come back," she said, "at 4 o'clock. You can have some of the birthday cake we've got for your dad." Harold Jr. returned at 4:00 p.m., too late for any party with his pop. The cake had been wheeled into Ballard's room earlier and posed with Yolanda and the patient. Then pictures of "Mr. and Mrs. Ballard" were distributed to the three Toronto newspapers. Harold Jr. didn't get any cake.

Mike Wassilyn is among the many who orbit around Ballard, more intimate with Harold than most. He is stocky and sturdy, at 38 the salient ticket host outside Maple Leaf Gardens. Police call him a scalper, a term Wassilyn resents.

"It's a dirty word, scalper," Wassilyn says. "I'm a street person from Cabbagetown. I hustle to make a living for my wife and four boys. It's not right that people look down on us." Wassilyn has been Ballard's pseudo son for several years, since he phoned Harold for solace after Wassilyn's father died. "He was warm to me," Wassilyn said. "God never made many like Mr. B. And Yolanda doesn't deserve all the knocks she gets. She's a wonderful woman."

There is gossip, on the street and in the Gardens, that Wassilyn's pipeline to Ballard and Yolanda gives him access to tickets. He denies the speculation as he stands in his office outside the front doors of the Gardens. During the hockey season, cars pull up to Wassilyn's office, the drivers turn down their car windows, hand Mike their tickets and take his money.

"Who are these people?" I asked Wassilyn as I watched an exchange. He said, "They are people who own season tickets to Leaf games. If they don't want to watch a certain game, they sell me their tickets." There is such demand for tickets to most Leaf games that Wassilyn sells the tickets he bought for more than he paid for them. The markup on a big night is impressive. When Wayne Gretzky led the Los Angeles Kings into Toronto during the 1988–89 season, Wassilyn could sell a pair of gold tickets, worth $57.00, for $500.00 or more.

Wassilyn has parlayed hustling on the city streets into a small farm in the country near Guelph, Ontario. He raises standard-bred horses and, by sheer coincidence, Bouvier dogs. Harold and Yolanda board their big Bouvier bow-wow at Wassilyn's farm whenever they travel out of Canada on vacation.

Mike Wassilyn was a constant visitor during Ballard's travail on the heart ward at Toronto General. "Mr. B. was
woozy," Wassilyn said, "and there was turmoil all around
him. There was a meeting on the ward with Bill Ballard and
some of the Gardens' directors. They thought Mr. B. was
incompetent. Bill was trying to wrest control of the Gardens
from his dad."

Don Crump, treasurer of the Gardens, discovered in early
August, 1988, that Michael Gobuty, in the bamboozling of
Ballard, had given Yolanda a cheque for $75,000. Ballard was
told about the cheque and, perhaps confused, yelled at
Yolanda, "I know you've been screwing around on me, by
God!"

Mike Wassilyn, on a visit, was orally assaulted by Bill
Ballard. "I'll chase you off the street," Bill said, "you fucking
scalper." Bill confronted Yolanda. "I'm going for a week's
fishing," he said, "but you'll be calling me back for my dad's
funeral."

Yolanda, no shrinking wallflower, wailed back. Nurses on
the ward tried to stop the caterwauling out of respect for
other heart patients disturbed by the Ballard bickering.
Metro Toronto police were called on August 9. Two security
officers were assigned to guard the door to Ballard's room.

On August 10, 1988, Canada's paper of repute had stories
on page one about two of the conspicuous characters in
hockey. The top headline in *The Globe and Mail* read:
"Gretzky goes to L.A." The report, bordered in black, related
the details of "the greatest player in National Hockey League
history" being bartered to the Los Angeles Kings. The
Edmonton Oilers swapped Gretzky for a cartload of cabbage,
said to be $5 million, and five Los Angeles players, three of
them future junior draftees.

Canadian fans were stunned, but not speechless at the
trading of a national treasure. The general tenor of the clamor
was "Picket Peter Pocklington!" directed at Peter Pocklington, a bearded, former used-car salesman who needed
millions to bolster his sagging Alberta empire.

Below the fold of page one, the *Globe* featured another
headline: "Companion kept away from Ballard." Bill Ballard
had told reporter Bill Houston that Yolanda was prohibited

from seeing his father. Locks had been changed in the Gardens to prevent her from returning to Ballard's studio apartment.

The story of Ballard's sanctions against his lover was dead within one day. I visited him in hospital on the evening of August 10, granted permission by the guards on the door. Harold was hearty but wan in the white overshift patients wear in hospital.

"You see the *Globe*?" he said, chortling. "How d'ya like it? The greatest hockey player of the day gets traded and, goddamn, I'm right on the front page with him."

I said, "The story's been around for two months that Gretzky'd be gone from Edmonton, to either Vancouver or Los Angeles. You didn't know that?" Ballard said, "If I'da known, I'd have given $20 million for Gretzky."

He opened his hospital gown to show, proudly, the length of the scar from his operation. "Look how they cut me. From the top of my chest to the bottom of my feet." The scar, thick and meandering and the color of dried blood, stopped at his left ankle. Dr. Tirone David had reached into Ballard's leg for the vein needed to bypass his distressed heart.

I said, "So how long are you good for now?" Harold said, "The vultures got to put up with me a damn sight longer than they want. The doc says I'm good for seven more seasons."

He seemed to have shrunk, somehow, but expressed vigor, ballsy as he used to be. "This was a hell of an operation I had," he said, "for somebody my age. Rich, you got any pull with the guys who run the *Guinness Book of Records*?"

"Why the hell," I said, "should you be in the *Guinness Book of Records*?"

Harold said, "Simple. I'm the oldest guy to have a quintuple heart bypass. Nobody older was ever bypassed more than me." He challenged, "You know anybody older had the operation I had?"

I told him I didn't know any other, for the indisputable reason that there aren't many 85-year-olds to write and broadcast about on the sports beat. There aren't any other 85-year-olds anywhere who are hands-on owners of a sports franchise, no other dinosaurs threshing around in the jock marshes.

I said, "So what about the affair with Yolanda. That over?"

Harold replied, "Yeah, I think it's over. Right now I think of my wife Dorothy every day."

I became aware of someone behind us, near the guarded door. I turned to see Yolanda, tremulous in a pink dress and white boots, weeping. Harold noticed her and said, "Why, Madame Queen. Come on in." She came in and I excused myself. Watching lovers make up is not a spectator sport.

The Battling Ballards became a staple on the Toronto media through the balance of August, 1988. I was phoned, as a friend of Ballard's, for comment by Dale Brazao, an award-winning reporter employed by *The Toronto Star*.

Brazao had heard all the raps against Yolanda, the speculation that she is clinging to Ballard because her path of disrespect leads but to the gravy. "For all the carping at Yolanda," I said, "I think she's good for Ballard. If she wasn't nursing him, his kids would have to put him in an old folk's home."

Brazao's story was published in the *Star* on August 11. The next morning, at 8:10 a.m., I received an abusive anonymous phone call at my hutch in Etobicoke.

"Beddoes?" an angry voice said. "If you see me before I see you, run or I'll pinch off your fucking head! I've read what you said in the *Star*, you cocksucker!" The agitated voice sounded like Bill Ballard's, a voice heard often as August subsided into September.

Don Giffin, Ballard's closest confidant among the Gardens' directors, called to confirm the reunion of Harold and Yolanda. "They're back together," Giffin said. "The locks have been unlocked at the Gardens. She's back in. All is love and kisses for the moment."

It occurred to me that I was involved in a watching brief on the Battling Ballards, with all its soap-opera overtones of sex, power and greed at the Gardens. I had the time for it; I had been fired as sports director at CHCH in Hamilton, for economic reasons, I was told. There had been no hint of criticism from the station's top management, just an abrupt dismissal. I suspect I wasn't servile enough to top management, but their severance pay was generous.

"What the fuck's wrong with those CH guys?" Ballard had said. "Well, what the hell. You can come and work for me.

Shake some hands, make some speeches about those old
Leafs you're always talking about. Maybe work on the radio
broadcasts of our games, talk us up, have fun like we used to
on CHCH."

I did work on broadcasts of the Leaf games in 1988–89,
thanks to Ballard's intercession. We did talk it up and have
fun, difficult as that is to do with a team that finished 20th in
a 21-team tournament.

On August 12, two days after Harold and Yolanda reunited, a
curious advertisement appeared in the three Toronto newspapers. "NOTICE TO MERCHANTS: Take notice that neither Harold E. Ballard nor Maple Leaf Gardens Limited will
be responsible for any debts, charges or expenses incurred by
or on behalf of Yolanda Ballard, also known as Yolanda Mac-
Millan, also known as Yolanda Babik."

The advertisement was signed by the solicitors for Ballard
and the Gardens, Miller, Thomson, Sedgewick, Lewis &
Healy. The ad wasn't placed by Ballard directly and did not
dent their steamy relationship.

Dick Duff, one of the Leaf alumni I admire, phoned on
August 13. "I work for H.B. and like him," Duff said. "Even
though he's changeable. One day he's all black. Next day, he's
sort of a shade of blue. The third day he's all white. You've got
to take him as a package deal." It's the best capsule comment
I've heard about many-sided Pal Hal.

Ballard was in his famous fettle when he was excused from
hospital in a wheelchair on August 13. Reporters and photographers clambered around the wheelchair, fended off by
Yolanda and two outriders from the Gardens.

"How you're feeling, Mr. Ballard?" a reporter politely
asked. "Wonderful, wonderful," Harold said. "Now fuck
off." He was taken a few blocks from the Toronto General to
the Westbury Hotel, where he was supposed to recuperate.
He refused to stay in the Westbury, demanding to be
returned to the Gardens. He was back in his studio apartment, isolated with Yolanda, three weeks after a serious,
complicated heart operation, anxious to be in the Gardens
where he wants to die.

"But I'm not dying anytime soon," he promised. I shared

his bantering mood. "You can't take all that money with you when you go," I said. Harold said, "Then I ain't going. I'll chain myself to my desk before you guys haul me to the boneyard."

On August 14, 1988, I was lazing around the den over a second cup of morning coffee when the phone rang at 9:15. Anna MacMillan, Yolanda's daughter, was on the line. "My mother wants you at the Gardens," she said. "She's got a crisis with Mr. Ballard. Come see me first at my place, 30A Dundonald."

Reporters get fascinated by stories, and I was absorbed in this one. An hour later, I'm on the front steps of 30A Dundonald, a townhouse five blocks from the Gardens, listening to a young, slim, attractive Anna MacMillan. "You can't guess what Bill Ballard's doing to us," she said. "I swear our phone is bugged. Somebody's always watching our house taking pictures. Now you better go help my mother."

A red door on the second floor of the Gardens opens on to a public corridor. Yolanda responded to my knock, frantic, but speaking in hushed tones. She led me into the cluttered apartment where Harold sat dressed and looking good, as though a hairdresser had applied a bright orange pomade to his haircut 15 minutes ago.

"You got problems?" I asked.

"It's these goddamn swollen feet, Rich. Yolanda can't get anything on my feet and I want to get to the cottage."

Ten or twelve pairs of shoes were scattered around, all too cramped for Ballard's bloated feet. I reached for a pair of slippers that were wider than a small barge. They fitted snug as a bug masticating a rug. Yolanda, ever sociable, brought two strawberry-flavored Royal colas from the kitchenette.

"No time for cola," Harold said. "C'mon, Yolanda, get a move on. I want to get to the cottage." She began to fill a large handbag with vials and pills and medicine for Harold's various ailments. She said to me, in a mysterious aside, "It's good to have witnesses. Harold's got $100,000 in cash on him. If it's lost, you are a witness that I didn't take it." She added, "Thank God you came to put his slippers on. Don't let Bill Ballard buy you. Thanks for the kind words in the *Star*."

Harold got to his feet with the aid of a thin, strong, brown cane carved for him, he said, by the Ojibwa Indians. Yolanda, perspiring in her loose summer chemise, walked towards the door. I followed, helping Harold navigate. There was a provocative swing to her hips.

Harold was appreciative. "Nice ass, eh, Rich?"

I agreed, also appreciative, "Harold, keep punching."

He ruminated. "I tell you, she's been damn good for me."

Out the door, Harold sat in his chair and I wheeled him to the top of the escalator moving to the main floor. Two of Harold's loyal outriders, Jonesy and Gunnar, supervised the safe transfer of the wheelchair to the escalator. At the bottom, they deftly loaded him into the front seat of the dark blue limo. Yolanda and T.C. Puck filled the back seat, the great off-white dog as eager to travel as Harold, lolling in splendor beside Yolanda, salivating.

Ballard bathos piled upon buffoonery. They stayed a day at the home on Georgian Bay and, on August 16, Ballard watchers read a headline in the *Star*: "Yolanda 'terrified' after finding Ballard's 4 guns."

The incident was more theatrical than serious. Shooting had not been added to the Gardens' mix of sex, power and greed. Yolanda was rummaging under Ballard's bed in the apartment when she discovered four hand guns, an antique arsenal. The guns were cashiers' weapons used 65 years ago in banks and hotels to frighten potential robbers. Two of the guns couldn't be fired because the hammers were missing.

To Yolanda, no expert on firearms, a gun is a gun. She had a secretary in the Gardens' hockey office put in a hurry-up call to the police. Two plainclothes officers and one uniformed constable from the Metro Toronto force came to confiscate Ballard's artillery. Harold couldn't find a permit for the pistols, which he bought at a long-ago auction. The officers went away with the guns stashed in brown paper envelopes. Cameramen from two Toronto television stations, alerted by someone in the Gardens, just happened to be there to record the removal of the rods.

Harold has done a lot of shooting in his lifetime, always from the lip, never from the hip. Yolanda had an explanation for her terror. She told Milt Dunnell in the *Star*, "I thought somebody might break into the apartment, find the guns and shoot us." She added, "Not that Harold and me ever had a problem. There's only one good Ballard. That's the one I live with. Whatever makes him happy makes me happy. It's the attitude of his family that devastates me."

Dick Duff and I visited Ballard at Thunder Beach on August 20, a sunny Saturday of high bright sky in the Muskokas. Yolanda was puttering in the flower beds, her thoughts not far from her battle with Ballard's boys.

"Bill Ballard's into snow, you know?" she said. Modern jargon eludes me.

"What," I said, "is snow?"

She couldn't believe a wise guy reporter didn't know that "snow" is a colloquialism for cocaine. "Bill Ballard," she said, "shovels snow in the summertime."

Harold was in the house, sitting in front of a wide picture window, gazing west towards the haze beyond Christian Island. He looked healthy, in a wisecracking mood, gregarious. For an hour, given an audience, he relived old Ballard glories, how he stole the flag at the Winter Olympics, and "put on preacher" Billy Graham, and the excitement he felt when he got the loan to buy the Gardens.

Yolanda was listening. She said to Harold, "I know somebody with a bigger ego than you have."

Harold lifted one swollen leg off the stool he was resting it on. "Who the hell is that bastard?" he asked.

Yolanda, triumphantly, said, "God."

Harold wanted to leave for Toronto. "I've got a car coming for me," he said.

Dick Duff asked, "How come you want to leave this resort on a day like today, Mr. B.?"

Ballard was emphatic. "I've got lots to do in Toronto. Letters to write, contracts to sign. I've got to keep moving." He seemed to think he'd lose his grip on the Gardens if he's not running the rink from his cramped studio apartment.

The Battling Ballards kept hanging their private story on public headlines. I dropped by the studio apartment on September 7, a clear day with a crisp hint of fall. Harold and

Yolanda wore matching nightshirts of green plaid. He was in good shape; Yolanda looked as though she'd had six fights with George Chuvalo and lost six times.

Her left eye was shut like the slot in a piggy bank. Her left cheek was puffed and discolored. She limped. I asked the obvious, "So who hit you?"

She whispered, "Ballard. Bill Ballard."

Yolanda claimed that the previous day, in Harold's office adjoining the apartment, Bill assaulted her. She said he said, "You fucking cunt! You're keeping him alive!" Then, she said, Bill punched her in the face and, when she fell down, kicked her in the abdomen.

Harold was in the apartment and did not necessarily see the alleged attack. He said, "All I know is that only a coward hits a woman." Ballard insisted that Yolanda lay assault charges against his son.

The headline on the front page of *The Toronto Sun* on September 9, 1988, blazoned the Ballard hostilities: BILL BALLARD CHARGED IN YOLANDA'S BEATING. Bill had been charged with assault causing bodily harm, which he called a "fabrication." He said, "I don't know anything about it and I don't care shit about it."

Yolanda admitted herself to Toronto General Hospital for repairs to her black eye, swollen cheek and bruised abdomen. The same day, Harold conducted a press conference in the Gardens to announce the signing of Borje Salming for the Swede's 16th season in a Maple Leaf uniform.

Salming was stale news compared to the assault charges. Harold denies knowledge of anybody attacking anyone in his presence. He responded to a radio reporter, "You say somebody hit Yolanda? Well, she's big enough to look after herself. And if I did know anything, I wouldn't tell you. So shove your microphone up your ass."

His private assessment of the assault charges was more restrained. In his office, after the press conference, Harold said, "I'm sad about Bill being charged. He phoned here this morning and lambasted Yolanda. Threatened to kill her."

Yolanda came into the office from the apartment, where she might have heard us talking. "Bill said he'd get me," she said. "He said he has a web of grungy underground guys who'll get me." Harold said, "I'm gonna phone Police Chief Jack Marks to send somebody out to the house in Etobicoke and tone Bill down."

Ballard was aware of irony in the apparent physical quarrel between his son and his live-in lady. "You know I'm a supporter of the Battered Women Society," he said. "I put on an exhibition game one time for battered women in Kitchener. You sort of set it up."

In 1983, when I was sports director at CHCH-TV in Hamilton, I had received a telephone query from a woman in Kitchener. She represented Anselma House, a home for abused women in that city. "Could you," she said, "get Mr. Ballard to play an exhibition game for us in Kitchener? We could sure use the funds." This was early September, when the Leafs were in training camp. I mentioned the woman's call to Ballard. "Tell her," he said, "that the Leafs will play an intrasquad game up there, for nothing."

The game was played and Ballard took no particular bows. He gave the receipts from the game to Anselma House, about $18,000, seed money to help Kitchener women abused by men. Harold didn't brag about it, lest it explode his image as a sexist.

Bill Ballard's mood was one of pure outrage. He phoned me at my house late on the night of September 9, riled and insulting. "Yolanda's crucifying me with those charges!" he said. "She's evil. She's against the whole social order. I want HER! I want HER in my parlor! When my case comes up, it will be my character against hers. I didn't hit her."

Bill's story was believed by a few executives in the Gardens. One of them confided, "I saw Yolanda after Bill is supposed to have struck her, and there wasn't a mark on her."

I said to the executive, "Well, she looks like somebody belted her."

He said, "Maybe she swung open a door and slammed it against herself to get the black eye."

Bill appeared in provincial court in Toronto's old City Hall on September 22. The case against him didn't proceed because the Crown lacked documentation. It was put over, as judges say, to October 13 for the setting of a trial date.

The atmosphere in old City Hall that brisk morning was

absolute carnival. Photographers and reporters jostled for position around Bill when he left the courtroom laughing with his brother and sister.

Mary Elizabeth quelled the rumors that the Ballards detest each other. "Here we are," she said gaily, "the warring Ballards." They walked along Queen Street towards Bay Street, surrounded by media, funny and festive. Mary Elizabeth stepped into the intersection, barely missing a car.

Bill held her back. "Look out, look out!" he shouted. "Yolanda is driving that car!"

The phone in my house rang at a barbaric hour the next morning, September 23. The bedside clock showed 3:47 a.m., an ungodly time when anyone abruptly aroused has sandpaper scraping the back of his eyeballs.

"Yeah?" I said, chummy as a bear caught in a beehive. The caller was Bill Ballard, chortling, on the line from Bregman's Restaurant on Yonge Street, owned by his friend, Marty O'Neill.

Bill said, "You should see the story in *The Globe and Mail*. Bill Houston wrote that stuff about Yolanda getting a cheque for $75,000 from Mike Gobuty on that loan business with H.B."

Bill was delighted to say he had phoned Yolanda in the Gardens and read the story to her. "You know how she talks in that husky conspiratorial whisper? I read the *Globe* story to her in the same sort of phony whisper. Then I reverted to my own voice and yelled, 'How d'you like them apples, Mommy!' Then I hung up in her ear."

Later the same day, in the Gardens, Don Giffin said to me, "All this family feuding has the Gardens on the verge of chaos." Giffin, as a director, and treasurer Don Crump are Ballard's closest financial advisers. "Poor Crump," Giffin said. "He's a damn good money man, but Yolanda has knives stuck all over his back."

Bill Ballard called me on September 23 with an idea for extending the story of the Battling Ballards. "You can write the script," he said. "You've been around us so much." I asked if he had a title for his made-for-TV movie. "Sure have," he said. "Come Home, Daddy."

Yolanda had hauled Bill into criminal court on the assault

charges and, on September 26, 1988, hit him with a million-dollar civil action. Her solicitors, Thomson, Rogers, began legal proceedings in the Supreme Court of Ontario, Yolanda Ballard v. Wm. Ballard.

Yolanda, as plaintiff, claimed "damages in the sum of $500,000.00 ... and punitive, aggravated and exemplary damages in the sum of $500,000.00." The specifics of the alleged assault seemed more grave in legalese than they had in earlier newspaper accounts.

> The plaintiff claims as a result of the assault and/or battery negligence of the defendant ... the plaintiff Yolanda Ballard has suffered severe external and internal injuries, including damage to her entire skeletal system, bruising, tearing and damaging of the nerves, muscles, tendons, and ligaments throughout her body and more particularly to her face, injury to her left eye, internal injuries, contusions to her abdomen, fear and nervous shock to her system.
>
> As a result of these injuries, the plaintiff Yolanda Ballard suffers from headaches, pain in her left cheek, teeth and jaw, impairment of vision in her left eye, and internal bleeding. The plaintiff has sustained great pain and suffering and her enjoyment of life has been permanently lessened. ...

Bill Ballard appeared in Provincial Court on October 13 to have a court date established for his trial on the assault charges. Judge J.P. Kerr set the trial for February 16, 1989. Then, in civil court, Bill's lawyers answered Yolanda's million-dollar claim.

His defence, as presented by barristers Fasken & Calvin, was a denial of the charges.

> ... The defendant was conferring with his father in Maple Leaf Gardens. While the defendant was engaged, the plaintiff entered the office, suddenly and without warning, and demanded that the defendant leave. ...
>
> As the defendant attempted to leave ... the plaintiff advanced upon the defendant with her arms raised, as

though ready to attack him. The plaintiff's shocking and
threatening behavior created in the defendant a reasonable apprehension of imminent harmful or offensive
contact.

When he saw the plaintiff advancing on him, the
defendant raised his own hands in a protective manner
and demanded that the plaintiff stop her menacing
approach so he could leave. ... The plaintiff lunged at
him in a manner that left him in no doubt that she
intended to harm him physically.

The defendant tried ... to keep her at arm's length.
If, in doing so, any part of the defendant's body made
contact with the plaintiff's body, then such contact was a
natural consequence of the plaintiff's own attack ...
unintentional and unavoidable, having regard to the
plaintiff's conduct.

Bill's defence concluded: "The defendant therefore pleads
that the plaintiff has suffered no damages. In the alternative,
the damages claimed by the plaintiff are exaggerated, excessive and remote. In addition, the plaintiff aggravated her
own damages by reason of her own conduct. ... "

The legalese, all very learned and whereasinine, did not
impede the beginning of the 1988–89 season. The Leafs
opened with a rush, fast enough to snatch the early lead in
the NHL. Ballard came out of the eye of Hurricane Harold to
forecast a Stanley Cup for Toronto. "This year," he said,
"we're going to fool you. We're going to win it."

Rose-colored glasses were discarded before the annual
meeting of Gardens' shareholders, on November 23, 1988.
The Leafs collapsed as through a gallows' floor, still more
gloom than gleam. The shareholders were unconcerned, 62
of them on the lower floor of the Hot Stove Lounge to see and
hear the act Scott Morrison of *The Toronto Sun* calls "Harold
Ballard, the prince of putdown."

The annual accounting sessions are run as Ballard dictates,
cognizant as he is that no other shareholder argues with the
man who controls 2,952,455 shares. Harold worked the room
as a caustic comic might.

"The stock goes up when I get sick," he told his minority

partners. "If you want to make money, give me the word. I'll go on an extended vacation to Florida and get very ill."

A shareholder asked about offers to buy the Gardens. "Stand in line," Harold said. "I hear from all kinds of schemers, almost every day, trust companies and banks and breweries. I file all that stuff in the garbage basket."

Another shareholder asked if Harold will ever allow a Russian hockey team to play in the Gardens. "Not till I'm dead," he said. "The stock will be at a million bucks when the Russians get in here, and I'll be gone by then."

The Leafs have won 11 Stanley Cup banners, but Harold does not intend to hang them in the rafters as gongs from old glories. "We've got the banners in storage if you want them," he said. "I'd fly them, but they collect too much dirt and dust. If it gets windy, I don't want the dust to come on me and the ice."

He looked at the shareholder who'd asked about the banners. "If you want to hang them," he said, "buy the building. I'll give you a good price."

The shareholders didn't get any banners; many settled for Ballard's autograph. He signed their annual reports with a fairly steady hand, "Harold E. Ballard." Business writers are amused at such a homey touch. They cover the annual meetings of cutthroats in banking and brewing and mining and oil and doughnuts and never see a shareholder ask for the president's signature.

There were two other strokes of Ballard business before 1988 went out one year and in another. On December 19, against his personal feelings, he fired John Brophy as Leaf coach. "I'm not really firing him," Harold said. "I'm just asking him to take a scouting job instead." George Armstrong, against his desire, accepted the coaching task, still willing to do the bidding of a man he's known for 40 years.

On December 23, Harold was driven to Park Lawn Cemetery to place Christmas wreaths of holly and cedar on the graves of his parents and wife. "The kind of year I've had," he said, "the only peace I got was when I saw the plot where we buried Dorothy. It's hell when you gotta go to a graveyard for some peace."

Peace, most times, is merely a word in the hurly-burly of

Ballard's existence. He was born to commotion. The odds are long against anyone living to 85, let alone living to 85 still squabbling, refusing to mellow.

He refuses, as well, to cater to his body. On February 14, 1989, he fell heavily to the floor between his office and apartment. He was carrying a large bag of red candies, and sprawled in a heap of sweets. "Goddamn it, Yolanda," Harold said. "Help me up."

Another morning, as Harold sat high in a red seat watching the Leafs at practice, Yolanda hurried towards him with a small syringe. "Harold," she said, "you forgot to take your insulin shot." It is normal to remove your pants when you give yourself a shot, the better to see the skin you're going to hit.

"Give me that syringe," Harold said. Then, removing no clothing, he plunged the needle through pants and underwear into a fleshy part of his upper leg. Milt Dunnell watched, amazed. "I hope," Milt said, "those pants weren't dirty. What about germs?" Harold whooped, "Haw, haw, haw!"

Ballard had a date in Provincial Court on February 16, 1989, to give evidence at a preliminary hearing into the charges of aggravated assault in the case of Bill Ballard v. Yolanda Ballard. He was in his wheelchair, wan and cranky, as Yolanda rolled him through the deadbeats and deadheads, the rabble and riffraff, the cops and lawyers who swarm daily through the court corridors. They were shepherded by Yolanda's lawyer, Allan Rachlin, serious, tense, wearing glasses.

I'd covered Ballard at his own trial 17 years earlier, before he was assigned to a vacation in the Crowbar Motel. "You're not totally foreign to the courts," I said.

Harold brightened briefly. "That's right," he said. "This is just like old home week for me."

There had been confusion over which courtroom would be used for the hearing. Reporters pursued the principals as Yolanda rolled Harold into a courtroom where Judge John Kerr was hearing another case. Judge Kerr recognized Ballard and paused in the proceedings before him. He informed Harold that the case had been adjourned until June 26, after

Crown Prosecutor Sal Meranda had reduced the charge to common assault. Then Kerr, gray and courteous, permitted Ballard to speak, curious to hear the man he'd heard so much about.

"Your Honor," Harold said, across 40 feet of courtroom, "I'm objecting to this being a really small situation. This has escalated into a top-notch case, but there's just two people involved. We should be able to settle it in five minutes."

Lawyer Rachlin offered Judge Kerr a letter from a doctor stating that delays in the trial could affect Ballard's health. "I'm worried," Harold said, "they're stalling this thing till I croak. They're betting on how long I'll be around."

"I can't see why we're extending this business," Harold said. "I work at Maple Leaf Gardens. If a guy gets a shot there, he's tried the next day."

Harold was taking rhetorical liberty with the facts. There have been assault cases in the NHL that have dragged on longer than the NHL playoffs. Judge Kerr said he didn't think his courtroom was the forum to discuss hockey violence although he'd heard Alan Eagleson, boss of the NHL players union, waxing wise on the subject on radio.

"If you listen to Eagleson," Harold said, "you'll go nuts. Now, Your Honor, I hope you'll use a little turpentine to speed this case up. I don't mind much, as long as you're in our corner."

Judge Kerr hastened to say, "Oh, I'm impartial." Pal Hal said, in a chummy groove, "We'll see about that. We'll go out some night and settle this case over a drink." It was one of the quaintest propositions ever put to Kerr and, smiling faintly, he bid the Ballards goodbye.

On the street, followed by eight reporters to a taxicab, Harold had a harder line. "I'm ashamed of my kid," he said. "He hit a girl and socked her black and blue."

A man with a microphone stuck it in Ballard's face as Yolanda rolled him toward the cab. The man said, "But isn't what happened sort of minor?"

Harold snorted as though hit by a live wire. "Minor, my ass! My kid ought to go to jail for life!"

Another reporter said, "You mean you wouldn't want to have your son paroled?"

Harold was adamant. "No, no. My son's no fucking good!" Then Yolanda and an obliging Gardens' hand named Henry loaded Harold into the cab and they drove off through the February chill.

A lyric from the Harry Chapin song, "Cat's in the Cradle," seemed to fit a father who thinks his son is callous and uncaring, yet, " my boy was just like me. . . ."

Bill Ballard called me later that day to find out what his father had said in court. I told him and Bill said, gentler than he is known to be, "He's lost it, Dick. He's really lost it."

The Leafs lost it on the last night of the 1988–89 schedule, eliminated from playoff contention for the fourth time in eight seasons. Pal Hal had his own problems staying in contention in April. He was in hospital twice, once for removal of fluid from his lungs, once for treatment of his swollen toes. *The Toronto Star* heard a rumor that both of Ballard's feet had been amputated.

I visited him to check the rumors and found him sounding fit and looking frail. He was pared down to 180 pounds, slimmer than his former 250-pound oval silhouette of an Easter egg.

"Amputation, hell," Harold said. "The doctors haven't amputated so much as a toenail. I've got enough spare toes that I can give you some, if you need a transplant."

Yolanda came in the room, a rhapsody in pink with her signature white boots. Harold had been waiting for her. He called her "princess" and "sweetheart" and when people get cooing like that, I grab my hat and run.

Pal Hal was back in the Gardens in May, still in charge. He had just borrowed $15.5 million from Molson Breweries to buy out his daughter, Mary Elizabeth. The loan, coupled with Molson paying the interest on earlier Gardens' debts since 1980, gave the brewery a large corporate toe inside the Gardens — about 20 per cent.

Unless the loans are extended, Molson will call the money back in the fall of 1990, or, more likely, attempt greater control of the old Cashbox on Carlton Street. In June, concerned that his two sons might attempt a hostile takeover, Ballard borrowed $21.5 million from the Toronto-Dominion Bank to purchase the stock of Harold Jr., Lightbulb Harold, as his father calls him, lit up as Canada's newest multimillionaire.

In late June, in courtroom 121 in Toronto's Old City Hall, Pal Hal testified on behalf of Yolanda Ballard in the charges of common assault against Bill Ballard.

Judge Walter Bell of London permitted wide scope in the questioning of Yolanda by Bill's lawyer, the able and aggressive Clive Bynoe. The judge's forbearance allowed Bynoe to detail Yolanda's involvement in the phony will fraud in an attempt to impugn her credibility in the assault case. Judge Bell allowed Ballard similar latitude in responding to Bynoe's cross-examination.

"I saw him slug her on the jaw, a dandy," Ballard said. "Then he kicked her in the stomach and ran out the door like a deer. She never touched him."

Bynoe said, "I suggest that Yolanda has brainwashed you."

Ballard barked, "That's a lie! Why don't you get your facts straight? . . . The facts are that my family fought like cats and dogs with Yolanda when I was full of hop in the hospital. They thought I was going to croak and wanted the money right away. . . . I think my kids would have administered drugs to get it done."

Bynoe said, "I suggest you told the press, after the alleged incident between Yolanda and Bill Ballard, that you didn't see it."

Ballard retorted, "That's a lie! I didn't want to talk about something I was ashamed of. I was so bloody ashamed. I didn't want to be associated with it."

During a recess in the trial, Ballard mentioned Bill. "Where," he demanded, "is the toughest guy in the girls' schoolroom?" Judge Bell adjourned the trial to late September, 1989, at which time Bill Ballard would come to bat and tell his side of the family squabble.

Ballard passed his 86th birthday in July, heartier than he had been in two years, able to preside over a Sunday party at his summer home on Thunder Beach. It was a day of sun and high sky on Georgian Bay. Overhead a small plane towed a banner proclaiming, "Happy Birthday, Harold, From Yolanda, Puck & Friends."

Puck is their great bouncing slobbering Bouvier pooch who, unaltered, jumps all over guests in an eager effort to

mate with their legs. The dog mingled with the people closest to Ballard in his waning days, notably Allan Lamport,
former ebullient mayor of Toronto. Four months older than
Harold, Lamport had been with him at Upper Canada College when they were teenagers and the world was a new
deck of cards.

Pal Hal enjoyed Don (Duck) Crump, the careful treasurer
of the Gardens for 19 years before Crump left late in 1989 to
become commissioner of the ailing Canadian Football
League. Ballard's other favorites among the Gardens directors were there: Steve Stavro, an ambitious farmer from the
Knob Hills, and Don Giffin, a sheet-metal king and the largest shareholder in the Gardens besides Ballard himself.

Giffin is in his early seventies and considered a giant in the
Canadian construction industry. He helped arrange the
loans Ballard needed from the Toronto-Dominion Bank to
buy John Bassett out of the Gardens in 1971 and to settle the
Stafford Smythe estate in 1972.

The Gardens' switch to Toronto-Dominion from the Imperial Bank of Commerce was abrupt. The Commerce had been
associated with the Gardens since the arena was built in
1931, but the bank was reluctant to loan Ballard the
$5,886,600 required to buy Bassett's 196,200 shares.

After Giffin obtained the loan from Toronto-Dominion,
Ballard got on the blower with Neil Mackinnon, who had
been his contact at the Commerce. Pal Hal said, "I wouldn't
take the fucking Commerce money, Neil, if it was interest-
free. G'bye. I'm going to the T-D."

Ballard appreciated Giffin's intercession with the T-D
Bank. He heard in the summer of 1972 that Giffin Sheet
Metals, having been outbid on some building contracts, was
strapped for cash.

Giffin, opening the mail one morning in August, was
surprised to have a cheque for $50,000 pop out of one enve-
lope. The cheque was from Ballard, with a note: "Hear you
might be able to use this. You got it interest-free. And there's
lots more where this came from, if you need it."

Giffin did not need to cash Ballard's cheque. "We won a
contract or two, so I didn't need Harold's money. But I never
cashed it. I framed the cheque and later, when we had a beef

on the Gardens directorate, I'd say, 'Harold, behave yourself, or I'll cash that cheque.'"

Ballard cut up with Giffin at his last birthday party, and with the chief ticket speculator at the Gardens, Mike Wassilyn, a scalper believed to be in league with Yolanda.

Don Giffin said, "We as Gardens directors think Yolanda would go to the box office and get tickets, which she said were for Harold. Then, we think, she turned the tickets over to Wassilyn, who hustled them on the street."

Ballard shuffled around his birthday party with the aid of a walker, which he'd grip and then move forward with each slow step. It seemed, on a pleasurable day for good food and lively conversation, to be his only concession to disease and age.

Yolanda bustled around choreographing the celebration, constantly sidling her freeloading friends up to Ballard to have their pictures taken with him. She intruded into his space, annoying him enough when it came to cutting a massive cake that he finally pointed the knife at her. He was petulant. "Get the hell away from me," he said.

Epilogue

♦

The trial of Bill Ballard on charges of assaulting Yolanda, held over from June, resumed on September 25, 1989, a sunburned fall day in Toronto. Courtroom 141 in Old City Hall was packed with the media, the curious and the gawkers entranced by the Battling Ballards, a farce of unarguable potency.

Judge Walter Bell of London, bald and benign, listened attentively to Bill Ballard's side regarding the alleged assault. Clive Bynoe, an aggressive lone gun among Toronto defence lawyers, led Bill through the confrontation with Yolanda MacMillan Ballard on September 6, 1988.

Bill slouched in the witness box, boyishly rumpled in a dark sports jacket and yellow tie. He is a graduate lawyer who has never practiced and, on this day, was not about to sound contrite.

Bynoe asked, "You went to see your father on September 6, 1988. Where was this?"

Bill responded, "It was in Maple Leaf Gardens. Concert Productions International, the company I own with Michael Cohl and Labatt, had two shows coming into the Gardens. I went into the box office and then went up to see my father in his quarters, on the second floor. He was in his office and I showed him pictures of my daughter, Maryke. He liked the pictures. Then he said, 'Bill, what's this beef between you and Yolanda?'

"I said, 'Look, Dad, throw that garbage out. I don't want to talk about it.' Then Yolanda appeared in the door between his office and their living space. She said, 'You've been here long enough. Get the fuck out!'"

Bill said he told the lady, known as Yo-Yo, "Lots of people

think you're running this building, not Harold. . . . She uses gutter language that is unparalleled. . . . I reminded her of her jail term."

Bill continued, "Then I turned and went down the hall leading to a door which opens into the hockey offices. It's six or seven feet from my dad's desk. I was walking out when I heard a weird noise — hoo-a! — and saw Mrs. MacMillan had her fingers bent in claws and came at me. . . . One of her hands came down the side of my face.

"I reached out and locked her hands with mine. I squeezed her fingers. She said, 'Look, Harold, he's assaulting me.' I said, 'If I assaulted you, there wouldn't be enough left of you to make a hot dog.'"

Bill's story was vivid: "I told her, 'Get the fuck away from me and leave me and my family alone.' I threw her hands down. As I got to the door, I turned, and damned if she wasn't coming at me like a steamroller. . . . She was charging me again."

Listening, spectators in the courtroom could imagine a short dumpy overweight woman of 56 rushing at a husky 42-year-old man, fingernails at the ready.

Bill said. "I looked back. . . . She came at me. . . . I raised my left leg. . . . I was wearing slip-on loafer shoes. I love those kind of shoes. . . . She ran into my leg. . . . Then I slammed through the door to get out there."

Clive Bynoe, Bill's lawyer, asked, "Why did you lift your foot?"

"Because," Bill said, "I didn't want my eyes scratched out. . . . Then I went down to the Hot Stove Lounge in the Gardens and had lunch."

Bill said later the same day he returned to Pal Hal's office. No, he told Bynoe, there were no hard feelings: "We were father and son. Harold asked, 'What's this about you beating up Yolanda?' I said, 'She's fucking crazy.'"

Bill added, "There was a press conference late in the afternoon in the Gardens, for my dad to announce the signing of a Leaf draft choice. . . . A reporter asked my dad about the brutalizing of Yolanda. . . . He said it was nonsense."

Metro Toronto police laid assault charges on Bill Ballard on

September 15, 1988. He admitted to a questioning sergeant that "I may have kicked out at her. . . . "

In court Bynoe asked: "Did you punch Yolanda's left eye?"

Bill: "No, never. I never punched her anywhere on her anatomy."

Sal Merenda, a stocky crown attorney, cross-examined Bill, acting for the alleged victim, Yolanda, who was not in court. One of Pal Hal's earlier consorts, Sylvia Train of the *Toronto Sun*, attended the hearing in support of Bill and his siblings, Mary Elizabeth and Harold Junior.

Merenda referred to a portion of Yolanda's testimony in June, 1989, in which she claimed that Bill kicked and struck her. Bill responded with an insolence guaranteed not to ingratiate himself with Judge Bell. He said, "Yes, I heard her say I gave her a good whack on the cheek. I saw pictures of her black eye . . . and her very big stomach. . . . But I've had much more serious injuries in football and hockey. . . . I've had broken ribs."

Merenda, probing, sought to emphasize the physical disparities between a big man and a small woman. Question: "How tall are you?" Answer: "Five feet ten or six feet. I hunch a little." Question: "What do you weigh?" Answer: "One hundred and seventy-five pounds."

The crown clinched the size argument. "You'd agree she's smaller and shorter than you?"

Bill said, "I don't know how tall or wide she is. . . . Yes, she's shorter than me. . . . I'm a man."

Merenda stated, not quite taunting: "But men don't fight with women. . . . You made her submit when your hands were locked."

Bill repeated his earlier declaration. "I had trouble restraining her, yes. She charged at me making a weird noise. . . . She went 'Aahg-g-g.' I pushed her down. . . . I didn't want my eyes scratched out. . . . I was afraid of her, yes."

Merenda shuffled through the photographs Yolanda had submitted showing her with her left eye and cheek puffed up as though she had had six fights with George Chuvalo and lost every one. "Look at the pictures," Merenda said. "There was no reason for you to cause these injuries. . . . Did you give her the black eye?"

Bill demurred: "My foot connected with her gut area, but not her eye. . . . It would be a minor thing for her to get herself a black eye. . . . Nothing she would do would surprise me."

Merenda persisted. "You caused these injuries, didn't you?"

Bill: "I said, 'Look, Yolanda, if I assaulted you, there wouldn't be fucking anything left over to make a hot dog.'"

Merenda: "Did you strike her?"

Bill: "I did not strike her. I threw her back. . . . I turned around, and she's coming at me again. . . . I stuck my left foot out."

Merenda: "She said you kicked her."

Bill: "She ran into my foot. It was about three feet off the ground. . . . I didn't want to get hit by her. I was off-balance."

Merenda suggested that Bill "hated" Yolanda. Bill insisted, "I'm not capable of hating. It's one of my downfalls. . . . I did say to her, 'Get away from me, you lunatic!'"

Merenda continued to press Bill on the second day of the trial "Yolanda does take care of your father?"

Bill said, "I hear she's in charge of Harold E. Ballard's medication and cleaning up his messes."

Question: "But your father's not a child."

Answer: "He's a very old man. . . . I question the medication given him by Yolanda MacMillan."

Pal Hal took daily injections of insulin to combat the diabetes that left his feet feeling numb. Yolanda walked around behind him in public carrying a large handbag which she claimed contained the pills he needed to sustain his heart.

The crown attorney said, "She's closer to your father than you are? She's keeping him alive?"

Bill countered, "She has a great deal of control over him. . . . But he's tough enough to keep himself alive."

Bill maintained his innocence in the alleged assault. "I did not hit that woman. . . . She could have inflicted the injuries on herself. . . . I know nothing about her black eye. I didn't punch her. . . . My foot made contact with her belly. . . . She was screaming. . . . It took a lot of strength for me not to hit her."

Merenda said, "Did you call her a cunt and a fucking whore?"

Bill answered, "No. . . I call her human garbage. I didn't consider it a serious matter at all. It was all part of the history of the exploits of Yolanda MacMillan. . . . I did contact her stomach."

Yolanda had said, inside and outside the courtroom, that "Billy Ballard said he had megabucks to buy police, judges and crown attorneys." She later expanded her list to include Willian Houston of the Toronto *Globe and Mail* and me as two more of those people bought off by Bill.

The last is ludicrous, a bad-mouthing tune played on a cheap tin whistle. Rich as Bill Ballard may be, he doesn't have enough money to buy me, nor, I suspect, William Houston of the *Globe*. Yolanda Babik MacMillan Ballard doesn't seem to understand people who play by rules different from her standard.

Sal Merenda implied that Bill could buy his way through life. "You do have several million in assets?"

Bill said, "Actually, my wife has my assets. My wife owns our house. If the business I'm in goes broke, I'm broke. . . . I may be a very rich boy, or I'm a very poor boy."

Merenda wondered aloud about Bill's relationship with his sister, Mary Elizabeth, and his brother, Harold Junior, in the family company, H.E. Ballard Limited. "Didn't you call your sister Mary Lizard?"

Bill replied, offhandedly, "My dad called my sister a rep- tile.' So I called her 'Lizard.' . . . My brother and sister left me high and dry. . . . My sister got $15-million from the family company. My brother got $21-million. . . . I don't get divi- dends from the company. . . . But I'm not motivated by money. . . . I'm lucky. I'm not a shrewd brilliant business- man. I just run into the right situations."

Merenda finished his cross-examination with a reference to a rowdy scene on the heart ward of Toronto General Hos- pital, after Pal Hal had his crucial quintuple bypass operation in July, 1988. He said to Bill, "You pushed Yolanda in the hospital?"

Bill denied he had shoved the lady. "She was sprinkling holy water over my dad. I said, 'Yolanda, leave.' . . . She was dying to have me hurt her. . . . She doesn't exist in my eyes. . . . "

Bill was excused from the witness box and his lawyer, Clive Bynoe, called Donald Crump as a witness for the defence. Crump's appearance masks a sharp intellect: he was a gray man in a gray suit, with less hair than he once had, who could blend into any background anywhere. He has been a chartered accountant for 32 years, 19 of them in the service of Pal Hal and the Gardens.

Bynoe said, "Mr. Crump, did you see Yolanda after Bill Ballard's alleged assaulting of her?"

Crump said, "Mr. Ballard called me to his office on a business matter not long after Bill left. . . . He was sitting at his desk, with Yolanda beside him. She had brought some lunch to his desk and he said, 'Yolanda, get this goddamn stuff out of here.' . . . I noticed nothing different about Yolanda."

Bynoe: "You noticed nothing different about her face or her walk?"

Crump repeated, "I noticed nothing different in her face or how she walked. I'd have noticed if she had a black eye. . . . "

Yolanda had detested Crump from an earlier episode. He had discovered the cheque for $75,000, made out to her by Michael Gobuty for, she told me, "jewelry." Crump and others at the Gardens believed the $75,000 was payment for persuading Ballard to back Gobuty's loan from the National Bank of Canada.

The lawyers summed up their arguments on September 27, 1989, a clear, brisk Wednesday. Clive Bynoe, articulate and confident, spoke eloquently for one hour and 29 minutes.

He began, "Your Honour, this trial is a matter of credibility between Bill Ballard and Yolanda Ballard. . . . I submit there are grounds for disbelieving Yolanda. . . . She is not a credible witness."

A courtroom is the theater of the law and Bynoe, moving easily, commanded his stage. He reminded Judge Bell, "We know that Yolanda MacMillan was involved in a well-planned scheme to forge a will with Robert Irwin 10 years ago.... I submit that she was the brains behind the fraud with Irwin...."

Irwin, a lawyer, had been described in the fraud trial as Yolanda MacMillan's "lover." He was sentenced to four years in prison and disbarred from the legal profession. In 1989 he was seen around the Toronto townhouse occupied by Yolanda's daughter, Anna MacMillan.

"Now, then," Clive Bynoe said, quite deliberately. "The hallmark of Yolanda Ballard is that there is something pathological about her make-up.... She interprets things to suit herself.... She testified that Bill Ballard hit her, but Don Crump said that he saw no marks on her. She wasn't limping. She didn't go to the hospital for three hours afterward.... What was her motive, Your Honour? I submit she had a million reasons, and every one was a dollar bill...."

Bynoe was alluding to the $1-million action launched in civil court by Yolanda's lawyers against Bill Ballard on September 26, 1988, twenty days after the alleged assault. Yolanda as plaintiff claimed damages "in the sum of $500,000.00 ... and punitive, aggravated and exemplary damages in the sum of $500,000.00."

She claimed she suffered "severe external and internal injuries," damage to "muscles, tendons and ligaments" so extensive that the description sounded as though she'd been run over by a regiment of Zamboni ice-making machines.

Bynoe referred to Pal Hal's testimony supporting Yolanda as "unbelievable." In one of his last public appearances Harold had perjured himself, a brazen and bizarre performance. At one point during the cross-examination, Pal Hal advised Bynoe, "Why don't you sit down? You're not only deaf, dumb and blind, but you've also got water on the brain."

Now, summing up, Bynoe said, "I submit, Your Honour, that Harold Ballard has only a nodding acquaintance with the truth.... He isn't a credible witness.... He corroborated Yolanda's testimony by saying, 'Bill upped and slugged her on the jaw and gave her a hell of a kick.' Yet on tape he said,

'Something happened that I couldn't see. . . . I didn't see the actual punch. All I heard was the scuffle.'"

Bynoe reviewed the alleged assault of September 6, 1988. "Yolanda took a swipe at Bill Ballard. . . . Her fingers were as claws. . . . They tussled back and forth. . . . She came racing at him. . . . He kicked out. . . . She went off balance . . . and fell down like a bag of potatoes."

Bynoe stressed the issue of credibility. "I believe the accused is entitled to defend himself, and he did. He got his foot up and pushed out. . . . So, Your Honour, your task is to find the truth. . . . I remind you of Yolanda's evidence, her possible motive, her character. . . . How can you believe her when she said Bill Ballard punched her?"

He also admitted, "Bill Ballard was a little flamboyant. . . . He was upset. . . . " Then, to wind up, he said, "Your Honour, anyone hearing this case . . . would have difficulty deciding on the evidence what actually occurred. . . . I'm in the middle ground. I'm not sure what happened, but I believe the case against the accused has not been proved beyond a reasonable doubt. . . . "

Bill Ballard had listened intently to Bynoe's stirring defence, delighted. When Bynoe finished, Bill sprang up to shake his hand. I remarked to a colleague in the press section, "If I was going to hang, I'd get Bynoe to pitch my case."

Sal Merenda, attorney for the crown, did not match Clive Bynoe's passion or his vivid command of language. He attacked Bill Ballard's evidence with a laid-back certainty.

Merenda said, "Under oath, Your Honour, the accused said when he got through with Yolanda, there wouldn't be enough left of her to make a hot dog. That's pretty potent."

He argued, "Yolanda's doing a lot for Harold Ballard. . . . She is taking care of him. . . . It takes a lot of tolerance for her to do what she is doing. . . . A lot of this trial has been to discredit Mrs. Ballard for her earlier jail term for fraud. But she presumably has been rehabilitated."

Merenda claimed the testimony from police officers and two doctors, heard in the trial in June, was pertinent. "The accused did admit, to the police, that he kicked her. . . . Doctors pointed out that bruises to Mrs. Ballard would not be

apparent from one to four hours after the attack . . . which is
why her injuries were not apparent to Don Crump. . . . The
accused claimed he acted in self-defence. If you accept that,
Your Honour, it still doesn't explain the damage to her cheek
and eye. . . . I submit that he punched her and kicked her. . . .
To suggest that she inflicted the wounds on herself is refuted
by the doctors' testimony that her injuries were 98 per cent
consistent with having been pushed. . . . "

The crown again contrasted the size and sex of Yolanda
and Bill Ballard. "Was this 56-year-old woman a threat to
him? . . . He lost control. He kicked and punched her. He
considered her human garbage. . . . "

Merenda concluded his 30-minute summation firmly:
"The accused did say to the police that 'I kicked her, but
certainly not that hard.' He couldn't explain the injury to her
eye. If he did hit her, he has no self-defence. . . . You may not
like Mrs. Ballard. You may think she'd drive one to drink. But
that can't justify her injuries. . . . "

Judge Bell, owlish behind his rimless glasses, declared a
half-hour recess before rendering his decision. Milling
around outside the courtroom, observers agreed that Clive
Bynoe's stirring plea for Bill Ballard would result in a verdict
of not guilty.

The courtroom was jammed when Judge Bell returned to
review the extravagant evidence he had heard during six
days in June and September, 1988. He could have been for-
given for feeling any pain in his ears.

Judge Bell said, "The accused denied most of Yolanda
Ballard's testimony . . . how she said he 'smashed me in the
face' and 'kicked me in the stomach.' . . . Yolanda Ballard was
prolix . . . and Mr. Bynoe proved she is a convicted criminal."

But, Judge Bell said, a doctor testified "that Yolanda was
admitted to hospital with a bruised face at 4:15 p.m. on
September 6, 1988. He said her puffed-up cheek and eye was
[sic] consistent with a blow of 'substantial force'. . . . A police
constable testified that her 'left eye and cheekbone were
swollen and purple.' Anna MacMillan testified that her
mother's face was 'badly bruised.' . . . I believe the testimony
of the police and doctors."

The judge said, "The accused found Yolanda 'despicable'

. . . but that was unrelated to the subject of the testimony. . . .
I allowed great latitude in the testimony. . . . I found Harold
Ballard capricious, disputive and scurrilous, devoid of objec-
tivity. . . . "

Judge Bell concluded, "The Crown has proved guilt
beyond reasonable doubt . . . and I therefore find the
accused GUILTY. . . . " In the courtroom, in the collective
silence at a judgment few anticipated, you could have heard
a defence lawyer drop.

Clive Bynoe, recovered, had a word before Judge Bell pronounced sentence. "I submit, Your Honour, that it would not
be in the public interest to hold the accused . . . and that a
discharge be granted."

Sal Merenda, the victorious crown, offered other words:
"The accused, Your Honour, showed no remorse. He treated
her like garbage. . . . Harold Ballard has the right to be with
who he likes. . . . If the accused is discharged, he can kick
and hit who he likes. . . . This man lost control and went
much, much too far. He committed a brutal attack on a
defenceless 56-year-old woman. . . . Perhaps a fine won't get
him to keep his hands to himself. . . . I ask you to impose
community service upon him . . . and prohibit him from
further contact with Yolanda and her family."

The last words were Judge Bell's. "The maximum fine for
this offence could be $2,000.00. I impose a fine of $500.00, to
be paid within 15 days."

As Judge Bell departed, Clive Bynoe murmured to a court
reporter, "So much for eloquence." Bill Ballard paid the fine
and, upon reflection, decided to appeal the verdict. He
wanted to erase the blot on his record and perhaps enhance
his chances of defeating Yolanda's bid for $1-million in dam-
ages from him in civil court. The Ontario Court of Appeal
upheld the assault conviction against Bill on June 28, 1990.

On September 30, 1989, after midnight, I was awakened at
home by a telephone call from Yolanda. She said, "Harold
wants to speak to you."

He came on the phone, gruff, hearty, "Rich, about that
book you're writing on me . . . "

"Yeah," I said. "What the hell are you doing up at this
hour? You wet the bed or what?"

"Haw, haw, haw! No, I want to sell our book in the Gardens. Come and see me about it. We'll sell it and give the proceeds to battered women."

Ballard received the first copy of *Pal Hal*, but Yolanda was not too battered to grab it from him and read it first. She was dismayed to read the account of her past, angered enough to kill any chance of the book being sold in Maple Leaf Gardens.

Pal Hal was apologetic when I visited him to seal the book deal. "I'm sorry, Rich," he said. "I've got to cancel what I told you. You took some cracks at Yolanda, which she didn't like." He looked up from his wheelchair, his refuge during the waking hours of the last year of his life. "And I've got to live with her, not you."

The Maple Leafs, under new administration, began the 1989–90 season with renewed enthusiasm and conquests. Pal Hal had one last stroke of luck. He replaced Gordon Stellick, whom he fired as general manager, with a thorough hockey operative, Floyd Smith, the team's chief scout for nine years.

George Armstrong, an old Ballard retainer, reacted to suggestions that he keep the coaching portfolio like a tremulous virgin on the verge. Pal Hal, impatient, shunted him into the scouting department and ordered Smith to find another coach.

There was Maple Leaf irony in Smith's selection. Doug Carpenter had been in the Toronto system in the early 1980s, as coach of the St. Catharines Saints. He was Punch Imlach's choice to coach the Leafs before Imlach was fired. Imlach's successor, Gerry McNamara, passed him over in favour of Dan Maloney in 1984. Carpenter rebounded to the NHL as coach of the New Jersey Devils, was dismissed in 1987 and landed on the first bounce in Halifax as foreman of the Quebec farm in the American Hockey League.

Floyd Smith found Carpenter in the Maritimes, persuaded Quebec to release him, and the Leafs finally had the coach they had intended to get five years earlier. Carpenter is smoother than John Brophy, scholarly to the point of being pedantic, and bears a fleeting resemblance to Pal Hal. His hair is a lively carrot color compared to the ripe peach of Ballard's pompadour.

Pal Hal's pace in the fall of 1989 had slowed to the hesitant roll of his wheelchair, which he parked every morning at the top of the red seats in the Gardens to watch the Leafs practice. Pals, old pals, would sit with him: Armstrong and Dick Duff from the champion squads of the 1960s, or Milt Dunnell, almost as venerable as Ballard, from *The Toronto Star*, or me.

Ballard would gaze around the Gardens with the affection of long familiarity, from the time the old cold-storage locker was built in 1931. Here he was truly at home. His wander years were gone, his world shrunken, as he was, to the size of a walnut.

Players do not wear names or numbers on their practice shirts, a fact that caused confusion for Pal Hal. "Who's that bastard laying on the ice?" he'd ask.

"Oh," I'd say, "that's Al Iafrate joking around." Or, "That's Wendel Clark gagging it up."

Clark was a Ballard favourite, often out of the lineup because of injuries to his back. "You think Wendel's swinging the lead?" Pal Hal would say. "You think he's kidding us?"

I said, "If you had 21 players with the guts of Wendel Clark, you'd be a hell of a lot closer to winning the Stanley Cup than you are. He cares like the best who ever played in Toronto."

"The Stanley Cup," Ballard mused. "If I won it one more time, I'd die happy and they could bury me at center ice."

Pal Hal was only half kidding. At center ice in the Gardens, directly below the massive time clock, Ballard had his initials — H.E.B. — carved into a circular cement slab. When the cement was fresh, many years ago, he also slapped down his palm prints. Then he stepped into the cement and left his footprints. The slab, I thought, would have made the most fascinating gravestone in the history of Canadian burials.

"No kidding, Rich," Pal Hal said one morning. "Don Crump and I've talked about burying me at center ice. We thought we'd sell tickets to the funeral and give the proceeds to charity."

He mused about his sons during the last fall days of 1989,
about Harold Junior, called Bobby when he was younger to
distinguish him from Harold Senior. Harold Junior had been
charged with breaking into the Ballard family home in a
fashionable section of Etobicoke and stealing hockey memorabilia valued at $18,000.00. The vacant house, worth per-
haps $700,000 to $1-million on the Toronto real estate market,
was where the Ballard children were raised.

"I can't believe that damn kid," Ballard said of his youngest
son. "I bought out his stock in the family company for $21-
fucking-million and he got it, cash. That's enough to buy a
country. Yet he breaks a window in my house to steal some
Stanley Cup replicas and stuff. If he'd asked for the key, I'd
have given it to him. He must have been high on something."

Harold Junior was 41 when he was charged, an entirely
agreeable individual when sober. He has a talent for painting
and commercial art, but has never earned money from his
avocation. Angry, he assaulted two Metro police officers
when they arrested him. He will answer charges of theft and
assault in an Etobicoke courtroom on December 19, 1990.

Ballard meditated on the court action his older son, Bill,
had instigated for control of the Gardens. He always seemed
closer to Bill than Harold Junior, perhaps because Bill acts as
though he is cut from the same tough roll of Ballard baloney.

"Only one real problem with Bill," Pal Hal said. "He thinks
he's got to outdo me. He ought to know he can't outdo his old
man. Now he's suing us, for Christ's sake."

The lawsuit was filed by a numbered company, 820099
Ontario Incorporated. Bill Ballard was listed as chairman of
the board and his partner in Concert Productions International, Michael Cohl, as president. They sought a mandatory
injunction that would overturn the $21-million sale of 33.98
per cent of the outstanding stock in Harold E. Ballard Ltd.

Pal Hal and his pals were among the defendants: Don
Crump and Don Giffin, directors of H.E. Ballard Ltd., and
Harold G. Ballard, alias Bobby or Harold Junior. As an alternative to a surrender of the shares, the numbered company
sought $170-million in damages.

In the breakdown, Harold Junior was sued for $50-million.
Crump and Giffin, as directors of the family company, were

sued for $50-million for "inducing Harold Jr. to break a con-
tract with the plaintiff" and for another $50-million in dam-
ages for conspiracy. An additional appeal of $20-million "in
aggravated and punitive damages" was sought against all
defendants.

The plaintiffs, Bill Ballard and Cohl, claimed to have
obtained an option from Harold G. Ballard, on February 15,
1989, that would permit the numbered company to purchase
the 35 shares owned by Harold Junior in H.E. Ballard Ltd.
The numbered company would also acquire the 34 shares
held by Bill Ballard. The plaintiffs maintained that the numbered company was poised to acquire "beneficial ownership" of the majority of outstanding shares in Harold E.
Ballard Ltd. and control of Maple Leaf Gardens for $40-
million.

The brotherly agreement, Bill Ballard and Cohl claimed,
stipulated that neither Bill nor Harold Jr. would "engage in
any action to transfer ownership of their shares." They also
claimed that Harold Jr. was informed on March 17, 1989, that
the agreement was being extended from April 5, 1989 to June
30, 1989.

The statement of claim declared: "At a time unknown to
the plaintiff, the defendants . . . became aware of the option
agreement and entered into a conspiracy to injure the plaintiff by inducing Harold Jr. to breach his obligations under the
option agreement. In or about late May, 1989, Harold E.
Ballard Ltd., through Harold Ballard Sr., Donald Crump and
Donald Giffin, offered to purchase the shares of Harold Jr.

"In breach of his agreement, Harold Jr. entered into dis-
cussions with Ballard Sr., Crump and Giffin. On or about
June 20, 1989, they succeeded in getting Harold Jr. to enter
into an agreement to sell his shares for $21,075,000. The
agreement of sale closed on June 21, 1989."

Bill Ballard and Cohl contended, "In furtherance of the
conspiracy, Ballard Sr., Crump and Giffin caused Harold E.
Ballard Ltd. to buy 350,320 common shares of Maple Leaf
Gardens, owned by Ballard Sr. and, in return, issued him an
unknown number of common shares in Harold E. Ballard
Ltd."

Bill and Cohl informed Harold Jr. on June 29, 1989, that

they were exercising their option. The purchase was to have taken place in the office of a Toronto law firm, but Harold Jr. did not appear. As a consequence, Bill and Cohl said they would "suffer irreparable harm if the defendants are not ordered to sell to the plaintiffs 33.98 per cent of the common shares of stock in H.E. Ballard Ltd. at the price set out in the option" of $20-million.

The statement of defence for Pal Hal, Don Crump and Don Giffin contrasted the perceived differences between the Ballard brothers. Bill and Cohl were described as "wealthy and sophisticated businessmen." They claimed the option "relied upon by the plaintiffs ... purportedly was made on February 14, 1989. At this time, Harold Jr. was unemployed and unable to meet his living expenses.

"He was anxious to realize on the 34 common shares he owned in H.E. Ballard Ltd. He was dependent upon William Ballard and Cohl for both emotional support and business advice, particularly in relation to the common shares, which represented his only asset. William Ballard and Cohl were aware of this dependency. Harold Jr., unlike Cohl and William Ballard, is not a sophisticated businessman and he received no independent legal advice with respect to the option agreement. . . .

"In fact, the option agreement, insofar as William Ballard purported to grant an option to purchase his shares in H.E. Ballard Ltd., was nothing but a sham and a ruse calculated to induce Harold Jr. to execute the option agreement.

"Further, the stated financial consideration to Harold Ballard Jr. for entering into the option agreement is a nominal sum of $10, which, in fact, was never paid to Ballard Jr. At all times, Cohl acted in the interests of himself and William Ballard and not in the interests of Harold Jr."

The lawsuit itself and the statement of defence were further proof that the Ballards are in court more than some Ontario judges. The controversy focused on the Ballard family company that Pal Hal established in 1966 to reduce estate and succession duties following the death of Harold Sr. This was before Dorothy Ballard's death, in 1969, and before the arrival of Yolanda, in 1983.

There were 103 shares in H.E. Ballard Ltd., 102 of them

transferred to trusts for the three children, Harold Jr., Bill and Mary Elizabeth. Dorothy Ballard owned one share, which she left to Harold Sr. when she died.

The statement of defence stressed the family's appreciation of Pal Hal's power. "Each of the children understood that the common shares carried no entitlement to control of H.E. Ballard Ltd. and that such control would remain with the preferred shares owned by Harold Ballard Sr.

"The children also understood there could be no transfer of common shares without the approval of Harold E. Ballard Ltd. which, in practical terms, meant the approval of Harold Ballard Sr.

"From time to time, various children indicated a wish to sell their common shares and realize on their inheritance. Ballard Sr. indicated, at all times, he did not wish any shares of Harold E. Ballard Ltd., which he had given to the children, to be sold outside the family group or have strangers become shareholders in the corporation. . . . "

Harold Jr. attempted to sell his shares to his father or Don Giffin several times beginning in 1982. He did sell to H.E. Ballard Ltd. on June 20, 1989, for about $21-million, 10 days before the expiration of the apparent option he had given brother Bill and Michael Cohl.

Pal Hal had a particular reason for buying out Harold Jr. It allowed H.E. Ballard Ltd. more corporate room to move if its shares in the Gardens were diluted by the exercising of an option held by the Molson Companies of 19.9 per cent of all stock in Maple Leaf Gardens. The option will expire in November 1990.

"Let's recapitulate," I said one day to Pal Hal. "You've made your daughter a multimillionaire because her name was Ballard by buying her stock. You've made one of your sons a multimillionaire because his name is Ballard. Bill's a cinch to get multimillions because his name is Ballard. For God's sake, Pal Hal, adopt *me!*"

Ballard gazed at my vacant expression and seedy appearance. "You," he said, "are too old and ugly to adopt."

He talked about where the residue of his wealth would go. "People thought I was kidding a couple of years ago when I said I'd leave a lot to charity. I guess they won't believe me until they read my will."

His last will and testament, dated March 30, 1988, in Toronto, established the Harold E. Ballard Foundation to dispense funds to assorted charities. He has been a major donor to the Canadian Cancer Society, the Charlie Conacher Cancer Research Foundation, the Salvation Army, the Hospital for Crippled Children and the Scott Mission in Toronto.

The Scott Mission is a haven for the homeless on Spadina Avenue, a teeming street west of downtown Toronto, not far from where Pal Hal had a machine shop for fixing sewing machines. He never said how much he gave the Mission, and the Mission has kept his secret.

Garnett Martin, executive director of the Mission, once said, "We never disclose who gives what to us. But I have a lot of respect for Mr. Ballard. He knew how much we dispensed in food and clothing to the homeless."

One of Pal Hal's charms, I thought, was that he rarely took bows for his charitable contributions. On television I once said to him, "I hear you give to charities privately. D'you want to talk about that tonight?"

"Knock that crap off, Richard," he said. "Don't make me seem like a hell of a guy. I want to be known as a rogue and renegade."

His last gesture as a renegade was to impede a Russian team from playing in the Gardens on New Year's Eve, 1989. He had not renewed diplomatic relations with the Soviet Union in spite of the goodwill exhibited by Mikhail Gorbachev, the latest general manager of the U.S.S.R.

"This guy, Gorby," I said to Ballard, "you know he's trying to make friends. Pretty soon you'll have Russians back in this building."

"That's crap, too," Ballard said. "I'm still mad at the Russians for shooting down that Korean airplane. This guy Gorby, I look on him as another Red Square. Haw, haw, haw!"

The NHL, sucking up to the Soviets, agreed to have Russian teams play NHL teams in a series of year-end exhibitions in 1989. Ballard was committed, against his profane wishes: "It's like I'm in a fucking war against the Russians by myself," he said. "Well, the hell with it. I've always been a loner and I'll take on the Russians alone."

He said perhaps he'd schedule the game at 2:30 a.m. on New Year's morning. "And I won't let my team wear the Maple Leaf uniforms against the Russians. It would be a disgrace if I let them do that."

One night, wandering around his cluttered apartment in the Gardens, he had Yolanda put him through to my hutch. "Rich?" he said. "How the hell are ya! How's it hanging? Haw, haw, haw!"

Then he said, "Tell me, does the Toronto Harbour freeze over in the wintertime?"

"Sometimes," I said. "Sometimes they've got to use an icebreaker to get the ferries moving between the mainland and the Toronto Islands."

He said, "I hope she freezes like a bastard this December."

"Why's that?" I asked.

"Because maybe I can play that goddamn Russian game on the Toronto Harbour. We could wheel out portable seats for the fans. You think it's a hell of an idea?"

"If you announce that stunt," I said, "people'll think you're smoking the same stuff you say your sons are."

"Fuck off," he said, and hung up.

The Leafs did play a Soviet side, on New Year's Eve in the Gardens, at the usual Saturday night time of 8 p.m., and lost. By then Pal Hal was in the Cayman Islands and beyond comprehending, sunburned, sluggish, in the worst physical shape of his life.

He was in sufficient shape, on December 5, 1989, to hit Yolanda with his cane. The witness was Roseanne Rocchi, a bright tough lawyer for the Gardens, whose practice concentrated on Pal Hal's affairs.

"They were at Toronto Hospital," Rocchi remembers. "I arrived to find him hitting her and shouting he wanted her out of his life. He told me he was sick and tired of having Yolanda running his life."

Rocchi wrote down her recollections. "She monitored his phone calls. She kept his friends away. She was rude to employees of Maple Leaf Gardens. She caused employees to

be afraid. She would not let him take calls. She would inform
people that he was not available."

Rocchi said, "Ballard told me he wanted Yolanda committed, or arrested. He didn't want her giving him his medicine.
He didn't trust her.

"They started to fight in the hospital. She muttered something about him having Alzheimer's disease. He told her she
was crazy. . . . She said if she left, no one would take care of
him. Mr. Ballard and I said that was his problem, that he
would make his own care arrangements."

Yolanda began to weep tears, of the purest crocodile. She
bawled that she had been with Pal Hal for seven years. He
said it wasn't seven years; it was six. He reminded her that
she had been well paid for the care she had given him.

Rocchi, stepping into the family scuffle, suggested that
Yolanda take a winter vacation as a trial separation from
Ballard. "I mentioned a few weeks, and he said he'd like to
send her away for two years."

Yolanda said, in effect, nuts to that idea: "I won't leave
him, because I want to keep him alive until he is 102."

Pal Hal retorted, "I don't want to live until 102, if it means
living with you."

"Would it be better," Yolanda asked, "to be 102 or under
the sod?"

"Better under the sod," he said.

The Cayman Islands are three heaps of sand directly south of
Cuba, in the Caribbean. In the last years of his life Ballard
was accustomed to going on winter vacation in the Caymans,
or south Florida.

Yolanda, bustling in and out of Ballard's home in the Gardens, complained in the fall of 1989 that "poison gas" was
being pumped into their apartment. Don (Shanty) MacKenzie, the building superintendent, took the complaint seriously enough to have experts from the City of Toronto's
health department check Pal Hal's pad. Yolanda refused to
believe the experts when they reported no traces of gas. She
kept the windows of the apartment open, permitting wind to
blow in December cold.

Arctic conditions were not guaranteed to improve the

health of Pal Hal, who had already had fluid drained from his system earlier in the year. He may have had pneumonia on December 14, 1989, the day they left for the Caymans.

By that time Yolanda had offended many of the functionaries around the Gardens. Henry Hayek, in charge of pushing Pal Hal's wheelchair, had been dismissed — "fired by Yolanda," he said. Her one ally was 18-year-old Denise Banks, whose real name is Banka.

The Banka girl, from the cottage country near Midland, Ontario, had been summer caretaker of the Ballard home on Thunder Beach. Yolanda "adopted" Denise and brought her to Toronto, where she served as her Girl Friday every day of the week. Banka accompanied Yolanda and Pal Hal when they escaped to the Caymans.

Ballard was customarily driven by a Gardens chauffeur in a blue Lincoln limo, with the license plate MLG-1 — Maple Leaf Gardens Number 1. For his last Cayman trip, he was driven to Pearson International Airport by his barber, Joey DeFrancesco. The barber was responsible for landscaping Pal Hal's locks and coloring them a becoming shade of pumpkin.

There was something covert and fly-by-night about Ballard's departure. His secretaries did not know where he was until they were called by Jack Johnson, an officer for Canada Customs at the airport. He later told *The Toronto Star*, "Ballard didn't look well enough to travel. I was there at curbside with a wheelchair when they arrived at the airport. I was so concerned about him that, after the plane left, I phoned Maple Leaf Gardens. They were shocked to find out that Ballard had left the country."

Johnson said Yolanda asked him not to tell anyone where they were travelling, but Johnson ignored her request. "Ballard didn't look good at all, so I called the Gardens. He was so weak he could hardly sign the U.S. declaration form. His signature was merely a scrawl."

Johnson asked Ballard, "Do you think you are well enough to travel? You're going to have to go to Miami, then make connections to the Grand Cayman."

Ballard said, "Why don't you and your wife come along, too?"

Johnson said thanks, and goodbye. He said, "When I got home I told my wife, 'That might be the last time we'll see H.B. He really didn't look good.'"

Yolanda and Pal Hal settled in the Casa Carib, a tropical bivouac near the Cayman capital of Georgetown. Medical care on the Caymans is even primitive for tourists who only risk sunstroke.

People at the Gardens, aware of Pal Hal's preference for the Caymans, phoned the Casa Carib to be certain of his whereabouts. Staffers of the hotel switchboard said the Ballards had been there, but had left for Hawaii. That was a lie.

Toronto reporters, all too aware of the Battling Ballards as the stuff of titillation, checked with one of the few law firms on Grand Cayman. The firm revealed that a marriage license had been filed with a justice of the peace in Georgetown. Yolanda had set a wedding date for January 3, 1990, the day she would be 57.

In Toronto, disturbed at the notion of wedding bells tolling for Pal Hal, lawyer Roseanne Rocchi sent Ballard an urgent warning that his will, which she had witnessed, would be invalidated if he married. As his wife, Yolanda could get $75,000 off the top of his estate, plus at least one-third of it.

Yolanda, grabbing for the gold ring, lost her slippery hold. The nuptials were cancelled on the morning of January 3. Yolanda told Toronto reporters, "the marriage was called off because Harold became suddenly sick." The justice of the peace, Vernon Jackson, was quoted in the *Toronto Sun* as saying "Ballard was a very sick man and not fit to proceed." A Caymans doctor, Robert James Efford, advised that Pal Hal be flown immediately for care in a Miami hospital.

Ballard was admitted on January 3, 1990, to the Baptist Hospital, among the best medical-care facilities in North America. He came under the supervision of Dr. Joel Mann, a careful man behind glasses, his sparse dark hair combed straight back.

Dr. Mann told me, "When I got Mr. Ballard he was fairly close to dying. He was comatose. His heart was failing. His kidneys weren't working. He was sunburned. If that lady'd got him to me 36 hours later, he'd have been dead. He was totally confused, disoriented and lethargic."

"That lady" was Yolanda. Throughout Pal Hal's sojourn in Baptist Hospital, from January 3 to March 13, 1990, Dr. Mann kept a snug rein on his enthusiasm for Yolanda. He said, "Ballard shouldn't have been taken away from the quick-care he could get in Toronto hospitals. Here in Baptist's she interfered with his rest. She caused tumult and created anxiety in the patient."

The patient could be kept alive only by machinery. He was hooked to a tube which gave him nourishment intravenously. He was hooked every other day to a dialysis machine to cleanse the poisons from his blood that his malfunctioning kidneys could not filter. Dying was dismal, but he mumbled random thoughts about the love of his life, his wife Dorothy, dead since 1969. He couldn't bring her back, he could only join her.

Yolanda, followed by the obedient Denise Banka, haunted Baptist Hospital. She was permitted occasional visits to Pal Hal's third-floor private room. When she wasn't allowed near him, by the order of Dr. Joel Mann, she phoned him from the hospital lobby.

Yolanda would breathe into the mouthpiece, "Harold, say I love you. Harold, say I love you."

She would not stop gnawing until Ballard, scarcely aware of who he was talking to, would mutter, "I love you." Michelle Mandel put it best in the *Toronto Sun*, "Pal Hal, Toronto's own Scrooge, is now a frail puppet, fraying strings jerked and pulled."

Bill Ballard moved from Toronto to a hotel in Miami Beach, there to monitor his father's health every day. He took sustenance from cigarets and Michelob beer. "That woman," he said of Yolanda, "has nine fucking lives. She broke up the Ballard family and brainwashed our dad."

Bill was convinced that Yolanda did not always live with his father in the Gardens. "I think," he said, "she'd leave the Gardens late at night and go a few blocks north to where her daughter lived, on Dundonald Avenue. Then she'd come back early in the morning to make Dad's breakfast. She made it look like she was living in the Gardens."

Then Bill's sister took command of Pal Hal's waning weeks. Mary Elizabeth Flynn is 48, as elegant as her mother was, tough-minded, fair-haired and able, married for a sec-

ond time and living in the expensive Toronto nook of Forest
Hill. She had not been as close to her father in recent years as
either of her brothers. She sought and got a Florida guardian
for her father, a tall young Miami lawyer, Paul Cowan. In
court documents she described Yolanda as "untruthful and
dangerous." In her affidavit she said, "When I spoke to my
father in hospital, he said 'You don't know what I've been
through.' He said he wanted me to take him to my home."

She also declared, "I feel very strongly that the treatment
and neglect which he received at the hands of Yolanda sub-
stantially contributed to, if indeed it did not directly cause,
my father's extremely poor condition when he was admitted
to hospital in Florida. . . . I have grave concern for my father's
welfare."

Grave concern by Ballard-appointed directors of the Gardens prompted them to assume operating control of the Old
Cashbox on Carlton Street. Pal Hal's imprimatur was erased
on January 5, 1990.

Yolanda, hollering insults from Miami, implied that the
directors, led by Don Giffin, were greedheads. "Vultures"
was her word. She told George Gross, corporate sports editor of the *Toronto Sun*, "Even vultures have the decency to
wait until the body becomes a carcass before they start picking at it."

She kept insisting, against all medical evidence, that Pal
Hal would recover. "I want the vultures to know," she said,
"that Harold was in much worse shape than he is now and
survived. He'll survive this, too. His heart is all right. He has
a kidney problem and has to be on a dialysis machine. But
he'll overcome it."

In truth, she was whistling past the Ballard family plot in
Park Lawn Cemetery in Etobicoke. She sought legal control
of him in Florida, and lost. Bill Ballard, spotting her in Baptist
Hospital, would derisively whistle or hum "Here comes the
bride, short, fat and wide."

Her control of Pal Hal, which had been absolute when she
whisked him to the Caymans, was indeed waning. She was
rebuffed when she attempted to pry a priest into Ballard's
cramped hospital room to pray for him. Paul Cowan, Pal

Hal's court-appointed guardian, refused to allow him admittance when Ballard said, "Get that fucker out of here!"

Yolanda begged through the closed door, "Please open it a crack, so this priest can pray for Harold." The door was slammed shut in her face.

She had been occupying a suite in the Dadeland Marriott Hotel, at $360-a-day, accompanied by the subservient Denise Banka. She refused to move to a single room priced at $136-a-day. Accordingly Marriott's management threatened to disconnect her telephone and turn off the water.

In Toronto, Paul McNamara spoke as chairman of the board of Gardens directors. "Harold's in a deep stupor most the time," McNamara said. "He can't comprehend what's happening, which is why the board is running the Gardens. Yolanda? She's a very loose cannon."

McNamara might have said a very loud loose cannon. She claimed to her Toronto lawyer, Howard Levitt, that she was broke. The Gardens, through lawyer Roseanne Rocchi, countered that Yolanda received an allowance from Ballard of $25,000 a year and got $100 a day while in Florida.

The sad turbulence rolled around the dying patient. Yolanda, permitted to see Pal Hal one day, tried to forcefeed him a banana, which, sputtering and gagging, he spit out. Bills charged by Yolanda's children to Ballard's accounts began to appear at the Gardens, to the indignation of Don Crump.

Her daughter, Anna MacMillan, charged merchandise and a cash advance on Ballard's bill at a Toronto pharmacy, Novack's on Church Street. Her son, Bill MacMillan, charged several hundred dollars' worth of clothes cleaned at Best Serve Cleaners on Yonge Street.

Don Crump, helping with the Gardens' finances while learning how to run the Canadian Football League, said, "Ballard's away and they're charging up things in his name. What galls me were the birth control pills being charged to Maple Leaf Gardens."

Crump said Ballard frequently scolded Yolanda for permitting her adult progeny to bill the Gardens for their personal goods, "but they persisted anyway."

Yolanda wilfully punched the Gardens meal-ticket as well.

Crump refused to pay a florist's bill for $86, for a bouquet Yolanda sent to Donald Mazankowski, the deputy prime minister in Canada's floundering Tory goverment. So far as anybody knew, Mazankowski was too busy propping up his prime minister, Brian Mulroney, to render Yolanda any favors.

Yolanda's solid losing streak continued on February 7, 1990, when she returned to Toronto to contest the legal wrangling over guardianship of Pal Hal. On arrival she was detained by customs agents for allegedly trying to smuggle jewelry worth $3,000 into Canada.

A customs officer said, "Our guys went through her bags and found gold jewelry. It wasn't declared and we seized the stuff until taxes are paid." Yolanda would have had to pay about $1,200 in taxes if she had declared the jewlry up front.

Bill Ballard, angry at Yolanda for extravagant spending of his father's money, had apparently tipped off Canada Customs to inspect Yolanda's luggage. "We're paying for it," he said, "so we want to know what she's bought."

Ten days later Yolanda lost her battle to become Ballard's guardian. She yelled, "I want an appeal!" after an Ontario district court judge, Donna Haley, appointed a former Supreme Court Justice, Willard Estey, as Ballard's personal Toronto guardian. Estey used to be known as Bud when he was involved in ratepayer affairs in a rich, palmy community in Etobicoke, Ontario.

Yolanda protested, "Harold lives and I live for him. His kids never cared for him. They're chomping at his coffin and he isn't even in it yet."

Then, calling on her erudition in the classics, she called the Ballard siblings "Hades Hal, Cyclops William and Medusa Mary." Hades Harold for Harold Junior was fairly straightforward, even for old sports writers whose reading is exclusively reserved for the *Hockey News*.

Cyclops Bill, I discovered, referred to the Cyclops in Greek mythology who were giant shepherds on Sicily, equipped with only one eye in the center of their foreheads. Perhaps Bill Ballard's habit of popping out a front false tooth gives him a Cyclopian smile.

Mary Medusa was a cheap shot, also out of Greek mythology. Medusa, in myth, was a female figure with staring eyes, protruding fangs for teeth, and writhing snakes for hair. As well Yolanda was accustomed to calling Bill Ballard "B.B.B.," which, she implied, meant "Billy Bogota Ballard." Bogotá is the capital of Columbia, the primary South American source of cocaine.

On March 6, 1990, Yolanda continued her ill-advised oral assault on the Ballards during a two-hour open-mouth program on CFRB, Canada's major radio station on the AM dial. The host, Wayne McLean, permitted her to slander Ballard's offspring. Their reaction was to slap Yolanda with a lawsuit for defamation, $5-million in total — $2-million in general damages and $3-million in punitive damages.

Mary Elizabeth Flynn said, "I will not stand by while she is given a platform to make outrageous allegations against me in public. . . . I have always thought CFRB was a responsible radio station . . . and was therefore shocked and hurt that CFRB would allow Yolanda Ballard to say absolutely false things about me."

Bill Ballard, in Florida, added, "I wouldn't have blamed Mary Liz if she'd sued Yolanda for $50-million."

The Ballards sought a retraction from the station, and received it. Wayne McLean, too, was obliged to read a profuse apology, written by the Ballards' lawyer, three times on the air. "Both CFRB and I wish to apologize without qualification or reservation to Mrs. Mary Elizabeth Flynn, Mr. William, Ballard and Mr. Harold G. Ballard," he said. "We're sorry for the hurt which our broadcast caused Mrs. Flynn and her brothers." CFRB's atonement, in addition to McLean's abject apology, included paying Mary Elizabeth's legal costs of $5,000, and donating another $5,000 to the Daily Food Bank in Toronto in the name of the Ballard children.

In mid-March Ballard was declared "mentally incompetent" by Judge Donna Haley, who appointed CFL commissioner Don Crump and Gardens directors Don Giffin and Steve Stavro guardians of Pal Hal's wealth. Judge Haley ruled, "Yolanda is too close to Mr. Ballard's estate to be chosen his personal guardian. It would be unwise in the extreme to appoint a person who could make a claim against the estate. It would make Mr. Ballard's welfare a bargaining chip in any dispute with the estate."

In Florida, Ballard's welfare was a daily concern of Allan Lamport, his old schoolmate from Upper Canada College, who has a winter retreat in Palm Beach. Lampy said, "My kidneys are in good shape. If the doctors want, they can take one of my kidneys and transplant it in Harold."

Lamport's offering was well-meant, a gesture of rare generosity, but he was quietly turned down, an indication from Dr. Joel Mann that Ballard was too far gone for more than a feeble physical fight. Still, when dialysis cleansed his blood, Pal Hal was conscious enough to enjoy brief raps with old friends who travelled south to visit.

"Hi ya, Rich," he said to me on March 12, 1990. "Where the hell's the party?"

"Any party we're going to have will be right in this hospital," I said. "We're both locked up here."

He asked about the hardcover edition of *Pal Hal*. "How the hell's our book doing? Are we selling it well in the Gardens?"

"I wish we were selling it in the Gardens," I said. "But Yolanda wouldn't allow it. Remember?"

"Oh, yeah," he said. "More trouble from the trouble-maker."

"Well, you're coming home to Toronto," I said. "You'll catch a few playoff games, I hope." The hope I felt was only veneer-deep, the fiction you express even as death closes in. He had the reluctant look the dying cast upon you when they gaze at you for the last time.

However, it was not quite the last time. Pal Hal was flown to Toronto by air ambulance on March 13, 1990, and transferred immediately to Wellesley Hospital, about six blocks north of the Gardens. Before she left Florida, Yolanda directed a tirade at Allan Lamport.

"Why has everybody turned against me?" she blurted. "Lawyers kept me away from Harold in the hospital so they can make a million in fees. You act like you're on Bill Ballard's payroll, too."

Lamport, rarely dignified as a Toronto civic politician, had a somewhat stately response: "My dear girl," he said, "you're turning me against you with your disgusting behavior. You are digging your own grave."

Ballard's condition did not improve in Wellesley, although the fiction was maintained that he might return to the Gardens. If he had, he would have noticed renovations.

Against her will, Yolanda was removed from Pal Hal's unkempt apartment by edict of the directors. She left clutching two green plaid-patterned nightgowns, his and hers, and a religious statuette. She did not depart quietly. "They are," she said of the directors, "evil greedy mongrels to do this to me while Harold's still alive."

The directors moved to end the perks enjoyed by the ticket scalpers in the Gardens lobby. There is a bank of pay telephones in the lobby where, Mike Wassilyn, among other ticket speculators, conducted his affairs. He would use the phones to call out, and wait for his patrons to call in; the lobby was his office. The directors had the phones altered so that no one could call in.

The directors honored tradition, which Pal Hal did not, by hanging banners representing the 11 Stanley Cups won by Maple Leaf teams. They did not hang the crest worn by those teams, the one on which the maple leaf really looks like a maple leaf. Instead, the banners have the modern emblem, a leaf designed by some lunkhead apparently unaware of what an actual maple leaf looks like.

The post-Ballard directors also intend to open a room in the Gardens for the Maple Leaf alumni. Similar rooms exist in the arenas of teams who care about what their retired players were, in Detroit and Montreal. Perhaps even Jim Thomson, the former Leaf captain called "a traitorous Quisling" by Conn Smythe in 1957, will visit the alumni room. The directors intend, too, to retire some player numbers and hang the jerseys of, say, Ted Kennedy or Frank Mahovlich from the rafters.

Pal Hal, expiring in Wellesley Hospital, was beyond caring what his successors were doing by this time. The countdown to the coffin began on April 5, 1990. He stopped breathing at 8:30 in the morning and was rushed into the hospital's intensive-care unit. He was hooked to life-support systems and revived, able to breathe only with the aid of a ventilator.

"Mr. Ballard is seriously ill," said Dr. Anthony Graham, a heart specialist. "He responded to the assist of a ventilator and began breathing again. . . . He is unconscious at times, at times rouseable."

Reporters with notebooks, microphones and cameras jostled together on the main floor of Wellesley. "So what are Pal Hal's chances?" someone asked.

Dr. Graham replied thoughtfully, "Immortality is not a business that we are in. We do the best we can for every patient."

Bill Ballard said, "He's back, what can I say? He's making little grunt sounds." He added, "But you can only pull through so many times."

A motley lot of people congregated. Yolanda was allowed to visit when Ballard's children weren't in the hospital. Monsignor Kenneth Robitaille arrived in a white Mercedes convertible from St. Michael's Cathedral. Mike Wassilyn, the ticket hustler, came in a half-ton truck. Ballard's guardian, Willard Estey, late of the Supreme Court, talked with former Toronto mayor Allan Lamport, who said, "I think he'll pull through. . . . Harold's got a powerful carcass."

As Pal Hal turned for the worse, shares in the Gardens took a turn for the higher on the Toronto Stock Exchange. The price of the shares jumped by $1.50, up to $44.25. The shares were dropped to $30 in June, 1990, a more realistic value.

Late on April 10, Ballard's condition seemed to improve and he was taken off a respirator. The next morning doctors suggested that he be hooked again to the life-support device. "No," he said. He died at 2:49 p.m. on April 11, "peacefully," the hospital said. By then he was a physical wreck racked by diabetes and failure of heart and kidneys. He was three months and 19 days short of his 87th birthday.

Ballard's children, in concert with the Gardens directors, decided that Pal Hal would rest in state in the directors' lounge on April 16, a clear cold Monday. External civilities were preserved. Yolanda was permitted a private hour with the closed coffin before fans and gawkers trooped into the Gardens to pay their final respects.

Yolanda, fenced off from the public and the Ballard family,

was accompanied by Denise Banka, her teenage companion. Denise had Yolanda's dog, the big bouncing Puck, on a leash. Lawyer Roseanne Rocchi, guarding the door, snapped, "Get that dog out of here. You can't bring that thing inside!"

Denise, cowed and crying, reluctantly gave the leash to a Gardens employee, who locked the peppy pooch in a storage room while Yolanda and Denise grieved. They were asked to leave exactly one hour later.

More than 3,000 fans traipsed past Pal Hal's coffin through the day, strolling through the residue of Ballard's life. Mary Elizabeth, recalling happier times, had festooned the room with pictorial mementoes of a remarkable life.

A blue-and-white flag, Maple Leaf colors, was draped over the coffin. On the wall above was a picture of the best friend Pal Hal ever had, his late wife Dorothy. There were pictures of Ballard's teams through the years, the senior Toronto Marlboros of 1948–49, the Stanley Cup Leafs of the 1960s, Pal Hall gleefully holding the Stanley Cup with his late partner Stafford Smythe, Ballard in his bunker at one end of the Gardens with his last male chum, King Clancy. There was not the slightest hint that anyone named Yolanda Babik Mac-Millan had ever caused family chaos.

In the last hour before the directors' room was closed, a shaggy poet from Hamilton sat in a corner mumbling a requiem for Pal Hal. "With the help of God," Arthur Ronald Mitchell recited, "I may do some good, I hope/ Before I'm dead...."

We left the room, the few of us loitering and somehow lost, to permit Bill Ballard and his sister to have the coffin opened for a final look at their father. "I don't want to remember him looking like that," Mary Elizabeth said. Then a shiny black hearse drove Pal Hal out of the Gardens on his last ride.

Yolanda and the Toronto media were not invited to the funeral the next day, a service of thanksgiving at Grace Church-on-the-Hill, an Anglican sanctuary where Mary Elizabeth worships in Forest Hill. She was determined that her father, who had lived in excitement and agitation, would be permitted to pass quietly into a state of grace. There were no cameras, no microphones, no old lovers permitted to disturb the dignity of the service.

One line from the minister's eulogy captured the tumult-ous person most of the mourners knew: "Harold lived with great zest and great power ... and understanding a world we did not know."

Officials at Park Lawn Cemetery, instructed by the Ballard children, had arranged for police cars to guard the gates. The family was determined to prevent Yolanda from causing any disturbance at the graveside. Reporters and cameramen were also kept outside the high wire fence. Nothing interrupted the ashes-to-ashes moment as Pal Hal's coffin was lowered into the ground beside his wife and parents. Bill Ballard, reconciled at last with the father he'd feuded with, stood in the cold under a leafless maple tree and saluted.

Postscripts beyond the grave began with the reading of Ballard's will on April 18, 1990. Somewhere Pal Hal was laughing. Most of his estate, with an estimated net worth of $50-million, was left to charity, as he had said it would be when nobody believed him. His estate includes controling interest in the Gardens and the Maple Leaf team. By law the foundation must sell all but 10 per cent of the Gardens shares within seven years.

He left his jewelry and furniture to his children. They were also given the first option to buy his Etobicoke home, his Toronto condominium unit and his Thunder Beach cottage.

He left his best regards and $50,000 a year to Yolanda MacMillan for life, or until she marries. Most of us, aware that the bequest would net about $39,000 a year after taxes, would have run to the nearest florist and ordered a fresh rose placed every day on Pal Hal's grave until we died. That is not Yolanda's way of going.

"It's too funny," she said of the will, in a tone indicating it wasn't funny at all, to her. At Ballard's grave a few days earlier, kneeling with Denise Banks and Puck the Pooch, she had said, "Harold, you'd better kick some ass down here."

Her lawyer, Patrick Schmidt, implied that it was Yolanda's ample ass that had been kicked. Her lifestyle of chauffeur-driven cars and travel, he said, cannot be maintained on $50,000 a year. Another of her lawyers, Seymour Iseman, told Yolanda she should seek between $100,000 and $120,000 a year. She is.

Don Giffin, rich from his sheet-metal business, was elected president of Maple Leaf Gardens by his fellow directors: Jake Dunlap of Ottawa, Norm Bosworth, Edward Lawrence and Paul McNamara of Toronto, and the ambitious farmer, Steve Stavro from the Knob Hills. Giffin will be paid $300,000 a year for the five years he hopes to remain as president.

Bill Ballard, not anxious to sell his stock, is suing for control of the Gardens and will acquire it if the courts decide he had a valid option to buy his brother's shares. With his show-business connections, Bill would seem the ideal person to operate the Gardens.

Lurking off there behind a beer barrel are the Molson brewers. The Ballard estate owes Molson about $40-million in loans obtained since 1980. Molson has a 19.9 per cent interest in the Gardens and, unless the loans are repaid by October 31, 1990, they can exercise options to buy Ballard stock.

One scenario suggests that Molson may co-operate with the prosperous Weston companies, who own the Loblaw supermarket chain. So Molson beer could be sold in Loblaw stores and Weston could build a new Maple Leaf Gardens for Molson on Weston property at Yonge Street and Highway 401, at the top of Toronto.

Pal Hal now has become the stuff of speeches at sports banquets. Rob Ramage, the Toronto captain, was getting laughs in the spring of 1990 with the tale about the last team picture Ballard sat for. He was accompanied on the ice by Puck the Pooch.

The dog sat beside Ballard in some discomfort. His hinder parts were being chilled by the ice. Pal Hal noticed Puck's shivering and called to equipment manager Smokey Lemelin, "Goddamn it, Smoke, bring over a towel for Puck to sit on. His balls are getting cold."

In June, 1990, the Toronto management attended the drafting of fresh young junior meat, in Vancouver. For the first time since 1961-62, Ballard was not at the Maple Leaf table. General manager Floyd Smith was free to pick whatever players were available, from anywhere on earth.

Smith broke Pal Hal's pattern of refusing to draft players from the Soviet Union. In the fifth round, fishing the 115th player from the pool, Smith said, "Toronto takes Alexander Godynuk, defenceman, Soviet Union."

The next day, wandering near Ballard's grave in Park Lawn cemetery, I fancied that the ground heaved. Pal Hal would not have chosen a Russian over his own dead body.

Index

Roy MacGregor

CHIEF

Billy Diamond has been called a hero, a saint, and a self-serving tyrant. He has fought with prime ministers and premiers, called upon the United Nations and Pope John Paul II for help, brought about the first modern constitutional amendment in Canada's history — and in the process created a self-sustaining aboriginal nation that stands today as an inspiration to the world.

Businessman, politician and charismatic leader, Billy Diamond combines the instincts of a great entrepreneur with the business savvy to bring his visions to fruition. Among his successes are the creation of a Cree owned and operated airline, Air Creebec, and a joint venture with Yamaha to redesign the historic Hudson's Bay canoe.

Despite his political and business successes, Billy Diamond was consumed by self-doubt and threatened by alcohol. It is Diamond's own brush with tragedy that gives his life new direction: economic self-determination for his people, evangelical inspiration for himself. There has never been a more significant native leader than Billy Diamond — nor a more remarkable personal story.

" . . . a story of hope and even triumph, the victory of an extraordinary Canadian, narrated by an extraordinary story-teller."

Walter Stewart, *The Toronto Sun*

"With the dash of a great journalist and the art of a first-rate novelist, Roy MacGregor evokes the tortured ego and awesome dignity of Billy Diamond — Canada's northern Iacocca."

Peter C. Newman

"Billy Diamond's remarkable life story, as told in stunning detail by Roy MacGregor, reveals Diamond as that rarest of Canadian creatures, a true-blue, larger-than-life hero."

The Toronto Star

David Cruise and *Alison Griffiths*

LORDS OF THE LINE

Six tough, arrogant and supremely powerful men, creators of Canada's greatest institution — the CPR.

George Stephen — A man of grace and elegance — and a supreme manipulator.

William Cornelius Van Horne — Canada's greatest railroader, a man of enormous energy and charisma.

Thomas Shaughnessy — Stern and frugal, Shaughnessy held the CPR's creditors at bay while turning the company into a money-maker.

Edward Beatty — Tough and shrewd, with the looks of a film star, Beatty ran the CPR as if he owned it.

Buck Crump — The man who unceremoniously replaced the beloved steam engine with the noisy, dirty diesel.

Ian Sinclair — Notoriously acquisitive and a canny negotiator, Sinclair ruled with the power of a feudal lord.

"Fascinating, well-researched and readable."
The Globe and Mail

"*Lords of the Line* has all the extravagant emotions, plot twists and sheer drama expected of a novel."
Montreal Daily News

"One word of warning: you can't scan this book. It is a book to be read right down to the last toothsome footnote."
The Vancouver Sun